The Serendipitous Evolution of the Balfour Declaration of November 2, 1917

The Serendipitous Evolution of the Balfour Declaration of November 2, 1917

By

Paul Goldstein and Eyal Lewin

**Cambridge
Scholars**
Publishing

The Serendipitous Evolution of the Balfour Declaration
of November 2, 1917

By Paul Goldstein and Eyal Lewin

This book first published 2021

Cambridge Scholars Publishing

Lady Stephenson Library, Newcastle upon Tyne, NE6 2PA, UK

British Library Cataloguing in Publication Data
A catalogue record for this book is available from the British Library

Copyright © 2021 by Paul Goldstein and Eyal Lewin

ISBN (10): 1-5275-7055-X
ISBN (13): 978-1-5275-7055-9

TABLE OF CONTENTS

PREFACE

The Balfour Declaration was one of the most important events in the history of the Jewish people prior to the Holocaust, signaling the beginning of a new era of self-determination in the reconstituted Jewish homeland after nearly 2000 years of life in exile. While commemorated every year as a milestone in the history of the Jewish nation, very few of the celebrants have any knowledge or awareness of the momentous historical background that led to this historic event.

The purpose of this study is to provide an all-inclusive understanding of the complex geopolitical elements that had shaped the facts on the ground in the Middle East. Analyzing the chain of events that led to the Balfour Declaration in a unique holistic approach, we demonstrate how the national interests of the nations involved in the World War I theatre intersected with those of the Jewish nation in the final phase of its long march towards political sovereignty. Like the multiple parts of precision clockwork, each element, regardless of shape or size, played an essential part in the functioning of the whole, while the absence of one of them could have altered the outcome of the entire process.

Even scholars of Israel studies have little awareness to what this comprehensive study validates, and that is – that the Balfour Declaration was not merely the product of a short-lived diplomatic episode during the penultimate year of World War I. The process that led to the Balfour Declaration was largely driven by the relentless persecution of Russia's Jewish population which activated and fueled the development of political Zionism during the 128-year period that started with the French Revolution and culminated with the promulgation of the Declaration in 1917.

This study started with an extensive review of the secondary literature dealing with the Balfour Declaration and any of its aspects. Most of the secondary accounts were found to provide only episodic fragments of the subject matter and were often tainted by hindsight-driven subjective biases. By limiting their research to specific aspects and episodic time frames, the various authors did not provide an overall explanation of the processes that led to the proclamation of the Balfour Declaration. Consequently, the focus of this study moved to seek information in primary sources. These included archives, diaries, autobiographies and first-hand accounts. Major sources included *The Complete Diaries of Theodor Herzl*, without which it is impossible to draw a realistic picture of the man's personality, ideas, diplomatic skills and unsparing efforts towards the realization of his objectives; and the complete minutes of the 1917 British War Cabinet meetings which covered all the issues related to the final wording of the Balfour Declaration.

To avoid any distortion of the historic realities that constituted the background to the Balfour Declaration, each episode of this study was insulated from rearview mirror interpretations of the geopolitical developments that unfolded in the wake of its proclamation post-November 2, 1917.

A large body of literature was found to be devoted to the roles played by the British government and the other World War I participants in the development of the Balfour Declaration. This has allowed this study to develop a detailed answer to the question as to what led the British government to commit itself to a Jewish homeland in Palestine.

By methodically tracking the stages that transformed the Jewish ethos from the amorphous stage of social and political impotence in the oppressive world of the Diaspora to the politically dynamic pursuit of the return to sovereign nationhood in the land of their forefathers, this study has identified three major developments that fueled this arduous journey and which are mostly wanting in the existing literature. Without the development of these crucial independent variables there would have been no political Jewish representation for the British government to engage with as part of its World War I strategy in the Middle East, and no Balfour Declaration.

The first was the gradual emergence of the emancipation of the Jews, triggered by the French Revolution which resulted in the Declaration of the Rights of Man and of the Citizen, in 1789. Jewish emancipation brought forth the *Haskala* [Jewish Enlightenment]. It was the cultural transformation inspired by the *Haskala* which led to the development of political Zionism which turned out to be the lodestar of the Jewish path to the Balfour Declaration.

The second shortcoming in the existing literature about the Balfour Declaration is the general failure to identify the cruel conditions of Jewish life in nineteenth century Russia, which had the largest Jewish population of any country in the world, as one of the major game-changing episodes that provided the critical mass for the development of political Zionism. Hence, we also describe in this book the relentless persecution of Russian Jewry by the tyrannical tsarist regimes and how it gave rise to the Zionist political awakening that paved the way to the Balfour Declaration.

The third major deficiency brought to light by this study is the insufficient recognition of the role played by Theodor Herzl in the conception and development of the Zionist movement as an internationally recognized political entity. This book, therefore, includes a complete description of Herzl's unique personality, ideas, social and diplomatic skills, and of his unsparing efforts to obtain the backing from the major European powers and leaders in the financial world in his quest for a sustainable homeland.

The identification of the essential components of the geopolitical clockwork that made the Balfour Declaration possible would not be complete without the inclusion of the vital role played by the Americans. Our study shows how their entry into World War I assured the defeat of the Central Powers and the liberation of the Middle East from Ottoman control. It also covers the diplomatic process that led to President Wilson's decision to support the Balfour Declaration, thereby satisfying one of the major conditions that had to be met before the British War Cabinet would authorize Foreign Secretary Arthur James Balfour to issue the Declaration.

To have a clear understanding of what was achieved by the Balfour Declaration, it is essential to have a clear perception of the political etymology of the verbal material that went into its deliberately ambiguous fabric. Rothschild submitted a Zionist draft declaration to Balfour on July 18, 1917, but on November 2, 1917 Balfour sent Rothschild the text of the declaration approved by the War Cabinet, which was substantially different. In poking into the nature of the challenges that caused this change in wording we show how the progressive exchange of versions between the Zionist leadership and the British government reflected the considerations that influenced both sides.

ACKNOWLEDGMENTS

Pericles, the prominent Greek statesman, wrote some 2,400 years ago: *"What you leave behind is not what is engraved in stone monuments, but what is woven into the lives of others."*

I am especially indebted to my friend and assistant of 20 years, Mary Arangio, whose support and dedication were vital to the successful completion of this study. In addition to her invaluable computer skills, she also contributed many helpful editing suggestions. During our many brainstorming sessions, she proved to be an excellent and productive sounding board. Being both uncompromising perfectionists, we sometimes argued stubbornly until we found common ground, and always with the best possible results in mind.

In terms of motivation and inspiration, I was driven by the memory of my heroic mother, Nessie Tiger Goldstein, who saved my life during the Holocaust and by the spirit of my beloved wife of over 50 years, Naomi, who passed away three years ago, halfway during my research for this project. Until the end, she took a great interest in the project as it progressed, and made many insightful and useful comments. The spirit of her unwavering love and support provided me with the energy and determination to keep extending myself to the limit of my capabilities to the completion of the many life-enriching projects we embarked on together.

In the final analysis, I was strongly motivated by the martyrdom of the Jewish people in the Diaspora, before, during and after the period covered in this book. The overriding impetus that cemented my determination to pursue the exploration of this seminal episode in the history of the Jewish people, was the responsibility that I felt my own survival bestowed on me to help ensure that their story be known and never forgotten.

Dr. Paul Goldstein

INTRODUCTION

On Wednesday October 31, 1917, the British War Cabinet agreed to authorize the United Kingdom's Foreign Secretary, Arthur James Balfour, to convey the historic eponymous policy statement that has become known as the "Balfour Declaration" to Lord Lionel Rothschild, head of the British Zionist Federation (National Archives, CAB 23/4/35).

On November 2, 1917, Balfour sent the following letter to Rothschild:

> Dear Lord Rothschild,
> I have much pleasure in conveying to you, on behalf of his Majesty's Government, the following declaration of sympathy with Jewish Zionist aspirations which has been submitted to, and approved by, the Cabinet.
> His Majesty's Government view with favour the establishment in Palestine of a national home for the Jewish people, and will use its best endeavours to facilitate the achievement of this object, it being clearly understood that nothing shall be done which may prejudice the civil and religious rights of existing non-Jewish communities in Palestine, or the rights and political status enjoyed by Jews in any other country.
> I should be grateful if you would bring this declaration to the knowledge of the Zionist Federation. (Gauthier, 2007, p. 272)

The Balfour Declaration was one of the single most important events in the history of the Jewish people. Without the Balfour Declaration, there would not be a sovereign Jewish nation today. The British had made many pledges to the major players involved in the political jockeying that was driven by the perils and opportunities unleashed by the Great War. The Balfour Declaration was, however, their only promise made to a nation that had been separated from its homeland, dispersed around the world, without a territory of its own for close to two millennia, constantly subject to persecution and for whom accession to a national home had an existential urgency that was unique among all the nations aspiring to self-rule under the opportunities created by the historic geopolitical changes generated by World War I.

Why did the British government, in 1917, address the Balfour promise to the Zionist Federation, which represented only a small number of the general Jewish population, and not to the Jewish population as a whole? This question can only be answered in the context of the state of the world in the years preceding World War I. The fact that the promise of the

Declaration was made to the Jewish people but that it was addressed to the Zionist Federation reflects the emergence and mobilization of a new socio-political animus in the Jewish diaspora, the development of which constitutes the bedrock of this book.

This study traces the activities of all the parties involved that led from the Zionist hope of a homeland for the Jewish people to the unprecedented substantiation of that aspiration by the leading world power at the time, which brought the Jewish people from the depths of their politically impotent existence on the peripheries of the societies to which they had been driven by the currents of relentless sectarian hatred to the status of recognized participants at the diplomatic negotiating table with the most powerful nation in the world at the time. Among history's great occurrences, the fertilization of the dormant seed of the Jewish return to their ancestral homeland can truly be considered *sui generis*. As we shall see in the sequence of events covered in this book, the unrelenting and ever-ready to erupt "Lethal Obsession" of antisemitism, which kept burning in the hearts and minds of European Christendom, was the toxic social lubricant that defined the nature of both the Christian oppression and the Jewish resistance. This tangled web of elements that interacted to lead to the historic Balfour Declaration contained the socio-political DNA that shaped the Declaration's meaning, interpretations and ensuing developments.

To avoid the pitfalls of relying on often contradictory bias-driven interpretations of the same events by secondary sources, we have based our research to the fullest possible extent on primary sources, i.e. archives, diaries, autobiographies and first-hand accounts. Where second-hand data were the only ones available, we have reviewed their sources and analyzed the discrepancies between contradictory accounts.

The Balfour Declaration produced the first ray of light at the end of the nearly 1,900-year-long dark tunnel of persecution in the Jewish diaspora communities and signalled the beginning of a new era of self-determination in their reconstituted Jewish homeland. The Declaration was born in the geopolitical petri dish of World War I and marked the intersection of the national interests of the United Kingdom and the aspirations of the Zionist liberation movement. By breaking the mould of the colonial world order, which was characterized by the control of the majority of the world's people by a handful of industrialized European powers, World War I unleashed a Pandora's box of suppressed national identities and big power territorial rivalries.

A vast number of scholars have dealt with one or more of the independent variables that led to the Balfour Declaration, but in our review of writings on this subject by, among others, Jonathan Schneer, Leonard

Stein, Jacques Paul Gauthier, Doreen Ingrams, Victor Kattan, Walid Khalidi, Richard Ned Lebow, Donald Lewis, Ian Lustick, Michael Makovsky, William Mathew, Edwin Montagu, Joan Peters, Barbara W. Tuchman and Chaim Weizmann, we have not come across a comprehensive identification of the range of structural conditions and agency-driven elements that led to this unlikely event.

The 33rd Annual Conference of the Association for Israel Studies held at Brandeis University in Waltham, MA, on June 12–14, 2017 under the theme *A Century after Balfour: Vision and Reality* served as a telling barometer of the current level of awareness of the significance of the Balfour Declaration as a symbol of the lengthy and complex process that had transformed the political structure of the Jewish world during the 128 years preceding its promulgation.

Of the 321 presentations delivered by academics representing 92 universities and 40 academic learning centres from around the world, only 12 made any reference to the Balfour Declaration. Their observations focused primarily on the Declaration itself and on the impact of the Declaration on various aspects of political and social life in Israel in the post-Balfour Declaration era. These 12 academics, and the titles of their presentations, were as follows: Martin Kramer, Shalem College, *The Allied Balfour Declaration*; Ian Lustick, University of Pennsylvania, *The Balfour Declaration 100 Years Later: A Radically and Accidentally Relevant Document*; Leon Wieseltier of the Brookings Institution, who delivered the keynote address *Reflections on the Balfour Declaration*; Gershon Shafir, University of California at San Diego, *A Century of Balfour Declarations*; Maria G. Navarro, Universidad de Salamanca, *Preventive vs Proactive Policies: An Interpretation of Balfour Declaration's Political Vision*; Avital Ginat, Tel Aviv University, *Shifting Loyalties: The Balfour Declaration in the Transition towards British Orientation during and after First World War*; Itamar Rickover, Bar Ilan University, *From Balfour Declaration to the Six Day War-Changes in the Character of the Jewish Warrior*; Meron Medzini, Hebrew University of Jerusalem, *The Reaction of the Asian Nations to the Balfour Declaration*; Khinvraj Jangid, Jindal Global University, *Indian National Movement and Zionism: In the Light of Balfour Declaration*; Judah Bernstein, New York University, *From the Balfour Declaration to Cleveland: The 1921 ZOA Convention Reconsidered*; Walker Robins, University of Oklahoma, *The Influence of Judah Magnes on American Liberal Protestant Interpretations of the Balfour Declaration*; and Lindsay Katzir, Louisiana State University, *Rainbows Built of Bitter Tears: Anglo-Jewish Zionism Before The Balfour Declaration*.

This listing does not imply any reflection on the quality of the few presentations that did refer to the Balfour Declaration. Its sole purpose is to illustrate the fact that this massive assembly of academics, meeting under the promising banner *A Century after Balfour: Vision and Reality*, did not provide any new knowledge or insights that would reduce the serious shortcomings in the existing literature about the Balfour Declaration that this study has undertaken to identify and correct.

This serious lacuna in the coverage of the past prevents an objective appraisal of the heavily politicized misinterpretation of the present. We intend, in this book, to amend this deficiency by tracing and connecting the causal elements that played a significant part in the conception and development of the Balfour Declaration.

What is new and unique in our analysis of this subject is that the holistic approach that we have adopted allows a clearer understanding of the complex geopolitical elements that have shaped the facts on the ground in the Middle East. Like forensic pathology that can trace the fundamental causes of current happenings by identifying common DNA patterns going back over long periods of time, so an objective scholarly analysis can connect the genetic political patterns that were established in 1917 with the dynamics of the Arab-Israeli conflict today. The Balfour Declaration, as a result of its politically contrived ambiguity, the nature of which is described in detail in *Chapter 6: What's in a Word – Political Word-Craftsmanship*, was the spark that set off the chain of political upheavals that followed in its wake. It is impossible to deal with geopolitical challenges without understanding their roots.

This study demonstrates how the national interests of the nations involved in the World War I theatre intersected with those of the Jewish nation in the final phase of its long march towards political sovereignty. Like the multiple parts of precision clockwork, each element, regardless of shape or size, played an essential part in the functioning of the whole, while the absence of one of them could have altered the outcome of the entire process. While the Declaration itself embodied the fusion of the interests of two nations, the British and the Jewish, this political joint venture would never have come about if these two partners had not been able to circumnavigate the competing challenges of the other powers vying for the same spoils as the British and who, for their own geopolitical reasons, were opposed to the Zionist aim of redeeming their ancient homeland. They would only allow themselves to be induced to support the Declaration if it furthered the realization of their own territorial ambitions.

It is impossible to effectively identify the human dynamics that led to the dramatic social change that was embodied in the Balfour Declaration without infusing the narrative with a graphic portrayal of the human experiences that ignited and fuelled the actions and counter-actions that drove the process. Merely recording events reveals only that they happened and reduces the narrative to an easily forgotten compendium of lifeless data. Only a qualitative cause-and-effect analysis can contribute to the understanding of how they impacted the actions of the leaders and the lives of their subjects. This book traces the episodic stages that transformed the Jewish ethos from the outwardly amorphous stage of socially and politically impotent stagnation in the oppressive world of the diaspora to the politically dynamic pursuit of their return to sovereign nationhood in the land of their forefathers.

The promise of a haven from persecution embodied in the Balfour Declaration was the outcome of a number of events occurring in different parts of the world which, while caused by totally unrelated political currents, were connected by one common thread, the fate of the Jewish communities which the diaspora has lodged among often hostile majorities. During the nearly 1,900 years that their ancestral homeland was occupied by intolerant despotic regimes, their own lives in the diaspora were subjected to harsh and restrictive conditions and any physical escape from persecution was out of the question; the "next year in Jerusalem" ritual incantation was just a ceremonial religious practice.

To fully understand why the Jews were treated in such a destructive manner, it is necessary to recognize the omnipresence of the social handicap of antisemitism that was the yeast that fermented and the social energy that ignited the Judeophobic outbursts of the host populations. It must not be forgotten that the embers of nationalism had been kept alive among diaspora Jewry, despite centuries of brutal attempts to deprive them of their identity and to stifle any manifestation of political activity. The scattered Jewish nation was like a dormant social volcano, with the tectonic plates of political and religious Judeophobia clamped down as firm lids on any manifestation of Jewish political self-assertion, precluding any possibility to translate their never-extinguished yearning for their ancestral homeland into political action. The tectonic shift that lifted this heavy lid and propelled the captive magma of Jewish self-assertion to the surface was the emancipation.

This seminal stage on the long Jewish path that led to the Balfour Declaration is the first of three major developments that fuelled this arduous journey that has been largely ignored by the academic world. The emancipation of the Jews was triggered by the French Revolution, which resulted in the Declaration of the Rights of Man and of the Citizen in 1789. The Jewish emancipation brought forth the *Haskala*, the Jewish enlightenment, which provided its followers, the *Maskilim*, with the conceptual apparatus that made other movements such as nationalism and socialism comprehensible. It was the cultural transformation inspired by the *Haskala* which led to the development of political Zionism, without which there would have been no Balfour Declaration.

The second shortcoming in the existing scholarship about the Balfour Declaration is the general failure to identify the inhuman conditions of Jewish life in nineteenth-century Russia – which had a larger Jewish population than any other country in the world – as one of the major game-changing episodes that provided the critical mass for the development of modern political Zionism. This lacuna is filled in this book through a description of the relentless persecution of Russian Jewry by the tsarist regimes of the nineteenth century which gave rise to the Zionist political awakening that paved the way to the Balfour Declaration.

The third major deficiency in the existing scholarship is the insufficient identification of the vital role played by Theodor Herzl in the conception and development of the Zionist movement as an internationally recognized political entity. Leonard Stein and Jonathan Schneer, while generally considered major authorities on the subject, fail to adequately address these organic parts of the genesis and development of political Zionism. Hence, we include in this volume a complete description of Herzl's unique personality, ideas, social and diplomatic skills and of his unsparing efforts to obtain the backing of the major European powers and leaders of the financial world to succeed in his endeavours to obtain Palestine as a sustainable home for his people

While all the elements necessary for the development of the Balfour Declaration eventually became interconnected, the process and its outcome were completely unpredictable. A number of social and political dynamics that were totally independent came together, in ways that could not have been foreseen, in a historically highly significant document called the Balfour Declaration. The development of this landmark promise combined the interconnectivity of a geopolitical clockwork with the serendipity of an unplanned but felicitous outcome for those who aspired to its fulfilment. As noted by University of Pennsylvania political science professor Ian Lustick in referring to the Balfour Declaration:

> Trivial accidents of policy, casual ideological or personal prejudices by colonial officers and relevant ministers, and other minor factors, often drove massive impactful interventions. (Lustick, 2017, p. 2)

It is important to realize that the various entities that played a part in the shaping of the future political map of the territory of Palestine conducted their affairs for the sole purpose of serving their own national interests and ambitions. These included not only the British Empire and the Zionist movement but also the Ottoman Empire, Germany, Russia, the United States and France, as shown in *Chart I-1: The Clockwork Evolution of the Balfour Declaration*. By following the concomitant but not necessarily parallel paths pursued by the various factions and by identifying the crossover points, one can obtain a more realistic awareness of the cause and effect dynamics of the major events that played a seminal role in the creation of the Balfour Declaration.

Chart I-1: The Clockwork Evolution of the Balfour Declaration

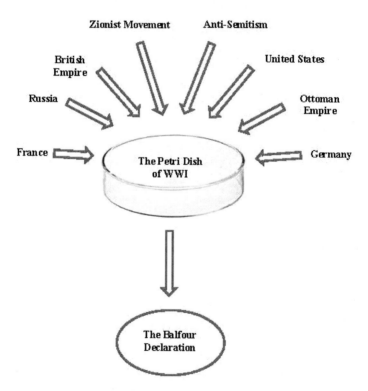

While the Balfour Declaration itself was a promise by the British government, the other participants in World War I also had a significant impact on the formulation of the wording of the Declaration, which had to take into account their political and strategic interests. Although the Arabs were also participants in the conflict, they did not play a significant role in the development of the Balfour Declaration. In 1917, they were embarking on their own phase of nationalism and had been appeased by the British promises made during the secretive Hussein-McMahon negotiations. It was only after the Balfour Declaration had been issued and the implementation process began that the Arab reaction became a crucial element of the Arab-Israeli conflict.

We review the roles played by the various protagonists as well as their motivations, specific activities and decisions that shaped the fates of the unwitting populations involved. Our intention is to identify the major political tributaries that coalesced into the mainstream that led to the undertaking by the international community to foster the reconstitution of the ancestral homeland of the remnants of the Jewish diaspora, including the part played by antisemitism in shaping the events that marked the build-up to the Balfour Declaration.

This research provides the basis for a comprehensive understanding of the significance of the Balfour Declaration, on which it is now possible to construct a more realistic picture of the events that followed in the wake of its issuance. This book aims at liberating the pivotal critical juncture of the Balfour Declaration from the suffocating layers of Judeophobic distortions that have blurred its true meaning and betrayed the expectations it generated.

Elizabeth Noelle-Neumann, Professor of Communications Research at the University of Mainz and founder of the Public Opinion Research Center in Allensbach, Germany, developed the concept of "the spiral of silence" in her comprehensive theory of public opinion. Her findings provide a useful tool for understanding how truth and facts can be distorted to serve the prejudices of the majority at the expense of a targeted minority. Her research led her to conclude:

> Even when people see plainly that something is wrong, they will keep quiet if public opinion (opinions and behavior that can be exhibited in public without fear of isolation) and, hence, the consensus of what constitutes good taste and the morally correct opinion speaks against them. (Noelle-Neumann, 1993, p. x)

Accordingly, our work is also essential, then, to liberate the agendas of the social and political entities which have a stake in the ongoing Arab-Israeli conflict from the propaganda-driven "spiral of silence" described by Noelle-Neumann (1993) so that the vital elements of truth and justice can be applied to the morally just treatment of the populations involved.

It is unfortunate that the current generation of Jews in Israel and in the diaspora have not been provided with a comprehensive account of how the recreation of a sovereign Jewish state on the site of their ancient homeland came about. There is no greater proof of the importance of the need to reconstruct the events that led to this historic development than the deplorable fact that the 128-year transformational period that paved the way has been completely ignored by the Israeli education system. The book *Israel – A Jewish and Democratic State*, the textbook authorized by the Israeli Ministry of Education that serves teachers in every Israeli high school, except for the ultra-Orthodox ones, and on which the matriculation exams are based, devotes barely half a page to the Balfour Declaration. It reads as follows:

> At the beginning of 1917 negotiations took place between representatives of the British Foreign Ministry and Zionist representatives headed by Haim Weizman concerning a declaration that would express encouragement of the Zionist aspirations. At the end of these consultations the British government issued on November 2, 1917, the document later known as the Balfour declaration, in the form of a letter written by the British Foreign Minister Lord Balfour to Lord Rothschild, who was Honorary President of the Zionist federation in England.
>
> In the Balfour declaration, for the first time in modern Jewish history, a major power acknowledged the national aspirations of the Jewish people in the Land of Israel. The declaration determined that the British government ruled that a Jewish national home would be established in the Land of Israel. Notably, Britain would not establish the national home, but it would encourage political and other essential infrastructure that would make it easier for Jews to establish their national home.
>
> What is a national home? The origins of this expression are within the Zionist Basel Plan. It was also offered by the Zionist representatives, for tactical reasons – to make it easier for the British government to issue a declaration with no commitment to a Jewish state.
>
> In the Balfour declaration there is nothing about sovereignty, authority or borders, but it formed a framework – one that was later shaped in the international post-WWI arrangements, such as the San Remo agreement and the British Mandate, which the Jews were eventually expected to fulfil. (Shahar, 2013, pp. 15–16, trans. E. L.)

It is regrettable that the sovereign Jewish state which resulted from the struggles and sacrifices of their forefathers has not produced a comprehensive textbook account of the costly path that led to this modern-day miracle.

To avoid any distortion of the realities that constituted the background of this historic event, each episode covered in this study is insulated from rearview mirror interpretations of the geopolitical developments that unfolded in the wake of the proclamation of the Balfour Declaration. We demonstrate how seemingly unrelated social and political currents drove different national protagonists, each navigating their own course in pursuit of their particular socio-political agendas, into the all-encompassing political vortex of World War I. Prior to the war, the various national actors who would eventually enter the stage created by the conflict were like sails passing in the wind, unaware of their potential connection to the transformational changes that were starting to influence social and political agendas around the world.

This book analyzes how this multi-faceted process developed and gave rise to the promulgation of the Balfour Declaration, which was a one-off event that resulted from the interaction of a multitude of political developments unleashed by the politically liberating but physically devastating impact of World War I. While the Balfour Declaration was not the main theme of World War I but a sub-plot which became a consideration for the Allies only halfway through the conflict, it was of existential importance for the Jewish people in their historic quest for the recovery of their status as a sovereign nation.

In this study, we provide a holistic description of the process that brought about the Balfour Declaration. We identify each contributing component which, if absent, would have prevented the Balfour Declaration from happening. Our main thrust is that the Balfour Declaration was the result of the fortuitous convergence of geopolitical interests of a significant array of national entities, the dynamics of which brought about this historic document.

The Jewish path to the Balfour Declaration was significantly more complex than the British motivation. The British motivation developed over a relatively short time span. Britain's practical involvement only emerged and became mobilized towards the end of War World I and primarily preoccupied the members of the War Cabinet. By contrast, the Jewish path, which had its wellspring in the French Revolution, ran through different phases, time frames and complex social political patterns caused by the dispersion of the Jewish people among different nations, geographical areas and political regimes.

The impact of Germany, the Ottoman Empire, France and Russia, which also played a significant part in the complex narrative of the evolution of the Balfour Declaration, was of a dual nature. These nations had two motivations. One was to deal with the Jewish populations in their midst who were trying to survive and eventually escape the oppressive antisemitic grip in which they were held. The other motivation was the fact that they were in constant strife with each other to either expand or protect their territories in their native states as well as in the colonial world. Their connectivity to the core issue of this study was of a quasi-organic and episodic nature and not the result of any national political agenda.

The impact on the Balfour Declaration of all the nations involved is fully covered within the various chapters in this book. *Chapter 1: The British Motivation* addresses the British motivation behind the development of the Declaration. It describes the competing territorial ambitions of the British and the Germans which triggered the devastating conflict of World War I, with the ensuing drives by both sides to enlist every possible source of support, leading to the duplicitous political deal-making between the British and the Arabs, the British and the French, the British and the Jews, and the British and the Ottoman Empire.

Chapter 2: Emancipation shows how the French Revolution, by triggering the emancipation of the Jews, started the first phase of the awakening of the Jewish mind from its nearly two-thousand -long political slumber.

Chapter 3: Persecution – Tsarist Russia, the Nineteenth-Century "Egypt" describes the relentless persecution of Russian Jewry by the tyrannically tsarist regimes of the nineteenth century, which led the persecuted Jewish people to ride the waves of emancipation, which started in central Europe, towards more tolerant environments and gave rise to the Zionist political awakening that paved the way to the Balfour Declaration.

Chapter 4: The Development of Zionist Political Thinking traces how the Zionist project developed from the first manifestations of Zionist political thinking during the second half of the nineteenth century to its full-blown development into a dynamic political movement. This chapter also covers the thirteen-year period following Herzl's death in 1904 to the issuance of the Balfour Declaration on November 2, 1917. While the Zionist efforts to secure a territorial solution to the desperate plight of European Jewry failed to make any progress prior to the outbreak of World War I in 1914, significant positive developments in respect of resolving its internal ideological conflicts occurred within the Zionist movement during this period. This chapter also explains how the outbreak of World War I broke the political impasse and kindled the hope that the Zionist dream might be realized after all.

Chapter 5: The American Factor reviews the impact of the United States' entry into World War I on the diplomatic process which drove the development of the Zionist project. The perilous military situation in Europe caused the British and French to pursue the American participation in the war against the Central Powers, while the Germans attempted to keep the Americans out through devastating assaults on the American merchant navy and the abortive attempt to induce Mexico to declare war on the United States.

Finally, *Chapter 6: What's in a Word – Political Word-Craftsmanship* describes how the political interests of all the players involved in the process, which included the British Empire, the Zionist movement, Germany, the Ottoman Empire, France, Russia and the United States, influenced the arduous process of the wording of the Balfour Declaration.

As we can see in these chapters, the forces at work inside these separate socio-political entities reached out beyond their own spheres of interest with significant, often unintended effects on each other's fortunes.

CHAPTER ONE

THE BRITISH MOTIVATION

Introduction

In this chapter, we explore the political and cultural factors that motivated the government of the largest power in the world, at the onset of World War I, to make the historic promise that turned the Jewish diaspora's centuries-old spiritual dream of the return to their ancient homeland into a political reality.

The British government did not suddenly find itself in support of a Jewish homeland in Palestine on November 2, 1917, the day the Balfour Declaration was issued. The road that led to this juncture had been a long and arduous one, a tangled web of international diplomatic and internal political manoeuvres. While British support of a Jewish homeland in Palestine was enhanced by the cultural and spiritual background of the leading class of British statesmen that happened to hold the reins of power at the time of the Declaration, the strategic consideration that public endorsement of the Zionist political aspirations would significantly bolster Britain's imperial ambitions was the fundamental impetus. The ultimate objective of the British was to come out as the victors of World War I so that they could consolidate their world power status, retain control over the international routes and territories that constituted the British Empire, including their vital oil resources, and expand this dominion by strengthening their grip on the soon to be conquered Middle Eastern territories of the Ottoman Empire.

During World War I, the British found, however, that they were no longer an island unto themselves. Not only did they have to deal with the devastating military stalemate on the Western Front, they also had to contend with the competing ambitions of friend and foe alike. This chapter will show how their dogged pursuit of their ultimate objectives led them to subordinate integrity to expediency, especially in their dealings with the Arab populations of the Middle East, with their French allies and, eventually, with the fledgeling Zionist movement.

The following sections address the religious, military and political dynamics that drove the British government's wartime agenda and led it to issue the historic Balfour Declaration.

Religion

While the need to muster any military, economic and political support that could tip the scales in their favour was the main motivation that drove the British political agenda at the time, these geopolitical considerations were not the sole British motivators behind the Balfour Declaration. An extensive study of the subject cannot fail to take into account the influence of biblical prophecy and the evangelical movement in shaping the mindset of the British Cabinet in approving the Balfour Declaration on November 2, 1917. According to church history professor and author Donald M. Lewis, it is only by understanding the phenomena of Christian philosemitism and Christian Zionism that one can make sense of the religious and cultural influences that worked together to create a climate of opinion among the political elite of Britain that was well disposed to the Balfour Declaration (Lewis, 2010, p. 10).

In his elaborate historiography of the British evangelical interest in the Jews, Lewis focused on the role of Anthony Ashley-Cooper, 7th Earl of Shaftesbury (known as Lord Ashley), as the "leading proponent of Christian Zionism in the 19th Century and the first politician of stature to prepare the way for Jews to establish a home in Palestine." Shaftesbury's devotion to the Jews was a manifestation of his concern for the plight of ethnic minorities in general, but it was greater than his concerns for the Welsh, the Scots or the Irish as it was rooted in his religious identity, which he derived from his Anglican heritage (Lewis, 2010, p. 107).

Lewis noted that there had been Gentile projects to resettle the Jews in Palestine and to establish them in their ancient homeland long before the Zionist movement began to pursue these ideas as practical political possibilities in the late nineteenth century. Shaftesbury was the chief advocate of the idea to return the Jews to Palestine as a nation, well before it gained currency with the British political and imperial establishment (Lewis, 2010, p. 114).

Lewis' main objective was to understand why Christian support for the idea of a Jewish homeland in Palestine was so prevalent in Victorian Britain and how this forms an important part of the background to the Balfour Declaration of 1917 (Lewis, 2010, p. 8). His exploration led him to conclude that historians had not been giving sufficient consideration to the importance of the religious and ethnic backgrounds of the British War

Cabinet. Lewis notes that, significantly, the War Cabinet was dominated by non-English members: David Lloyd George, although born in England, had been raised in Wales and was thought of as Welsh. Scotland had four members (Balfour and the two Labour members, Arthur Henderson and George Barnes, plus the New Brunswick-born Andrew Bonar Law, who from the age of 12 had lived in Scotland). Edward Carson was an Irish Protestant. Six of the ten members were thus from the Celtic fringe. A seventh member was Jan Christian Smuts, born in the Cape Colony, and the eighth non-English member was the German-born Alfred Milner. The resulting spiritual inclination of the British War Cabinet, in 1917, was the first indispensable thread that contributed to the process that brought about the Balfour Declaration. The fact that seven of the nine Gentile members had been raised in evangelical homes or personally embraced evangelicalism disposed them to think of the Jews as a "people," a "race," and a "nation," and thus inclined them towards the idea of a Jewish homeland and the idea that Britain had a special role in enabling this to happen (Lewis, 2010, pp. 332–334).

A number of other scholars have also traced the origin of this evangelical strand in the mindset of the 1917 British War Cabinet and identified Lord Ashley as the leading proponent of Christian Zionism in the nineteenth century. According to history professor Isaiah Friedman, it was Shaftesbury who, on August 1, 1838, propounded the scheme for the promotion of Jewish settlement in Palestine to then British foreign secretary Lord Palmerston, who became a determined advocate for the evangelical idea that Britain was to be "a chosen instrument of God for the Restoration of the Jews to the Holy Land" (Friedman, 1968, pp. 28–29).

Zionist historian Leonard Stein similarly referred to the body of devout and high-minded English Christians who, as early as the 1840s, believed that the time was at hand for the fulfilment of prophecy with the return of the Chosen People to the Holy Land and that it was God's will that the British nation should be His instrument for achieving His purpose. While acknowledging Shaftesbury as the most eminent representative of the early nineteenth-century movement for the restoration of the Jews to Palestine, Stein expressed a dim view of Shaftesbury's evangelically inspired philosemitism and held that, rather than being a friend of the Jews, he was primarily motivated by his purpose to see the Jews lose their identity by becoming Christians. Not only was Shaftesbury no friend of the Jews in domestic politics, neither did he demonstrate any sympathy with the ideas that later led to the politicization of the Zionist movement. "It is an illusion to suppose that he was a Zionist before his time" (Stein, 1961, pp. 10–11).

According to diplomatic history scholar and author Dr. Michael Makovsky, England had, since the sixteenth century, been receptive to the prospect of a revival of the historic connection between Jews and the Holy Land. He found that various English writers, clergymen, thinkers and politicians have thought about Jewish restoration to the Holy Land and their conversion to Christianity as part of a millennial vision. Lord Ashley saw Britain as God's chosen instrument to restore Jews to the Holy Land and trigger the Second Coming. This prompted Lord Palmerston to encourage the Ottoman Sultan to allow Jews to return to Palestine and to establish the British consulate in Jerusalem in 1839 (Makovsky, 2007, pp. 51–52).

International relations professor Alan Dowty, in describing the various motivations that led the British government to issue the Balfour Declaration, similarly noted that "some British leaders, including Prime Minister David Lloyd George, were Gentile Zionists drawn to the idea of Jewish revival in the Holy Land on religious and biblical grounds" (Dowty, 2012, p. 74).

Norman Bentwich, the British-appointed attorney-general of Mandatory Palestine, characterized the British people as a Bible-reading nation, which led many of them to believe the fulfilment of the prophecies of the Old Testament about the return of the Jews and the British government to recognize that purpose in its Near East policy. This political support began with the appointment in 1837 of a British Council in Jerusalem, which had the function of protecting Jews generally in Palestine. That function gradually evolved to support the foundation of a national home (Bentwich, 1960, cited in Gauthier, 2007, p. 279).

International law specialist Howard Grief, in his comprehensive legal case for the legitimacy of Israel's sovereignty over Mandated Palestine, traced the religiously minded support for the restoration of the Jewish people to Palestine to the days of Shaftesbury and Palmerston in the context of the synergy between their evangelical form of Zionism and their relations with Ottoman Turkey. While Palmerston's efforts to encourage the Jewish resettlement of Palestine were not successful at the time, they did pave the way towards the British policy which, 75 years later, resulted in the Balfour Declaration of November 2, 1917 (Grief, 2008, p. 534).

While it is clear that the British evangelical mindset, whether driven by philosemitic or antisemitic sentiments, was in harmony with the Zionist credo and thus facilitated this politically motivated nexus embodied in the Balfour Declaration, in the final analysis, as we shall see in the following sub-chapters, the Declaration resulted almost entirely from purely pragmatic political considerations. The implementation of the British political agenda hinged on the developments on the battlefronts, where the physical realities of the political dynamics were being played out.

The Military Picture

In 1917, WWI was still in full swing, with staggering casualties on all sides. The state of affairs on the Western Front showed the cumulative effects of the debilitating war of attrition that had brought the opposing sides there to a stalemate. American historian and author Barbara Tuchman goes back to the Battle of the Marne in September 1914 as the beginning of the exhausting battle of attrition that characterized the state of the war between the Allies and the Germans during the first three years of the conflict. While this is not the place to replicate the detailed description she provides of this pivotal battle (Tuchman, 2004, pp. 479–524), she effectively encapsulated its significance when she stated:

> The Battle of the Marne, as all the world knows, ended in a German retreat. Between the Ourcq and the Grand Morin, in the four days that were left of their schedule, the Germans lost their bid for "decisive victory" and thereby their opportunity to win the war. For France, for the Allies, in the long run for the world, the tragedy of the Marne was that it fell short of the victory it might have been. (Tuchman, 2004, p. 518)

During 1916, which John Keegan, an English military historian and author, referred to as "The Year of Battles," the protracted trench warfare took a heavy toll in casualties on the armies of Germany, France and Great Britain. The Battle of Verdun, which pitted the Germans against the French, started on February 21, 1916. By May 8, French and German casualties already exceeded 100,000 killed and wounded each. By the end of June, with over 200,000 men killed and wounded on each side, Verdun had become a place of terror and death that could not yield victory. On July 11, after a final effort by the Germans was beaten off, they ceased their attempt to destroy the French Army at Verdun and relapsed into the defensive. The Battle of Verdun ended on December 15, 1916, with the French recapturing much of the ground they had lost since the beginning of the battle (Keegan, 2000, pp. 284–286).

During the same year, on July 1, 1916, "while Verdun still raged," nineteen British and three French divisions had launched the Battle of the Somme. Keegan provides a detailed description of this ill-planned and recklessly executed attack, which he referred to as a catastrophe and the "greatest loss of life in British military history." He noted that the advance achieved nothing; most of the dead were killed on ground the British had held before the offence began. The Battle of the Somme exemplified the war of attrition, where "fresh divisions were sent in monotonous succession only to waste their energy in bloody struggles for tiny patches of ground. [...] By July 31, the Germans on the Somme had lost 160,000, the British and French over 200,000, yet the line had moved scarcely 3 miles since July 1" (Keegan, 2000, pp. 295, 297).

By November 19, 1916, when the Allied offensive was officially brought to a halt, the furthest line of advance, at Les Boeufs, lay only 7 miles forward of the front attacked from July 1. Yet, the losses suffered by both sides were staggering: "The Germans may have lost over 600,000 killed and wounded in the effort to keep their Somme positions. The Allies had certainly lost over 600,000; the French casualty figure being 194,451, the British 419,654. [...] To the British, it would remain the greatest military tragedy of the 20th century, indeed of their national military history." Keegan concluded his observations about the Battle of the Somme with the statement that "The Somme marked the end of an age of vital optimism in British life that has never been recovered" (Keegan, 2000, p. 299).

By the onset of 1917, what had been, until then, mainly a war of attrition in its various theatres reached the phase of desperate final efforts to call on the last reserves of physical strength and willpower to break the stalemate and hopefully administer a decisive knock-out blow. In Germany, in Britain and even in France, so grievously wounded by losses of life in defence of the homeland, the popular will nevertheless remained intact. In Germany, there was still no thought of accepting an unsatisfactory outcome. In Britain, the *Annual Register* recorded that "The prospect of [...] sacrifices [...] appeared to be quite powerless in effecting any modification of the national resolution to prosecute the war to a successful conclusion." Even in France, the bond of "sacred union" that united all segments of the nation had also persisted until the end of 1916, on the basis that "France had been the target of foreign aggression and had therefore to be defended. [...] Illogically, the belief that the war might be ended quickly, by a German collapse or a brilliant French victory, persisted as well" (Keegan, 2000, p. 321).

In 1917, the situation was nearing the point wherein the will to fight was not sufficient by itself to lead to victory if it was not backed by adequate human and material resources. Unfortunately, before this critical point was reached, none of the warring sides were prepared to face reality and were willing to spend whatever resources they could muster to force the issue. It was in this spirit that the British, assisted by the French, launched the Third Battle of Ypres, which Keegan referred to as Britain's "most notorious land campaign of the war" (Keegan, 2000, p. 355). This battle takes on specific importance as it illustrates the growing disconnect between political considerations and military hubris. Prime Minister David Lloyd George was oppressed by the rising tide of British casualties; already a quarter of a million dead, a high sacrifice in lives without significant military returns. Field Marshal Sir Douglas Haig, the Commander-in-Chief of the British Army on the Western Front, on the other hand, favoured a counter-offensive that would break the German line. During a session of the Committee on War Policy on June 19–21, when Haig outlined his plans and asked for their endorsement, Lloyd George wondered how the offensive could succeed without significant superiority in infantry and artillery. Yet, despite Lloyd George's fears about casualties, compounded by the difficulties of finding any more men from civil life to replace those lost, Haig insisted that it was necessary to go on engaging the enemy. The nub of the difference was that Haig wanted to fight, while Lloyd George did not. The Prime Minister could see good reasons for avoiding a battle: it would cause many men to be lost for little material gain, it would not win the war, neither the French nor the Russians would help, the Americans were coming, and, in consequence, the best strategy was for a succession of small attacks rather than a repetition of the Somme. His chief failing, unexpected in a man who so easily dominated his party and parliamentary colleagues, was a lack of will to talk Haig down. In the end, he felt unable, as a civilian prime minister, to impose his strategic views on his military advisors and was therefore obliged to accept theirs (Keegan, 2000, p. 358).

After a fifteen-day bombardment of the German positions, at 3:50 a.m. on July 31, 1917, the assaulting troops of the Second and Fifth Armies, with a portion of the French First Army, moved forward, accompanied by 136 tanks. By late morning, the familiar breakdown of communication between infantry and guns had occurred. By two in the afternoon, the German counter-attack was unleashed with an intense bombardment so heavy that it drove the leading French troops to flight. A combination of German shells and a torrential downpour soon turned the battlefield to mud (Keegan, 2000, p. 361).

Rain and lack of progress prompted Sir Douglas Haig to call a halt to the offensive on August 4 until the position could be consolidated. While total casualties, included wounded, numbered about 35,000 on the Allied side and the Germans had suffered similarly, Haig nevertheless insisted to the War Cabinet in London that the attack had been "highly satisfactory and the losses slight." The Germans, however, remained in command of the vital ground and had committed none of their counter-attack divisions.

On the evening of July 31, Crown Prince Rupprecht, who commanded the Sixth Army opposite the British in Flanders (Keegan, 2000, p. 180), recorded in his diary that he was "very satisfied with the results" (Keegan, 2000, p. 362).

By September, after many casualties and little success, Lloyd George, reviewing the whole state of the war, argued that, with Russia no longer a combatant and France barely so, it would be strategically wiser to husband British resources until the Americans arrived in force in 1918. Haig insisted that it was precisely because of the other allies' weakness that the battle must continue. Keegan comments that since there was no obvious successor to Haig, in spite of his ill-judged strategy and its harmful effect on his long-suffering army, the campaign was to be continued for want of a better man or plan. The "battle of the mud at Ypres – Passchendaele" would therefore continue, but not with British soldiers in the vanguard. Those had fought themselves out in August and early September, and the only reliable assault divisions Haig had left were in his ANZAC and Canadian Corps, which had been spared the worst of the battles in the year before. Between October 26 and November 10, 1917, the New Zealanders had suffered nearly 3,000 casualties, and the Canadian Corps, 15,634 killed and wounded (Keegan, 2000, pp. 365–368).

Keegan concluded that the Germans had another army in Russia with which to begin the war in the west all over again, while the British had given their all and had no other army. Like France, it had, by the end of 1917, enlisted every man that could be spared from farm and factory and had begun to compel into the ranks recruits that included "the hollow-chested, the round-shouldered, the stunted, the myopic and the over-age. Their physical deficiencies were evidence of Britain's desperation for soldiers and Haig's profligacy with men. On the Somme he had sent the flower of British youth to death or mutilation; at Passchendaele he had tipped the survivors into the slough of despond" (Keegan, 2000, p. 368).

On October 13, 1917 – three weeks before the Balfour Declaration – the British commanding generals approved a plan for a tank offensive on Third Army General Sir Julian Byng's front, which ran across dry, chalky ground on which tanks would not get bogged down, as they would on the muddy grounds of Flanders, where the main battles had so far taken place. By early November, with the battle at Passchendaele lapsing into futility, Haig was anxious for a compensatory success of any sort and, on November 10, at Byng's urging, gave his consent to the offensive at Cambrai (Keegan, 2000, p. 369).

The lack of proper coordination between men and machines on the British side and the formidable counter-attacking power of the German

Army caused the British offensive to fail in its mission. Over 300 tanks, massed on a front of 10,000 yards, were to advance in dense formation, with infantry following close behind to consolidate the ground conquered. General G. M. Harper, who commanded the infantry formation at the centre of the front of the attack, "did not like tanks but loved his Highland soldiers." He believed that tanks would attract German artillery fire on his infantry and so, instead of insisting that they follow closely, ordered them to keep 150–200 yards behind (Keegan, 2000, p. 370). In the centre of the front, the 51st Highland Division, gingerly following the tanks at some hundred yards' distance, entered the defended zone of the German 54th Reserve. Its gunners began to engage the British tanks as they appeared, unsupported by infantry, over the crest near Flesquières village, and knocked them out one by one. Soon, eleven tanks were out of action, and by the time the 51st Division's infantry at last got up with the tanks, it was too late for the division to reach the objective set for it for the day (Keegan, 2000, p. 371).

After ten days of slow and laborious progress, the British troops ran into a massive German counter-attack on November 30. In the following ten days, twenty divisions had been assembled by Crown Prince Rupprecht, the local commander. Not only did they take back much of the ground lost to the tanks on November 20 but an additional British-held portion as well. The Cambrai battle, which should have yielded a deep pocket driven into the German front, ended on ambiguous terms along the line of the Drocourt-Quéant Switch, a sinuous double salient which gave both the British and the Germans some of each other's long-held territory. It was an appropriate symbol of the precarious balance of power on the Western Front at the end of 1917 (Keegan, 2000, p. 371).

The desperate British military situation in 1917 was corroborated by military history professor Matthew Hughes. With reference to the Western Front, Hughes notes that Britain's military efforts from 1917 ended with an advance of only several miles and the capture of the village of Passchendaele in November. The attritional Third Battle of Ypres marked a new low in the battles on the Western Front. Men drowned in the mud of a grotesque, mangled landscape to capture territory the Germans quickly retook in ensuing offensives. The awful casualties incurred to capture a few sodden acres of Flanders from the Germans appalled Lloyd George, and he redoubled his efforts to redirect the conduct of the war and made the Palestine campaign a more attractive alternative (Hughes, 1999, p. 29). He wrote that 1917 raised the biggest challenge to date for the Entente: Russia had collapsed and sued for peace at Brest-Likovsk; mutinies in the French Army in 1917 following the failed Nivelle Offensive seriously weakened France's offensive potential; the Italians had been routed at the Battle of Caporetto in October 1917 and needed Anglo-French reinforcements; unrestricted German submarine warfare threatened to starve Britain into submission; and the build-up of American troops had yet to gather pace. As a result of all these negative developments, Britain was left bearing the brunt of the fighting. By October 1917, Britain had been fighting for over three years, casualties were mounting, and the situation looked grim. It looked as though the war would continue not only into 1918 but into 1919 or even 1920. With the other Allied armies collapsing and the Americans yet to arrive in strength, Britain could not afford to squander its army. This caused Lloyd George to look for alternatives to operations in France (Hughes, 1999, pp. 27–28).

It is important to note that the events which eventually transpired in 1918 were totally unforeseen the year before and thus could not affect the political decisions made in 1917 when, in view of the anticipation of the extended duration of the war, the British Army needed to be husbanded for a prolonged struggle. This situation led to the British government's political and military decisions that shaped the background and context that illuminates the path that led to the Balfour Declaration.

Hughes succinctly encapsulated the political mindset that arose from the dire situation the British were facing on the Western Front and which caused the British policymakers to shift their attention to the Middle East. He notes that the Palestine campaign provided an alternative to the devastation of the Western Front. The involvement of romantic figures such as Lawrence of Arabia, cavalry charges, the capture of historic cities, leadership by the mercurial General Sir Edmund Allenby, who was given command of the Egyptian Expeditionary Force in June 1917, and fighting in lands with deep religious attachments for three great monotheistic faiths combined to stir the emotions of a generation weary of the misery of trench warfare (Hughes, 1999, p. 2).

There was considerable propaganda value for Britain in success in Palestine at a time when operations in France offered little except long casualty lists. While cities such as Beirut, Damascus, Homs, Hama or Aleppo had none of the religious significance of Jerusalem and meant nothing to most British people, Jerusalem was a different matter in an area where people had a far more detailed grasp of the Bible, and Allenby's capture of the city was a great coup for Britain (Hughes, 1999, pp. 40–41).

Hughes points out that at the time Allenby sailed for Egypt, there was a civil-military struggle in London that demonstrated a lack of focus in the matter of British strategy. While Lloyd George was looking for alternatives to the debilitating grind of the Western Front, Field Marshall

Sir William Robertson, Chief of the Imperial General Staff, preferred to concentrate all efforts on the war in France. He and his generals argued that this was where the war would be won or lost. This disagreement in London complicated Allenby's task in Palestine as the political and military strategists were unable to agree on the objectives of the Palestine campaign (Hughes, 1999, p. 23). Hughes observed, interestingly, that those at the centre of power such as Lloyd George and Robertson were astute and able to see the complexities surrounding the prosecution of the war and that the conflict between them was more of a power struggle over who would direct the war (Hughes, 1999, p. 24). Hughes also identified the quintessential source of Britain's promise in favour of the reconstitution of a Jewish homeland in Palestine when he writes that

> Britain's support for Zionism expressed in the Balfour Declaration of November 1917 ... tightened her hold on Palestine as Zionism was a bridgehead for British interests.... Military occupation, added to Zionism, allowed Britain to extend her area of control in Palestine and negate her obligations to France as embodied in the Sykes-Picot agreement. (Hughes, 1999, p. 94)

Politics

The implications of the Balfour Declaration cannot be properly understood without an appreciation of the political context in which it was created. The final wording of the Balfour Declaration was the result of countless discussions and deliberations among all those who had an interest in its purpose and a say in the tenor of its terminology. The British government, while holding the upper hand, was not as uninhibited as the Zionist leadership in the formulation of the Declaration. While the Zionists were striving for the recovery of their ancestral homeland, to finally put an end to 2,000 years of statelessness, the British had to take into account the commitments they had made elsewhere regarding the same corner of the Middle East. To appreciate the nuances that were forged in the wording of the Declaration, one has to be aware of those concurrent self-serving but strategically understandable deals and commitments. Also critical to the understanding of the contrived ambiguity of the Balfour Declaration is the chronology of the deal-making efforts conducted by the British throughout World War I. The promises made first to the Arabs and then to the French preceded and significantly impacted the wording of the Balfour Declaration.

British historian William Mathew substantiated the theme of this study when he argued that Britain's endorsement of a national home for Jews in Palestine reflected both the unpredictability of the events of World War I and the concerns and personalities of the British politicians involved (Mathew, 2011, p. 26). While it was critical for the Zionist project that Prime Minister Herbert Asquith, who found the idea of a Jewish Palestine under British suzerainty particularly unappealing, was replaced in December 1916 by the pro-Zionist Lloyd George, this transfer of power might never have taken place if Asquith and Lloyd George had been able to work out their political differences (Mathew, 2011, pp. 30, 39).

Asquith's negative attitude towards the Zionist project manifested itself when Herbert Louis Samuel, the first Jew ever to sit in a British Cabinet, outlined a scheme to Foreign Secretary Sir Edward Grey for setting up a Jewish state in Palestine. In January of 1915, he submitted a memorandum to Asquith on the future of Palestine and, two months later, he circulated a second memorandum to the Cabinet in which he referred to the possibility of establishing an autonomous Jewish state in Palestine. Nothing came of his proposal because of the opposition of Asquith (Grief, 2008, p. 86).

It is important to keep in mind the two stages on which World War I was conducted: the virtual and the real. The map-gazing diplomatic arena was the mirror image of the blood-soaked physical battle fronts. The ebbs and tides of both shaped the outcome of both, perhaps somewhat haphazardly on an episodic basis but inexorably from the cumulative historical perspective.

During World War I, the British had separate diplomatic negotiations going on with different parties involved in the war. They made promises and deals that were often in conflict with each other and known only to them. A copious amount of writing has been devoted to the Machiavellian plots that underpinned the political tugs of war between the participants in World War I. We are alluding in particular to the three major British undertakings which contextualize the complex political process that led to the promulgation of the Balfour Declaration. By running concurrent conflicting agendas with different audiences and in the process making irreconcilable promises and commitments, primarily for serving their own war exigencies, the British sowed the seeds of discontent which would eventually undermine the fulfilment of the expectations raised by the Balfour Declaration. As put succinctly by Nick Reynold:

> Britain had been involved in political shenanigans throughout the war. It had made promises (McMahon) in 1915/16 to the Arabs, led by Sherif Hussein, that they would get their own independent state in a part of Palestine after the war. This was followed a year later by an agreement (Sykes-Picot) with France and Russia that would carve up the Middle East, with fair shares for all. The French would have a coastal strip from the

north as far as Haifa, and the Jerusalem area would be shared among
different countries, including France. A year later the Zionists had been
promised British support for the establishment of a Jewish homeland in the
same small piece of land. (Reynold, 2014, pp. 4–5)

Promises to the Arabs

British history professor Jonathan Schneer referred to the much-debated
Hussein-McMahon correspondence as the first of these three opportunistic
political manoeuvres in which Lieutenant-Colonel Sir Vincent Arthur
Henry McMahon, High Commissioner of Egypt, offered ambiguously
worded territorial inducements to the Grand Sharif of Mecca to tempt him
into an anti-Ottoman rebellion. Such a rebellion, from the British
perspective, would aid the British war effort (Schneer, 2010, pp. 57, 69).

By the beginning of 1915, a new man was running Britain's Cairo
operation. McMahon had been brought in from his last posting in India to
fill in for Lord Kitchener, detained by war work in London. Here we
encounter a telling example of the political differences that existed
between major power centres of the British Empire. British officials in
India strongly opposed Cairo's plan for an uprising led by Sharif Hussein.
They especially opposed Kitchener's suggestion that an Arab might
repossess the caliphate from the Turks and specifically discounted the
sharif's personal influence and abilities. They considered their existing
relations with the principalities running along the Arabian coast of the
Indian Ocean, from Aden to the Gulf of Oman, sufficient for their
imperialist purpose. The establishment of a great Arabian state headed by
Sharif Hussein would preclude their annexationist dreams. So far as they
favoured any Arab leader for a larger role, it was Ibn Saud, who, as chief
of the sectarian Wahhabis, could never become caliph. Having sent troops
across the Indian Ocean into Mesopotamia, they intended to keep that
territory after the war. They assumed that McMahon, so recently one of
them, still supported their position (Schneer, 2010, p. 56).

Once McMahon arrived in Cairo, however, the British intelligence
community there soon converted him to their position. Sir Francis
Reginald Wingate, the governor-general of Sudan and commander-in-chief
of the Egyptian army, was among those who strongly believed that an
Arab rebellion would aid the British war effort. Moreover, he cherished a
secret personal ambition: that Cairo would "mother" a great Arab Empire,
as Delhi had "mothered" Britain's Empire in India, and that he would be
its viceroy (Schneer, 2010, p. 57).

In one cable after another, Wingate urged first Gilbert Clayton, at that
time British director of military intelligence for the Middle East, then

McMahon, and then, through McMahon, both Foreign Secretary Sir Edward Grey and Secretary of State for War, Lord Kitchener, to make Hussein an offer he could not refuse. Meanwhile, from Delhi, Viceroy Lord Hardinge urged the opposite, that the sharif not be encouraged. Wingate and Hardinge sent each other conflicting cables setting out their positions as well. Debate raged in the Foreign Office, but in the end, Cairo and Khartoum and their belief that an Arab rebellion would aid the British war effort prevailed. Foreign Secretary Grey informed Wingate that if he thought it necessary to achieve a peace agreement with Hussein, he was authorized to promise him that the Arabian Peninsula and its Muslim Holy Places would remain in the hands of an independent sovereign Muslim state (Schneer, 2010, p. 57).

The interplay between the nascent Arab nationalist movement and the political intrigues of the Ottoman Sultan's court provided the opportunity for Great Britain to seek what it hoped would be vital support in its daunting military situation. From the British perspective, the Arab overtures came at a precarious phase of the war. Bulgaria's entry on the side of the Central Powers provided them with not only an increment of strength, but also a direct overland route from Germany to Constantinople. At Gallipoli, the British prospects looked bleak as well; losses mounted daily, morale had plummeted, and their beachhead remained insecure, and so withdrawal seemed increasingly likely. Meanwhile in Mesopotamia, British forces were overextended and were on the verge of devastating military setbacks at Ctesiphon and Kut (Schneer, 2010, p. 63).

While the British were highly motivated to play the Arab revolt card against their Turkish masters, the Ottomans were pressing Grand Sharif Hussein to raise an army to throw his soldiers against the British at the Suez Canal. Even more alarming was their demand that Hussein endorse their call to jihad, which would inspire millions of British Muslim subjects in Egypt, Sudan and India to rise up against their colonial infidel masters, making Britain's worst nightmare come true (Schneer, 2010, p. 49).

While the grand sharif was playing for time so that he could feel out the main Arab leaders about their intentions and their likely reaction if he were to launch a rebellion against the Ottoman government, new developments of direct concern hastened his thinking. In January 1915, Hussein's oldest son, Ali, while on a military mission into Medina, found out that the Turkish governor of the Hejaz, who accompanied him, was carrying documents that showed that he intended to depose Hussein and to assert ultimate control over the Hejaz (Schneer, 2010, p. 50).

We have entered the phase during which an undercover level of activity, aimed at overthrowing the Ottoman regime, was developing within the ranks of the Sultan's military establishment. The plans of the secret Arab society al-Fatat, which believed that Arab autonomy required complete independence from Turkey, were already well advanced. Its members' views had altered considerably since the outbreak of the war. Arab autonomy within the Ottoman Empire would no longer satisfy them, since the Ottomans likely could no longer protect Arabia from European imperialist designs. They now believed that Arab interests required complete independence from Turkey. Thus, the war hastened the society's transition from Ottomanism to Arabism. In Syria, al-Fatat combined forces with another major secret society, al-Ahd. Together the two groups planned a rising. Arab army officers stationed in Damascus would lead their soldiers into a revolt that Syrian desert tribes whose sheikhs already belonged to the societies would join. The leaders hoped the revolt would spread to the Arabian Peninsula as well (Schneer, 2010, p. 50).

Al-Fatat's mission to sound out Grand Sharif Hussein at the time that he was seriously considering the British offer of helping to overthrow the Ottoman regime in exchange for an independent Arab kingdom is indicative of the growing development of the drive towards Arab nationhood. As Ali was arriving back in Mecca, another young man, Fauzi al-Bakri, was setting out from Damascus for the same city. The Turks had conscripted him, but he belonged to a prominent Syrian family that had long been friendly with the family of Grand Sharif Hussein. Unknown to them, however, Fauzi had recently joined al-Fatat. Just before his departure from Damascus, the society commissioned him to find out if, in the event Arab nationalists rose against the Turks in Syria and Iraq, the grand sharif would consent to be their leader and, if he agreed, if he would send a deputy to work out plans with them beforehand (Schneer, 2010, p. 50).

After hearing out Fauzi, Hussein held a family council with his sons to discuss the matter. While his oldest son Feisal distrusted Western imperialist designs in the Middle East and had hitherto favoured maintaining relations with the Ottomans, Abdullah had held anti-Turk and pro-British views since at least early 1914. Abdullah largely accepted the Arab nationalist position, but his father remained, as always, more a pan-Islamist than an Arab nationalist, although he was increasingly doubtful that he could continue to cooperate with the Ottoman regime. The result of the meeting was a decision to send Faisal to Constantinople to convey to the Ottoman authorities his father's outrage at the governor's double-dealing. En route, Faisal was to stop at Damascus and meet clandestinely with representatives of the secret societies in order to gauge them and their plans. Then he was to report back to his father (Schneer, 2010, p. 51).

Feisal's secret meetings with emissaries from al-Ahd and al-Fatat impressed him deeply. He changed from thinking that his father should stick with the Ottomans and have nothing to do with Arab nationalist schemes to being of the belief that his father should lead the Arab nationalist attempt to throw off the Ottoman yoke even if it led to a strengthened role for Britain in the Middle East. Feisal promised the support of the Hejazi tribes – without consulting his father. What the plotters wanted was for the Grand Sharif of Mecca to lend his prestigious support to their uprising and for Feisal himself, the grand sharif's most effective general, to become their visible leader (Schneer, 2010, p. 53). They had settled, too, the question of Great Britain's role in their rebellion and its aftermath, which they outlined in what became known as the Damascus Protocol, which included:

> The recognition by Great Britain of the independence of the Arab countries lying within specific frontiers running along parallel 37° North from the Mediterranean coast to the border of Persia northeast of Baghdad, all the way down to the Indian Ocean with the exception of the port of Aden, and back up with the Red Sea and Mediterranean Sea as the Western frontier up to the Anatolian seaport of Mersin on the 37° North parallel.
>   The abolition of all exceptional privileges granted to foreigners.
>   The conclusion of a defensive alliance between Great Britain and the future independent Arab state.
>   The grant of economic preference to Great Britain. (Schneer, 2010, pp. 53–54)

In essence, the Damascus Protocol, which Schneer refers to as the foundation document and lodestar of the Arab revolt, envisioned a federation of Arab countries organized within a single independent Arab state or empire, containing Palestine, and backed by Britain, which would receive in return economic preferences. Implicit in the document was the inference that Grand Sharif Hussein would preside over the great state (Schneer, 2010, p. 54).

In July of 1915, Hussein sent a message to Cairo, which repeated the Damascus Protocol and asked whether the British approved it and warned that, if they did not, "we will consider ourselves free in word and deed from the bonds of our previous declaration" (Schneer, 2010, p. 59).

The British were delighted with Hussein's promise of cooperation, until they realized that Hussein had copied the proposed borders of the new Arab state verbatim from the Damascus Protocol, which the British found far too expansive. McMahon, after much consultation with London, tried to square the circle by confirming in a letter to Hussein on August 29, 1915 "the British desire for the independence of Arabia and its inhabitants, together with our approval of the Arab Caliphate when it should be proclaimed." McMahon dodged the questions of limits, frontiers and boundaries by adding that it would appear premature to discuss such details in the heat of war (Schneer, 2010, p. 59).

In his angry response on September 9, Hussein argued that "the borders he had indicated were essential for the well-being of any future Arab state" (Schneer, 2010, p. 59). The two parties had apparently arrived at an impasse, with both sides seemingly unwilling to compromise. What broke the stalemate was the appearance on the scene of 24-year-old Muhammed Sharif al-Faruqi, an Arab Ottoman staff officer from Mosul who in the autumn of 1915 deserted the Ottoman forces at Gallipoli and crossed over to Allied lines. As related by both Fromkin (2009, p. 176) and Schneer (2010, p. 60), he claimed to have important information for British intelligence in Cairo and was promptly sent to Egypt for interrogation. In his debriefing by Gilbert Clayton, the chief British intelligence officer in the Middle East, he claimed to be a member of the secret Arab military society al-Ahd. His unverified claim that he was a spokesman for the organization was believed by British intelligence, although it turned out later that he was not in fact a representative of al-Ahd or indeed any other group and that Clayton had been duped.

Faruqi assured Clayton that the reach of the secret society extended to Damascus and Beirut provinces, with branches being started in every important town or station (Schneer, 2010, p. 60). He claimed full awareness of the real military situation of the two contending forces and that siding with the Allies would greatly weaken the enemy. He alleged he was aware of the negotiations between the British and the sharif and of their willingness to give the sharif the necessary arms and ammunitions for the attainment of his object. He also maintained that his people had found out that the British had given their consent to the sharif establishing an Arab empire but that the limits of this empire were not defined. He added that the secret societies had renounced allegiance to the Sultan of Turkey and sworn instead to support Hussein, who would lead their rebellion (Schneer, 2010, p. 61).

Faruqi knew the terms of the Damascus Protocol and McMahon's response to it. He had deserted in part to argue for the boundaries allocated in the Protocol. Although he was not authorized to speak for the secret societies, he acted as though he was, and the British came to treat him as such. He asserted that the scheme he was promoting embraced all the Arab countries, including Syria and Mesopotamia, but if his people could not have all, then they wanted as much as they could get. More specifically, he said that the plotters insisted on keeping in Arabia the purely Arab districts of Aleppo, Damascus, Hama and Homs. Schneer points out that this was the first mention of a geographical caveat that would prove a stumbling block to all future understanding and goodwill. The formulation appears for the first time in a cable reporting on the discussion with Faruqi that McMahon sent to London on October 19, 1915 (Schneer, 2010, p. 61).

Faruqi even went so far as to state that Turkey and Germany were fully alive to the situation, had already approached the leaders of the Young Arab party, and had promised them the granting of their demands in full. He assured Clayton, however, that the party leaders were still strongly inclined towards Britain (Schneer, 2010, p. 62).

While historians have found no archival evidence that the Turks and Germans were prepared to grant the Arab demands, events would soon put the lie to Faruqi's assertion. Far from wanting to woo Arab nationalists, the Turks wanted only to destroy them, as a series of brutal trials, imprisonments and hangings in Damascus would disclose in a matter of months (Schneer, 2010, p. 62).

What mattered in October 1915, however, was that Clayton believed that the Arab plotters were powerful and that Germany and Turkey were near to winning them over. Clayton disagreed with McMahon's strategy to postpone discussion of future boundaries and pushed instead for defining the boundaries immediately and in a way that would satisfy Arab aspirations. He thought that this was necessary if Britain hoped to outbid the Germans. He warned London that to reject the Arab proposals entirely, or even to seek to evade issues, would throw the Young Arab party definitively into the arms of the enemy and that their resources would be employed against Britain throughout the Arab countries. Clayton warned of the danger that the religious element would come into play and that the jihad, so far a failure, might become a very grim reality, the effects of which would certainly be far-reaching and potentially disastrous (Schneer, 2010, p. 62).

This unlikely episode only makes sense if seen in the context of concurrent developments. Faruqi appeared before Clayton almost simultaneously with Hussein's chilly letter of September 9, 1915, and his claims were in sync with the sharif's claims. He claimed that he was not speaking for himself but for a larger movement that had established the boundaries of the future Arabian federation (Schneer, 2010, p. 63).

Faruqi's multiple claims and assertions, as inflated and unverified as they were, ended up convincing Clayton that it was necessary that the disputed boundaries be defined immediately in line with the Arab aspirations. Clayton thought it was necessary if Britain hoped to outbid the Germans. In memos and cables, the Cairo contingent stressed Britain's dire predicament in the Middle East and the grim consequences of inaction. Reginald Wingate did so from Khartoum, and political advisor to the Foreign Office Sir Mark Sykes echoed the same message at the war committee meeting. McMahon prepared to write the most important letter of his career, one that would induce Hussein finally to throw down the gauntlet to Turkey (Schneer, 2010, p. 62).

The end game of the Hussein-McMahon diplomatic episode was embodied in what is generally recognized as "the most important letter in the Hussein-McMahon correspondence" (Schneer, 2010, p. 63; Gauthier, 2007, p. 218; Ingrams, 2009, p. 3). The letter was dated October 24, 1915. It is generally agreed, by historians on both sides of the Arab Israeli conflict, that the most crucial words were contained in the following paragraphs:

> The two districts of Mersina and Alexandretta and portions of Syria lying to the West of the districts of Damascus, Homs, Hama and Aleppo cannot be said to be purely Arab, and should be excluded from the limits demanded.
>
> With the above modification, and without prejudice to our existing treaties with Arab chiefs, we accept those limits.
>
> As for those regions lying within those frontiers wherein Great Britain is free to act without detriment to the interests of her ally, France, I am empowered in the name of the Government of Great Britain to get the following assurances and make the following reply to your letter: that subject to the above modifications, Great Britain is prepared to recognize and support the independence of the Arabs in all the regions within the limits demanded by the Sharif of Mecca. (Ingrams, 2009, p. 2)

Lebanese-Egyptian historian George Antonius considered McMahon's letter of October 24, 1915 the most important international document in the history of the Arab national movement, as it contained the pledges which brought the Arabs into the war openly on the side of the Allies (Antonius, 1939, p. 217).

While an attempt to describe all the arguments about the true meaning and intent of this particular letter would produce a cornucopia of exegetic pyrotechnics, Ingrams provided a succinct synopsis that seems to encapsulate the essential points. She argued that the letter's omission of Palestine by name led the Arabs to argue, in later years, that it was not geographically possible for Palestine to be included in the "portions of Syria lying to the West of the districts of Damascus, Homs, Hama and Aleppo." The British government, however, maintained that it had always intended to exclude Palestine from the area of Arab independence. The imprecision of the McMahon letter might have been intentional because, while it encouraged Arab hopes for independence, the British government also had to consider its French ally's long-standing cultural links with Syria and Lebanon and its consequent claims to those countries after the Turks were defeated (Ingrams, 2009, p. 2).

The Hussein-McMahon correspondence episode finally ran its course with the Grand Sharif's reply of January 1, 1916. In it, he accepted McMahon's suggestion that the future be decided at a later date in deference to the alliance between Great Britain and France in the agreement made between them during the present war. To underline his ultimate objective, he declared that, after the war, no deviation ceding any amount of territory to France or any other power would be tolerated (Schneer, 2010, p. 73).

Schneer attributed Hussein's willingness to postpone settling the border issue to the fact that his deteriorating relations with the Turks, coupled with his strengthening relation with the plotters, pointed to rebellion as the most likely and hopeful course and that he wanted the British on board as much as they wanted him (Schneer, 2010, p. 73). As Schneer concluded:

> This would have to do, it was good enough. Now the spring was wound up and the plot would move forward. But the deferred question of Syrian, Lebanese, and especially Palestinian borders, and Britain's role in Mesopotamia, remained a stumbling block to future understanding and good relations. (Schneer, 2010, p. 74)

As we mentioned earlier, the Balfour Declaration was not created in a vacuum. It was the third in the sequence of three major strategic diplomatic manoeuvres the British were engaged in during World War I. Each of these episodes contained elements that impacted on the evolution of the other two. The principal seed of contention was the unsettled question of whether Palestine was part of the spoils of war promised by the British to the Arabs.

While the promises made by the British to the Arabs on October 24, 1915 to elicit their support against the Turks had a significant bearing on the other two strategic negotiations the British conducted during World War, they could not result in binding obligations on the nations or parties concerned unless officially adopted and incorporated in some international instrument. Negotiations on the partition of the Turkish territories between Great Britain, France and Russia only commenced a few months after the McMahon-Hussein correspondence of October 1915 (Gauthier, 2007, pp. 221–222).

The British-French Territorial Tug of War

All the authors referenced in this chapter have painted detailed narratives about the tenor and contents of these new negotiations, all under the rubric of the Sykes-Picot Agreement. The common denominators between these various studies are succinctly encapsulated by John Strawson, in whose view the defeat and collapse of Europe's traditional enemy, the Ottoman Empire, opened the entire Middle East to the victorious powers:

> The discovery of oil in Arabia and the conversion of the British fleet to the new fuel underlined its critical role.... The secret deal by Mark Sykes and George Picot sought an orderly replacement of Ottoman rule with Britain and France dividing the region between them. Under the Sykes-Picot agreement some of what became Palestine would fall under the French, but most under the British – although there was a provision that the area could come under international supervision. The implementation of the agreement would remain a contentious issue between both powers during and after the war. (Strawson, 2010, p. 9)

To establish the policies on which they would base their negotiations with the French, the British set up a committee in April 1915 at the request of Prime Minister Asquith. This committee, chaired by Sir Maurice de Bunsen, former British Ambassador to Vienna, and which would be known as the Bunsen Committee, was given the responsibility of making recommendations regarding the interests and entitlements of Great Britain relating to the Turkish territories in the event of the victory of the Allies. A report was published on June 30, 1915. The committee concluded that the destiny of Palestine must be the subject of special negotiations involving both belligerents and neutrals. According to the international lawyer and author Jacques Paul Gauthier, some British political leaders believed in full control over Palestine while others realized that such control would have to be shared or the area would have to be under international administration (Gauthier, 2007, p. 225).

David Fromkin described the committee as being composed of one representative each from the Foreign Office, the Admiralty, the India Office and other relevant departments. Field Marshal Horatio Herbert Kitchener, who had been appointed Secretary of State for War on August 5, 1914, was represented on the committee by General Sir Charles Calwell, Director-General of Military Operations. In addition, Kitchener placed Sir Mark Sykes on the committee as his personal representative, and through Sykes, the Secretary of State for War dominated the committee's proceedings. Thereafter, Sykes remained the London bureaucrat

charged with responsibility for Middle Eastern affairs throughout the war
(Fromkin, 2009, p. 146). Kitchener required a young politician who knew
the Middle East, and the young Sykes was one of the handful of Members
of Parliament who knew the area. As a Tory, he shared many of
Kitchener's sentiments and prejudices (Fromkin, 2009, p. 147).

While Sykes did not work with Kitchener directly – all two-way
communications were passed through Kitchener's close friend and
personal military secretary Lieutenant-Colonel Oswald FitzGerald – the
other members assumed that he spoke with the full weight of Lord
Kitchener's authority. The relatively inexperienced M.P. controlled the
interdepartmental committee. He was outspoken and opinionated. He was
the only member of the committee who had been to most parts of the
Ottoman Empire; he alone could speak from first-hand knowledge
(Fromkin, 2009, p. 147).

After discussing the relative advantages of the alternatives available to
Britain, the committee, led by Sykes, proposed the creation of five largely
autonomous provinces in the decentralized Ottoman Empire which they
envisaged. They were to be Syria, Palestine, Armenia, Anatolia and
Jazirah-Iraq (the northern and southern parts of Mesopotamia). As the
committee saw it, British influence or control would be desirable in a wide
swath across the Middle East from the Mediterranean to the Persian Gulf.
A British railroad was to be constructed from a Mediterranean port to
Mesopotamia to provide the overland road to the East. Kitchener
continued to insist on Alexandretta as the port, but Sykes demanded that it
be Haifa, and FitzGerald, mediating between the two, let Sykes have his
way (Fromkin, 2009, p. 148).

In all other respects, Sykes hewed close to the Kitchener line, though
with slight modifications of his own. Like Kitchener, he advocated moving
the caliphate to the south to put it out of the reach of Russia's influence;
but he added that it would also put it out of the reach of France's financial
control, for he assumed that Ottoman finances would be largely controlled
by the French in view of their large investment in the Ottoman public debt
(Fromkin, 2009, p. 149). The overall approach, however, was Kitchener's.
Sykes, who had been a conspicuous member of the pro-Turkish bloc in
Parliament, abandoned his conviction that the integrity of the Ottoman
Empire ought to be maintained (Fromkin, 2009, p. 149).

While it was one thing for the British to discuss their postwar strategic
ambitions among themselves, they were, in spite of their imperial hubris,
not really an island unto themselves and had to take into account the
strategic imperatives of friend and foe alike. As the veteran war
correspondent and author Scott Anderson pointed out, McMahon had

"unobtrusively" inserted what amounted to an escape clause in his October 24, 1915 letter to Sharif Hussein to the effect that the promises made to the Arabs only applied to "those regions lying within those frontiers wherein Great Britain is free to act without detriment to the interests of her ally, France." This meant that if the French had a problem with some aspects of the McMahon-Hussein deal, their resistance might override British acceptance (Anderson, 2012, p. 162).

The British knew only too well that the French were likely to have such a problem. The previous summer, the French ambassador to Great Britain had spelled out to Foreign Secretary Grey precisely what territory his nation intended to grab in the Middle East. This included all of greater Syria, or the most valuable lands now promised to Hussein (Anderson, 2012, p. 162).

To get around this dilemma, the British decided not to tell the French of the deal struck with Hussein. Instead, in late November, French diplomats were invited to London to discuss their wish list for the Near East. British officials expressed surprise when the French reiterated that they wanted pretty much the whole thing: Lebanon, Palestine, the Syrian interior, Iraq. Thus the stage was set for one of the strangest and – with the advantage of hindsight – most destructive diplomatic accords ever penned: the Sykes-Picot Agreement (Anderson, 2012, p. 162).

Anderson saw this egregious diplomatic high-stakes wheeling and dealing episode as a telling portrayal of the cynicism with which the British and French pursued their post-WWI geopolitical objectives. The future map of the Middle East was cobbled together in just a few days, in early January 1916, by two mid-level diplomats: Sir Mark Sykes and Francois Georges-Picot, the French consul general in Beirut. This map bore no resemblance to the one envisioned by Emir Hussein. The French and British imperial ambitions reduced the promised independent Arab nation to the desert wastelands of Arabia and turned control of Greater Syria over to the French and possession of Iraq to the British. The remainder of the land north and inland of Hussein's kingdom of the Hejaz would remain under indirect British and French control, with "priority of right of enterprise." Sykes and Picot felt that they could pledge independence for these so-called Zone A and B enclaves since neither of them believed the Arabs were truly capable of governing themselves. They felt secure that these territories would end up as British and French vassal states. They even came up with a new designation for Palestine. Rather than be part of the future Arab nation, it was now to fall under the joint administration of France, Great Britain and Russia (Anderson, 2012, p. 162).

Anderson acknowledged that, in Picot's defence, he could not have known how much his territorial demands conflicted with those of Emir Hussein, because his British counterpart never chose to tell him. In any event, during those crucial days of early January 1916, when much of the future map of the Middle East was being drawn, Sykes was the only person in the world who knew the full details of both the McMahon-Hussein correspondence and the emerging Sykes-Picot concord and who might have grasped the extent to which Arab, French and British goals in the region had now been set on a collision course (Anderson, 2012, p. 163).

While the labyrinthine machinations required to keep the various parties affected by these conflicting diplomatic manoeuvres in the dark make fascinating reading, they are referred to in this analysis only to illuminate the tortuous political path that led the British government to turn a minuscule portion of the soon to be conquered Middle East into a thrice-promised land.

Reams of scholarly pages have been devoted to the purpose, nature and ultimate effect of the Sykes-Picot Agreement. The major elements from the discussions contained in the analyses of different academics who have investigated this chapter of World War I diplomacy can be summarized as follows.

While the British and French diplomatic activities during the Sykes-Picot episode did involve Tsarist Russia and its territorial ambitions, these did not extend to the part of the Middle East covered by the McMahon-Hussein agreement. Therefore, they need not be taken into account when discussing the dynamics of the British motivation for the Balfour Declaration. Russia was involved only to the extent that "some regions of the Ottoman Empire (Kurdistan and parts of Armenia) would be annexed or ceded to it" (Grief, 2008, p. 20). As we shall see further on, however, the revolutionary developments in Russia in 1917 did have a significant impact on the British handling of the Zionist aspirations.

Grief observed that the Sykes-Picot Agreement could never have been relied upon from a legal point of view since it had been conceived secretly prior to the break-up of the Ottoman Empire and was never publicly announced by Britain and France even after they ratified it (Grief, 2008, p. 44). As a direct result of the Allied Supreme Council decision at the San Remo Peace Conference on April 24, 1920, the secret Sykes-Picot treaty of May 1916 was officially replaced and terminated and "the title of sovereignty over Palestine was exclusively vested in the Jewish People and not in any other nation, state or entity [...]" (Grief, 2008, p. 19).

In political studies professor Efraim Karsh's assessment, even after the Ottoman entry into the war, London was reluctant to divert the necessary resources for its defeat from the European war theatre and for months remained wedded to the Muslim empire's continued existence, leaving it to a local Meccan potentate – Sharif Hussein Ibn Ali of the Hashemite family – to push the idea of its destruction. Impressed by Hussein's promises to raise the Ottoman Empire's Arabic-speaking subjects in revolt against their Muslim suzerain, the British accepted his main territorial demands, albeit in a highly equivocal fashion, then persuaded their French and Russian allies to endorse them in what came to be known as the May 1916 Sykes-Picot Agreement. And while Hussein never came close to fulfilling his end of the bargain and the Sykes-Picot Agreement never saw the light of day, the sharif's false pretences would have a considerable impact on the future shape of the Middle East (Karsh, 2015, p. 3).

Karsh argued that there was nothing deceitful about the Anglo-French talks. With the two war allies engaged in a mortal struggle over their destiny, it was only natural for them to coordinate strategies, in accordance with the September 1914 Declaration of London obliging the Anglo-French-Russian Entente to coordinate its peace terms. If anything, it was France that should have harboured a grievance against Britain for breaching the terms of their wartime alliance by making unauthorized promises to a minor third party that had not even decided to ally itself with the Entente. It was precisely to staunch this grievance that the British initiated talks with the French, not to renege on their tentative understanding with Hussein but to give it the widest possible international recognition. According to British historian Albert Hourani, it seems clear that the intention of the British government, when it made the Sykes-Picot Agreement, was to reconcile the interests of France with the pledges given to Sharif Hussein (Karsh, 2015, p. 22).

While the significance of the Sykes-Picot Agreement has drawn an endless stream of interpretative commentary, it cannot be denied that it was overtaken by events and never reached any legally enforceable status. It did, nevertheless, raise considerable unrequited political expectations which would become a source of claims and counterclaims of the parties enmeshed in the enduring Middle East conflict. Modern history scholar and author Harry Defries notes that in April of 1917, the sub-committee of the Imperial War Cabinet deliberated on the territorial desiderata of the terms of peace. In its report on April 28, the sub-committee concluded:

> The acquisition by Germany, through control of Turkey, of political and military control of Palestine and Mesopotamia would imperil the communication between the United Kingdom and the East and Australasia

through the Suez Canal, and would directly threaten the security of Egypt and India. It was considered of great importance that both Palestine and Mesopotamia should be under British control. It was therefore desirable that the government should secure a modification of the Sykes-Picot agreement with France of May 1916 in order to give Great Britain definite and exclusive control over Palestine. (Defries, 2001, p. 64)

The Zionist Card

Leonard Stein traced the beginnings of the nexus between political Zionism and the Jewish community in Great Britain to Theodor Herzl's initial steps to introduce his concept of a Jewish homeland to the political arena. He had done everything in his power to interest them in his ideas about the nature of the Jewish problem and the way to deal with it and had, in his own mind, cast them for the leading role in the execution of his plans. As it turned out, the leaders of Anglo-Jewry were, with few exceptions, alarmed rather than attracted by his proposals, but he had begun with high hopes of the support to be expected from them (Stein, 1961, p. 17).

In November 1895, during a visit to London, Herzl met some prominent members of the Anglo-Jewish community and ended by addressing a select group known as the Maccabeans, the first audience to hear a considerate exposition of his views. A few months later in Vienna, he published his pamphlet *Der Judenstaat*, the English version of which, *The Jewish State*, was published in the same year in London. In it, as he stated in its preface, he developed the idea of the restoration of the Jewish State (Herzl, 2010, p. 1)

In 1899, Herzl showed his desire for a foothold in England, and his respect for London as the world's financial centre, by incorporating the Jewish Colonial Trust, which was to be the main financial instrument of his movement, as an English company. The precedent was thus set and would be followed in the next two years by the Jewish National Fund and other important Zionist institutions. There was some significance in the choice of London as the venue of the Fourth Zionist Congress. "England," Herzl declared in his opening address, "England, great and free, looking out over all the seas, will understand us and our endeavours" (Stein, 1961, p. 18).

This is not the place to describe Herzl's failed attempts between 1898 and 1902 to obtain assistance from Germany and Turkey towards the creation of a home for the Jewish people in Palestine. Nor is it the place to discuss the suggested alternatives in Sinai, Cyprus and East Africa, which faltered in the face of the opposition against Jewish immigration by the established settlers in those territories. What set the Zionist narrative back on its course was the adoption by an overwhelming majority of a statement by the Seventh Zionist Congress on July 30, 1905, in which it affirmed its rejection of all Zionist activity outside Palestine and its immediate neighbourhood and, while thanking the British government for its offer to make land available for a Jewish settlement in East Africa, resolved not to engage itself further with the proposal (Stein, 1961, p. 32).

After the liquidation of the East African project in 1905, it was some years before the Zionist leaders attempted to re-establish contact with the British government. The first Zionist toe dips in the murky waters of pre-World War I British politics occurred "in the summer of 1912, when Nahum Sokolow, a Russian-Polish member of the Zionist Executive, the directorate of the Movement, was sent from Berlin to take some soundings in London." While he did not get to meet with any British government officials, he returned to Berlin with nothing much to report beyond his impression that in English public life, and especially in religious circles, Zionism had some influential friends (Stein, 1961, p. 41).

A few months later, when war broke out in the Balkans, the Powers were once more confronted with the Eastern question in acute and urgent form, and there was a strong feeling in some Zionist circles that now was the time for a fresh approach to the British government (Stein, 1961, p. 41). A brief description of this Balkan war episode brought out its significance in the scheme of things. In what Fromkin referred to as the First Balkan War (1912–13):

> The Balkan League (of Bulgaria, Greece, Montenegro, and Serbia) defeated Turkey and annexed almost all of the territory the Ottoman Empire still held in Europe. In the Second Balkan War (1913), the Ottoman Empire managed to regain some territory in Thrace, immediately across the water from Asiatic Turkey; but that looked to offer merely a brief respite in the empire's continuing disintegration. In Constantinople, the band of Young Turk adventurers who had seized power and who ruled the empire as the Sultan's ministers, feared that their domains were in mortal danger and that the European predators were closing in for the kill. (Fromkin, 2009, p. 45)

The view that this development in the Balkans presented the Zionist movement with a timely opportunity to pursue its cause with the British government was pressed on the Executive by Dr. Chaim Weizmann, who, though not yet in a position of leadership, was one of the British members of the Zionist General Council and already an important figure in the Zionist world. In November 1912, he wrote to Berlin urging that Sokolow should come to England without delay. He asked that, in the meantime, he himself should be authorized to approach certain important personages, to whom, he said, he could get access – among them Balfour and Lord Chancellor Richard Haldane. The Executive declined to sanction such conversations, but early in 1913 arranged for Sokolow to spend some time in London on his way to the United States. Sokolow had the advantage of a letter of recommendation from the British Ambassador in St. Petersburg, which enabled him to establish direct contact with the Foreign Office. Although he met with a number of senior officials of the Department – there is no record of his having been received by any Cabinet member – he felt that he had at least broken the ice and left London satisfied that "in case the question of Palestine is put before any future Conference, this will prove to have been a preparatory step." Sokolow reported:

> Zionism has no longer the attraction of novelty which it had before. [...] One is also to pay attention to the general increase of antisemitism. This has now become an epidemic in France and also in England. (Stein, 1961, p. 42)

He also realized that even though the Foreign Office had seemed interested in what he had to say, he felt that with the Balkan crisis at its height, the Jews and their aspirations in Palestine were hardly a priority for the British government (Stein, 1961, p. 42). To the Foreign Office, in the early stages of the War of 1914–18, the Zionists and their claims were of little practical importance. While, in some higher quarters, the Zionists enjoyed from the start more sympathy than they themselves realized, at the official level, the Foreign Office was not disposed to give them any encouragement (Stein, 1961, p. 43).

In the Sykes-Picot Agreement of May 1916, the Zionists were ignored. The British government and its advisors, notably Sir Mark Sykes, were alive to the strategic importance of Palestine, both from a military and naval point of view, and had done their best to keep it out of exclusive French control, but so far as Zionism was concerned, the government was still uncommitted (Stein, 1961, p. 115).

The candle that nevertheless kept the flame of Zionism flickering in the arena of British politics was Herbert Samuel, a Liberal politician who became president of the Board of Trade and then Home Secretary in Asquith's Cabinet. While he came from the cousinhood of wealthy assimilated Jewish Britons, he secretly nurtured Zionist beliefs, which he revealed to Asquith's Cabinet and to Weizmann early in the war. Later, he helped bring Weizmann into contact with other important British officials.

After the war, he served for five years as Britain's first high commissioner in Palestine (Schneer, 2010, p. xxi).

It is axiomatic that the wheels of social change are usually set in motion when social and economic pressures threaten the established order and provide the opportunity for new political thinking and leadership. At the beginning of his political career, Samuel showed no signs of becoming a strong advocate for the Zionist project in British government circles. According to Stein, Samuel's public personality, background and environment showed no signs of any interest in Zionism. In the family circle to which he belonged, Jewish loyalties and traditions were cherished, but there was little sympathy with Zionism. After Samuel had left Oxford in 1893, he had entered the House of Commons in 1902, been given a junior office when the Liberals returned to power some four years later, and in 1914, at the age of forty-four, had a seat in the Cabinet which he kept for the next five years. He had remained in the fullest sense a member of the Anglo-Jewish community, but, immersed as he had been in politics, he had never taken an active interest in its affairs. He had a mind of his own and did not participate in the anti-Zionist campaign conducted by a group of influential British Jews. As long as Palestine was in Turkish hands, his interest in the whole question was only academic. It was only when Turkey entered the war on the side of the Central Powers that Samuel moved into action. He explained in later years that earlier in his career he had had no connection to the Zionist movement and felt that prospects for its success seemed remote. These conditions changed once he became the first member of the Jewish community to sit in a British Cabinet. He now felt an obligation to study the aims of the Zionist movement and its achievements (Stein, 1961, pp. 105–106).

We know from Lord Samuel's memoirs that at a meeting of the Cabinet on September 5, 1914, Lloyd George referred to the ultimate destiny of Palestine. According to Samuel, Lloyd George assured him that "he was very keen to see a Jewish state established in Palestine." On the same day, in a conversation with Foreign Secretary Sir Edward Grey, Samuel suggested that the rivalries between the European powers would preclude allocating Palestine to any of them, which would create the opportunity to fulfil the Zionists' dream by restoring a Jewish state in their ancestral homeland (Stein, 1961, p. 103). Dr. Weizmann, president of the English Zionist Federation, recalled that in December 1914 when he was breakfasting with Lloyd George (then Chancellor of the Exchequer), Herbert Samuel, M.P. (then President of the Local Government Board) said that he was preparing a memorandum for the Prime Minister (Asquith) on the subject of a Jewish state in Palestine (Ingrams, 2009, pp.

3–4). Submitted in January 1915, Samuel's memorandum started out by saying:

> The course of events opens a prospect of change, at the end of the war, in the status of Palestine. Already, there is a stirring among the twelve million Jews scattered throughout the countries of the world. A feeling is spreading with great rapidity that now, at last, some advance may be made, in some way, toward the fulfillment of the hope and desire, held with unshakable tenacity for eighteen hundred years, for the restoration of the Jews to the land to which they are attached by ties almost as ancient as history itself. (Ingrams, 2009, pp. 3–4)

Fromkin noted that in March 1915, the revised version of Samuel's memorandum was circulated to the Cabinet, and he refers to Asquith's private comment that:

> Curiously enough, the only other partisan of this proposal is Lloyd George, who, I need not say, does not care a damn for the Jews or their past or their future […]. (Fromkin, 2009, p. 270)

Herbert Samuel's pioneering government-level pro-Zionist activities are also corroborated by Schneer, who noted that on November 9, 1914, a week after Turkey entered the war, Samuel met with Foreign Secretary Grey. Schneer makes the significant observation that this encounter represented an historic first in that Samuel "was no unfamiliar Jew from Poland, seeking audience with a distant and disdainful official. He was a member of the government. For once, a Zionist had entered the inner sanctum on equal terms to discuss the future of Palestine" (Schneer, 2010, p. 125).

Samuel prepared carefully for the interview and came right to the point when he suggested to Grey that Turkey's move might offer the opportunity for the fulfilment of the ancient aspiration of the Jewish people and the restoration (in Palestine) of a Jewish state. Samuel added, most importantly from the British point of view, that Britain should support this ancient aspiration because the geographical location of Palestine, so close to Egypt, would render its goodwill to England a matter of importance to the British Empire. Furthermore, almost equally significant in the present wartime circumstances, if Russia could be induced to back the Zionist policy, then Russian Jews would have some reason to support their government. That would benefit Russia's ally Britain. For that matter, Samuel argued, a pro-Zionist policy would rally Jewish opinion throughout the world on behalf of the Allies (Schneer, 2010, p. 125).

Samuel introduced an additional and more altruistic reason why Britain should support the establishment of a Jewish state in Palestine when he suggested that it might become the centre of a new culture, the source of great literature, art and the development of science. If the Jewish population could see their own people achieve great things, it would greatly enhance their outlook. This would in turn benefit their Middle Eastern neighbours as well: "Raising their [the Jews'] character would add to their usefulness to the peoples among whom they lived" (Schneer, 2010, p. 126).

With Turkey having chosen the wrong side in the great conflict, Grey could make only one response. "Zionism, which would undermine Turkey in the Middle East if given free reign, finally had entered the realm of practical politics, from the British point of view – or at least got its toe inside the door." So, without actually committing himself to a specific policy, Grey smiled upon a proposal that his Foreign Office subordinates had rejected, politely but scornfully, just a few months before when put to them by Nahum Sokolow. Samuel recalled Grey telling him that he had always felt had a strong sentimental attraction to the idea and that its historic appeal was very strong. Grey added that he was quite favourable to the proposal and would be prepared to work for it if the opportunity arose (Schneer, 2010, p. 126).

In retrospect, this meeting between Samuel and Grey turned out to be a critical juncture on the tortuous road to the Balfour Declaration. It was one of those rare serendipitous combinations of the variables of conducive agency and propitious structure that set and pointed the political process in the direction aspired by the champions of the reconstitution of the Jewish homeland.

Later that day, Samuel raised the same matter with another Cabinet colleague, Chancellor of the Exchequer David Lloyd George. Whereas the previous April, Lloyd George had described Samuel as a "greedy, ambitious, grasping Jew, with all the worst characteristics of his race," on November 9, when Samuel mentioned the "ancient aspiration" of the Jews to establish a state in Palestine, Lloyd George replied that he was "very keen to see a Jewish state established there." Thus encouraged, Samuel prepared a memorandum on the subject for circulation among the other Cabinet ministers (Schneer, 2010, p. 126).

While the British government and its advisors were alive to the strategic importance of Palestine both from a military and naval point of view and had done their best to keep it out of exclusive French control, in respect of Zionism, the government was still uncommitted. Samuel refused to be discouraged, and in November 1916 he seems to have been preparing

the ground for a fresh approach to Grey. However, with the change of
government, both Samuel and Grey had followed Asquith out of office,
and the issue was left to be finally decided by a Cabinet of which he was
not a member (Stein, 1961, p. 115).

Out of office, Samuel continued to exert his still considerable influence
in the same direction as before. He brought his proposals to the notice of
Lord Milner, a leading British imperialist member of Lloyd George's War
Cabinet. Though not himself a member of the Zionist Organization,
Samuel was present, and played a leading part, at the important conference
at which, in February 1917, Sir Mark Sykes exchanged views with a group
of representative Zionists for the first time. The following October, when
the fate of the Balfour Declaration was in the balance, he was consulted by
the War Cabinet and in his reply set out, with all the weight of his
authority, the case for the policy which, in and out of office, he had
consistently advocated for nearly three years (Stein, 1961, p. 116).

Karsh argued that it was the ability of the Zionist movement to exploit
a unique convergence of factors to harness British support to its national
cause that produced the Balfour Declaration of November 1917. These
factors included Lloyd George's belief that the Jews might be able to
render more assistance than the Arabs in easing the French out of
Palestine; the widespread conviction of British officialdom that Zionism
held the key to the goodwill and support of "World Jewry," which, the
British hoped, would, through Jewish influence within revolutionary
circles, counteract calls for Russia to leave the war; and the growing
approval of Zionism as a working national movement, rather than as a
merely handy tool, in the higher reaches of the British political and
administrative establishment. The British desire to undo the Sykes-Picot
Agreement created a unique opportunity that the Zionist leader, Weizmann,
was quick to exploit (Karsh, 2015, p. 28).

Until the end of 1916, the impact of Zionism on British public opinion
had been insignificant. While in the select circle in which policy was
made, the Zionists could already count on some important friends, nothing
had been decided, nor did they themselves believe that any firm
commitment was in sight (Stein, 1961, p. 298). When, on December 5,
1916, Lloyd George became Prime Minister and Balfour moved from the
Admiralty to the Foreign Office, the tide began to turn. Soon afterwards,
the war with Turkey entered a new phase, in which Palestine became of
cardinal importance. In March, the Russian Revolution set in train a
succession of events which, though not in all respects advantageous to the
Zionists, worked, on the whole, in their favour (Stein, 1961, p. 305). The
antisemitic tsarist government had just been overthrown with the help of

Russia's significant Jewish population, which had been the unremitting target of brutal persecution. Aside from a genuine belief in the righteousness of the Zionist cause held by Lloyd George and most of the members of his Cabinet, they also hoped that, in light of these events, a formal declaration in favour of Zionism would help gain Jewish support for the Allies in the United States and especially Russia. They assumed that by throwing their support behind the new regime, Russian Jewry would exert a powerful influence on the Russian government not to withdraw from the war against the Central Powers.

As far as the United States was concerned, its declaration of war on Germany in April 1917 ensured that it would play a decisive part in the shaping of the post-war settlement (Stein, 1961, p. 350). The Zionist leadership in London and the British government had, therefore, a common interest in inviting the American Jews to endorse the idea of a Jewish Commonwealth in Palestine under British protection (Stein, 1961, p. 358).

These expectations were based on exaggerated British perceptions of Jewish/Zionist power, which were the result of the widespread antisemitic myths that had been propagated around the world. The fact that the opposite was true was later borne out by the absence of any impact of Jewish influence on the Russian government not to withdraw from the war against the Central Powers, as well as by the negligible impact American Jewry had on the U.S. participation in the war effort. History teaches us that unchallenged fiction assumes the mantle of fact, with the same action-stimulating power. The reality remains that the British government in 1917 did act on the assumption that Jewish influence could, if properly motivated, have a decisive impact on the outcome of the war. The question of whether the British were aware that the extent of worldwide Jewish influence was vastly exaggerated but that they found it convenient to act as if they believed it, so as to provide themselves with a noble fig leaf for their true ambitions, deserves further examination. Whatever the answer, it does not affect the outcome of the Balfour Declaration development process.

Even though Samuel followed Asquith out of office, the change of government was, on balance, immeasurably to the advantage of the Zionists and another step forward on the road to the Balfour Declaration. While Asquith had never given them the slightest encouragement, Lloyd George, the new Prime Minister, and Arthur James Balfour, the new Foreign Secretary, were strongly predisposed in their favour and were men whom Weitzman could approach with the knowledge that he had already won their confidence (Stein, 1961, p. 309).

Stein noted that under the new regime instituted by Lloyd George, final decisions on questions of high policy rested with a small War Cabinet presided over by the Prime Minister and composed of ministers free from departmental duties. Although Balfour was not a member of the War Cabinet, he had all the authority attached to his office as Foreign Secretary and to his standing as an elder statesman of the highest eminence. He often attended War Cabinet meetings and enjoyed a privileged position by dint of his close relations with the Prime Minister (Stein, 1961, p. 310).

As identified earlier in this chapter, the majority of the War Cabinet's members in the Lloyd George government in 1917 were conceptually already favourably disposed towards the reconstitution of the Jewish homeland. Their ranks were reinforced at the last moment by Lord Milner who, as a result of the change of government, had been offered a seat in the War Cabinet by Lloyd George. Lord Milner had become a firm supporter of a pro-Zionist policy and, in the end, shared with Balfour and Lloyd George the main responsibility for the Balfour Declaration. Lloyd George's co-option of Lord Milner to the War Cabinet can only be appreciated in the light of Milner's background and credentials. Milner had recently returned to England after seven years of service under the Crown in South Africa where, as High Commissioner, he had shown marked consideration for the Jews in his handling of various problems affecting their interests (Stein, 1961, pp. 310–311).

Soon after joining the War Cabinet in December 1916, Milner received from Samuel a copy of his Palestine memorandum. He wrote to Samuel that the alternative he found the most attractive was some form of British protectorate for Palestine coupled with the encouragement of Jewish immigration, so that eventually, when the Jewish inhabitants had grown into a majority, they would be entitled to a corresponding degree of self-government. Stein suggests that it was the Samuel memorandum that triggered Milner's active interest in Zionism (Stein, 1961, pp. 314–315).

Milner's positive attitude towards the Jews was not due to any feelings of guilt or any dreams about the restoration of a Jewish homeland in Palestine. His prime motivation was the question of whether Great Britain, in the context of the approaching break-up of the Ottoman Empire, stood to gain from cooperating with the Zionists. The combination of Milner's pro-Zionist thoughts and his natural British interest-guided state of mind led him to play an important role in the determination of the final wording of the Balfour Declaration (Stein, 1961, p. 316).

Towards the end of October 1917, after four months of consideration by the Foreign Office and at Cabinet level, it looked as though at last the way was clear. U.S. President Woodrow Wilson had now agreed to a declaration. The anti-Zionist British Jews had had their say and could not complain of not having been heard. The War Cabinet had been assured by the Chief Rabbi that the proposed declaration would be welcomed by the overwhelming majority of Anglo-Jewry and, as a result of the campaign set on foot by the English Zionist Federation, resolutions in support of the Zionist programme had poured into the Foreign Office from hundreds of Jewish bodies in various parts of the country. At this point, the Foreign Office was anxious that the declaration should be approved by the War Cabinet without further delay (Stein, 1961, p. 543).

The extent to which the strategic war considerations were part of the British motivation was shown by the thrust of the memorandum submitted to Balfour, on October 24, 1917, by Sir Ronald Graham, head of the Eastern department of the Foreign Office. Graham urged Balfour that there should be no further procrastination, "since the result might be to throw the Zionists in the arms of the Germans and put an end to the prospect of attracting valuable support for the Allied cause from the Zionist forces in Russia and the United States" (Stein, 1961, p. 544).

It is important to note that what the War Cabinet was considering at this point was not whether, in the eventual peace settlement, Great Britain should try to do something for the Jews in Palestine, but whether the British government should there and then enter into a public undertaking to the Zionists. According to Lloyd George, Balfour did not think it necessary to dwell on the larger aspects of the Zionist question. Nor did he say anything about strengthening the resistance to French pretensions in Palestine or about any long-term advantages to be expected from a British association with the Zionists. He chose to rest the case for the declaration mainly on its value as propaganda (Stein, 1961, p. 546).

That Balfour viewed the declaration more as a product of war expediency than of sympathy for Zionism is evidenced by his politically tempered choice of words. As to the meaning of the words "national home," to which the Zionists attached so much importance, Balfour understood it to mean some form of British, American or other protectorate, under which full facilities would be given to the Jews to work out their own salvation and to build up, by means of education, agriculture and industry, a real centre of national culture and focus of national life. It did not necessarily involve the early establishment of an independent Jewish state, which was a matter for gradual development in accordance with the ordinary laws of political evolution (Stein, 1961, p. 547). Finally, on October 31, 1917, the War Cabinet came to a decision, which was embodied in the final text of the Balfour Declaration.

Conclusion

As this exploration of the British motivation behind the Balfour
Declaration has shown, it was the product of a blend of religiously
inspired sentiments and self-serving political pragmatism. The course of
the British diplomatic and military activities during World War I was
driven solely by Britain's perception of its national interests. The
strategies it resorted to in the pursuit of those objectives were influenced
by the mindsets of the decision-making government members in charge.
Serendipitously for the proponents of the Declaration, in October 1917,
most of the Cabinet members were already favourably disposed, albeit on
religious grounds, towards the idea of a Jewish homeland in Palestine.

The diplomatic process that led the British to issue the Balfour
Declaration consisted primarily of pragmatic geopolitical considerations,
greatly influenced by the horrendous human toll on the battlefields and the
need to accommodate the aspirations of its allies and thwart those of its
foes. First, there were the Hussein-McMahon negotiations, which led to
the promises made by the British to the Arabs, aimed at bringing them into
the war on the side of the Allies. Next came the British competitive
dealings with their French allies over the spoils of war, resulting in the
Sykes-Picot Agreement of May 1916. It must be remembered that, due to
the conflicting nature of the arrangements the British forged with their
negotiating partners, they kept each secret from the other.

The subject of the Zionist aspirations in Palestine did not actively enter
the arena of British politics until the end of 1916. During the previous two
years, Lord Herbert Samuel, the first Jewish member of the British
Cabinet, who had embraced Zionism at the outbreak of World War I when
he saw the possibility of the realization of the Zionist aspirations with the
entry of Turkey into the war, had kept the embers of the movement alive
in London.

The Russian Revolution added an additional dimension to the British
motivation to support the Zionist objectives by kindling the exaggerated
perception of the influence of Russian Jewry on the Russian government
with regard to keeping Russia in the war against the Central Powers.

This analysis of the fabric of the British motivation to issue the Balfour
Declaration notes that the tide in its favour began to turn on December 5,
1916, when Lloyd George replaced the anti-Zionist Herbert Asquith as
Prime Minister and Balfour moved to the Foreign Office.

The main theme that runs through this chapter about the British
motivation is the one that characterizes Lord Milner's attitude in favour of
the Declaration. His prime motivation revolved around the question of

whether Great Britain, in the context of the approaching break-up of the Ottoman Empire, stood to gain from cooperating with the Zionists (Stein, 1961, p. 316).

The next chapter, *Chapter 2: Emancipation*, traces the beginning of the arduous path that led the Jewish population of Europe to the Balfour Declaration back to the French Revolution of 1789. By extending equality under the law and access to higher education and the professions to all citizens, the French Revolution allowed the development of a Jewish intelligentsia which, by discovering the concepts of nationalism and self-determination, led to the birth and development of political Zionism.

CHAPTER TWO

EMANCIPATION

Introduction

This chapter shows how the French Revolution, by triggering the emancipation of the Jews, started the first phase of the awakening of the Jewish mind from its eighteen-century-long political slumber. It also demonstrates how the asynchronous socio-political developments on the European continent caused the impact of emancipation and enlightenment on the fate of the geographically separated segments of the Jewish population to be totally different between those living in Western and Central Europe and the vast majority that were trapped within the confines of the tsarist regime.

The Asynchronous Development of Jewish Emancipation

It is crucial for a proper understanding of the role of the emancipation in the awakening of Jewish political consciousness to remember that, as noted by Hebrew University political science professor Shlomo Avineri, most Jews in the nineteenth century lived within the confines of the Russian Empire which, in addition to Russia proper, also contained Central and Eastern Poland, Ukraine, Bessarabia and the Baltic countries. While Jews in the West experienced emancipation and equal rights, those living under the authoritarian regime of the Tsar were still suffering under the yoke of anti-Jewish government policy, which confined them to the traditional Pale of Settlement and excluded them from professions and from public service (Avineri, 2017, p. 59). This total disparity between the social conditions of the Jews living in the West and those trapped in the East constitutes the principal cause of the different responses within the Jewish world to the political Zionist imperative during the period leading to the Balfour Declaration.

The first step on the evolving social ladder of the Jewish diaspora was the French Revolution, which resulted in the Declaration of the Rights of Man and of the Citizen in 1789, under which every citizen was promoted to equal treatment under the law. This ushered in the period of emancipation that provided all citizens with equal human rights, which included equal access to secular higher education and professions. James Gelvin, Professor of Middle Eastern History at the University of California, noted that during the eighteenth century, with the emergence of the absolutist state, the monarchs of France, Prussia, Russia and Austria asserted the primacy of the ruler over their subjects, which led them to dismantle all structures that mediated between the ruler and the ruled. These included the corporate structures that gave to groups of their subjects, including the Jews residing among them, whatever local autonomy they enjoyed. Since the modern state emerged from the absolutist state in Western and Central Europe before it did in Eastern Europe, the subsequent history of the two regions and their Jewish communities began to diverge. Nevertheless, the year 1791 marks a watershed in the history of Jews in both regions. In Western and Central Europe, the destruction of the legal distinctions that separated Jews from their compatriots is referred to as "Jewish emancipation." The highpoint of Jewish emancipation occurred in France in 1791 during the time of the French Revolution, when the promise of "liberty, equality, fraternity" came to replace (at least in theory) aristocratic privilege and rigid social hierarchies (Gelvin, 2005, p. 36).

After the Jewish emancipation in France in 1791, other nations of Western and Central Europe granted full emancipation to their Jews: Great Britain (1858), Switzerland (1866), Austria (1867), Italy (1870), and Germany (1871). While much of the Jewish population of Western and Central Europe welcomed Jewish emancipation, that of the Jews of Eastern Europe would have to wait. Russia did not emancipate its Jews until 1915. Nineteenth-century Tsarist Russia, with the largest Jewish population of any country, was also the place where antisemitism and Jewish persecution were at their most disastrous level (Gelvin, 2005, p. 37).

We have encountered no more apt description of this socio-political time warp than the one contained in the renowned historian Simon Dubnow's unpublished introduction to his account of Alexander III's reign. Fortunately, Simon Dubnow's translator, Israel Friedlander, deemed Dubnow's account significant enough to quote it in his preface to volume II of Dubnow's work. In essence, Dubnow put forth that Russian Tsardom began its consistent role as a persecutor of the "Eternal People" at the end of the eighteenth century, when it took over vast areas of Central Europe and, with it, the vast Jewish population of disintegrated Poland. Consequently, when Western Europe had just begun the emancipation of the Jews, in Eastern Europe, the Jews were subjected to every possible medieval experiment. The reign of Alexander II, who slightly relieved the civil disfranchisement of the Jews by permitting certain categories among them to live outside the Pale and by a few other measures, formed only a brief interlude in the Russian policy of oppression. His tragic death in 1881 marked the beginning of a new terrible reaction which superimposed the system of wholesale street pogroms upon the policy of disenfranchisement and again threw millions of Jews into the dismal abyss of medievalism (Dubnow, 1918, pp. 6–7).

This is how Russia created a lurid antithesis to Jewish emancipation at a time when it was consummated not only in Western Europe but also in the semi-civilized Balkan states. Dubnow acknowledges that the rise of Russian Judeophobia was paralleled by the appearance of German antisemitism in which it found a congenial companion. Yet, Dubnow observes, the antisemitism of the West was only a weak aftermath of the infantile disease of Europe – the medieval Jew-hatred – whereas culturally retrograde Russia was still suffering from the same infection in its acute, "childish" form. While the social and cultural antisemitism of the West did not undermine the modern foundations of Jewish civil equality, Russian Judeophobia, more governmental than social, being fully in accord with the entire regime of absolutism, produced a system aiming not only at the disfranchisement but also the direct physical annihilation of the Jewish people. "The policy of the extermination of Judaism was stamped upon the forehead of Russian reaction, receiving various colors at various periods, assuming the hue now of economic, now of national and religious, now of bureaucratic oppression" (Dubnow, 1918, pp. 6–7).

Haskala – Product of the Jewish Emancipation

Like the European enlightenment, from which it derived its principles, the *Haskala* asserted the primacy of science and rationality over religion and tradition. The devotees of the *Haskala* – the *maskilim* – believed that the laws governing human society were just as discernible by reason as the natural laws that governed the physical universe. The *Haskala* provided its followers with the conceptual apparatus that make other movements, such as nationalism and socialism, comprehensible. The *Haskala* began in Germany during the final quarter of the eighteenth century. From there, it spread to the Austrian Empire and the Pale. To end the stranglehold of traditionalist rabbis over the cultural life of the Jewish community, *maskilim* advocated immersion in both biblical Hebrew and the languages of Europe. By mastering biblical Hebrew, *maskilim* hoped to bring to biblical scholarship the critical tools their non-Jewish counterparts were using in the analysis of classical texts. This also served the purpose of enabling the Jews of Western Europe to assimilate into the societies in which they lived without the fear of losing their Jewish cultural identity. *Maskilim* established schools to teach modern European languages and spread the gospel of science and progress among the younger generation (Gelvin, 2005, p. 47).

Acting in concert with the social, political and economic transformation of Jewish life during the nineteenth century, the cultural transformation inspired by the *Haskala* provided fertile ground for a number of modern ideologies to take root among the Jews of Europe. One of these ideologies was Zionism. Gelvin argues that Zionism is not simply a spontaneous outgrowth of the *Haskala*. Before Zionism can emerge, someone has to take the ideas pioneered by enlightenment thinkers and not only translate them into a nationalist idiom but put them in the service of a nationalist programme. "In other words, nationalism is impossible without nationalists" (Gelvin, 2005, p. 49). Jewish nationalism was triggered by the ideas and social structures unleashed by the French Revolution, modernism and secularism. Being a response to the challenges of liberalism and nationalism, it could not have occurred at any time before the nineteenth century (Avineri, 2017, p. 11).

Shlomo Avineri identified the paradox which lies at the root of Zionism as a deep feeling of attachment to the land of Israel unmatched by any practical or operational efforts towards converting the belief in the return to Zion into a political reality. Until the second half of the nineteenth century, during eighteen centuries of exile, while the link to the Land of Israel always loomed large in the collective consciousness of Jewish communities everywhere, the belief in the return to Zion acted as a powerful component of group identity, but was almost totally passive as an activating element in changing reality. Jewish religious thought legitimized this passivity by denying any active intervention in the divine scheme of things. The redemption of the Jews from exile and their return to Zion had been left to Divine Providence, until now (Avineri, 2017, pp. 2–3).

What was different at this time was that, by the end of the nineteenth century, the world had seen the emergence of pockets of freedom and opportunity for its citizens and, as such, these also extended to the Jewish minorities among them. This time in history constitutes a critical junction in the history of the Jewish people. For eighteen centuries, Jews had been ostracized from mainstream society, excluded from positions of public service, and barred from schools and universities and from most professions. They had mostly been relegated to "finding a living in the niches and crevices of a society which excluded them even when it tolerated their religious beliefs." Now, with the French Revolution and emancipation, they were, for the first time, admitted into European society on equal footing. This meant equality before the law and gradual access to schools, universities and professions (Avineri, 2017, pp. 4, 6).

The ideology of Zionism was so removed from the social and cultural constraints of ghetto life in Eastern Europe that it took the rolling out of the bridge of Jewish emancipation in the West to carry the seeds of modernity to the arid intellectual soil of the Jewish ghetto world in the East. The fertilizing intellectual soil carried across this bridge was the *Haskala*, the Jewish enlightenment.

Whereas the emancipation which sprang from the French Revolution had liberated the Jewish mind from the paralyzing ghetto mentality and awakened the possibility of developing a more liberating political awareness, the widespread pogroms from 1881 in the dense Jewish population centres in southern Russia became the tipping point in the Jewish realization of the futility of trying to find acceptance in hostile Gentile environments in spite of, or perhaps because of, the effects of the emancipation (Avineri, 2017, pp. 63, 69–70, 77).

Conclusion

Emancipation in Western Europe preceded Russia's de jure enactment by at least a century, while de facto, under the tsarist absolute monarchy, which outlasted its French counterpart by about the same length of time, it never fully emerged from its cocoon. In reality, although the Russian Revolution resulted in the official emancipation of its Jewish population in 1915, this did not put an end to their persecution, which went on relentlessly. The social, economic and political impact of emancipation on the Jewish populations in these two regions followed asymmetric paths, both chronologically and qualitatively. Eventually, through the development of a modern Jewish intelligentsia in the East and their exposure to their Western counterparts, these two currents coalesced into the same mainstream of Zionist political development.

As will be shown in the following chapter, the Jewish path to the Balfour Declaration was paved by the one-hundred-year-long stretch of relentless persecution under the tsarist absolute regimes of the nineteenth century.

CHAPTER THREE

PERSECUTION –
TSARIST RUSSIA,
THE NINETEENTH-CENTURY "EGYPT"

Introduction

The Jewish roots of the Balfour Declaration contain two major elements which initially ran their own course and eventually merged into a mainstream that carried the crucial elements of the composite parts. One element is the tormented history of the Jewish people in Tsarist Russia. It constitutes the background that gave birth to the anguished cries for salvation which became the wellspring of the Zionist movement. The Jews of Russia, through their obstinate struggle to preserve their national identity, provided the critical mass. This chapter will fill a lacuna in the literature by providing a detailed account of the century-long genocidal persecution by the tsarist regime of its Jewish population.

The other crucial element is the development in Western Europe of racial antisemitism with its emancipation-stifling impact, which gradually forged a consensus among the leading Jewish thinkers of the time that the only long-term solution to the Jewish predicament was the reconstitution of the ancient homeland in a sovereign Jewish state.

Without the synergy between these two elements of ideological agency and social structure, there would not have been a Jewish path leading to the Balfour Declaration. The general omission of these foundational elements from the identification of the roots of the political expression of the return to Zion embodied in the Balfour Declaration has left us with a deficient account of the genesis of one of the most important destiny-shaping episodes in the history of the Jewish people. A holistic analysis of the genesis of the Balfour Declaration requires the inclusion of these all-important elements.

The quality of life of the Jewish diaspora was in direct proportion to the level of emancipation of the host nations. In those countries where they were extended civil rights and where some of the barriers to education and enterprise had been lifted, the Jews were quite content to live as loyal citizens and to practice their religion as a spiritual aspect of their lives only. The memory of their pre-diaspora history inspired their cultural but not their political identity. Jewish emancipation, which had been inspired by the age of enlightenment and had liberated the Jewish minds in Western Europe following the French Revolution, had, however, not reached the areas where the majority of Jewish populations were centred at the time. Nineteenth-century Tsarist Russia, which had the largest Jewish population of any country, was also the place where antisemitism and Jewish persecution were at their most disastrous level.

The major road to the Zionist awakening that led to the Balfour Declaration was paved with the relentless persecution of Russian Jewry by the tyrannically tsarist regimes of the nineteenth century. Gelvin noted that about 75 percent of the world's Jews lived in Eastern Europe during the nineteenth century and that most of those Jews lived within the boundaries of the Russian Empire (Gelvin, 2005, p. 38). Author and journalist Ben Zion Goldberg notes these Jews had come to Poland several centuries before on the invitation of the Polish kings to fill the social gap between the feudal landlords, who regarded any gainful employment, even management of their own estates, as beneath their dignity, and the serf-like peasants just below subsistence level. The Jews were to be the traders, artisans and administrators – in a sense, a bridge to the new bourgeois society. But the Polish kings failed to suppress the feudal lords to make the birth of the new society possible, and the obsolescent Polish feudal state was crushed under its own weight (Goldberg, 1961, pp. 4–6). The presence of so many Jews in the Russian Empire was a relatively new phenomenon. Before the eighteenth century, Russian tsars had attempted to keep Jews outside their domains. However, the consolidation and expansion of the state under Peter the Great and Catherine the Great soon rendered that policy futile. The territories annexed by Russia, Austria and Prussia between 1772 and 1795 contained large numbers of Jews who had lived there for centuries (Gelvin, 2005, p. 38).

The Russian merchant classes, to avoid mercantile competition, insisted that the Jews of the annexed territories be confined to the provinces of their origin, the so-called Pale of Settlement. Within the Pale, conditions had already been worsening in the face of the growing population, narrowing economic opportunities and widening competition. The inevitable result was overcrowding and pauperization, and thus a Jewish problem arose (Goldberg, 1961, pp. 4–6).

This sudden appearance of large numbers of Jews within their empire was a matter of concern to Russian imperial elites. In 1791, Catherine the

Great hit upon a novel plan to deal with them. Henceforth, Jews living within the empire were to reside in a specially designated area on the empire's western fringes. The Jewish Pale of Settlement stretched from the Baltic Sea to the Black Sea and included the contemporary states of Latvia, Lithuania, Belarus, Ukraine and parts of Poland. Catherine was motivated to establish the Pale by the Russian political elites' fear that the integration of a large number of Jews into Russia proper would have deleterious effects on the body politic. Some argued that Jews should be kept separate until they had been "Russified." The Russian government permitted the Jews to live outside the Pale only under special circumstances. Most Jews of the Pale lived in poverty in small towns and villages (shtetls), the targets of periodic violence inflicted by their non-Jewish neighbours. Culturally segregated from those neighbours, they used Yiddish – a blend of mostly German and Hebrew with a smattering of Slavic and even Old French – as their lingua franca (Gelvin, 2005, pp. 39, 40). It is impossible to understand what caused the Jews in Russia to abandon what they considered their homeland without a realistic awareness of the severity of the relentless persecutions they suffered under the tsars during the nineteenth century.

Nicholas I (1825–1855)

During the thirty-year reign of Nicholas I, the Jews had been targeted for assimilation into Russian society with total conversion to Russian Orthodoxy as the Tsar's ultimate objective. Even though the Jews were deprived of civil rights, the Tsar resorted to the use of military service as an educational and disciplinary agency for his Jewish subjects. The treatment of the Jewish population of Russia during this period was a reflection of the tsarist regime's attempts to obliterate the identity of this minority nation. The infamous expression *Judenrein* comes to mind. It is essential to identify this episode as an egregious exercise of what are considered crimes against humanity (Berk, 1985, p. 3; Gelvin, 2005, p. 40).

Simon Dubnow, in his monumental three-volume *History of the Jews in Russia and Poland: From the Earliest Times until the Present Day*, included an in-depth account of Jewish life in Tsarist Russia. The fact that he not only lived at the time and on the scene of the events addressed in this chapter but that he also passionately devoted himself to provide a scholarly, in-depth account of how they occurred and played out makes him a valuable source of information on the subject (Dubnow, 1916, pp. ix–xi).

According to Dubnow, the most odious of the government policies towards this end was the *rekrutschina*, the conscription system introduced by Nicholas I in 1826. Against the protestations and warnings of his closest advisors, he instructed his ministers to draft a special statute of military service for the Jews, which was different from the laws applicable to the rest of the population. The ukase imposing a term of military service of twenty-five years upon the Jews was signed on August 26, 1827 (Dubnow, 1918, pp. 16–17). The eighth clause of the special statute prescribed that "the Jewish conscripts presented by the Jewish communes shall be between the ages of twelve and twenty-five." In addition, clause 74 stipulated that "Jewish minors, i.e., below the age of eighteen, shall be placed in preparatory establishments for military training" (Dubnow, 1918, pp. 18–19).

While the institution of minor recruits, called *cantonists*, also existed for Christians, in their case it was confined to children of soldiers in active service, whereas the conscription of Jewish minors was to apply to all Jewish families without discrimination. In addition, the years of preparatory training in the case of the Jewish recruits were not included under the terms of active service, which started at the age of eighteen. Consequently, the Jewish cantonists had to serve six extra years in addition to the obligatory twenty-five years. To make it easier to recruit as many Jewish youth as possible, the normal fitness standards for serving did not apply to them. All that was demanded for their qualification to serve was that they be "free of any disease or defect incompatible with military service" (Dubnow, 1918, p. 19).

Every Jewish community was compelled by law to supply a definite number of recruits. They had to elect between three and six executive officers, or "trustees," in every city to carry out this responsibility. Due to the fact that none of the potential recruits were eager to submit themselves to the horrific fate reserved for them in the military, the communities and the recruiting trustees, who had to answer to the authorities for any shortage in recruits, were practically forced to act as police agents, whose function it was to "capture" the necessary quota of recruits. Many young men and boys of the lowest economic class, which under Russian law was referred to as the burgher class and which could not be exempted from military service, took flight to other cities, or to forests and ravines (Dubnow, 1918, pp. 22–23).

The recruiting agents hired by the community hunted down these fugitives to capture them for the purpose of making up the shortage. If this failed to meet the quotas, little children, sometimes no more than eight years old, were seized, even though they were below the legal age limit for conscription. Due to the fact that regular birth registers were not yet in existence, it was easy for the agents to misstate their age. The agents acted with incredible cruelty. Houses were raided during the night, and children were torn from the arms of their mothers, or lured away and kidnapped (Dubnow, 1918, p. 23).

After being captured, the Jewish conscripts were kept in confinement in the recruiting jail until their examination at the recruiting stations. The enlisted minors were then dispatched to their places of destination, which were located in the faraway eastern provinces, including Siberia, at a safe distance from all Jewish influences. The juvenile cantonists were packed into wagons like sheep and carried off in batches in a military convoy. They were torn from their families and sent off for a quarter of a century; in the case of children, it was for an even longer term (Dubnow, 1918, p. 24).

The following eyewitness account provides a telling illustration of the level of inhumanity Russian society had sunk to in their treatment of the Jewish minority in their midst. In 1835, Alexander Hertzen, a famous Russian writer who was himself being exiled for propagating liberal doctrines, happened to meet a batch of Jewish cantonists at one of the post stations in a remote village in the province of Vyatka. The following account of his conversation with the officer guiding the children provides a poignant description of their plight:

"Whom do you carry and to what place?"

"Well, sir, you see, they got together a bunch of these accursed Jewish youngsters between the age of eight and nine. I suppose they are meant for the fleet, but how should I know? At first the command was to drive them to Perm. Now there is a change. We are to drive them to Kazan. I have had them on my hands for a hundred *versts* [ca. sixty-six miles] or thereabouts. The officer that turned them over to me told me they were an awful nuisance. A third of them remained on the road (at this the officer pointed with his finger to the ground). Half of them will not get to their destination," he added.

"Epidemics, I suppose?" I inquired, stirred to the very core.

"No, not exactly epidemics; but they just fall like flies. Well, you know, these Jewish boys are so puny and delicate. They can't stand mixing dirt for ten hours, with dry biscuits to live on. Again, everywhere strange folks, no father, no mother, no caresses. Well then, you just hear a cough and the youngster is dead. Hello, corporal, get out the small fry!"

The little ones were assembled and arrayed in a military line. It was one of the most terrible spectacles I have ever witnessed. Poor, poor children! The boys of twelve or thirteen managed somehow to stand up, but the little ones of eight and ten.... No brush, however black, could convey the terror of this scene on the canvas.

Pale, worn out, with scared looks, this is the way they stood in their uncomfortable rough soldier uniforms, with their starched, turned-up collars, fixing an inexpressibly helpless and pitiful gaze upon the garrisoned soldiers, who were handling them rudely. White lips, blue lines under the eyes betokened either fever or cold. And these poor children, without care, without a caress, exposed to the wind which blows unhindered from the Arctic Ocean, were marching to their death. I seized the officer's hand, and, with the words: "Take good care of them!" threw myself into my carriage. I felt like sobbing, and I knew I could not master myself.... (Dubnow, 1918, pp. 24–25)

After arriving at their destination, the juvenile conscripts were put into the cantonists battalions, where the true purpose of their conscription was carried out under the guise of preparing them for military service. It began with their religious re-education at the hands of sergeants and corporals, who used every means to lead the children to the baptismal font. The children were first sent for spiritual admonition to the local Greek Orthodox priests, whose efforts, however, proved fruitless in nearly every case. To succeed where the priests failed, the soldiers, with the tacit approval of their superiors, resorted to all kinds of torture. A favourite procedure was to make the cantonists get down on their knees in the evening after all had gone to bed and to keep the sleepy children in that position for hours. Those who agreed to be baptized were sent to bed; those who refused were kept up for the whole night until they dropped from exhaustion. The children who continued to resist were flogged and, under the guise of gymnastic exercises, subjected to all kinds of torture. Those who refused to eat pork or the customary cabbage soup prepared with lard were beaten and left to starve. Others were fed on salted fish and then forbidden to drink until the little ones, tormented by thirst, agreed to embrace Christianity (Dubnow, 1918, p. 26).

The majority of these children, unable to endure the tortures inflicted on them, saved themselves through baptism. But many cantonists, particularly those of a maturer age (between fifteen and eighteen), bore their martyrdom with heroic patience. Beaten almost into senselessness, their bodies striped by lashes, tormented to the point of exhaustion by hunger, thirst and sleeplessness, the lads declared again and again that they would not betray the faith of their fathers. Most of these obstinate youths were carried from the barracks into the military hospitals to be released by a kind death. Only a few remained alive (Dubnow, 1918, pp. 26–27).

As for the adult recruits, the objective of ethnic cleansing by forced conversion to Christianity was pursued with the same tragic consequences for the older recruits who were drafted at the normal age of conscription (18–25). The impending twenty-five-year service in far off regions was designed to cause total alienation from family and faith. Many recruits, before leaving home, gave their wives a divorce to save them from perpetual widowhood (Dubnow, 1918, pp. 27–28).

From the moment they were captured, they were tossed into a totally unfamiliar environment. Their years of military service were spent under extreme duress caused by an extremely hostile Judeophobic environment. They were beaten and ridiculed because they could not speak the Russian language, because of their refusal to eat non-kosher food, and because of their difficulty in adapting to the military mode of life. In the end, it became clear that the underlying proselytizing agenda of the Nicholas I regime overruled any humanitarian and legal principle when it came to Russia's Jewish population. Even those Jewish soldiers who managed to adapt to their new environment and to the military way of life were denied any deserved promotion, as any higher rank was available only to those who accepted to be baptized. The government's hypocrisy was demonstrated by the fact that even while the Statute on Military Service promised that the Jewish soldiers who had completed their term in the army with distinction would be admitted to the civil service, this promise was not kept as long as the candidates were loyal to Judaism. The ultimate blow of Russian infamy was delivered when the Jews who had completed their military service were not even allowed to live out their lives in the localities outside the Pale in which they had been stationed as soldiers (Dubnow, 1918, pp. 28–29).

Education was another method viewed by the government of Nicholas I as an effective device to assimilate and ultimately convert the Jews of the empire. Special government schools were established for Jewish children. His government also created new institutions of higher learning to train rabbis and teachers. The Jewish masses, extremely suspicious of the government that had visited the *rekrutschina* upon them, resisted this attempt to convert the Jews to Russian orthodoxy, and most refused to send the children to the government schools or to accept the graduates of the state-sponsored seminaries (Berk, 1985, p. 5).

Berk noted that, in the end, the government schools did have an impact on the subsequent course of Russian Jewish history. The small number of students in those schools, who came from either poor families or upwardly mobile middle-class Jewish homes, received an education that was totally different from the overwhelming majority of their coreligionists. Whereas the latter attended the traditional *heder* and *yeshiva,* with their total emphasis on religious studies, those who attended the government Jewish schools received a more secular education, distinguished primarily by the teaching of the Russian language. The graduates of these schools, who numbered in the thousands, were among the first Jews to have a familiarity with Russian culture. They were the first to enter the broader Russian society and to create a new Russian Jewish culture (Berk, 1985, p. 5).

The number of Jews who had acquired secular knowledge was also increased by the spread of the *Haskala* to Eastern Europe. With its connotation of secular learning and religious reform, it had been carried from Germany, its place of origin, to various Eastern European areas, most significantly to Galicia in the Habsburg Empire. By the end of the 1830s, the *Haskala* had reached the Russian provinces that bordered upon Galicia. The creation of the new schools for Jewish students, where they would be taught arithmetic, science, the Russian language and Russian history, provided an essential element for the implementation of the objectives of the Russian *Haskala*. The Russian *maskilims'* pursuit of Jewish emancipation included the writing of new religious textbooks to teach the fundamentals of Judaism to offset what they considered to be the harmful influence of the Talmud, the teaching of manual trades to young Jews and the wearing of the same clothes as the rest of the Jewish people (Berk, 1985, pp. 5–6).

It was the synergy of the discovery of modern political and scientific concepts resulting from the spreading of the *Haskala* and the increasingly oppressive anti-Jewish policies of Nicholas I's regime that triggered the awakening of the Zionist political thinking among the Jews of Eastern Europe.

The new city of Odessa played a significant role in raising the hopes of Russian Jewry in the benefits of the *Haskala*. Established at the end of the eighteenth century in an area recently taken over from the Ottoman Empire, Odessa was free of the constraints of tradition. As a major seaport, it was exposed to new ideas and diverse people. It was in this cosmopolitan environment that the first Jewish school for secular education in Russia opened in 1826 (Berk, 1985, p. 6). This relatively open and liberal urban enclave with a non-Jewish population that was relatively better educated and tolerant than within the rest of Russia attracted an influx of forward-looking Jewish businessmen, entrepreneurs, professionals and members of the intelligentsia who were more or less emancipated from the traditional Orthodoxy of the Pale of Settlement. Odessa became the capital of Hebrew letters and Jewish enlightenment in Russia. Odessa had become a beehive of Jewish intellectual activity focused on the advocacy of emancipation and enlightenment for the Jews (Avineri, 2017, p. 60). Here were fostered the dreams of a society where Russified Jews could participate in building a multi-national and multi-religious Russian homeland, free from tsarist autocracy and religious bigotry. These dreams were encouraged by the reforms of the 1860s under Tsar Alexander II, whereunder the serfs were emancipated, a relatively enlightened bureaucracy started to open Russian society to Western ideas, and Jews were gradually allowed into schools, universities and the professions (Avineri, 2017, pp. 60–61).

Alexander II (1855–1881) – The Calm before the Storm

While conditions were terrible for Russian Jewry under Nicholas I, they seemed to improve under the new tsar, Alexander II, who succeeded Nicholas I in 1855. The main trigger for the positive changes that occurred under Alexander II was the impact of Russia's humiliating defeat, in 1856, in the costly sixteen-month Crimean war. It was Russia's first major defeat since the early eighteenth century and caused the Russian government and educated classes in Russian society to look for the internal causes that led to this unexpected outcome. By the end of the decade, they had reached the conclusion that Russia needed drastic structural reforms to strengthen the state against international threats and to ensure internal tranquillity (Berk, 1985, p. 7).

The most famous of the ensuing reforms was the emancipation of the serfs in February 1861. As a result of his transformational development, Tsar Alexander II became known as the "Tsar Liberator." Just as the French Declaration of the Rights of Man applied, in theory, to all French citizens regardless of faith, the Russian government officials concerned with the Jews believed that their emancipation and the improvement of their position was consistent with the contemporary spirit (Berk, 1985, p. 7).

Although Alexander probably did not hold the Jews in high esteem, he still allowed his officials to implement significant reforms. The most impactful piece of legislation affecting Russian Jewry was issued on the very day of the new tsar's coronation, August 26, 1856. It abolished juvenile conscription, the worst feature of the *rekrutschina*. On December 2, 1857, the Russian government reopened the fifty-*verst* [ca. thirty-three-mile] zones along the Prussian and Austrian frontiers in the west and, after October 27, 1958, through Bessarabia in the east, all of which had been closed to Jews in April 1843. Jews would now be allowed to live in these frontier zones (Berk, 1985, pp. 7, 8).

In 1859, Jewish merchants of the First Guild were granted the right to trade and reside all over Russia. In 1860, Jewish soldiers who completed their term of service in the guard regiments were permitted to remain permanently in the capital (Berk, 1985, p. 8).

On November 27, 1861, a new law granted Jews who finished a university programme and received a higher academic degree to live and work outside the Jewish Pale and to receive government employment (Berk, 1985, p. 8).

On December 11, 1861, merchants of the First and Second Merchants' Guilds were granted the right of permanent residence in Russia's main city of Kiev, while all Jews were permitted temporary residence in certain quarters (Berk, 1985, p. 8). The long list of new laws affecting the Jews included the opening of all of Russia, on June 28, 1865, to Jewish artisans and their families (Berk, 1985, p. 8).

While this and many other new laws concerning the Jews were hedged with all sorts of qualifications and provided substantial advantages for only a very small segment of Russian Jewry, leaving the rest of the community in the same abysmal conditions as before, it appeared that government policies towards the Jews were moving in a totally new direction (Berk, 1985, p. 9).

The Russian press, including government organs, reflected the new philosemitic mood of the late 1850s. In 1858, an article in the *Russkii Invalid* (Russian Veteran), published by the Ministry of War, spoke of the need to view the Jews in a new light:

> Let us be worthy of our age; let us give up the childish habit of presenting the Jews in our literary works as ludicrous and ignominious creatures. On the contrary, remembering the causes which brought them to such a state, let us not forget the innate ability of the Jews for the arts and sciences; and by offering them a place among us, let us utilize their energy, readiness of wit, and skill as new means for satisfying the ever-growing needs of our people. (Berk, 1985, pp. 9–10)

These apparently positive developments boosted the morale of the Jewish intelligentsia in Russia. They were optimistic that emancipation would soon be enacted and bring with it the *sblizhenie* (rapprochement) between Jews and Russians that would bring an end to the degrading treatment of Russian Jewry. The various Jewish periodicals in Odessa concurred in their view that a new age had dawned for the Jewish people, that the fruits of emancipation would put an end to their history of degradation and persecution, and that the Jewish people were about to take their rightful place in the family of nations (Berk, 1985, p. 10).

The greatest influence on the Jewish intelligentsia was exerted by the small group of writers and poets whose books and poems appeared in the

Jewish periodicals on a serialized basis. Their writings reflected and shaped the attitudes of many in that generation of the 1860s and 1870s. Writing primarily in Russian, but also in Hebrew and Yiddish, they were the first in a long and distinguished line of Russian Jewish literary personalities who sought to lead their people to a better life. These were the leading intellectuals who believed that embracing the social opportunities promised by the *Haskala* would bring an end to the status of the Jews as a persecuted minority. While constituting only a small part of the Jewish population, they were the philosophical pioneers who believed in the promise of Russification and secularization (Berk, 1985, p. 12).

In his Hebrew poem "Awake My People!" published in 1866 in the periodical *Ha-Karmel*, Yehudah Leib Gordon praised Russia for opening its arms to its Jewish citizens and urged them to become an enlightened people by opening their hearts to wisdom and knowledge and to embrace the Russian language as their own. Gordon encouraged the mastering of all manner of arts and crafts for the brave to serve in the army and for the farmers to till the land. The Jews should be brothers to their countrymen and servants to their king (Berk, 1985, pp. 12–13).

Berk singled out Lev Levanda as the man whose literary endeavours best expressed the mood of the new generation and probably had the greatest influence on it, as well as upon those Russians interested in Jewish affairs. Graduate of a government rabbinical school, teacher in a crown school, and later attached to the governor-general's office in Vilna, Levanda became a passionate advocate of internal reform, an ardent Russian patriot, and an equally enthusiastic Russifier (Berk, 1985, p. 13).

In an article published in the very first issue of the fervently pro-*Haskala* Jewish periodical *Razsvet* (Dawn), Levanda wrote that it was the Jews themselves and not the Russian government who were responsible for their problems. He urged the Jews to change their values and attitudes, including the economic bases on which they constituted their lives. The Jewish male's total absorption in the study of the Talmud, to the point of abdicating his responsibility for the economic well-being of his family, was, according to Levanda, at the root of the problem (Berk, 1985, pp. 13–14).

Levanda expressed his passion for Russification in his novel *Goriachee Vremia* (Turbulent Times), wherein he praised Russia and advocated full rapprochement between the Jewish and Russian people in the belief that this would lead to a brilliant future for Russian Jewry (Berk, 1985, p. 14).

Another prominent advocate for linguistic Russification and internal reform was Ilia Orshanskii, who, Berk noted, was an extremely talented young scholar of the late 1860s and 1870s, who wrote for the Odessa

Jewish periodical *Dyen* (Day) and who died at the age of twenty-nine. Unlike Levanda, who used fiction, Orshanskii wrote insightful, scholarly articles on the economic, social and legal aspects of Jewish life in Russia. His book *Russkoe Zakondatel'stvo o Evreikh* (Russian Legislation Concerning the Jews), in which he describes the history of the legal disabilities of Russian Jewry, was considered a classic by his contemporaries. While he was convinced that the integration of Russian Jewry was desirable and inevitable, he, unlike the more fervent Russifiers, believed in a natural process of assimilation without the stimulus of coercive government policies. He was among those who argued that the existing Russian legislation concerning the Jews was counterproductive. If the Jews were allowed to be emancipated first, all the needed social, economic and religious reforms would follow as a matter of course (Berk, 1985, p. 14).

What distinguished Orshanskii from other writers and gave him great popularity was his passionate defence of the Russian Jewish community against its many detractors. In his studies of contemporary Russian Jewry, he depicted them as a creative and productive people who played significant roles as artisans, in agriculture, and in livestock farming. He also rejected the idea that the Jews were responsible for the great poverty and perpetual inebriation of the Russian peasantry. He had the courage to attribute their condition to the general backwardness of Russian society, which had to end before their condition could be improved. While he was a firm believer in Russification, Orshanskii maintained a powerful emotional tie to the Jewish masses and, like most of the Russian Jewish intelligentsia, hoped that Jewish institutions would be preserved after emancipation (Berk, 1985, p. 15).

Ideas have no social traction unless they activate the mindsets of a significant segment of the population they target. Both Levanda and Orshanskii were speaking to a growing audience. In the 1860s and 1870s, Russification spread rapidly among Russian Jewish youth. They were motivated by the apparent liberalism by Alexander II's reign, by the heightened attractiveness of Russian literature and culture, and by the granting of rewards and privileges by the government to Jews possessing Russian diplomas that contributed to this process. Jewish enrolment figures in the gymnasium of the empire testified to the strength of the movement. In 1859, for example, 159 Jewish students constituted less than 1.5 percent of total enrolment. By 1863, 3.8 percent, or 547 students, were Jewish. In 1870, Jews constituted 5.5 percent of the student body, numbering 2,047. The figure reached 11.5 percent in 1880 (Berk, 1985, p. 15).

While all the leading intellectuals who were advocating the Russification of the Jewish population were proponents of the *Haskala*, there were some significant differences in their approach and emphasis during this period. While Moshe Leib Lilienblum and Isaac Joel Linetski both urged familiarity with Russian society and civilization, they were also much concerned with reforming the basic structure of Russian Jewry. Lilienblum began his public career as an outspoken champion of religious reform. In his writings in the Hebrew newspaper *Ha-Melits* which emphasized the values that he proposed, he argued that Judaism was not a stagnant religion and that Talmudic authorities had always sought to reconcile Judaism with the spirit and needs of the time. He appealed to prominent Russian Jewish religious leaders to begin the task of interpreting Jewish religious law in a rational and modern way so as to eliminate the traditional obstacles that stood in the way of modernizing Russian Jewry. Like many of his contemporaries, Lilienblum suffered for his liberal views. Orthodox religious leaders in his wife's town of Vilkomir harassed him to the point that he had to flee to Odessa. This city, as we have seen, was a young and dynamic seaport and a centre of the Russification movement. Here, Lilienblum switched his focus from religious reform to the need to restructure the economic underpinnings of Jewish life. He preached the need for Jews to learn a manual trade and became an advocate for agricultural work among Jews. He also suggested that Jews would benefit from knowledge of the laws of nature through the study of the natural sciences (Berk, 1985, pp. 15–16).

Unlike many of the other proponents of the *Haskala* who were educated in crown schools and had quickly entered the world of the new Russian Jewish intelligentsia, Isaac Joel Linetski was born into a Hasidic family, educated in the traditional way and married at the age of 14 to a young girl of 12. His most important literary work, *Dos Poylishe Yingel* (The Polish Lad), written in Yiddish, was a hilarious, if biting, satire of Hasidic life. The importance of Linetski's book lies in the fact that, because it was written in Yiddish and in an entertaining satirical style, it was one of the few works, outside of some religious tracts, which were read by the Jewish masses of Eastern Europe and enjoyed a readership probably greater than that of most other literary publications of the period (Berk, 1985, pp. 16–17).

Berk noted that Linetski was able to elucidate, better than anyone else, the internal dynamics of Hasidic life and its harmful impact on the Jews of the empire. Linetski laments the sad lot of traditional Jewish women, oppressed and held in contempt and yet, at the same time, doing their Herculean labour in the home and the business. In his criticism, Linetski spares no aspect of Hasidic life that he considers an obstacle to the improvement of their social and economic status. He attacked the superstitious faith in miracle-working Hasidic rabbis, their greed and hypocrisy, and the slavish devotion of the *hasid* to his rabbi, even at the expense of his own family. He harshly criticized traditional Jewish education in the *heder* and lamented the lack of secular knowledge among the Jews. He did not close his eyes to those aspects of life in the Pale that even the most radical critics of traditional Jewish life were reluctant to touch: alcoholism, sexual promiscuity, and cowardly and obsequious behaviour on the part of the Jews in their dealings with Gentiles (Berk, 1985, p. 17).

Levanda, Lilienblum, Orshanskii and Linetski, each in his own way, pursued the same objectives. While they were in favour of Russification and substantial internal reform, they also believed in maintaining communal Jewish identity (Berk, 1985, p. 17).

At the same time, some Jews, as a result of their secular education, became aware of the nationalistic impulse in European civilization and the growth of national movements throughout the European continent. It can be said, therefore, that Jewish nationalism and the drive for rapprochement and assimilation were both products of the *Haskala* (Berk, 1985, p. 18).

Not all the leading Jewish writers during the reign of Alexander II believed that emancipation through Russification provided the only way to relieve the Jewish population from the relentless burden of Judeophobic oppression. Berk notes that in the 1860s and 1870s, Jewish nationalist sentiments were an important element in the thinking of at least part of the Jewish intelligentsia. He hints at the growing antisemitism of the 1870s as the accelerator of this process (Berk, 1985).

Abraham Mapu, considered the father of the modern Hebrew novel, was, at the time, also a champion of the Russian *Haskala*. In his novels, he too espoused the cause of knowledge, manual labour and the cultivation of the soil. His major contribution, however, was to include a yearning for Palestine in the sense of national consciousness found among Russian Jews. In his two romantic novels, *Ahabat Sion* (The Love of Zion) and *Ashmat Shomron* (Guilt of Samaria), he contrasted the pastoral beauty of the ancient homeland with the squalid towns and villages in which they were currently quagmired. He thus paved the way for the development of the national idea which emerged in response to the tragic events that would occur following the death of Alexander II (Berk, 1985, p. 18).

Russian-born Perez Smolenskin, who published his Hebrew periodical *Ha-Shahar* (Dawn) in Vienna, was also a partisan of the national idea. In the mid-1860s, through his novels and essays, Smolenskin warned that all

Jewish attempts to ingratiate themselves with governments and host populations through enlightenment and rapprochement would not result in Jewish equality. Smolenskin believed that the preservation of the Jewish people was so symbiotically bound up with the Hebrew language that there would be no Judaism without it (Berk, 1985, pp. 18–19). Smolenskin's ideas resonated with a large portion of the Russian Jewish youth, against the background of the increase in antisemitism and the gradual erosion of the signs of goodwill towards the Jewish community Alexander II and his government had displayed during the first half of his reign.

The Gathering of the Dark Clouds

The young generation who had grown up during the years that *Haskala* was moving in a positive direction were disappointed by the failure of the government to grant the Jews civic equality and discouraged by the growing anti-Jewish campaign by the Russian press after the Russo-Turkish War (1877–1878). The acute economic crisis following the bad harvests from which Russian Jewry suffered in the late 1870s also awakened interest in the plight of their own people. Yet, while Smolenskin leaned in the direction of Zionism and attracted a wide response, he did not go so far as to voice an equivocal call for Jewish settlement in Palestine (Greenberg, 1944, p. 143). This task fell on the shoulders of one of his most prominent disciples, Eliezer Pearlman, known as Ben-Yehuda.

Ben-Yehuda turned out to become the outstanding figure in this period of national resurgence. Inspired by the sentiments of racial solidarity expressed by the Russian press in regard to the Balkan Slavs for whose national freedom Russia was fighting during the Russo-Turkish War, he asked himself why the Jews should be any less worthy of being a nation with their own language and their own land than any other people. This thought motivated him to devote himself wholeheartedly to the resettlement of Palestine. It was Ben-Yehuda who took Smolenskin to task for suggesting only halfway measures. In an open letter to Smolenskin's own periodical, Ben-Yehuda criticized the latter for his failure to preach a return to Zion. Ben-Yehuda argued that the Jews were not merely a spiritual nation but a nation like any other and, as such, were entitled to a land of their own. He believed that the revival of the Hebrew language by itself was not enough to revive Jewish national consciousness and that the Jewish nation can exist only on its own soil (Greenberg, 1944, pp. 143–144).

In his article "She'elah Nichbadah" (An Important Problem), which appeared in *Ha-Shahar*, Ben-Yehuda pointed out that the Jews possessed all the attributes of nationality, such as common history, common memories and a common language, Hebrew. He asserted that their unique religion and the antagonism of other nations, which were the two factors that had saved the Jews from national extinction, could no longer save them from national death. He called on Jewish writers to organize a society for the promotion of colonization in the Holy Land. In effect, nineteen years before the First Zionist Congress launched Zionism as a political movement, Ben-Yehuda had already formulated the Zionist programme (Greenberg, 1944, p. 144).

Greenberg concluded that as the hope of achieving the status of equality was fading for the Jews in Russia, a new hope was kindled in many hearts by the ideas of Smolenskin and Ben-Yehuda; the former by awakening an interest in their own national culture, the latter by holding out hope of an independent life on the soil of their ancestors (Greenberg, 1944, p. 145).

Berk concluded his observations about the situation of the Jews in Russia in the 1870s on a mixed note. The affluent and educated Jews were predominantly optimistic; they were adamantly opposed to emigration and still believed in rapprochement and assimilation, which would lead to emancipation. Meanwhile, the vast majority of the Russian Jews, who had received few of the benefits of the Era of the Great Reform, were still suffering from the cruel Russian reality, remained in their state of passivity, and were willing to bide their time in the hope of better things to come (Berk, 1985, pp. 32–33).

This brings us to a critical junction in the development of Jewish social consciousness, the assassination of Alexander II on March 13, 1881, which triggered two significant developments: the ascent to power of Alexander III and the 1881–1882 pogroms. These, in their unexpectedness and extreme severity, completely dashed the hope that the path to liberty and equality lay in the embrace of the cultural values of the Gentile majority.

Alexander III (1881–1894) – From Bad to Worse

The unprecedented new wave of pogroms was triggered by two connected upheavals: the shockwave created by the assassination of Alexander II and the violence-accelerating catalyst of the much more repressive regime resulting from Alexander III's accession to the throne.

Alexander III was trained primarily for a military career and was, as characterized by one of his close friends, a man of "limited education and lacking in mental keenness." He was totally imbued with the traditional faith in absolutism and in his own imperial destiny. This natural aversion to democratic innovations caused him to react to his father's assassination with increased resistance to the popular demands for sharing government (Greenberg, 1951, p. 2).

The powder keg of pent-up hatred for the impoverished Jewish minority which had been maligned and vilified to a fever pitch needed only the fuse of an opportune event to explode into a wave of violence. The assassination of Alexander II on March 13, 1881 turned out to be a major critical juncture in the history of Russian Jewry. Earlier that day, he had signed the Loris-Melikov constitution, which held out the possibility of democratic rule in Russia. Although Alexander II was not less autocratic than his predecessors, through the reforms he had granted during the first part of his reign as well as by signing this constitutional document, he had proven that he was not insensitive to the currents of the time and to the demands of enlightened public opinion. Unfortunately, his assassination and the personality of his successor turned out to pre-empt the possibility of a constitutional monarchy (Greenberg, 1951, p. 2).

To identify the socio-political dynamics that led to the watershed 1881–1882 pogroms, it is essential to focus on what Dubnow called "the decided drift toward political reaction in the second part of Alexander's reign." During the first liberal years of Alexander II's reign, Russian Jewry began to look upon commerce as a beneficial pursuit. The economic advancement of the Jews was due not only to the privileges bestowed upon them by the authorities but even more so to the impact of changes in the economic environment. It was primarily the expansion of the railroad industry during the 1860s and 1870s that brought new opportunities to the Jewish business class. When the old system of farming out the sale of liquor was abolished in 1861, some Jewish capital moved from the liquor trade into railroad building. Jewish entrepreneurs who had been engaged in the collection of excise on liquor became shareholders, supply merchants or contractors in the railroad industry. This first manifestation of economic success caused jealousy and fear among the Russian mercantile class, who urged the curbing of what they called Jewish exploitation. While the trend towards Russification was strong in the new Jewish intelligentsia of the 1860s, the vast majority of Jewry was totally oblivious to this tendency. The government began to doubt whether the hopes of a fusion of the Jews with the original population were justified by the events. Russian officialdom also started to question whether it was worthwhile to extend any rights to the Jews if it was not going to ensure their fusion with the Christians (Dubnow, 1918, p. 187).

The slippery road which led to the complete reversal of the liberal direction during the early years of Alexander II's reign was fueled by a flood of antisemitic propaganda, unprecedented in volume and virulence.

One of the occurrences that were instrumental in causing the government to embark on a new policy of thoroughly investigating the workings and activities of the Jewish population was the arrival on the scene of the nefarious figure of Jacob Brafman. His role in fuelling the antisemitic tendencies among Russian officialdom was so pernicious and invasive that it has received extensive coverage in the scholarship on that period. Brafman, a Jewish convert to Russian Orthodoxy, did more than any other individual to poison the minds of the Russian population against the Jews. Born into an extremely poor Jewish family, Brafman belonged to the generation of unfortunate boys who were chosen by Jewish community officials for recruitment into the army. He deserted his race and religion rather than endure the horrible fate of Jewish child recruits in nineteenth-century Tsarist Russia. Embittered against the Jewish community agents who had become recruiting tools for the government, he set out to unchain his wrath against the very idea of a Jewish communal organization by offering his services to the authorities. His greatest success came with the publication of the book *Kniga Kagala* (the Book of the Kahal). *Kahal* was the term for the executive agency of the local Jewish community. This agency had been in charge of taxation, internal policing and the administration of justice for the Jews but had been abolished in 1844 by the government. In practice, however, it continued to function until the end of the nineteenth century. Brafman's book, which contained a collection of his newspaper articles published in 1866, established him, both in Russia and in the rest of Europe, as the leading expert on Jews (Berk, 1985, pp. 45–46.)

Brafman denounced the Jews as a Talmudic Republic, a state within a state, which did not recognize the law of the land. According to Brafman, all Jewish organizations throughout the world were part of this Talmudic Republic, which he called the Kahal, which had as its ultimate goal the subjugation of the Christian world to Jewish hegemony and exploitation. All the refutations by scholars of all denominations, which showed Brafman's falsification and misinterpretation of Talmudic and other Jewish writings, failed to stem his influence. His book was serialized in newspapers and became compulsory reading for government officials throughout the empire. The government published a second edition in 1878, which was soon translated into French, Polish, German and English.

Berk notes that Brafman's book might have inspired similar subsequent writings of Jewish cabals, such as *The Protocols of the Elders of Zion* (Berk, 1985, p. 46). It is symptomatic of the allure of antisemitic propaganda that Brafman achieved such a vast audience in spite of the fact that he had no real knowledge of traditional Jewish sources, knew little Hebrew and had to resort to the hiring of unsuspecting students at the Vilna Rabbinical Seminary to assist him in his research. The prominent Jewish scholar Abraham Harkavy, who worked for the State Library in St. Petersburg, provides a telling example of Brafman's lack of erudition when he cites the occasion when he was asked by Brafman to get him the book entitled Ibid or Ibidem, which had to be very important because it was cited everywhere (Berk, 1985, p. 46)

Nevertheless, the authorities of St. Petersburg seized upon Brafman's fictitious revelations of Jewish separatism as justification for the methods they saw fit to apply to the solution of the Jewish problem (Dubnow, 1918, p. 191)

It is symptomatic of the visceral antisemitic appetite for Judeophobic fodder that Brafman's work, despite its total lack of erudition and factual content, managed to contribute so significantly to the growing hostility towards Jews, which manifested itself in both private and public levels of Russian society. Accusations of Jewish exploitation of the lower classes and the growing inundation of Russia by Jews were becoming the predominant themes of the Russian press. In the late 1860s and 1870s, the Jew had become, in the eyes of Russian antisemites, "a cunning spider whom it was necessary to crush in the name of general security" (Berk, 1985, p. 47).

Brafman's attacks on the Jews were echoed by more prominent literary figures. The famous Slavophile Ivan Aksakov also repeatedly accused the Jews of exploiting ordinary Russians. He urged them to enter the world of European civilization by converting to Christianity (Berk, 1985, p. 47)

Similarly, A. S. Suvorin, the new publisher of the once prominent liberal newspaper *Novoe Vremia*, turned it into a vicious instrument of anti-Jewish propaganda. In 1880, he wrote an article entitled "The Yid is Coming," wherein he accused the Jews of leading the revolutionary movement as well as of exercising a destructive influence on Russia by participating in the evils of both capitalism and socialism. He feared that Jewish participation in the gymnasiums and universities was so great that it would lead to Jewish domination of the liberal professions and hence to the control of Russia itself (Berk, 1985, p. 47).

Even Fyodor Dostoyevsky was caught up in the revived spirit of antisemitism. He deplored the Jews' nefarious influence not only in

Russia, where, he claimed, they were sucking the peasants dry, but in all of Europe and the United States as well. Dostoyevsky expounded that the Jews had no respect for Gentiles, whom they were humiliating at every opportunity, and that they wanted to exterminate or enslave the non-Jewish populations of the world. He predicted that the Jewish banks would inherit the property of a world plunged into anarchy by the Jews. He expressed the fear that Jewish world dominance was totally assured (Berk, 1985, p. 47).

As always, the irrational impulse of Judeophobia was impervious to responses of reason and truth. The vast amount of evidence produced by, among others, the talented young scholar Ilia Orshanskii, whose penetrating analyses of life in the Pale of Settlement revealed that non-Jews living in the Pale were better off economically than those living outside of it, did not alter the perception of Jewish exploitation. Neither did Bliuch's massive study, which confirmed that peasants living in areas inhabited by Jews were much better off than those living in areas where there were no Jews. What mattered was not reality but the perception of reality, such as the reference in the periodical *Syn Otechevsta* (Son of the Fatherland) to Jews as that "mass of usurers and hucksters of dubious honesty, who enriched themselves by exploiting the gullible Russians" (Berk, 1985, p. 47).

It was this intensified atmosphere of anti-Jewish fervour that fueled the retrogressive changes, from the initial spurt of beneficial legislation during the first half of Alexander II's reign to the introduction of new restrictions on the Jewish populations of the cities and towns of the Pale. While the rural self-government and judicial reform laws promulgated in 1864 included no restrictions on the Jews, the proclamation in 1870 of the decree on the municipal *dumas* (self-governing city councils) reflected the growing government hostility towards the Jews. Under the new Municipal Duma Law, only one-third of executives could be non-Christians and no Jew was eligible to be mayor, even though Jews were disproportionately present in the cities and towns of the Pale (Berk, 1985, p. 48).

This reinvigorated anti-Jewish spirit was similarly evident in the comments and reports of the members of the Committee for the Amelioration of the Condition of the Jews, established by the Ministry of the Interior in 1871. In discussing whether Jews should be allowed to live and work beyond the Pale, one member, V. Grigoriev, said that it would be dangerous to let Jews reside outside of the Pale because "the plague which has thus far been restricted to the Western provinces will then spread over the whole empire." Grigoriev's opinions were shared by others on the committee, a number of whom picked up on Brafman's lead by harshly attacking the pernicious influence of the Talmud (Berk, 1985, p. 48).

The reach and influence of Brafman's book are illustrated in the report submitted, in 1872, to the Tsar by the governor-general of Kiev, Prince A. M. Dondukov-Korsakov, wherein he states that "the cause of every last Jew is also the cause of the worldwide Jewish kahal... that powerful yet elusive association" (Berk, 1985, p. 48).

Scholarly consensus sees in the Russo-Turkish War of 1877–1878 another opportunity eagerly seized upon by the right-wing anti-Jewish press to intensify antisemitic sentiment. Although Beck erroneously dated it to 1873–1874, he concurred that it was accompanied by intense pan-Slavism and that it heightened xenophobia and hostility towards the minorities living within the empire. The press accused the Jews of corruption, embezzlement and cowardice and for being responsible for starting the war. In his novel *Tamara Ben-David*, the popular Russian writer Vsevolod Krestovskii maintained the Jews had wanted the war for the purpose of increasing business (Berk, 1985, pp. 48–49).

The relentless inciters of anti-Jewish sentiment never missed an opportunity to invent and publicize a treacherous Jewish hand in any internal or external political turn of events affecting Russia's national interests. They seized upon British Prime Minister Benjamin Disraeli's role at the Congress of Berlin, which was held to check Russia's territorial ambitions in the wake of its victory in the Russo-Turkish War, to turn Disraeli's Jewish ancestry into the suggestion that the Russian Jews had set him against Russia to avenge their lack of civil rights (Berk, 1985, p. 49).

The Jew-hating publisher Alexei Suvorin saw Russian Jewry and Disraeli linked in a plot to fulfil Jewish national aspirations. He saw in both of them a tribal disposition towards the Turks, whose resurrection they envisaged as the path towards the fulfilment of their 2,000-year-old dream of the revival of a Jewish kingdom (Berk, 1985, p. 49).

The fires that kept stoking this anti-Jewish mood continued to be fanned relentlessly throughout the end of the 1870s and beyond. In 1876, Ippolit Liutostanskii, a defrocked Catholic convert to Russian Orthodoxy, successfully produced a new book libelling the Jews. Entitled *Ob upotreblenii evreiami kristianskoi krov dlia religioznykh tseli* (Concerning the Use of Christian Blood by the Jews), it raised, once again, the blood libel charge of the Jewish use of Christian blood for the baking of unleavened bread, the *matzoh*, at the time of Passover. He managed to present a copy to the heir to the throne, the future Alexander III, and to receive from him a grateful acknowledgement. High-ranking police officials embraced the book and disseminated a large number of copies to police officials throughout the country. In 1879, Liutostanskii published another defamatory work, *Talmud i Evrei* (The Talmud and the Jew), which further stirred up the by now hackneyed charges about the Talmud (Berk, 1985, p. 49).

Unfortunately, as unfounded as these charges were, they found a large audience and caused a lively reaction. The well-documented refutations by Jewish and non-Jewish commentators, to the effect that Liutostanskii, like Brafman, had forged the facts on which he based his accusations, were of no avail. Berk suggested that Liutostanskii's publications may have inspired the blood libel trial in the city of Kutaisi in the Caucasus, where ten local Jews were accused of the death of a girl who went missing just before Passover. The spuriousness of this typical case of Jew-baiting is demonstrated by the fact that the defence attorneys for the accused successfully challenged the evidence used to support the indictment (Berk, 1985, pp. 49–50).

Berk concluded his examination of the antisemitic background that fueled the new wave of pogroms starting in 1881 by noting that in the few years just prior to the pogroms, the anti-Jewish press hammered at a new theme: the relationship between Jews and the revolutionary movement. Unfortunately, by cramming this important element of antisemitic fomentation into a single paragraph of quoted commentaries, he fails to provide an adequate understanding of one of the underlying causes of the rising intensity of antisemitic feelings among the Russian population during this critical period (Berk, 1985, p. 50).

Greenberg, however, provided a detailed, elaborate and complex picture of the extent, nature and consequences of Jewish participation in the revolutionary movement. The Russian socialists of the 1870s referred to themselves as *Narodniki* (Populists) because their programme called for revolutionary propaganda among the masses of the Russian population. They were not motivated to fight for Jewish rights but by the plight of the Russian peasantry. As an expression of solidarity with the Russian revolutionary movement, a Jewish revolutionary of the period stated in his memoirs, "We are *Narodniki,* the mujiks are our natural brothers" (Greenberg, 1944, p. 147).

Alexander II's refusal to grant a constitutional regime and his failure to solve the land needs of the peasantry marked the start of secret anti-government activity and of the spirit of rebellion which spread to the non-Russian "racial" minorities of the empire, caused the Polish uprising of 1863, and led to signs of unrest in Ukraine and the Caucasus (Greenberg, 1944, p. 146).

Of the major ethnic minorities in the Russian Empire, the Jews were the most loyal to the government of Alexander II. While their economic condition and legal status had not shown much improvement under his reign, they were grateful for the abolition of some of the cruel laws of Nicholas I. Lev Deich, an important Jewish revolutionist, ascribes the absence of the will to revolt among the Jewish masses to their isolation and to the centuries of oppression which had crushed any spirit of rebelliousness out of them (Greenberg, 1944, p. 146).

The educated and wealthy among the Jews displayed the same lack of any spirit of unrest. While their contact with Russian thought should have made them more susceptible to revolutionary ideas, the government had secured their goodwill through the special privileges they enjoyed (Greenberg, 1944, p. 146).

It befell a converted Jew, Nicholas Utin, to play a conspicuous role in the 1861 anti-government student demonstrations. To avoid arrest, he fled to Geneva, where he became editor of the periodical *Narodnoe Delo* (The Case of the People), founded by the Russian anarchist Mikhail Bakunin. By supporting Marx in his struggle with Bakunin in the First (Socialist) International, Utin added fuel to the anti-Jewish sentiments of Bakunin, who regarded the Jews as enemies of Russia and the Slavic races (Greenberg, 1944, p. 147).

To most of the early Jewish revolutionists, the only unhappy, dispossessed people were the tillers of the soil and the Russian speaking factory workers. These revolutionists looked upon their own people with contempt, labelling them as bourgeois and orthodox. They harboured the same feelings towards the Jewish workers, who were mostly artisans who often engaged in petty trade which, therefore, made them part of the exploiting class. All specifically religious, cultural or national Jewish matters were anathema to them. According to their spokesman, the Russian revolutionary movement took precedence over the struggle for Jewish emancipation. They were confident that the Jewish problem would be solved with the liberation of the Russian masses (Greenberg, 1944, p. 148).

According to Greenberg, in spite of their openly pro-Russian and anti-Jewish posture, deep down their interest in the revolutionary movement was motivated by the sufferings of their own people. This latent motivation manifested itself more openly towards the end of the 1870s as a result of the increasing anti-Jewish attitude of the government. The Jewish *Narodnik* H. Magat expresses this sentiment tellingly in a letter he wrote in 1879: "I see two and half million people in bondage, and I say: one must stand up on behalf of this humiliated and defenceless people and fight for its freedom" (Greenberg, 1944, pp. 148–149).

Greenberg went to great length to detail the Jewish contributions to the revolutionary movement. Due to their isolation in the ghetto, from which they were just beginning to emerge, there was a total absence of Jews among the original leaders of the movement. They had no share in the creation of the movement and did not produce a single outstanding philosopher or theoretician among the *Narodniki*. Nor were they particularly well suited for the terroristic activities the *Narodniki* engaged in during the late 1870s after they had failed to stir up rebellion among the peasantry. Centuries of submissiveness to force, coupled with a religious training that bred an abhorrence of bloodshed, explains their reluctance to engage in violent action (Greenberg, 1944, p. 149).

Official data culled from tsarist archives show that in the middle of the 1870s, Jewish representation in the revolutionary movement constituted about 4 percent of the total Russian participation, which corresponded to their percentage of the population (Greenberg, 1944, p. 149).

Even though most Jewish revolutionaries had completely disassociated from Jewish life, the entire Jewish community was reviled both by the anti-Jewish press and by the government for the activity of the revolutionists (Greenberg, 1944, p. 158).

Ironically, even though the Jewish masses were resentful of the activities of the Jewish rebels and were genuinely loyal to the regime of Alexander II, the increased activities of the revolutionaries in the later 1870s intensified the hostility of the press and the government against the Jews. "Everyone knows," declared the antisemitic organ *Novoe Vremia* (Modern Times), "that these Jews, since time immemorial the representatives of the revolutionary spirit, now stand at the head of the nihilists" (Greenberg, 1944, p. 159).

It was natural that the Russian Jewish youth were attracted to the national revolutionary movement. In light of the fact that their people had been cruelly and systematically tormented and humiliated, one could have expected that they would contribute a large number of desperate terrorists. In reality, their number was insignificant compared with the atrocities which were constantly perpetrated against them. Most of them joined the ranks of the Social Democratic organization, which disapproved of political assassination. Numerous Marxists among the young Jewish men and women who had been turned away from the Russian institutions of learning had gone to Western Europe to learn the doctrines and methods of German Social Democracy. On the whole, the number of active Jewish revolutionaries was an insignificant by-product of the Russian revolutionary movement (Dubnow, 1920, p. 68).

According to author Irwin Michael Aronson, in 1877–1878 and thereafter, the Russo-Turkish War also intensified nationalist feelings and resulted in numerous newspaper articles attacking Jewish contractors who supplied the Army, claiming that these purveyors robbed the government and harmed Russia's military might by their various chicaneries. Finally, the 1879 Kutaisi blood libel trial added more fuel to the fire and led to serious discussions in the press as to whether Jews actually did use Christian blood for religious purposes, blatantly ignoring the fact that the accused Jews were acquitted (Aronson, 1990, p. 42).

All the interlocking attitudes and events affecting Russian Jewry during the second half of Alexander II's reign, as described in the previous pages, built the socio-political climate that only needed the fuse of an exceptional event to launch the period of relentless anti-Jewish violence that started with the pogroms of 1881.

The 1881–1882 Pogroms and the Collapse of the *Haskala* Illusion

While the immediate triggers of the pogroms were the assassination of Alexander II on March 13, 1881 by Russian revolutionaries, the ensuing press orgy and the proximity of Easter, the perennial occasion for violence against the Jews, the underlying causes were embedded in Russian history and in the social and economic conditions in Russia in the 1870s and 1880s.

One of the participants in the attack on the Tsar was a Jewish woman named Gessia Gelfman. The antisemitic press capitalized on her ethnicity with such enthusiasm that it provided the final stimulus for the pogroms. Impoverished masses of artisans, merchants, peasants and workers formed a vast number of migrants and created a situation of rising prices, substantial unemployment and intense competition. In the heated atmosphere of the post-assassination period, they lashed out at a group whose economic behaviour was held to be abhorrent and whose very existence was viewed with contempt. Religion, law and a new secular antisemitism combined with economic factors to make the Jews visible, ostensibly contemptible and inferior and, most significantly, vulnerable. The explosion, when it came, was spontaneous. The inaction of local civilian authorities, police officials and the military transformed limited violence into pogroms (Berk, 1985, pp. 54–55).

68

Chapter Three

One day after the murder, the *Vilenskii Vestnik* designated the Jews as being guilty of the Tsar's death, calling it "their affair." In St. Petersburg, *Novoe Vremia* took particular note of the fact that one of the assassins had an "Eastern demeanour and a crooked nose." On March 20, in Odessa, the *Novorossiskii Telegraf* published an article reporting a rumour that people would gather on Easter Sunday to attack the Jews because of their responsibility for the assassination and for the terrible economic situation. The Kiev journal *Kievlianan*, in a series of articles ending on April 5, spoke not only of Jewish participation in the assassination but dwelled at length on the great economic harm caused by the Jews and on the "holy necessity" of simple people to struggle against them. In Elizabethgrad, where the pogroms began, the local newspaper, after the assassination, carried articles accusing the Jews of obnoxious economic behaviour. On the eve of Passover, it gave prominent space to rumours of ritual murders and to the blood libel, all calculated to inflame the local population (Berk, 1985, pp. 54–55).

The pogrom on April 15, 1881 in Elizabethgrad was a seminal event in the history of the Jewish people. It started the day following the Greek Orthodox Easter celebration when a drunken Russian was ejected from an inn by its Jewish owner. This innocuous event was all the mob, which was waiting nearby for provocation, needed. They raised the hue and cry that the Jews were beating Russians and began attacking Jewish pedestrians. This signal for an attack launched the smashing and looting of Jewish stores in the market place. While that night the police checked the riots, they resumed the next day with increased vigour and the police assuming a neutral attitude (Greenberg, 1951, p. 20).

It was the prelude of a reign of terror against the Jews in south Russia of such ferocity that it completely and irrevocably altered their social consciousness and the direction of their socio-political behaviour. Most students of this episode in Jewish history agree that it thrust the course of Jewish history in a completely new direction, as will be demonstrated in this chapter.

The anti-Jewish movement in Russia reached its peak in 1881–1882. Within this short time period, over two hundred communities in the Russian Empire were hit by pogroms. According to official accounts, hundreds of Jews were killed, wounded, mutilated and raped (Berk, 1985, p. 36). These figures were probably vastly understated since many Jews, for religious reasons, would not allow autopsies to be performed on their murdered relatives and the government would list only the pogrom victims who had been autopsied. Similarly, the number of rapes confirmed by government officials is probably not reflective of what really happened, since many women were unlikely to have admitted to being raped or been willing to submit to medical examinations to certify the attacks (Berk, 1985, p. 190).

Barbara Tuchman, in relating what happened in Russia in 1881, summarized that within three days, all of western Russia from the Black Sea to the Baltic was smoking with the ruins of Jewish homes. From Warsaw to Kiev to Odessa, through one hundred and sixty small villages, a mass savagery on a scale and with a degree of brutality unknown since the Middle Ages exploded upon the Jews. It echoed around the world through the horrified reports of foreign envoys and journalists. Adolf Hitler added the concentration camp and the gas chamber, but otherwise he invented nothing (Tuchman, 1956, p. 199).

P. Sonin, a non-Jewish social worker and author who lived in the south of Russia at the time, gave a revealing description of the pogrom technique he saw in action in Kirovo, the first city to initiate this savagery. According to his account, the pogrom was organized by a gang dispatched to Kirovo for that purpose. This was preceded by the visit of a high-ranking official from St. Petersburg who asked the local police commissioner whether in the event of a pogrom he could vouch for the safety of the non-Jewish population. The visitor from St. Petersburg noted that during the coming Easter season, due to the public mourning for Alexander II, all spectacles and festivities were strictly prohibited, and he wondered if the police chief was afraid that this might cause disorder. The emissary absolved the commissioner in advance for any blame for outrages perpetrated against the Jews, reassuring him that such assaults would be interpreted as "unexpected outbursts of the people's wrath." However, if the mob began to attack wealthy non-Jewish citizens and businessmen or German merchants, the police would be held responsible for neglecting their duties (Greenberg, 1951, p. 20; Aronson, 1990, p. 104).

A wave of pogroms soon spread to many other locations in south Russia. According to the testimony of General Vasily D. Novitsky, chief of the state gendarmerie, the pogrom in Kiev on April 23, 1881 was encouraged by the governor-general of the southwestern region, Alexander Drenteln. According to various accounts, the soldiers reacted to their commander's inaction and to the atrocities they witnessed by joining the hooligans:

> [Drenteln] hated the Jews from the bottom of his heart, and gave complete freedom of action to a savage mob which in the presence of the general and his troops continued to loot and plunder Jewish warehouses, stores, and market places. (Greenberg, 1951, p. 21)

The true horrors of the pogroms and their effect on the mindset of the Jewish population of nineteenth-century Russia cannot be fully understood without a graphic depiction of the physical assaults on the individuals, particularly the rapes of women and girls, some of them ten or eleven years old, and the murder of children, including infants who were often tossed out of windows to be crushed to death on the ground. The perpetrators of attacks on women were not loath to rape mothers and daughters in sight of each other (Berk, 1985, p. 36).

There was panic everywhere in Jewish communities in the Pale of Settlement, in Russian Poland and Lithuania and in the small Jewish communities in the Russian interior. It is important to realize that the Jews in Russia were traumatized not only by the pogroms but also by the oppressive changes in the social environment that followed in their wake. Every week, in the period from April 1881 to the autumn of 1882, the Russian Jewish press, such as *Russkii Evrei* (The Russian Jew), *Razsvet* (Dawn) and *Nedel'naia Khroniki Voskhoda* (Weekly Chronicle of Sunrise), reported individual cases of murdered Jewish families, Jews being beaten, and Jewish women being raped (Berk, 1985, p. 36).

After the physical violence of the pogroms, the anti-Jewish excesses took a different form. A wave of fires swept over the Pale of Settlement, bringing ruin and destruction upon the Jewish inhabitants of many cities. While they were officially described as accidents, it was believed that they were the work of the same elements that instigated and directed the pogroms (Greenberg, 1951, pp. 25–26).

Even in areas such as Lithuania and Russian Poland where pogroms did not occur, Jews often received anonymous letters threatening pogroms. Rumours of impending pogroms were everywhere, and local Christians told their Jewish neighbours openly that they would use the opportunity to take over their property. Soldiers sent to prevent violence instead treated Jewish entrepreneurs with contempt and took whatever they wanted without payment (Berk, 1985, p. 36).

The wave of antisemitic manifestations that were triggered by the pogroms spread in different forms throughout the Jewish communities. In schools, gymnasiums and universities, Jewish students were frequently beaten and verbally abused by antisemitic teachers (Berk, 1985, p. 36). The accession of Alexander III brought a permanent reign of terror to the Jews and added new disabilities. Prior to his rule, there had been a number of pogroms in the city of Odessa at widely separated intervals: the first in 1820, the second in 1859 and the third in 1871. Beginning with the regime of Alexander III, the pogrom became an established, frequently recurring feature until the fall of the tsardom in 1917 (Greenberg, 1951, p. 19).

It is difficult to get a realistic picture of the cause and effect dynamics of the pogrom phenomenon from any one work on the subject, as different writers give significantly different explanations. The arguments range from the position that the pogroms were orchestrated by an antisemitic government which incited and abetted violence against the Jews as part of its ethnocentric policies (Louis Greenberg, Ben Zion Goldberg, Simon Dubnow, James Parkes, Barbara Tuchman) to the opposite view that the Russian government, while antisemitic, was officially in favour of the equal treatment of all minorities and did its best to prevent these outbursts of mob violence, but could not control the overwhelming popular outbursts which, according to this school of thought, were often triggered by the visible, albeit very limited, success of Jews who had climbed the ladder of emancipation (Michael Aronson, Stephen Berk). A review of the range of arguments put forth by these writers, which included identifying the common denominators in terms of the areas they agreed on, determining the breadth of their sources and the degree of selectivity they exercised to prove their preconceived positions, leads to the conclusion that the dynamics of the pogroms were a fluid blend of both approaches, depending on location, demographics and the subjective attitudes of officials at all levels.

The dynamics of all the pogroms followed a similar pattern. The 1881 pogrom in Kirovo is a typical example and can serve as a blueprint for how the 1881–1882 pogroms were carried out. Before a pogrom started, a rumour would spread through the town about coming disorders scheduled for a particular day. Alarmed, the Jews would ask the authorities for protection. They would be reassured about their safety and told to go home, but no steps were taken to forestall the possible riots. Then, on the appointed day, there would appear at the railway station a band of out-of-town hooligans under the leadership of a literate ring leader who had a prepared list of Jewish homes and business establishments. Having fortified themselves with liquor, the howling ruffians would swoop down upon the Jewish quarter, and there would follow an orgy of pillage and looting (Greenberg, 1951, p. 19).

Like an erupting volcano which, after destroying and devastating its surroundings, will leave in its wake death and destitution, the pogroms of 1881–1882 had the same effect on the Jewish population in Russia.

The Jewish Reaction to the 1881–1882 Pogroms

The unprecedented outburst of violence against the Jewish population of Russia in 1881 dealt a fatal blow to the hope that obtaining emancipation would end discrimination and persecution. It caused the leading thinkers among the Jewish intelligentsia to abandon their advocacy of the Jewish embrace of the liberating fruits of the French Revolution and develop a new approach to the liberation of the Jewish diaspora.

Hebrew author, scholar and editor Peter Smolenskin, who was born in the Pale of Settlement, is considered as one of the archetypical members of the generation of Jews whose hopes were kindled and then extinguished after 1881. He left the famous Shklov yeshiva to earn a living as an itinerant house teacher in Odessa (Avineri, 2017, p. 60). Odessa had become a shining prototype of the development of social modernization within the reactionary framework of Russian society in the nineteenth century. As such, it played a leading role in the development of the Hebrew enlightenment. It was most unusual as a Russian city in that it was newly built by the tsars in an area captured from the Turks and that, in their attempt to develop and Russify the region, the government allowed Jews to settle there while continuing to deny them access to Russia's main cities: St. Petersburg and Moscow (Avineri, 2017, p. 60).

After a few years in Odessa, Smolenskin moved to Vienna, where he edited his journal *Hashahar* (The Dawn) and wrote most of his books and articles, which were mainly addressed to the Russian *maskilim* (Avineri, 2017, p. 61).

For Smolenskin's generation, the 1881 pogroms were a rude awakening. In one fell swoop, religious bigotry and intolerance, bureaucratic harassment and official connivance in the pogroms seemed to obliterate twenty years of slow progress. For the thousands of Jews who managed in the 1860s and 1870s to enter, through schools and universities, the ranks of the Russian intelligentsia, the pogroms vividly demonstrated how fragile and shallow all this development was. Beneath the thin veneer of relative tolerance, an abyss of deep hatred continued to exist. A key phenomenon was that the pogroms did not distinguish between Orthodox Jews and the enlightened emancipated Jews. The fact that both became victims to the pogroms undermined the central belief of the *maskilim* that it was only the strangeness of the Orthodox Jew that made him a target for fear and hatred. The pogroms targeted religious and secularized Jews alike, the pious as well as agnostics. When the official reaction was to reimpose the old restrictions relating to residence permits and access to secondary and higher education, it became clear that the enlightenment slogan – "educate yourselves!" – had become meaningless (Avineri, 2017, p. 61).

The 1881–1882 pogroms marked the beginning of massive Jewish emigration from Russia. From 1882 to 1914, almost three million emigrated from Tsarist Russia to the West – to North America, England,

South Africa and Argentina. This demographic and sociological change in the structure of the Jewish diaspora was paralleled by the fundamental intellectual transformation of the members of the Russian Jewish enlightenment. Just as 20 years earlier Moses Hess had recognized that the groundswell of modern, nationalist antisemitism in Germany had cast doubt on the ability of liberalism to solve the Jewish question, so the events of 1881 confronted the Russian *maskilim* with the inadequacy of the liberal and humanist dreaming in the Russian context. Whereas the Jewish masses reacted in 1881 in the traditional Jewish fashion of emigration, the intellectuals were forced into an agonizing reappraisal (Avineri, 2017, pp. 61–62). As noted by Stephen Berk, the pogroms of 1881–1882 signalled the end of Eastern Europe as a centre of Jewish life and led to the creation of two new ones in America and Israel (Berk, 1985, p. xii).

The Russian Reaction to the 1881–1882 Pogroms

The Russian government, stunned by the pogroms, did send investigators to search out the causes of these events. The most thorough government agent assigned to this task was Prince P. I. Kutaisov, who interviewed hundreds of ordinary people in the villages, towns and cities and whose report covered several hundred pages. Kutaisov found an enormous number of complaints against the Jews. Peasants and urban dwellers claimed that they were victims of Jewish exploitation, primarily through the sale of liquor, which took the peasants' hard-earned money from them. Jews were accused of speculating in grain and other products, which drove up their price. Jews acquired wealth through trickery, they claimed, by selling poor quality goods and giving incorrect weights on various commodities. They stole horses, dealt in stolen goods, and did not fulfil military or tax obligations. Jews were accused of being incapable of physical labour and living off the sweat of Christians, of diluting vodka and of adulterating the tobacco that they sold. Many business people charged the Jews with taking advantage of the ignorance and simplicity of ordinary Great Russians and Ukrainians. According to their detractors, the Jews were always taking peasants to court and winning their cases because the peasants did not know the law. On the other hand, the Jews did not fulfil their contracts to buy grain from the peasants (Berk, 1985, pp. 52–53).

Besides economic grievances, there were attacks on the social and political behaviour of Jews, such as that Jews are dirty, that they cause epidemics, and that they turn their Russian and Ukrainian female servants into prostitutes. The Jews made their Christian servants lazy and unfit for work for Christian employers. The Jewish communities were helped by their Kahal to help them bypass the law. Kutaisov was told that the Talmud creates a mentality that makes Jews different from Christians. Jews have no sense of honour. The Jews isolate themselves from the rest of the population, "they stand away from us and our social interest." Russian merchants complained to Kutaisov that Jewish women flaunted their clothing and jewellery, which made Russian women envious and caused them to make life miserable for their husbands. The Jews were a "dark force" that exercised a pernicious influence on all spheres of Russian life. Whatever their source and veracity, those charges testify to widespread antipathy in Ukraine towards Jews and turned southern Russia into a tinder box waiting to explode (Berk, 1985, pp. 53–54).

At first, the new tsar, Alexander III, acknowledged that the turbulence was the work of the anarchists. He said as much to a group of Jewish representatives in St. Petersburg in May 1881. It took less than 30 days, however, for the government to back away from this position and resume its traditional antisemitic mode by shifting the responsibility for the violence to the Jews. Because they exploited the peasants, the Jews were responsible for the violence. To understand this change of government attitude, it is important to realize the nature and mindsets of the new occupant of the throne and of the powers behind it. Foremost was the leader of the Russian Orthodox Church, Procurator of the Holy Synod Konstantin Pobedonostsev, who had been the tutor of Alexander III since the mid-1860s and was able, throughout Alexander's life, to shape his views on public issues. He was a fervent believer in autocratic rule, a staunch opponent of the revolutionary movement, and against the slightest form of liberalism. No sooner had the new tsar ascended the throne, after the assassination of his father on March 13, 1881, than Pobedonostsev was able to persuade him to drop Loris-Melikov, the Minister of the Interior and one of the most progressive members of the government, on the grounds that the latter's constitutional reforms would endanger autocratic rule. According to Pobedonostsev, constitutions were the tools and the source of all untruths and of all intrigue. He waged a ferocious assault on the entire reform programme of Alexander II's reign. Pobedonostsev held those reforms responsible for the upsurge in revolutionary activity that led to Alexander II's assassination (Berk, 1985, pp. 57–58).

Pobedonostsev showed even more loathing against the Jews. In his reported conversations with Dostoyevsky in 1879, he said that he was convinced that the Jews undermined everything, that they were at the root of the revolutionary movement and of regicide, that they owned the periodical press, that they controlled the financial markets and financially enslaved the people as a whole, and that they even controlled the principles of contemporary science which they strove to place outside of Christianity. In addition to all these faults, he also held them responsible, through their ownership of taverns, for much of the morality and crime among the peasants. For Pobedonostsev, the Jews were a "great ulcer." He was convinced that the Jews were responsible for the pogroms (Berk, 1985, p. 58).

This was the man who would now shape Russia's policy towards the Jews. As a result of Pobedonostsev's closeness to Alexander III, whom he saw two or three times a week, while often communicating with him in writing, the new tsar also began to speak of Jewish culpability. It was not a big leap for him to adopt Pobedonostsev's interpretation of events. As a fervent disciple of Russian Orthodoxy, he shared the view of the Jews held by conservative religious elements in Russia. In the 1870s, Pobedonostsev had already introduced Alexander to the antisemitic writings of Aksakov and Dostoyevsky. The anti-Jewish influence of the leading Russian intellectuals at the time, including his ecclesiastic mentor, inevitably moved the Tsar's reaction to the pogroms in an extremely anti-Jewish direction. In 1883 he expressed the opinion that the Jews are repulsive to the Christians because they exploit them and that this was the real cause of the pogroms (Berk, 1985, pp. 58–59).

The forging of the government's view that the pogroms were caused by Jewish exploitation was joined by other powerful Judeophobic influences in the Tsar's entourage. Foremost among these were the newly appointed Minister of the Interior Nicholas Ignatiev and the aforementioned Count Kutaisov, the main government agent tasked with investigating the causes of the pogroms (Berk, 1985, p. 59).

Kutaisov's mission provided the government with all the ammunition it needed to shift the blame for the pogroms entirely from the originally suspected revolutionaries to the Jews. In July 1881, Kutaisov travelled through the strife-torn region, where he interviewed hundreds of bureaucrats and ordinary people. His report was a compendium of the enormous number of complaints he had heard against the Jews and reflected the deep-seated animosity against the Jews, which predated the outbreak of the pogroms. Kutaisov's report provided the government with the excuse it needed to prove to the world that it was not responsible for the pogroms; that they were, in fact, a "popular judgment," vengeance wreaked upon the Jews by the Russian victims of their exploitation (Berk, 1985, p. 59).

Ignatiev incorporated Kutaisov's theory in a more elaborate form in his report to the Tsar on August 22, 1881. In his report, he expressed his opinion that the recent pogroms proved that the "injurious influence" of the Jews could not be suppressed by the liberal reforms pursued during the reign of Alexander II, which had allowed them to become increasingly harmful to the Christian inhabitants of Russia. To remedy the situation, he proposed the establishment of special commissions in each province with large numbers of Jews to discuss how to deal with the Jews' harmful activities. The Tsar immediately followed up on Ignatiev's advice with an imperial decree establishing provincial commissions consisting of representatives of the local urban and rural populations and presided over by the governor of the provinces. To ensure that the commissions' work would lead to an unfavourable outcome for the Jews, he instructed the governors-general not to try to be impartial in their formation of the commissions. In his memorandum of August 25, 1881, he included his own hostile views on the Jews and ordered the commissions to focus on two key questions: which economic activities of the Jews were especially injurious to the "native" population, and what new legislation would be helpful in curtailing the pernicious activities of the Jews (Berk, 1985, pp. 59–60).

From the start, the activities of the commissions were stacked against the Jews. Most of the commissions allowed only one or two Jews to participate, as tokens of the government's fairness. Dr. Max Mandelshtam, the prominent Jewish ophthalmologist who was one of the two Jews sitting among thirty-one non-Jewish members of the Kiev provincial commission, described the impossible position that the Jewish members of the commissions found themselves in. Mandelshtam and his Jewish companion found themselves listening to a rash of anti-Jewish accusations that were egregiously ignorant and bigoted. Mandelshtam saw that there were commission members who were surprised to find out that there were poor Jews and that their number was far greater than that of the wealthy Jews. Of particularly ominous tenor was one commission member's statement that Jews should not be allowed out of the Pale and into Russia proper because the Jews were immoral, proliferated like rabbits and would corrupt the whole empire (Berk, 1985, p. 60).

The position of the Jews became increasingly difficult due to the fact that both the secretary of the Kiev commission and the governor-general were conspicuously biased and acted diligently to censor any comments in defence of the Jews. Any speeches favourable to or in defence of the Jews were edited or completely omitted from the minutes (Berk, 1985, p. 61).

In the end, the enormous government pressure on the bureaucratic representatives and on the delegates from the villages to vote against the Jews resulted in a large majority consistently voting for increased restrictions on the Jews and against any improvement in their position in Russia (Berk, 1985, p. 61).

For Ignatiev, the provincial commissions were the first step in his plan to raise the government's anti-Jewish policies to a new level. On October 19, 1881, while the commissions were still engaged in completing their work, the Tsar approved Ignatiev's request to establish a Central Committee for the Revision of the Jewish Question under the jurisdiction of the Ministry of the Interior, under the chairmanship of its Deputy Minister D. V. Gotovtsev. Even though the committee was to base its recommendations on the work of the provincial commissions, it began its deliberations even before the commissions were finished with their work. The committee raised the government's anti-Jewish propaganda machine to a new level of virulence and intensity. Even Brafman's perfidious influence found its way in the committee's declarations when it raised the spectre of an international Jewish organization, based in Western Europe, established to advance Jewish hegemony and exploitation. With Ignatiev's friend, Gotovtsev, in charge, and the majority of the committee members being composed of bureaucrats, the committee was bound to follow the Minister of the Interior's lead on the pogroms. It endorsed the idea that the Jews exploited the population and that Alexander II's Jewish reforms had only made the Christian population more vulnerable to this exploitation. The committee concurred in the view that the attacks of the Jews by the local population were a natural response to the deleterious influence of the Jews (Berk, 1985, p. 62).

These contrived conclusions provided the committee with the assumed authority to deal a fatal blow to the possibility of a peaceful and humanitarian outcome for Russian Jewry. For the committee, this meant that they had to pursue two objectives. First, they had to rescind the reforms of Alexander II and regress to the restrictive policies of Nicholas I. Second, the government should act to separate the Jews from the rest of the population. To achieve these objectives, the committee proposed extremely harsh restrictions on Russian Jewry. In effect, the committee completely rejected the concept of emancipation and decided instead to dismember Russia's Jewish citizenry through repression (Berk, 1985, p. 62).

To achieve these extreme objectives, the committee developed a project which called for a prohibition on all Jews moving from the Pale to the interior of the empire. In the Pale, Jews were not allowed to settle in the villages, and those already in the villages could be expelled by a majority vote in the village assemblies. Jews were to be excluded from any form of liquor trade in the villages and towns. Jews were prohibited from buying or renting land in rural areas. Jewish businesses were to be closed on Sundays and Christian holidays, and the percentage of Jews in public schools could not exceed their percentage in the general population (Berk, 1985, pp. 62–63).

While these proposals would have led to the dislocation of a large number of Jews, they were not tough enough for Ignatiev. He amended the project to require the complete expulsion of Jews from villages and rural areas of the Pale, regardless of the village assemblies. Ignatiev and the committee were convinced that the Jews were guilty of bringing on the pogroms and that they had to be dealt with accordingly, even if it meant the removal of hundreds of thousands from their homes in the rural areas of the Pale of Settlement (Berk, 1985, p. 63).

The government behaved as mercilessly as the committee. It withheld any support to the victims of the pogroms and prohibited any help from Jews who were able and willing to assist their suffering brethren. To add insult to injury, the civil and military courts acted very leniently towards those who had committed the violence against the Jews during the pogroms and gave light sentences to those who were tried (Berk, 1985, p. 63).

At this point, the problem as to how to deal with the Jews in Russia had become so intractable that the thought of emigration as a way out had started to emerge on all sides. The conflicting opinions among key government officials created great confusion and uncertainty. On January 16, 1882, Ignatiev's statements created the impression that he favoured emigration and that the western frontier was wide open. In April 1882, he had changed his mind and stated that talk of emigration was incitement to treason. Pobedonostsev is alleged to have made the notorious pronouncement that the Jewish problem in Russia would be solved by having one-third of the Jews emigrate, one-third convert to Russian Orthodoxy, and one-third left to die off. A review of the provincial commissions' reports revealed that the majority of their members, including those most hostile to the Jews, still believed that the Jews could be successfully Russified (Berk, 1985, p. 64).

By the beginning of 1882, due to Ignatiev's increasingly harsh anti-Jewish agenda and the concomitant explosions of antisemitic violence, the outlook for Russian Jewry had reached a new level of desolation. Their worst fears were exceeded with the outbreak of a pogrom in the city of Balta, in the province of Podolia, which began on March 29, 1882 and which surpassed in savagery the riots of 1881. At first, the Balta Jews, who far outnumbered the non-Jewish population, caused the hooligans to retreat, but as soon as the police and troops arrived, the mob poured into the streets again, this time aided by the local police who beat the Jews with their swords and rifle butts. Someone then sounded the alarm bell as a signal to the local populace, who came streaming into the marketplace, accompanied by the local military commander, the police commissioner, the mayor and a detachment of the city battalion. They then turned toward the Turkish section of the city, where the sparser Jewish population was expected to offer less resistance. There, over the course of a few hours, they plundered and looted until there was nothing left. A cordon of soldiers controlling all access points to that section headed off any Jews who tried to come to their fellows' help while allowing all non-Jews free access. The Jews of Balta, expecting some assistance, were bitterly disillusioned when, the following morning, the local rabble were joined by about five hundred peasants called out from neighbouring villages by the district police captain to join them in a renewed attack. After looting a nearby liquor store, the intoxicated crowd of peasants, soldiers and police engaged in a frenzy of destruction, plunder, murder and rape (Greenberg, 1951, p. 22).

Until then, the horrible predicament of Russian Jewry had been kept secret from the outside world. News of the extent and savagery of the pogroms was not disseminated in Western Europe and the United States until several months after the first pogrom in Elizabethgrad on April 15, 1881. This delay was due to the Russian government's censorship and the small number of foreign correspondents operating in Russia. To avoid criticism and embarrassment, the government even put a lid on the deliberations of Kutaisov's provincial commissions. Yet the level of persecution had reached such an existentially ominous level that the need for outside awareness and possible assistance propelled its dissemination beyond Russia's borders (Berk, 1985, p. 65).

Of all the pogroms that occurred in 1881 and 1882, it was the one in Warsaw on Christmas Day in 1881 that helped bring the genocidal anti-Jewish agenda of the tsarist government to the attention of the world. While the other scholars referred to in this study made either scant or no reference at all to this unexpected outbreak of anti-Jewish violence, Simon Dubnow, who lived in Russia and devoted his entire life to the study of the history of Russian Jewry, realized its special impact and gave it extensive coverage. He noted that the news that a pogrom, lasting three days, had taken place in the capital of the Kingdom of Poland came as a complete surprise. While the Church of the Holy Cross in the centre of Warsaw was crowded with Catholic worshipers, someone shouted, "Fire!" Twenty-nine people were crushed to death, and many others were injured in the rush to escape the premises. It turned out to have been a false alarm; there was no trace of a fire in the church. It was generally believed that the alarm had been sounded by pickpockets who were known to resort to this trick to cause the public to panic. Suddenly, among the crowd outside the church which watched the bodies of the victims being carried out, a rumour was spread that two Jewish pickpockets had been caught in the church – which subsequently also proved to be unfounded (Dubnow, 1918, pp. 280–281).

As if on cue, the whistles which served as the signal for a pogrom were heard. The street mob started to assault Jewish passers-by and to attack Jewish stores and residences in the streets adjoining the church. The hordes were led by local thieves who were well-known to the police and by some strangers who gave signals by whistling to indicate in which direction to proceed. Dubnow notes that, as in all other cases in which authorities did not feel directly threatened, there were few policemen and soldiers on hand, which always stimulated the rioters to carry on. Following the well-established pogrom routine, the authorities waited until the third day before stepping in to suppress the riots, at which time the governor-general of Warsaw, Albedinski, ordered the troops to check all crowds and stop the disorder. By this time, however, the damage had already been done. Some fifteen hundred Jewish residences, businesses and houses of prayer had been demolished and pillaged, twenty-four Jews had been wounded, and the monetary loss had risen to several million rubles. Over three thousand rioters, including a large number of under-aged youths, were arrested. While most of them came from the dregs of the Polish population, a number of them turned out to be Russian-speaking (Dubnow, 1918, pp. 280–281).

The antisemitic St. Petersburg daily *Novoe Vremia* (New Times) emphasized the friendly attitude of the Polish hooligans towards the Russians in general and the officers and soldiers in particular. In light of the inveterate hatred of the Poles towards the Russians, especially the military and official class, Dubnow found this attitude rather suspicious. Dubnow also noted that the Polish patriots from the upper classes strongly resented the staging of a barbarous Russian pogrom in Warsaw. On the second day of the pogrom, in an appeal to the people, the representatives of the Polish intellectuals emphatically protested against this dreadful shaming of their capital. The Archbishop of Warsaw also joined the protests, and the Catholic priests urged the crowds to disperse. Nevertheless, the governor-general of Warsaw, in the midst of the pogrom, rejected the request of a number of Poles for permission to organize a civil guard, pledging to restore order in one day. Dubnow concluded that someone wanted the organized anti-Jewish violence in Kiev and Odessa to be repeated in the capital of Poland and bring the "cultured Poles" in line with the Russian barbarians and persuade Europe that the pogrom was not exclusively a Russian phenomenon (Dubnow, 1918, Volume II, p. 283).

In reality, this Russian-inspired manoeuvre achieved the opposite result. Of all the pogroms that occurred after the assassination of Alexander II, it was the Warsaw pogrom that made the strongest impression upon Europe and America. Unlike Ukraine, where the other pogroms took place, Warsaw had close commercial relations with the West, and the havoc wrought there had an immediate effect on the European market (Dubnow, 1918, p. 283).

The International Reaction to the 1881–1882 Pogroms

While first-hand stories from emigrants who had reached Central Europe were occasionally reported by major European newspapers as well as by a number of Jewish organs, the main source of information on the pogroms was a small but highly effective group of Orthodox Jews located in Kovno and Vilna in Russian Lithuania. Through their organization *Hayay im Pipiyot* (Inspired the Lips), named after a prayer said on the Jewish New Year, they gathered information on the pogroms as well as valuable data on the plight of Russian Jewry, which they secretly disseminated to prominent Jewish leaders in other countries in the hope that this would stimulate international protest. In the autumn of 1881, the written appeals from the organization's leader, Rabbi Yitschak Elhanan Spektor, came to the attention of Baron Nathaniel Rothschild. He was informed about the pogroms and the impending hard legislation and was urged to organize a protest movement (Berk, 1985, p. 66; Greenberg, 1951, p. 22).

Rothschild immediately turned the letters over to *The Times* of London, which incorporated the information in two articles on January 11 and 13, 1882. These articles aroused great interest and evoked remarkable responses. Even though they laboured under horrendous conditions and were faced with daunting obstacles, the Lithuanian rabbis provided information that was corroborated by subsequent studies (Berk, 1985, p. 66).

The following quote from the initial article provides an example of the style and tone that had such an electrifying effect on large numbers of the English public, both Jewish and non-Jewish:

> Men ruthlessly murdered, tender married women the prey of a brutal lust
> that has also caused their death, and young girls violated in the sight of
> their relatives by soldiers who should have been the guardians of their
> honour, these have been the deeds with which the population of southern
> Russia has been stained since last April. (Berk, 1985, p. 66)

In his articles, Joseph Jacobs included a detailed list of the towns in which
pogroms took place, as well as a description of the nature of the crimes
perpetrated against the Jews, including some horrible details of assaults on
women and children, and the number of victims of these attacks. The
articles relates how a young girl, Pelikoff, was gang-raped by soldiers in
Elizabethgrad, how the three-year-old son of Mordichai Wienarsky was
thrown out of a window in Kiev and torn to pieces, and how the house of
the Prescoff family in Kitzkis was burned to the ground and the father and
two children "were left to roast in it." According to Jacobs, in 1881, brutal
attacks on the Jews took place in over 160 towns and villages (Berk, 1985,
pp. 66–67).

The articles also contained a stinging indictment of the Russian
government at all levels, including its civilian and military personnel.
Ignatiev's provincial commissions were seen as extremely prejudicial
institutions that were preparing "legislation to return Russia to the Middle
Ages." What the articles found most infuriating were the officials,
especially the members of the police and the army, who violated their oath
to maintain peace and order and participated in the attacks against the Jews
(Berk, 1985, p. 67).

The Times went on to attribute the primary cause of the pogroms to the
"barbarous" Russian laws that were designed to deprive the Russian Jews
of their civil rights and freedoms and to set them apart from the rest of the
Russian population. The articles ended with the resounding conclusion that

> the only solution of the Jewish question is the granting of full equality [...].
> The Russian Jewish question may ... be summed up in the words: Are
> three and a half millions of human beings to perish because they are Jews?
> (Berk, 1985, p. 67)

The articles in *The Times* generated considerable discussion in British
society and triggered a series of demonstrations throughout the country.
The largest and most important demonstration took place on February 1,
1882 at Mansion House in London under the chairmanship of the Lord
Mayor. It attracted some of the most prominent personalities in the
country, including Members of Parliament, scholars, and leading church
officials. Speaker after speaker urged the Russian government to stop the

violence against the Jews. Cardinal Manning, head of the Roman Catholic Church in England, condemned the pogroms as well as the degrading legislation which has harassed the Jews for centuries. The Mansion House meeting passed a resolution condemning the pogroms as "an offense to Christian civilization" and appealed to the British government to approach the Russian government to act in the spirit of the resolution (Berk 1985, p. 68).

It is at this stage that the classic conflict between public morality and political expediency again manifested itself. In spite of the fact that these humanly inspired appeals had reached a wide and sympathetic public audience, from the government's point of view they were nevertheless seen to be moving into dangerous diplomatic terrain. While in the House of Commons, Prime Minister William Gladstone did acknowledge that the reports of the pogroms had inspired sentiments of pain and horror, he declared that the matter was an internal affair of another country and could not, therefore, "become the object of official correspondence or inquiry on the part of a foreign government." In the same vein, he refused to transmit a petition signed by Russian Jews and addressed to the Russian government. Consequently, there would be no approaches to the Russian government by Britain during the era of the pogroms. Gladstone could not even be swayed by the willingness of the United States to make a joint representation to the Russian government (Berk, 1985, p. 68).

Berk suggested that Gladstone's opposition was not only motivated by conventional diplomatic practice but also by the threat contained in Russia's harsh reaction to the persecuted Russian Jews themselves. He cites a statement condemning interference in the internal affairs of nations, published in the government's organ *Pravitelstvennyi Vestnik*: "Any attempt on the part of another government to intercede on behalf of the Jewish people can only have the result of calling forth the resentment of the lower classes and thereby affect unfavourably the condition of Russian Jews." In fact, the Jews were now being held hostage to forestall British diplomatic intervention. This determined Russian stance had its desired effect on the British government. Gladstone warned that British governmental representations as well as parliamentary debates about the situation of the Jews in Russia were "more likely to harm than to help the Jewish population." Gladstone assured the House that the Russian government shared the anguish of the people of Britain over the anti-Jewish disorder and that it would be better to influence it through private and unofficial contacts (Berk, 1985, pp. 68–69).

Berk argued that while the Russians appeared to have won by having succeeded in averting a British diplomatic initiative, they could in fact ill afford to antagonize British public opinion. No European state could disregard Great Britain with its vast empire, huge financial reserves and close proximity to Europe. Furthermore, Russia had entered the early period of its industrial development and had started to become dependent on foreign investment. It could not afford any significant deterioration in his relations with Great Britain. It was in Russia's interest to find a way to accommodate British concern for the Jews. While the Jew-baiting Ignatiev might not have been aware of these concerns, more perceptive Russian statesmen were (Berk, 1985, p. 69).

Russian statesmen also had to reckon with the fact that declarations of support for the Russian Jews were not limited to Britain. While demonstrations against the Russian pogroms were also held in United States, Italy, the Netherlands and Spain, the strongest outcry was heard in France. In July 1881, a weekly bulletin in Paris began to inform the public of the persecution of Russian Jewry. The pogroms were reported in leading French newspapers. Victor Hugo and other prominent French citizens participated in relief work for Russian Jewry. Paradoxically, the French Jewish community kept a low profile and did not participate in the public expressions of sympathy, nor did the leading Jewish personalities and institutions tend to make public pronouncements. The Alliance Israelite Universelle, at the time the foremost Jewish institution not only in France but in the world, was against calling for public protest in raising the issue in the Chamber of Deputies. Berk attributed this cautious trend to indigenous French antisemitism, as well as to increasing speculation in French government circles about the need for an alliance with Russia to end France's diplomatic isolation and vulnerability vis-à-vis Germany. Notwithstanding the silence of French Jews, the widespread declarations of support in France and elsewhere for the Russian Jews were additional factors Russian statesmen had to take into account (Berk, 1985, pp. 69–70).

It was the concern of the potential damage of the pogroms to Russia's own national interests that caused a growing opposition at the highest level of Russian society against this barbaric method of persecution. Pobedonostsev, in spite of his strong antisemitic disposition, had become strongly opposed to the pogroms. He firmly believed that the mobs attacking the Jews would end up turning against the state. As a true conservative, he abhorred popular movements of any kind. In June 1881, he sent a letter to Alexander III in which he expressed his opposition to the pogroms, and in early 1882, he condemned the Ministry of the Interior for allowing demagogues to instigate riots and demonstrations against the Jews (Berk, 1985, p. 70).

The prominent conservative Russian journalist Mikhail Nikiforovich Katkov was so appalled by the Balta pogrom of March 1882 that it caused him to break his silence. His newspaper, *Moskovskiia Vedomosti* (The Moscow Gazette), stated that "if Attila the Hun had passed through Balta […] he could not have done more." Katkov urged the Russian government to put an end to this "shameful scandal," which posed a great danger to Russia. The pogroms were extremely destructive to the Russian economy and could play into the hands of the revolutionaries. He was also highly critical of the government's policy of expelling the Jews from places they had inhabited for decades, leaving thousands of innocent people homeless and starving. He particularly lamented the fate of Jewish soldiers who had fought for the fatherland and were now rewarded for their efforts with expulsion. Katkov did not limit his criticism to calling for an end to the pogroms. He disapproved of those who so easily blamed the Jews for all of Russia's problems. It was nonsense to hold Jewish innkeepers responsible for the poverty of the peasants. He argued that the peasants of the Russian interior, where there were no Jews, were more inebriated and poorer than the peasants in the Pale. Katkov declared that the real poverty in the West was Jewish poverty (Berk, 1985, pp. 70–71).

Katkov was a prominent journalist with very close links to the government. He was considered as one of the most influential figures in the early years of the reign of Alexander III, who was a careful reader of his articles in *Moskovskiia Vedomosti*. His view that the pogroms were dangerous for Russia as well as his sympathetic defence of the Jews must have caught the attention of the highest circles of government (Berk, 1985, p. 71).

The commercial and industrial classes also wanted to see the government put an end to the anti-Jewish disorder. On May 30, 1881, I. S. Morozov, a leading Moscow textile manufacturer, wrote to Ignatiev about the harsh economic and potentially dangerous political consequences of the pogroms. Morozov told the minister that the violence in the south was causing the Jewish commercial elements in Ukraine to suspend active trading. Jewish merchants were afraid to appear at the various trade fairs, which led to a steep drop in business and made it impossible for some to make payments to the manufacturers in central Russia. This would soon force the Moscow producers to cut production, leading to increased unemployment and the risk of political instability (Berk, 1985, p. 71).

These apprehensions proved to be justified when, in early May 1882, representatives of fifty Moscow firms presented a petition to the Ministry of Finance detailing the great harm that the anti-Jewish disorder was doing to the Russian economy. The petition stated that, compared to previous

years, there had been a steep drop in goods purchased at the recent
Kharkov trade fair by Jewish buyers who constituted a majority of those
present. The petitioners informed the government that they had extended
credit worth tens of millions of rubles to retailers and wholesalers in the
south and that dire consequences would ensue if the economic situation in
that area did not improve (Berk, 1985, p. 71).

The economic and social impact had also cascaded down to the poorer
strata of Russian society. Diplomatic representatives of the Habsburg
Empire in the major Russian cities had noted and reported rising
unemployment in Moscow and St. Petersburg and the breakdown of
commercial activity in the south. In the pogrom-afflicted areas, the Jews
were reluctant to extend more credit to the peasants, artisans and small
shopkeepers. As a result of the slowing economic activity, the railroad
stations in central Russia were jammed with work-seeking peasant
migrants from the south. The diplomats warned that the government would
have to put a decisive stop to the violence, not so much for the sake of the
Jews as for the domestic tranquillity and economic well-being of Russian
society (Berk, 1985, p. 72).

The May Laws of 1882

The international as well as internal outcries against the pogroms had
raised awareness of their damaging effect on the economic and political
stability of the tsarist regime. Alexander III and his closest entourage
realized that it was in their own interest that Ignatiev's relentless
escalation of repressive anti-Jewish regulations not be allowed to continue,
as they were the main cause of the violent disorder.

At this point, Ignatiev realized that the growing opposition to his
repressive legislative proposals would hamper the implementation of the
inflammatory provisos of his Central Committee for the Revision of the
Jewish Question which, in essence, proposed the total elimination of
Jewish settlement from the rural areas of the Pale. Ignatiev, although
aware that by law all permanent legislation had to be approved by the
much larger and somewhat more progressive State Council, submitted his
proposal to the Committee of Ministers where, it being a smaller body, he
believed he had a better chance of success (Berk, 1985, p. 72).

It turned out that Ignatiev did not obtain the results he had anticipated
from the Committee of Ministers, with whom his project ran into
unanimous opposition. The Minister of Finance, N. K. Bunge, denounced
Ignatiev's proposals on a number of grounds. He claimed that their
enactment would dry up Russia's sources of credit, which were vital to the

well-being of the state. He also warned that Ignatiev's measures would devastate the Christian population, which had very extensive commercial relations with the Jews. He added that the implementation of Ignatiev's measures would not only be disastrous for the Jews, but would also place enormous burdens on the cities and towns of the Pale that would have to absorb them. Similar criticism of Ignatiev's proposed legislation was expressed by Mikhail Nikolayevich Ostrovsky, the Minister of State Domains; Dmitry Nabokov, the Minister of Justice, who also worried about Jewish resistance to displacement; and M. Solski, the State Comptroller, who called on Ignatiev to stop the libellous attacks in the press against the Jews which so stirred up the population and also upbraided him for the inaction of the police during the pogroms. The chairman of the Committee of Ministers, M. K. Reutern, also took aim at the Ministry of the Interior's behaviour during the pogroms. He was concerned that their behaviour would set a bad precedent. His words reflected the general mindset of the Committee of Ministers:

> Everyone should be defended against infringements of their rights. Today they bait and rob the Jews. Tomorrow they will turn on the so-called kulaks [rich peasants].... Then merchants and landowners would take their turn under the gun. In other words, given such inaction by the authorities, some may expect the development in the very near future of the most terrible socialism. (Berk, 1985, p. 73)

In the face of such strong opposition from the Committee of Ministers, Ignatiev had no choice but to back off from his original project. On May 3, 1882, after a period of negotiation with the Minister of the Interior, the Committee of Ministers produced the following "temporary decrees":

(1) As a temporary measure, and until a general revision is made of their legal status, it is decreed that the Jews be forbidden to settle anew outside of towns and boroughs, exceptions being admitted only in the case of existing Jewish agricultural colonies.

(2) Temporarily forbidden at issuing of mortgages and other deeds to Jews, as well as the registration of Jews as lessees of real property situated outside of towns and boroughs; and also the issuing the Jews of powers of attorney to manage and dispose of such real property.

(3) The Jews are forbidden to transact business on Sundays and on the principal Christian holy days; the existing regulation concerning the closing of places of business belonging to Christians on such days apply to Jews also.

(4) The measures laid down in paragraphs 1, 2, and 3 shall apply only to governments within the Pale of Jewish Settlement [that is, they shall not apply to the 10 provinces of Poland]. (Berk, 1985, p. 73)

In the final analysis, with this new "temporary" legislation, also known as the May Laws, Ignatiev had achieved most of the pernicious objectives embodied in his original project. The Jews would no longer be allowed to move from the cities and towns into the villages and rural areas of the Pale, and they were now prohibited from purchasing or leasing property in the rural areas. Even though they did not go to the extremes wanted by the Committee for the Revision of the Jewish Question – the village assemblies could not evict Jews and Jews were not barred from participating in the liquor trade – the May Laws had very adverse consequences for a growing Jewish population which was already confined to the Pale and now had its residential living space constricted even further. In reality, it turned out that Russian Jewry benefited very little from whatever small measure of protection the May Laws contained. In the years that followed, local officials would interpret the May Laws in an arbitrary fashion, generally to the disadvantage of the Jews. In some cases, Jews were already living in villages, and those who were to be left in place, according to the May Laws, were not allowed back into their homes if they were away even for a short time, such as people who worked in cities or towns. There were cases of local officials who acted in the spirit of Ignatiev and, in violation of the May Laws, followed the village assemblies that had voted to force the Jews out. From May 3, 1880 until the 1917 February Revolution, the May Laws were "a throttle around the neck of Russian Jewry" (Berk, 1985, p. 74).

Restricted to towns and forbidden to pursue certain occupations, over the course of the nineteenth century, the profile of the Jewish community became increasingly urban. In 1860, the Jewish population of Warsaw was 41,000 (about 1/4 of the population); in 1900, Warsaw contained 220,000 Jews (about 1/3 of the population). The urbanization of the Jewish population ensured that large numbers of Jews would be exposed to urban-based social and political movements, such as trade unionism, socialism and nationalism. It also provided future Zionists with positive proof that life in exile had made the Jewish nation aberrant and in need of redemption through the love of good nationalism. Gelvin concludes that in normal circumstances, urbanized artisans would have constituted the cream of Russian or any other nineteenth-century society. However, since Jews found themselves at the mercy of unpredictable eruptions of violence and the often debilitating restraints of imperial diktat, a disproportionate number of Jews decided to leave (Gelvin, 2005, p. 42).

One cannot avoid the question as to how the Committee of Ministers, after opposing Ignatiev's proposals so strongly, could issue rules that were still so extremely harmful to the Jews. Berk surmises that the anti-Jewish sentiments of some of the ministers had convinced them that, while they disagreed with Ignatiev's methods, they agreed with his view that Jewish exploitation was the root cause of the pogroms. Berk also finds it likely that, aware of the Tsar's intense dislike of the Jews, his bureaucrats were not prepared to present him with legislation that would make their lives easier rather than harder (Berk, 1985, pp. 74–75).

While the ingrained antisemitic disposition of the tsarist governments would never produce any improvements to the lives of Russian Jewry, their sense of self-preservation led them to deal more decisively with the pogroms, which, as we have seen, they realized were a threat to the economic welfare and political stability of the state. In this matter, the deliberations of the Committee of Ministers did, unintentionally, produce some positive results for the Russian Jews. It declared that attacks against the Jews and their property were not to be permitted and that the government must make it clear that such actions would be prosecuted and that measures would be taken to suppress the anti-Jewish disorder. On May 10, the Senate issued a declaration to provincial governors stating that local authorities would be held responsible if the violence continued and that officials who failed to deal effectively with the problem would be dismissed. The government had finally come to the conclusion that the continuation of the anti-Jewish attacks was dangerous for the maintenance of state order and that inefficient antisemitic local officials had acted as a spur to the pogroms (Berk, 1985, p. 75).

While the failure of local officials to deal effectively with the disorder was bound to reflect negatively on Ignatiev and his administration of the Ministry of the Interior, a more compelling reason for his demise lay in his support for the convocation of a Zemsky Sobor. The Zemsky Sobor was a throwback to the way Russia had been governed in the sixteenth and seventeenth centuries. It was an advisory assembly representing different groups from the upper stratum of Russian society and was convened on several occasions to express support for the Tsar's policies (Berk, 1985, p. 75, n. 59). As Ignatiev's increasingly stringent legislative initiatives were running into growing opposition from the existing established order, he must have felt that resorting to the revival of this more elitist legislative venue would allow him to bypass the existing branches of government. On May 30, 1882, Ignatiev was finally forced to step down and Count Dmitri Tolstoi was appointed as the new Minister of the Interior (Berk, 1985, p. 75).

While not less antisemitic than his colleagues in government and a fierce champion of autocratic rule, Tolstoi was also strongly opposed to mass eruptions of violence, regardless of their targets. In contrast to

Ignatiev, he officially threatened local officials with prosecution if they did not act effectively to prevent disorder. In the summer of 1882, a number of cases were brought to court and the guilty incurred severe penalties. The new policy produced remarkable results. According to Dubnow, during the next twenty years, the number of pogroms was reduced to ten isolated instances. There was no recurrence of the pogrom epidemic of 1881–1882 until the great Kishinev pogrom of 1903. Dubnow considers this as additional proof that systematic pogroms in Russia are impossible as long as the government and local authorities are determined to prevent them. In other words, the disastrous pogrom wave of 1881–1882 occurred because officials in the capital and at the local level refused to step in to restrain the population and protect the victims (Dubnow, 1918, pp. 314–315).

In essence, the objective of extinguishing Russian Jewry as a sub-state national identity had not changed. Only the method was adjusted as a tactical measure to achieve the same end without creating as much of a stir. The May Laws were meant to replace the pogroms as a means of continuing the persecution of Russian Jewry. Social asphyxiation was quieter than mob violence.

Jewish Reactions to the May Laws

The 1881–1882 waves of pogroms and the suffocating May Laws had such a traumatizing effect on all segments of Russia's Jewish population that they could no longer ignore the futility of their hope that they could gain acceptance as equal citizens of Russia. The Jewish students who were close to Russian culture and the Russian intelligentsia were hit particularly hard by the violence and by the growing manifestations of antisemitism they were encountering. In Odessa, Jewish students were told that the peasants were acting justly against the Jews who exploited them. As a result, a number of students had a total change of heart and acted in ways that would have been unthinkable for them before the onslaught of the pogroms. On January 18, 1882, when the leaders of Russian Jewry called a day of public prayers and fasting to appeal for both divine and government intervention on behalf of the Jewish community, Jewish gymnasium and university students participated in large numbers. In Kiev, they participated in the prayers offered in the synagogue and even offered their services to the members of the congregation affected by the violence in that city. Through songs and speeches, they gave encouragement to the thousands of Jews gathered in and around the synagogue. In St. Petersburg, students who had not only completely turned their backs on Jewish life but had often shown contempt for it now came to the main synagogue to participate in its prayers and meetings (Berk, 1985, p. 103).

In Odessa, Jewish students took the lead in the formation of Jewish self-defence organizations, in spite of opposition from all sides. Rich Jews tried to dissuade them out of fear that they would upset the authorities. The police assured them that there was no need as the local constabulary, together with the military, would deal effectively with any violence. They were also up against the fear of the Jewish masses and the problem of procuring weapons. Eventually, they managed to mobilize groups of butchers, carters and produce vendors and succeeded, in May 1881, in defending some of the poorest Jewish streets against the pogromists. They would have been more successful if the police had not stood idly by and even arrested some of the defenders, whom they accused of being the ones who had provoked the pogroms (Berk, 1985, p. 103).

This demonstration of unexpected zeal for Russia's suffering Jews was not limited to gymnasium and university students. On January 18, 1882, fashionably dressed businessmen, doctors, civil servants and members of the Jewish intelligentsia showed up in the Choral Synagogue in St. Petersburg. The perilous developments had been a signal call to all segments of Russian Jewry that it was time to return to the fold (Berk, 1985, p. 103).

In the areas directly affected by the pogroms, the reaction of the Jewish community rose to new levels of intensity. Jewish community leaders vigorously countered the hateful accusations voiced by the press and by the local citizenry. They unanimously rejected Jewish exploitation as being the cause of the pogroms. They told Kutaisov that Greeks, Armenians, Germans and Tatars were also accused of exploitation, but there were no attacks against them. They blamed their inferior legal position and the fact that they appeared as aliens to ordinary Russian citizens for being targeted by the pogroms. Legal discrimination, they claimed, tainted all Jewish activity as illegal and Jewish wealth as ill-gotten. They also denied the existence of a conspiratorial Kahal and declared that it was absurd for those unfamiliar with the Talmud to condemn it (Berk, 1985, pp. 103–104).

The provincial Jewish leaders attributed a share of the responsibility for the pogroms to the government for its failure to oppose the first ones in the spring of 1881. They accused Christian businessmen of inciting the pogroms to eliminate Jewish competition and the antisemitic press for its role in inciting the violence (Berk, 1985, p. 104).

The most consequential and, therefore, historically significant reaction came, however, from the grassroots of Russian Jewry. The terrible plight of the masses of ordinary, impoverished Jews who bore the brunt of the devastating wave of pogroms had reached the limits of endurance. Having been robbed of property, physically assaulted, their women violated, they were rendered mute and powerless. Most were too stunned to do anything. The more traditional resigned themselves to what they saw as another manifestation of divine will. For a growing number of these unfortunate victims, however, prayer, resignation and inertia were not the answer. On the contrary, they decided to leave their former homes to find safer refuge elsewhere. While some saw relief in the larger cities and towns of the Pale, others gave up on Russia and sought salvation in America, Western Europe and Palestine. This marked the beginning of the Russian Jewish emigration movement. It was not started by the wealthy Jews living in St. Petersburg, who actually strenuously opposed it – and not by the members of the Russian Jewish intelligentsia, even though in many cases they did support it – but by ordinary Jews who simply believed that the Jewish possibilities in Russia were played out (Berk, 1985, p. 104).

With the dam of inertia finally breached by the pressure of relentless and unendurable persecution, talk of emigration resounded throughout the Pale. It was encouraged by the belief created by some high-ranking Russian officials in late 1881, when Ignatiev was still relentlessly pursuing his increasingly oppressive anti-Jewish agenda, that Jewish emigration was still an option. Ignatiev himself declared, at the time, that "the Western frontier is open" and that the Jews were free to leave. When, on January 16, 1882, at a meeting with Dr. Isaac Orshanskii, he alluded to his statement of the previous year, he created the widespread impression that he was in favour of emigration and that the western frontiers were indeed open. The fact that Dmitri Tolstoi, who had replaced Ignatiev as Minister of the Interior after the latter's dismissal in May 1882, published a report against the emigration of Jews and threatened reprisals against those who instigated or assisted it did not alter the belief among Jewish leaders and ordinary Jews that the government did indeed desire the emigration of the Jewish population as a way to solve the Jewish problem in Russia. They were further encouraged in that belief by the speed with which officials responsible for granting emigration permits acted in issuing exit visas (Berk, 1985, pp. 63, 104).

At first, during the pre-pogrom days, Russian Jewry was split between those who clung to their traditional beliefs and those who sought a solution to their problems in assimilation and Russification. The realization that their Russian persecutors ignored this distinction and targeted all Jews with the same policies of rejection and oppression caused the common people and the intelligentsia to close ranks. Very often, university students, mostly from the middle class, provided leadership for the potential emigrants, articulating their aspirations and demands and championing emigration as the only solution to their problems. Jewish students at Novorossiysk University in Odessa expressed this nexus very aptly when they wrote to the Jewish periodical *Razsvet* in 1882 as follows: "Emigration – is the only way out from the present situation, an escape not dictated by the intelligentsia to the people, but by the people to their spokesmen." According to the students, the common people looked to the intelligentsia for information about America and Palestine. Students, teachers and simple Jews from every city and town bombarded the Jewish periodicals with letters supporting emigration as a solution for their intolerable predicament. They also appealed to intellectuals and wealthy Jews, particularly the Jewish plutocrats in St. Petersburg, to help the emigration movement with adequate funds and organizational expertise to bring some order and structure to the state of chaos it found itself in at this early stage (Berk, 1985, p. 105).

While the Jews of Russia were trying to come to grips with the perilous predicament they found themselves in, the Russian government was deliberately equivocal in its attitude towards Jewish emigration, leaving the impression that, while not in favour, it was turning a blind eye. In the early 1890s, it dropped all pretences and made the departure of Russian Jewry its official policy. To further the implementation of this new policy, the Russian government raised the intensity of the persecution of its Jewish subjects to a new level (Dubnow, 1918, p. 377).

The "Miraculous" Train Accident Survival of Alexander III – Another Persecution Pretext

During almost the entire first half of the 1890s, Russia was still ruled by Tsar Alexander III, whose ultra-reactionary regime continued unabated, especially in its persecution of the Jewish population. All levels of government were encouraged to devise increasingly harsh measures with the aim of physically ridding the empire of its Jewish population. Any catastrophic event that could be used to inflame public opinion was transformed into a drive to propel the anti-Jewish agenda to a new level.

The railroad accident near Borki on October 17, 1888 provided such a spark. The nature of this event provides a typical example of the dynamics of the Russian political and social culture at the time and of its systemic anti-Jewish orientation. The most reliable account of this incident was provided by Count Sergei Witte who, at the time, was Director of the South-Western Railroads, later becoming Minister of Finance and eventually Prime Minister. Witte was instructed to act as an expert in the

investigation of the causes of the accident that had just happened to the
imperial train. The investigation, which he conducted on-site, led to the
following account. The train had been running at an excessive speed, for
which its engines had not been built. Such excessive speed caused the
engines to sway and thrust a loose rail off the track beds and wrecked the
train. The train jumped the track and rolled down the embankment.
Twenty-one lives were lost and thirty-seven people were wounded. At the
moment of the catastrophe, the Tsar and his family were in the dining car.
The car was completely smashed and its entire roof fell on him, yet, owing
to his great strength, he supported it with his back, thus saving everyone in
the dining car from injury (Witte, 1921, p. 29).

The American journalist and novelist Harold Frederic (1856–1898),
who visited Russia in 1891 to investigate the persecution of the Jews, in
reporting on this accident, commented that:

> It was reported about that the Tsar regarded the escape alive of himself and
> his family from the terrible railway accident at Borki as a direct and
> miraculous intervention of Providence. (Frederic, 1892, p. 169)

Frederic totally ignored the fact that it was the Tsar's order to the engineer
to drive the train way beyond its speed limit that caused the derailment.
This incident was seized upon by Pobedonostsev and his associates to
convince the Tsar that this "miracle" was God's way of showing him how
to save Russia from Western reforms and return it to the fold of Russian
Orthodoxy. This conviction inspired the counter-reforms which aimed at
strengthening the power of the police, nobility and the church in Russia, as
exemplified by the curtailment of rural and urban self-government and the
large increase in Greek Orthodox parochial schools to the detriment of the
secular schools. Inevitably, the same spirit stimulated the growth of
Judeophobia and its increasingly malignant manifestations at the highest
government circles. When, in 1890, a high official submitted a report to
the Tsar, describing the sufferings of the Jews and pleading for the
necessity to end their oppression, he penned in the margin: "But we must
not forget that it was the Jews who crucified our Lord and spilled his
priceless blood." The court clergy publicly preached against friendly
relations with a Jew, since the gospel commanded "to hate the murderers
of the Savior" (Dubnow, 1918, p. 379).

The most widely read press organs were turned into well-subsidized
government mouthpieces and kept up a barrage of hideous accusations
against the Jews. The metropolitan news organs set the tone for the press
in the provinces, thus systematically poisoning public opinion in Russia
with the venom of Judeophobia (Dubnow, 1918, p. 380).

In the spring of 1890, the Ministry of the Interior, under the direction of Vyacheslav von Plehve, the sinister Chief of Police, elaborated a secret project which was circulated among the governors-general to solicit their opinions. Copies of the project found their way to London, Paris and Vienna. Alarming rumours of the enactment of some forty clauses designed to curtail the commercial activities of the Jews, to increase the rigour of the "Temporary Rules" inside the Pale, and to establish medieval Jewish ghettos in St. Petersburg, Moscow and Kiev elicited a terrible outcry in the foreign press against these contemplated new acts of barbarism. While the government denied these rumours, the Russian press continued to recommend ferocious measures against the Jews for the purpose of "removing them from all branches of labor" (Dubnow, 1918, p. 381).

The voice of protest was particularly strong in Britain. When appeals in favour of diplomatic representations in defence of the persecuted Russian Jews were introduced in both houses of the British Parliament, Premier Salisbury in the House of Lords and Under-Secretary of State for Foreign Affairs Fergusson in the House of Commons replied that "these proceedings, which, if rightly reported to us, are deeply to be regretted, concern the internal affairs of the Russian Empire, and do not admit of any interference on the part of Her Majesty's Government" (*The Jewish Chronicle*, August 8, 1890, reprinted in Dubnow, 1918, p. 382).

In 1891, a secret committee attached to the Ministry of the Interior was to formulate and execute a complete set of Jewish counter-reforms, which were designed to eliminate any rights certain categories of Jews had been granted by Alexander II. The main objective was to clear the Russian interior of any Jews who had been allowed outside the Pale by the privileges conferred upon Jewish First Guild merchants and artisans (Dubnow, 1918, p. 399).

While never short of motivation to act against the Jews, the reactionary cliques who orchestrated the execution of their sinister plots were equally adept at finding suitable pretexts. This time, it was the Tsar's decision to appoint his brother Grand Duke Sergius as the new governor-general of Moscow. The appointment of such a lofty member of the imperial household made a strong impression on the citizens of Moscow, who interpreted it as a sign that the rumoured transfer of the seat of government from the capital of St. Petersburg to the old Muscovite home of the more reactionary regimes of the past was imminent. The fact that this gambling-addicted prince was also a rabid antisemite assured him of Pobedonostsev's full cooperation. The solemn aura of the occasion, combined with the underlying purpose of ridding Moscow of its Jewish population, demanded that this objective be achieved in time for Prince Sergius' Majestic Investiture. On March 29, 1891, on the first day of Passover, with the synagogues of Moscow filled with worshippers, word spread of the publication of an imperial edict ordering the expulsion of the Jews from Moscow. The byzantine machinations contrived by the executors of the imperial decree were deliberately so ambiguous as to throw the Jewish community in a total state of confusion (Dubnow, 1918, p. 402).

For starters, the imperial order was issued in two stages. On March 28, 1891, it declared that "Jewish mechanics, distillers, brewers, and, in general, master workmen and artisans shall be forbidden to remove from the Jewish Pale of Settlement as well as to come from other places of the Empire to the city and Government of Moscow." The next day, the second half of the edict was published, extending the expulsion order to all the Jews of these categories of master workmen and artisans, even though they had lived in the city for many years. This virtually amounted to an illegal repeal of the law of 1865 that had conferred the right of universal residence upon Jewish artisans, and it ended with some twenty thousand Jews being forcibly removed to the Pale of Settlement (Dubnow, 1918, p. 406).

To provide an accurate and complete picture in all its horrendous aspects of this watershed episode in the history of Tsarist Russia's persecution of its Jewish population would require volumes of detailed descriptions of the government's efforts to rid the Russian interior and eventually the entire Russian Empire of its Jewish citizens. While the events in Moscow represent only a tiny fraction of the horrors perpetrated upon Russian Jewry in all parts of the empire, a few examples of the brutality and callousness with which the authorities carried out the expulsion of the Jews from Moscow can serve as a blueprint for what happened throughout the empire.

During the night following the promulgation of the expulsion edict, large detachments of policemen and firemen appeared in the section of the city where the bulk of the targeted Jewish residents were huddled together. The police invaded Jewish homes, aroused the scared inhabitants from their beds, and drove the semi-naked men, women and children to the police stations, where they were kept in filthy cells for a day, sometimes longer. Some of the prisoners were released in exchange for a written pledge to leave the city immediately. Others were sent out of the city like criminals, in a police convoy, and taken to the special transportation prisons in which convicts sentenced to deportation were kept pending their deportation. Many families, forewarned of the impending raid, spent the night outside their homes to avoid arrest. They hid in the outlying sections of the city, in the cemeteries, stiffened from cold, or in houses of ill repute. Ultimately, they all fell into the hands of the police inquisition (Dubnow, 1918, pp. 403–404).

Of all the writers we consulted on the history of the Jews in Tsarist Russia, none provided a more vivid description of the inhuman manner in which the expulsion from Moscow was carried out than the American author and investigative journalist Harold Frederic, who observed many of these events first-hand and received personal accounts from other eyewitnesses. Frederic went almost every afternoon to the Smolenski station to witness the departure of the seven o'clock train for Brest-Litovsk, by which practically all the refugees were making their way to the Pale. On January 26, 1892, the date of the Moscow expulsion, during the coldest week in years, the thermometer marked 34 degrees below zero Fahrenheit. Bonfires were kept blazing in the squares and on corners, at public expense, to prevent citizens compelled to be outside from freezing as they walked; the schools were closed and garrison drills were suspended. On January 22, orders had been issued that the forwarding of criminal convicts from the central prison should be stopped for the time being, owing to the terrible cold. The only people who were not spared were the nearly 2,000 Jews who were forced out of their homes that day. The fact that a police order was issued on January 28, two days after the expulsions had already taken place, deferring "the further expulsion of Jews from Moscow until February 1, in view of the extreme frosts," and that the officials shrugged their shoulders and laughed when this was pointed out to them illustrates the extreme sadistic bent of the Russian persecutors. They were totally oblivious to the fact that four little children were frozen to death in the streets on their way to the railway station and that there were scores of wretched children, clad only in linen smocks, whose hands and feet were frozen. Frederic concludes his narrative of the Moscow expulsions with the following memory-haunting final picture:

> The crowded platform [which] from early morning till midnight, offered at every step such scenes of heartbreaking misery of mind and wild physical anguish as belong to the battle-field alone. (Frederic, 1892, pp. 229, 243–244)

The main focus of this study is to identify the geopolitical dynamics which led to the history-making Balfour Declaration on November 2, 1917. It would take us too far afield and occupy an unlimited amount of space to describe the events in Russia after the Moscow expulsion in all their complex details. There is no question, however, that at no time did the Russian government recede from its intention to decimate its Jewish population. All efforts by the Russian authorities to replicate the events that happened in Moscow in other parts of the country were only occasionally briefly interrupted when the indignant reaction from around the world threatened Russia's economic interests.

Similarly, with Baron Hirsch's dream of transplanting millions of people to South America having resulted in total failure, with only some six thousand Jews emigrating to Argentina between 1892 and 1894 out of the 3,250,000 contemplated, this episode does not add any value to the focus of this study. Suffice it to say that the expulsion from Moscow as well as alarming rumours of impending persecutions, on the one hand, and exaggerated news about the plans of Baron Hirsch, on the other, resulted in uprooting tens of thousands of people, who flocked to Berlin, Hamburg, Antwerp and London, imploring to be transferred to the United States, which, with Canada, remained as the only practical destination (Dubnow, 1918, pp. 419–421).

Alexander III died on October 20, 1894. During his fourteen-year reign, the increasingly drastic persecution of the Jews went on unabated. The details of their continued economic strangulation and of the progressive restriction of their living space, especially during the three years following their expulsion from Moscow, would by themselves fill volumes. As Dubnow sums up with regard to Alexander's fourteen-year rule, "Having begun with pogroms, it ended with expulsions" (Dubnow, 1918, p. 429).

Pogrom-Driven Exodus – America or Palestine?

The Jewish emigration from Russia to the United States served as a barometer of the persecutions endured by the Jews in the land of bondage. In the empire of the tsars, the Jews were denied the right of residence and the privilege of a school education but were forced at the same time to serve in the army. In the United States, they at once received full civil equality and free schooling without any compulsory military service (Dubnow, 1918, p. 373).

With masses of Jews now streaming across the Pale on their way out of Russia, with America as their destination and with Jewish periodicals being deluged with letters, the Russian Jewish press felt compelled to address the burning issue of the day. Should the Russian Jews leave or stay, and if emigration was the answer, where should they go? To America or to Palestine (Berk, 1985, p. 106)? Jewish thought and intellectual history professor Paul Mendes-Flohr and modern Jewish history professor Jehuda Reinharz concurred that, for the Jewish intellectuals who favoured emigration, the main issue was: America or Palestine? They quote East Prussian socialist and poet Judah Leib Levin, who tellingly expressed this dilemma in 1881:

> In the Holy Land, our dream would be far from realized; there we would be slaves to the Sultan and the Pasha; there, as here, we would bear a heavy burden in the midst of a wild desert people, sustaining ourselves with a distant hope that if our numbers increased sufficiently we might perhaps, after many years, become another small principality that will, finally, in some ultimate utopia, [...] achieve its destiny. But in America our dream is closer to fulfillment [...] and our hope of attaining our independence and leading our lives in accordance with our beliefs and inclinations would not be long deferred.
>
> Kindly note, my friend, that I speak not only of the advantages in regard to spiritual rebirth; I have not mentioned the material advantages of America, as they are obvious and require no proof [...]. Our brethren beg for relief from oppression [...]. They must find a safe haven. Our rich and generous must [...] rescue the lost flock of Israel from the dwellings of lions [...]. Let [the rich] find any place that suits them if only they save our wretched brethren.
>
> The eloquence of the Bible, the piteous spectacle of the bereaved daughter of Zion, the emotion aroused by our ancient memories, all these speak for the land of Israel. The good life recommends America. You know, my friend, that many will yearn for the Holy Land, and I know that even more will stream to America. (Mendes-Flohr and Reinharz, 1995, pp. 413–414)

The Jewish masses of the Pale responded to the pogroms of 1881 with a panicked, spontaneous flight across the borders of Russia. Mendes-Flohr and Reinharz put the number of those penniless Jewish emigrants at approximately 200,000. An estimated 70 to 80 percent of them went to the United States; between 1881 and 1890, the actual number of Russian Jews that entered the United States totalled 135,003 (Joseph, 1914, p. 93, quoted in Mendes-Flohr and Reinharz, 1995). The bulk of the emigrate masses who went to the United States settled in the cities, primarily in New York. They worked in factories or in the trades, the most important of which was the needle trade; they engaged in business, peddling, farming and, lastly, the liberal professions. Many an immigrant passed successfully through all these economic stages before obtaining a secure economic position. By the end of the decade, they had created a 200,000-strong community, which formed the nucleus for the rapidly growing new Jewish centre in America (Dubnow, 1918, p. 374).

In contrast, the movement in the direction of Palestine was a more complex and longer process than the "pack and go" idea of moving to

America. While Palestine was the common ideological destination, it was at the time not a practical one. Not only was it underdeveloped with no infrastructure to accommodate any significant number of newcomers, it was also still under the strict control of the Ottoman government, who were adamantly opposed to the concept of allowing the Jews to return to their ancient homeland. The only possible practical destination at the time was America, which provided all the necessities for physical survival.

Nevertheless, the concept of abandoning the metaphysical, divine intervention-dependent concept of national redemption was, for the first time in two thousand years of diaspora impotence, activated by the agency-driven decision for the Jews to take matters into their own hands and to attempt physically, in the here and now, to reconstitute the homeland they had been expelled from eighteen centuries earlier. It is in this spirit that the leading Jewish minds began to pursue the politicization of the Zionist agenda. It was essential to keep the flame alive by incessantly increasing the number of followers and to keep them motivated until the time that the geopolitical stars were sufficiently aligned to turn this new objective into a practical reality.

Notwithstanding the aforementioned drawbacks, a small number of idealistic pioneers managed to establish a Zionist foothold in Palestine. In 1882, they established the colony of Rishon le-Zion, near Jaffa. Subsequently, a few more colonies were founded in Judea and Galilee. In spite of their enthusiasm, their lack of adequate resources would have led to complete failure if it had not been for the intervention of Baron Edmond de Rothschild in Paris, who gave these fledgeling colonies his support on apparently purely philanthropic grounds. He contributed vast amounts of money towards their education in the higher form of agriculture, particularly wine growing (Dubnow, 1918, pp. 375–376).

This state of affairs led to a situation that was not what the new Zionist colonists had had in mind when they went to Palestine. Gradually, Rothschild ended up owning most of these colonies, which turned the colonists into labourers or tenants under the complete control of the Baron's administration, a far cry from their dream of a free life in the Holy Land. Yet there can be no doubt that under the conditions prevailing at the time, the continued existence of the colonies was only made possible through the liberal assistance which came from the outside (Dubnow, 1918, pp. 375–376). As we shall see later, Rothschild was totally at odds with Herzl's idea of reconstituting a homeland in Palestine for world Jewry. Rothschild's motivation was purely philanthropic and not political.

As disillusioning as this outcome turned out for these first self-sacrificing idealistic pioneers, their efforts had not been in vain. By establishing a tenuous foothold in Palestine, they provided a tangible base for the popularization of the ideas of the first exponents of the territorial restoration of Jewry, Pinsker and Lilienblum, and for the organization by the "Lovers of Zion," who looked upon them as their leaders, of a number of societies in various cities. Towards the end of 1884, the delegates of these societies convened a conference, across the border, in the Prussian town of Kattowitz, as it was impossible to hold it in Russia due to the threat of police interference. They established a fund to channel the donations in favour of the Palestinian colonies. By winning over a number of prominent champions of rabbinical orthodoxy, such as Samuel Mohilever, the well-known rabbi of Bialystok, they weakened the opposition of the orthodox masses who saw in the political Zionist movement a rival of the Messianic idea of Judaism. Without government approval, the Hobebe Zion societies in Russia were hampered in their activities and had barely enough funds at their disposal for the upkeep of one or two colonies in Palestine (Dubnow, 1918, pp. 376–377). Consequently, there were not more than a few hundred Russian Jewish immigrants to Palestine for the period 1881–1882, and the annual trickle remained at that level for the entire decade (Berk, 1985, p. 120), compared to the 135,000 Jews who migrated to the United States from Russia during that same period (Greenberg, 1951, p. 73).

However, like the mighty oak tree that owes its existence to the tiny acorn, the historical realization of the eighteen-century-old dream of the reconstitution of the Jewish homeland would never have happened without them. These first immigrants and those who followed them in the later 1880s laid the foundation of the Yishuv, the modern Jewish community in Palestine. While their numbers pale in comparison with the mass exodus to America, it was they who took the first step on the long road to the political realization of the Zionist dream, which could not have occurred without them. As such, they constitute a vital link in the chain of events that led to the promulgation of the Balfour Declaration.

This brings us to the end of the 1880s. These ten years were marked by a transformational reaction from Russia's Jewish population to the unrelenting oppression by the Russian government. From the Jewish perspective, the ninth decade of the nineteenth century marked the transition from the older *Haskala* movement to the more modern national revival of which the steady growth of Russian-Jewish emigration was one of the prime manifestations (Dubnow, 1918, pp. 372, 377).

The social heterogeneity that characterized the Jewish population gave rise to a diversity of reactions by its various segments. While the Jewish intelligentsia were all facing the same problem, they were not unanimous in their choice of solution. The Jewish periodicals published in Russia provided a broad and democratic forum for the intense debates that raged over these questions. Regardless of their editorial board's own position, each newspaper opened its columns to participants of the opposing viewpoints, a tradition they carried over from the previous two decades when they published contrary views on the then-crucial issues of Russification and assimilation. While the Russian language *Razsvet* and the Hebrew language *Ha-Melits* were leaning in the direction of moving to Palestine, *Voskhod* and *Russkii Evrei* were still largely opposed to the idea of emigration altogether (Berk, 1985, p. 106).

Razsvet's complete change of position provides a characteristic blueprint for the socio-political dynamics that turned the 1881–1882 pogroms in Russia into one of the most important junctures in the history of world Jewry. At the start of this calamitous episode, *Razsvet* was still opposed to the idea of emigration. The first shock of the pogroms was not sufficient to shake off the old belief in assimilation and emancipation. At first, *Razsvet* rejected emigration as a viable solution to the problems faced by the Jews of Russia. It showed that it was still imbued with the old assimilationist patriotic sentiment when it questioned how Jews could "leave the sky unto which they were born, the land where they are buried…. The Jews will remain in Russia. Russia is their fatherland, the Russian land is their land. The sky of Russia is their sky" (*Razsvet*, May 8, 1881, pp. 730–731, quoted in Berk, 1985, p. 107). To emigrate would prove to the antisemites that they were right in claiming that the Jews were not loyal to Russia. This, in 1882, was also the theme vociferously pursued by the Jewish plutocracy (Berk, 1985, pp. 106–107).

In the ensuing weeks and months, under the impact of the pogroms and the reports of its own correspondents in the provinces, *Razsvet* reversed its earlier position and became a strong advocate of emigration, as evidenced by their statement on February 26, 1882:

> We […] consider it [emigration] in the present moment to be the only measure which corresponds to the material interest of the unfortunate mass and to the moral interests of all Russian Jewry which is now in a condition of the most shocking moral oppression. (*Razsvet*, February 26, 1882, p. 323, quoted in Berk, 1985, p. 107)

While its columns were now open to writers supporting emigration to either Palestine or America, *Razsvet* itself had, by now, become an unequivocal advocate for emigration to Palestine. In June 1882, it definitively underscored its position when it demanded that immigration to Palestine be made "a national, holy task" (*Razsvet*, June 27, 1882, p. 979, quoted in Berk, 1985, p. 107).

Razsvet's rationale for supporting migration to Palestine was their fear that one of two things would happen if the Jews went to America: they would either be lost through assimilation or, if they managed to preserve their Jewish identity, they would provide new ground for antisemitism and pogroms. The *Razsvet* writers' chief concern was how to achieve physical survival without falling prey to assimilation. They concluded that, as anti-Jewish sentiment had proven to be a permanent phenomenon, there was no future for the Jews in Russia or in Europe and that, by staying there, they would never see an end to their suffering. What the Jews needed to avoid this suffering and to successfully preserve their culture was a land of their own, which could only be Palestine, their ancestral homeland (Berk, 1985, p. 107).

The movement in support of immigration to Palestine was not limited to the Russified members of the Jewish intelligentsia and to the Jewish periodical *Razsvet*. It also included the old-style *maskilim*, progressive and secularized men of letters who wrote and conversed in Hebrew, as well as those Orthodox Jews who were not oblivious to contemporary events and modern patterns of thought. Hebrew-language periodicals such as *Ha-Melits* and *Ha-Magid* also published numerous articles in support of immigration to Palestine (Berk, 1985, p. 112).

In March and April of 1882, Alexander Tsederbaum, the editor and publisher of *Ha-Melits*, wrote that with the Russian government having decided that there was no place in Russia for the Jews, they were left facing the reality that they had no choice but to emigrate. Tsederbaum, in drawing a succinct distinction between the personalities of the two types of potential emigrants, inadvertently provides the basis for the argument that Palestine was an unrealistic destination for the desperate Jews of Russia who were seeking immediate relief from their perilous situation. He argues that those favouring America were so enamoured with nineteenth-century ideals and culture that they "can find satisfaction only in modern metropolitan centers, where there are great activity and vitality, railroads, steamboats and telegraph" (Berk, 1985, pp. 112–113).

In other words, what they needed at the time, not just in the future, was a land that would welcome them and have the infrastructure in place to accommodate millions of persecuted and destitute people. Tsederbaum and the other pro-Palestine intellectuals sounded as if opting for America represented a lack of faith in the ultimate destiny of returning to the ancestral homeland. When Tsederbaum described those who were looking to Palestine at the time as "being infused with religious fervour and love of their people, who would rather spend one hour in the Holy Land than all their lives in the land of dispersion: for them there is only Palestine," he rejected America as a place of settlement as it would lead the Jews to further dispersal and eventual assimilation. It would cause them to lose their sense of Jewish peoplehood, which could only be preserved by settling in their ancient homeland (Berk, 1985, p. 113).

One of the most perceptive articles to appear in *Ha-Melits* was written by Dr. Herman Schapira, the future founder of the Jewish National Fund, who put the dilemma of the choice of destination in a less divisive and more optimistic context. He was of the opinion that the fact that so many Russian Jews were going to America and other places besides Palestine would, in the long run, benefit the entire Jewish people, for, wherever they went and prospered, they would support the settlement of Palestine and influence the governments in its behalf to the prospect. The diaspora, therefore, was indispensable for the successful colonization of Palestine. He also felt that since settlement in Palestine was bound to be extremely difficult, it might be more advantageous for the ultimate success of the enterprise that masses of immigrants did not come at once (Berk, 1985, pp. 113–114).

The reality of the situation was that while the need for a safe haven was immediate, Palestine, unlike America, was at that time not in a position to absorb large numbers of immigrants. First and foremost, the Ottoman Empire would not allow Jewish settlement in Palestine out of fear that such settlement would lead to a call for an independent Jewish state, which would set a dangerous precedent for that multinational empire. As Charles Netter of the Alliance Israélite Universelle, the largest, wealthiest and best known of all the Jewish organizations, wrote to the *Jewish Chronicle* (London) on March 24, 1882, Palestine was too poor, the land too barren, and the population too hostile. It could not possibly absorb large numbers of immigrants (*Jewish Chronicle*, March 24, 1882, pp. 6–7, quoted in Berk, 1985, p. 120). Because of these unfavourable conditions, none of the major Jewish organizations, inside or outside Russia, endorsed the idea of a return to the Holy Land. The Russian Jews were fully aware of the poor prospects for settlement in Palestine. For centuries they had been providing charity for the small Jewish community in Palestine. The poverty of this community and the general backwardness of the area were confirmed in the letters from those who migrated there in early 1882 and in articles in the various Jewish periodicals. In summary, the backwardness, hardships and absence of the organizational sponsorship of settlements in Palestine were no match for the appeal of the free, dynamic, wealthy nation of America (Berk, 1985, p. 121).

Before we follow the course of Zionist political thinking from its wellspring in the cauldron of the tsarist genocidal oppression of Russian Jewry to its fruition in the seat of the British Empire on November 2, 1917, we must recognize the fact that while this new ideological development was a strong and compelling force in spirit, in practical numbers it represented an almost insignificant minority of Russia's beleaguered Jewish population. As mentioned before, because of the difficulties the Turkish government raised against Jewish immigration, as well as the slight absorptive capacity of the country at the time, the number of Jewish emigrants to Palestine in the 1880s was negligible (Greenberg, 1951, p. 72).

Nicholas II (1894–1917)

Dubnow describes Nicholas II, Alexander III's successor, as the most gloomy and reactionary of all the nineteenth-century tsars. A man of limited intelligence, he attempted to play the role of an unlimited autocrat, fighting in blind rage against the cause of liberty. The same champions of the savage antisemitic policies that marked the reign of his father Alexander III remained at the helm of Russian affairs, including Konstantin Pobedonostsev, the Head of the Holy Synod, Pyotr Durnovo, the reactionary Minister of the Interior, and Sergei Witte, the accommodating Minister of Finance. As he had done with the previous tsars, Pobedonostsev made sure to fill the new monarch's head with the classic hateful charges against the Jews so as to prepare him for a proper understanding of the Jewish problem (Dubnow, 1920, p. 9).

When, in 1898, the Council of the Jewish Colonization Association in Paris applied to the Russian government for permission to settle Russian Jews as agriculture farmers in Russia itself, Pobedonostsev turned them down on the grounds that he considered the Jews a very clever people, intellectually and culturally superior to the Russians, and, as such, dangerous to them: "The Jews are displacing us, and this does not suit us." On one occasion, when questioned about the future of Russian Jewry under the system of uninterrupted persecutions, Pobedonostsev gave the following infamous reply: "One third will die out, one third will leave the country, and one third will be completely dissolved in the surrounding population" (Dubnow, 1920, p. 10).

The pernicious "Temporary Rules" promulgated in 1882 continued to be applied with excessive zeal by the "faithful watchdogs of Russian reaction" – the successive Ministers of the Interior who occupied this powerful position between 1895 and 1904: Durnovo, Goremykin, Sipyaghin and Plehve (Dubnow, 1920, p. 16).

In the Pale of Settlement, the government continued its policy of keeping the Jews confined to the cities and towns. To solve the problem of those who had been allowed to stay in the villages before 1882, Finance Minister Witte sought to drive them out of the countryside by turning over the liquor trade, which had been their principal source of income, to the state. As a result, by the end of the 1890s, the rural Jewish population had been considerably reduced. The hair-splitting manipulation of the anti-Jewish laws by the lower courts always ended up in new punishments for the Jews (Dubnow, 1920, pp. 17–19).

By the second half of the 1890s, the entire area of the Russian Empire outside the Pale of Settlement, while open to foreigners of all nationalities, remained hermetically closed to the Jewish citizens of Russia. The borders between these two areas were guarded with unprecedented strictness, often to the most revolting extremes. A prime example is the law passed in 1896, which prevented Jewish soldiers from spending the brief leave of absence granted during their military service outside the Pale. A Jewish soldier serving in a regiment stationed in far-off Siberia was forced to travel thousands of miles to the Pale of Settlement to spend his month of furlough there. He was not allowed to remain in the city in which he was discharging his military duty, even if the furlough was granted to him for health reasons (Dubnow, 1920, p. 21).

The concerted efforts by the Russian authorities, during Nicholas II's reign, to complete the objective pursued by his predecessors of ridding Russia of its Jewish population had, by the second half of the 1890s, led to the complete economic collapse of Russian Jewry. To present a realistic picture of the diversity, complexity and insidious nature of this watershed episode in the history of Russian Jewry would require a book on its own. While such a voluminous treatment lies beyond the scope of this study, an awareness of the extreme deprivations inflicted on Russia's Jewry at this time is essential if one wants to comprehend the force of the Jewish counter-reaction which formed the foundation of the birth and development of the Zionist political movement.

The range of Jewish economic endeavour, which was already severely limited, kept being narrowed more and more. The government targeted all vital elements of Jewish economic survival: the liquor trade, the agricultural sector, the arts and crafts, the liberal professions (law, medicine), as well as all avenues of education required to improve the living standards of a society. The most severe measure, implemented between 1896 and 1898, of placing the liquor trade under government control deprived tens of thousands of Jewish families of their livelihood. While the upper strata of the Jewish population welcomed this reform, as they looked with disdain on the involvement of a large number of their coreligionists in what they considered a morally tainted business, it is important to remember that the Jews did not derive their livelihood from the liquor trade as a matter of preference. They would have gladly surrendered this ignoble trade to Russian hands if they had only been allowed to pursue other methods of earning a livelihood. While the government deprived two hundred thousand Jews of a livelihood in the liquor trade, it refused to lift the special restrictions which barred their way to other useful occupations (Dubnow, 1920, pp. 22–23).

Those members of the Jewish working class who were willing to take up agriculture found that avenue to earning a livelihood closed by the "Temporary Rules" of 1882 which blocked their way to the countryside, thus making it impossible for them to buy or even lease a piece of land. When Baron Günzburg and other prominent Jews of St. Petersburg petitioned the government to allow the Jews to purchase small parcels of land for personal use, their petition was rejected. The government went so far as to prohibit the Jews from buying or leasing parcels of land which were part of a city but happened to be situated outside the city limits. Thus, when, in 1897, a wealthy Jew of Minsk by the name of Pollak petitioned the local town council to sell him a piece of suburban property for the establishment of a Jewish agricultural farm, his petition was refused. To ensure that all possibilities of land use were denied to the Jews, the government upheld its prohibition of land ownership even in the case of the Jewish students who had completed a course in the school of the Jewish agricultural farm near Odessa (Dubnow, 1920, pp. 24–25).

The government would not even allow the Jewish working class to develop their widely practised occupation of arts and crafts, which was one of the last ways of earning a living left to them. The example of the Jewish millionaire Brodski of Kiev is a case in point. In 1895, he offered to open a trade bank to which he would contribute 120,000 rubles. When he submitted the constitution of the proposed bank to the local authorities for their approval, he was required to insert a clause that the directors and the chairman of the bank's council should always be Christians and that the council itself should not include more than one Jewish member. Unable to comply with the request that an establishment to be founded with his money and which was to bear his name should contain restrictions affecting his coreligionists, Brodski withdrew his offer. Dubnow comments that the fact that Kiev's failure to acquire a trade bank also affected the city's Christian artisans did not concern the authorities. By making the Jews suffer materially as well as morally, "the purpose of the highly placed Jew-baiters was accomplished (Dubnow, 1920, pp. 25–26).

The Russian authorities were equally determined to deprive the Jewish intellectuals of earning a livelihood. Being barred from the civil service, they were particularly attracted to the liberal professions. In keeping with the government's anti-Jewish agenda, these were also closed to the Jews. In 1889, the government had passed a law that effectively closed the legal profession to qualified Jewish candidates. It made their admission to the bar dependent upon the granting of a special permission by the Minister of Justice. The fact that this permission was granted to only one Jew in the course of a whole decade attests to the purpose and success of this discriminatory measure. In 1897, the government went a step further when it appointed a committee to consider the enactment of a 10 percent norm for Jewish lawyers. The reasons advanced by the committee attest to the underlying Judeophobic instincts that inspired the proposed legislation:

> The conduct of a lawyer is determined by the impulses of his will, of his conscience, – in other words, that sphere of his inner life which finds its manifestation in religion. Now the admission of Jews constitutes a menace, resulting from views peculiar to the Jewish race, which are contrary to the Christian morality. (Dubnow, 1920, p. 26)

The committee's conclusions inspired the staff of the Ministry of Justice to stop the admission of Jews to the bar altogether, with the result that the proposal regarding the percentage norm was shelved. Consequently, the hundreds of Jewish students who had completed their legal education at the universities were deprived of the opportunity to pursue their chosen profession (Dubnow, 1920, pp. 26–27).

Jewish physicians also had limited career opportunities. They were restricted to private practice and barred from occupying a government or public position (Dubnow, 1920, p. 27).

We have seen how, during the 1880s and 1890s, the fanatically Judeophobic tsarist regime continued to heap increasing hardships on its Jewish population. Remarkably, in spite of the shattering blows that were intended to destroy their bodies and souls, the resilient spirit of the Jews allowed them to rebound and to energize themselves into a social, spiritual and political regeneration. Like the icy summits of the Earth's glaciers generate the streams which ineluctably circumvent all obstacles to end up forming and maintaining the lakes and seas, the persecution of Russian Jewry produced two streams of liberation and reconstitution. The larger stream carried the desperate majority to the immediate relief provided by the American shores, while the smaller one flowed in the direction of the yet to be developed home in Palestine. By the early 1890s, the Zionist political movement aimed at the ingathering of the exiles in the yet to be rebuilt ancient homeland had gathered enough momentum and had developed sufficiently strong roots that it would be able to withstand all the political storms and obstacles that it was bound to encounter on its unwavering course. While the Russian government and Russian people continued their relentless persecution of the Jews throughout Nicholas II's rule, the roots of national liberation planted by the Jewish philosophers developed into the robust political movement that eventually brought the Jewish people to the negotiating process that culminated in the Balfour Declaration of November 2, 1917.

As we have seen, any major event, whether internal or external, that affected the Russian regime adversely inevitably led the tsarist regime to deflect any accusation of government mismanagement by diverting the blame onto the Jews, the perennial scapegoats in the rabidly antisemitic and easily inflamed Russian society. The most serious problem faced by Nicholas II's regime at the turn of the century was the growth of the Russian revolutionary movement led by the Social Democratic and Social Revolutionary parties, which had arisen between 1898 and 1900. For the lower strata of the Russian population, grassroots terrorism was the only answer to the ruthless application of state terrorism, which had used unrestricted violence against the faintest stirring for liberty, such as the demands for moderate constitutional reforms. Nocturnal raids and arrests were the order of the day. Prisons and places of penal servitude were filled to overflowing with "political criminals." The revolutionaries fought terrorism with terrorism. When one of their victims, the reactionary Minister of the Interior, Dmitry Sipyagin, was assassinated in April 1902, the Tsar replaced him with Vyacheslav von Plehve, who had earlier honed his skills as an efficient henchman of the Russian political inquisition in his role as Chief of the Political Police (Dubnow, 1920, pp. 66–67).

The fact that the tsarist government's treatment of the Jews had nothing to do with justice and fairness came into full play in its reaction to the Russian revolutionary movement. The Russian bureaucracy regarded the revolution as a personal threat, a menace to its own existence, and considered the Jewish participants in the revolution as their own individual enemies whose deeds had to be avenged upon the whole Jewish people. It was this warped mindset that led to Plehve's devilish plan to combat the non-Jewish revolution by waging war against the Jews, thus diverting the attention of the Russian public from the mounting revolutionary propaganda in the direction of the time-honoured Jewish scapegoat. The idea was to brand the Russian emancipatory movement as the work of the

Jews, as an anti-patriotic cause which was foreign to the Russian people. The plan to turn reality on its head required the staging of a barbarous anti-Jewish pogrom for the purpose of intimidating the Jewish revolutionaries and interpreting it as a protest of the "Russian people" against the "Jewish revolution." The site chosen for this particular anti-Jewish conflagration was Kishinev, the capital of Bessarabia (Dubnow, 1920, pp. 68–69).

The Kishinev Pogrom – April 6–7, 1903

Pogroms, as we have seen, always contained a set of specific elements, based on the formula that had been developed by their instigators, to ensure their successful execution. These included: a location which provided a propitious demographic mix of Jews and non-Jews; a well subsidized local newspaper committed to running a virulent hatemongering campaign against the Jews, designed to develop and raise an irrepressible Judeophobic bloodlust; the presence of well-trained *agents provocateurs*; the ensured compliance of the local civil authorities, police agencies and military; and a convenient pretext to light the fuse at the chosen time. The sequence of events during the Kishinev pogrom, described below, clearly follows this pattern.

Until the end of the nineteenth century, the 50,000-strong Jewish community of Kishinev had lived in peace and harmony with their 60,000 Christian neighbours. These friendly relations were brought to an end by the untrammelled antisemitic propaganda spewed by a local journalist named Pavel Krushevan. Since 1897, he had been publishing a local paper under the name of *Bessarabetz* (The Bessarabian). While it originally followed a moderate progressive policy, it was soon bought by the local antisemitic reactionaries from among the nobility and bureaucracy, whereupon it became subsidized by the government. From that time on, Krushevan's paper conducted an uninhibited public campaign against the Jews, accusing them of every possible crime: economic exploitation, socialism, hatred towards Christians, ritual murders, and being responsible for the "Godless revolution." The fact that the deputy-governor of Kishinev, who was in charge of news censorship, also had a proven track record of persecuting the Jews ensured *Bessarabetz* had immunity and complete freedom of action, even when it proceeded to print appeals calling on the Christian population to make pogroms upon the Jews (Dubnow, 1920, p. 70). This agitation was particularly perilous, as *Bessarabetz* was the only press organ in the province, the government having consistently refused the publication of any other newspaper. The results were predictable. Russian public opinion became increasingly inflamed by the unchallenged poisonous doses of hatred administered to it daily. At the beginning of 1903, Krushevan saw the opportunity to raise his pogrom campaign to a fever pitch. The mutilated body of a Russian peasant boy, Rybalenko, was found in the town of Dubossary. The judicial inquiry established that he had been slain by his uncle in the hope of inheriting his part of a bequest. Ignoring the facts, *Bessarabetz* immediately accused the Jews of ritual murder. The almost daily appeals of "Death to the Jews! Let all the Zhyds be massacred!" were read in all the saloons and public establishments of Bessarabia. While a first attempt at a pogrom in Dubossary was frustrated by the sturdy resistance of the local Jews, the events in Kishinev, which occurred soon thereafter, unfolded in line with the master plan (Dubnow, 1920, pp. 70–71).

On the eve of Easter 1903, rumours were circulating in Kishinev that the Jews had murdered a Christian servant girl. In fact, she had poisoned herself and died in spite of the efforts of her Jewish master to save her life. A secret criminal organization centred in the local Russian club, which was the gathering place of the province's officials, sprang into action. They were suddenly joined by an emissary of the political police, a gendarmerie officer named Levendahl, who had been dispatched from St. Petersburg. After Easter, when the bloody onslaught had been committed, Levendahl disappeared just as suddenly (Dubnow, 1920, p. 71).

The Krushevan-Ustrugov-Levendahl triumvirate provided the motivation and cover for the terrible antisemitic conspiracy in Kishinev. Printed handbills were distributed throughout the city, telling the people that an imperial ukase had been published, granting permission to inflict a "bloody punishment" upon the Jews during the three days of the Christian Passover. The police, who were later found out to have been part of the conspiracy, made no attempt to suppress these circulars. When, on the eve of the festival of Passover, representatives of the Jewish community implored the governor and the chief of police to provide them with protection, they were told that the proper measures for their safety were already in place. The anti-Jewish hate campaign had been so pervasive that, when the rabbi went to see the local Greek Orthodox bishop, the latter asked him whether it was true that a Jewish sect was using Christian blood for ritual purposes (Dubnow, 1920, p. 72).

The openly planned conflagration broke out on cue. On Sunday April 6, 1903, the first day of the Christian Passover and the seventh day of the Jewish holiday, as church bells began to ring at noontime, a large crowd of Russian burghers and artisans, seeing that the police were making no attempt to stop them, broke into the Jewish houses and stores to throw the contents onto the streets, where everything was destroyed or plundered.

Even then, the police and soldier detachments stationed on the streets remained passive. The mob saw this as final proof that the rumours that the Tsar had given permission "to beat the Jews" were correct. By evening, the looting had escalated to killing. Armed with clubs and knives, the rioters attacked the Jews on the streets and in their homes, resulting in many Jews being severely injured or killed. The police and military continued to stand idly by. The only time they did act was when they saw a group of Jews, armed with sticks, trying to fend off their attackers. They promptly stepped in to disarm the defenders (Dubnow, 1920, pp. 72–73).

At ten o'clock in the evening, the attacks suddenly stopped. Word spread that the pogrom organizers were meeting to plan the next move, which they intended to turn into a systematic butchery. The rioters soon received the necessary orders, which resulted in Kishinev becoming the scene of unprecedented bestialities during the entire day of April 7, from daybreak until eight o'clock in the evening. Unable to defend themselves, the beleaguered Jews tried to hide in their cellars or find safety in the houses of their Christian neighbours, where they were eventually tracked down by their determined murderers. No description of the barbaric fashion in which the Jews were slain during the Kishinev pogrom can be more telling than Simon Dubnow's own account:

> Most of them were not killed at once, but were left writhing in pre-mortal agonies. Some had nails driven into their heads or had their eyes put out. Little children were thrown from garrets to the pavement, and their brains dashed out upon the stones. Women had their stomachs ripped open or their breasts cut off. Many of them became the victims of rape. One gymnasium pupil who saw his mother attacked by these fiends threw himself single-handed upon them, and saved at the cost of his life his mother's honour, he himself was slain, and his mother's eyes were put out. The drunken hordes broke into synagogue, and getting hold of the Torah scrolls, tore them to shreds, defiled them, and trampled upon them. In one synagogue, the old *Shammes* (beadle), arrayed in his prayer-shawl, and shielding with his body the Ark containing the sacred scrolls, was savagely murdered by the desecrators on the threshold of the sanctuary. Throughout the entire day, wagons were seen moving in the streets, carrying wounded and slain Jews to the hospitals which had been converted into field-lazarettes. While these atrocities were carried out in plain sight, they were met by total indifference by the non-Jewish passersby, who continued their walks, leisurely and unconcerned. (Dubnow, 1920, pp. 73–74)

It was not until five o'clock in the afternoon that a telegram was received from Plehve, the Minister of the Interior, and at six o'clock, large detachments of fully armed troops appeared on the central streets. The sight of the soldiers was sufficient for the crowd to disperse without a single shot being fired. Only in the outskirts of the town, which had not yet been reached by the troops, did the plunder and massacre continue until late in the evening (Dubnow, 1920, p. 75).

Dubnow noted that had the police and military attended to their duty at the inception of the pogrom, not a single Jew would have been murdered nor a single house destroyed. Instead, by giving the murderers and rioters a free hand for two days, the government-inspired and -controlled Kishinev pogrom resulted in forty-five Jews being slain, eighty-six severely wounded or crippled, and five hundred slightly wounded, not counting the cases of rape, the number of which could not be determined. Fifteen hundred houses and stores were demolished and looted. The victims were mostly among the lower classes of the Jewish population, since many well-to-do Jewish families were able, by bribing the police heavily, to have the rioters turned away from their houses (Dubnow, 1920, p. 75).

When the news of the Kishinev butchery spread throughout Russia and abroad, it was met with a universal outcry of outrage and horror. The entire liberal Russian press was unanimous in its condemnation of the Kishinev atrocities. The great writer Leo Tolstoi, in a letter which the government's censors did not allow to be published, showed profound insight into the causes of the Kishinev barbarities, as demonstrated in the following extract:

My opinion concerning the Kishinev crime is the result also of my religious convictions. Upon the receipt of the first news which was published in the papers, not yet knowing all the appalling details which were communicated subsequently, I fully realized the horror of what had taken place, and experienced simultaneously a burning feeling of pity for the innocent victims of the cruelty of the populace, amazement at the bestiality of all these so-called Christians, revulsion at all these so-called cultured people who instigated the mob and sympathized with its actions. But I felt a particular horror for the principal culprit, our Government with its clergy which fosters in the people bestial sentiments and fanaticism, with its horde of murderous officials. The crime committed at Kishinev is nothing but a direct consequence of that propaganda of falsehood and violence which is conducted by the Russian Government with such energy. The attitude adopted by the Russian Government in relation to this question may only serve as a new proof of the class egotism of this Government, which stops at no cruelty whenever it finds it necessary to check movements that are deemed dangerous by it. Like the Turkish Government at the time of the Armenian massacres, it remains entirely indifferent to the most horrible acts of cruelty, as long as these acts do not affect its interests. (Dubnow, 1920, p. 76)

The tsarist government went out of its way to silence the humanitarian outcries from inside Russia. Plehve warned the papers who published even minor fragments of the horrible truth that he would discontinue their publication unless they ceased the "pursuit of an injurious policy," as happened in the case of the Russian-Jewish *Voskhod* in St. Petersburg and the legal journal *Pravo* (The Law). The government forced the entire Russian press to publish its falsified official reports, in which the organized massacre was toned down to a casual brawl and the number of casualties downplayed to an insignificant number (Dubnow, 1920, p. 77).

The Kishinev catastrophe had a greater soul-stirring effect upon Russian Jewry than the pogroms at the beginning of the 1880s and the Moscow atrocities at the beginning of the 1890s. It awakened the burning feeling of martyrdom, but with it also a feeling of heroism. Seeing that they could not depend on the government to protect them, they felt the urgent need for self-defence, which led to the organization of self-defence societies in a number of cities. Plehve felt that this development of organized Jewish resistance might present him with two new challenges. First, they might make it more difficult to engineer the pogroms, which would be no longer safe for the murderers and plunderers. Second, he was fearful that these self-defence societies might be used by the revolutionary movement for propaganda purposes and political activities (Dubnow, 1920, pp. 79–80). To deal with these two concerns, the minister instructed the governors that "no self-defence societies should be tolerated" and that the authorities should adopt measures for the "prevention of violence" and the "suppression of lawlessness." As it turned out, while the second order was never put into effect, the first instruction was carried out with relentless brutality; during the following pogroms, the troops' first business was to shoot members of the self-defence societies (Dubnow, 1920, p. 80).

Plehve was concerned that the Jewish outrage at the Kishinev massacre would drive the growing Zionist movement into the ranks of the Russian revolutionaries. On June 24, 1903, he issued a "strictly confidential" circular to the governors, ordering them to adopt strong measures against the "propaganda of the ideas of Zionism," which, the circular claimed, had departed from its original aim of transferring Jews to Palestine and was, instead, advocating "the organization of the Jews in secluded societies in the places of their present domicile." In response to these orders, the police began to persecute the Zionists in a number of cities, forbidding the sale of Jewish Colonial Trust shares, the collection of money for the Jewish National Fund, and the holding of meetings and conferences by the Zionist societies (Dubnow, 1920, pp. 82–83).

Theodor Herzl arrived in St. Petersburg on July 25, 1903, one month after Plehve launched his campaign against the Zionists. Herzl's immediate objective was to persuade the Russian authorities to halt these persecutions. His more important objective was to obtain a promise from the Russian government that it would exert diplomatic pressure on Turkey to permit the settlement of Jews in Palestine on a large scale. During his four interviews with Plehve, Herzl appeared to have convinced him that it was in the Russian government's interest to assist the Zionist movement. Plehve's reply, which he confirmed in writing, was that the Russian government was willing to help Zionism as long as it directed its political activity towards its aims outside of Russia, the creation of a Jewish centre in Palestine, and the emigration of the Jews from Russia. However, as soon as the movement turned inward, by propagating the Jewish national idea and the organization of Jewry in Russia itself, it would subvert the Russian national policies and could thus not be tolerated. Herzl assured Plehve that political Zionism's only aim was the creation of a centre outside of the diaspora (Dubnow, 1920, pp. 83–84).

With both Plehve and Herzl seemingly satisfied with their conversation and with Herzl also having met with the Minister of Finance, Witte, and the Minister of Foreign Affairs, Vladimir Lamsdorff, Herzl left St. Petersburg in a hopeful mood. While Herzl, during his trip to St. Petersburg, was greeted with rousing ovations by the Zionists, he was severely criticized by representatives of other Jewish political groups who felt that by negotiating for the salvation of the Jewish people with the man responsible for the Kishinev massacre, Herzl had lowered the national dignity of the Jewish people (Dubnow, 1920, p. 84).

The Zionist political movement, launched with such enthusiasm six years earlier at the First Zionist Congress, found itself stymied in its efforts to translate its lofty objectives into concrete realities by the seemingly insurmountable obstacles it was facing. Herzl's efforts in Russia, both in their causes and effects, reflect the true nature of this crisis. Unsuccessful in obtaining a charter from the Ottoman Sultan, Herzl felt compelled to pursue the glimmer of hope he perceived in the convoluted dynamics of the Russian government's political calculations concerning its Jewish population. He was obviously of the opinion that since the Russian government was using the pogroms for the purpose of ridding Russia of its Jewish population, they might be willing to achieve the same object by providing diplomatic assistance to the Zionist plans. As we have seen, Plehve actually gave such a pledge to Herzl. As it turned out, Herzl had, perhaps naïvely, overestimated the importance of the promises made by the Russian government officials, who had treated him as a well-intended idealist but not someone to be taken too seriously (Dubnow, 1920, p. 84).

The horrors of Kishinev invested the need to escape from Russian bondage with a new urgency. It was at this point that the Zionist movement gave rise to the Territorialist Organization, which called for the creation of an autonomous Jewish centre at any available point of the globe. In the meantime, emigration to the more readily accessible United States had, since 1881, already created a more than 1-million-strong Jewish centre in that country, which, given the circumstances, was expected to keep growing (Dubnow, 1920, pp. 84, 86).

The judicial investigation conducted in connection with the spring pogrom in Kishinev turned out to be a travesty of justice. The investigation's main objective was to mask the deliberate organization of the pogrom. The government functionaries and members of the upper class, who were known to be the true instigators, were deliberately eliminated from the proceedings. Only the hired assassins and plunderers recruited from the lower-class mob were brought to trial. To ensure that the truth would not leak out, the Ministry of Justice ordered the case to be tried behind closed doors. Echoes of the proceedings, which inevitably reached beyond the walls of the closed courtroom, showed that the successful efforts by the counsel for the defence, which succeeded in proving that the prisoners at the bar were merely the blind tools of the true perpetrators of the crime, were to no avail. When the court refused their demand that the case be probed in-depth, the lawyers, after stating their reasons, withdrew from the courtroom. The speech by Karabchevski, one of the withdrawing Christian lawyers, was particularly powerful and to the point. He openly declared that the pogrom was "the fulfillment of a criminal order given from above." In his words:

> The whole of Kishinev was converted during the excesses into an immense circus of antiquity, where, before the eyes of curious spectators from among the administration and the army, before a festively attired crowd, a terrible drama was enacted in the depth of the arena. From the one side defenceless victims were driven upon the arena, and from the other maddened beasts were set at them, until the signal to stop is given, and the frightful spectacle was ended at once. (Dubnow, 1920, p. 91)

The remaining advocates were the antisemite Shmakov and other wholehearted defenders of the Kishinev massacre, who regarded it as a manifestation of the honour and conscience of the Russian people. In the end, the court sentenced a few of the murderers and rioters in the dock to hard labour or penal service while at the same time dismissing the civil actions for damages presented by the Jews (Dubnow, 1920, pp. 91–92).

When, six months later, the Kishinev case came up before the Senate, with the Jews appearing as complainants against governor von Raaben, deputy-governor Ustrugov and the Kishinev chief of police, whom they held responsible for the pogrom, the bureaucratic defendants claimed that the Jews had been more than compensated by contributions from Russia, Western Europe and America. All the arguments presented on behalf of the victims failed to convince the judges of the Senate, and the petition for damages was dismissed. As von Raaben frankly admitted, the government did not wish to create a precedent for compensating pogrom victims out of public funds as this might make it necessary to increase the imperial budget by several million rubles a year (Dubnow, 1920, p. 92).

The Relentless Tightening of the Russian Judeophobic Juggernaut – 1903–1917

The foregoing account of the Kishinev pogrom in all its dimensions provides a telling example of the relentless determination of the tsarist regime to make the lives of its Jewish population of six million so intolerable as to force it to have to choose between physical and moral destruction as a national identity or massive emigration. It also provides a blueprint as to the manner in which the tsarist regime continued to carry out its Judeophobic policies until the end of its existence in 1917. While a detailed account of all the violent outbursts against Russian Jewry between 1903 and 1917 would require several volumes, a brief chronological summary will provide a necessary awareness of the continuing horrible plight of Russian Jewry and of its heroic resilience during that period.

In January 1904, a committee of governors and high officials of the Ministry of the Interior met to consider the Jewish Question. The conferees were made to understand that the government considered even the slightest improvement of the condition of Jewry out of the question. The only liberal member of the committee, governor Sergey Urusov, acknowledged afterwards that the Kishinev pogrom and the agitation surrounding it demonstrated that the hatred towards the Jews was personally shared by the Tsar and his inner circle of co-conspirators. As a result, instead of reforming Jewish legislation, the committee applied itself to systematizing the anti-Jewish code of laws (Dubnow, 1920, p. 92).

On January 27, 1904, upon the outbreak of the Russo-Japanese War, some thirty thousand Jews, a disproportionate number, were sent to the front. Jewish recruits were generally dispatched to Siberia, so that they would always be near the theatre of military operations. A disproportionately large number of Jewish physicians in the reserves were mobilized at once. Out of the thirty physicians who were mobilized in Kiev, twenty-six were Jews. In Odessa, twenty-one of the thirty mobilized physicians were Jewish. Not being allowed to occupy any state or public office, they could be dispatched much easier than the Russian physicians, who would have to be diverted from their administrative services. Hundreds of Jewish physicians had to work and face the deadly fire of the Japanese because of the unjust law that deprived them of their right to civil service in times of peace (Dubnow, 1920, pp. 94–95).

This time, the ever-ticking time bomb of Russian Judeophobia was ignited by the intensified chauvinism that occurs in times of war, especially when the war in question was marked by the rapid failures of the Russian army and the surprising military superiority of the Japanese. True to form, the reactionary press, headed by *Novoye Vremya*, turned on its vicious antisemitic rumour mill, spreading the most preposterous accusations. Jews were secretly helping the Japanese, their "kinsmen by race," as an act of revenge for the Kishinev massacres. The public press of the capital circulated its absurd accusations nationwide, on a daily basis, such as "The Jews are exporting gold abroad, they are purchasing horses for Japan, they are collecting money to build cruisers for the Mikado, they are provoking England and America against Russia." It is clear that the agitators were using the war situation to instigate anti-Jewish violence based on the accusation of "treachery." The Jewish periodical *Voskhod*, in its issue of March 11, 1904, warned its readers of these incitements. A week later, the same paper published accounts of the panic which had spread among the Jewish population, particularly in the south (Dubnow, 1920, pp. 95–96).

All this incitement led to a number of pogroms in the Russian south which, at the beginning, followed the conventional pattern outlined earlier in the section dealing with the Kishinev pogrom, but they soon took on a new dynamic. The mobilized Russian reserve troops, deeply distraught by their impending departure to the deadly Manchurian front, where the Russian army was suffering a string of defeats, directed their anger towards the Jews, the customary defenceless scapegoats. On September 6 and 7, a violent pogrom took place in the Ukrainian city of Aleksandriya. An intoxicated horde of soldiers, accompanied by the street mob, set upon the looting of Jewish homes and attacking their inhabitants. On the sacred day of Yom Kippur, they invaded the synagogue, which was crowded with worshippers, and savagely butchered twenty people. The police made no attempt to stop the killings and looting. Only on the second day, when the violence continued unabated, were the Cossacks brought in to restore order (Dubnow, 1920, p. 100).

A month later, the pogroms perpetrated by the mobilized Russian reservists spread to the northern region of White Russia. During the pogrom in the city of Mogilev, committed by soldiers and local hooligans on October 10, the rioters attacked even the families of Jewish reservists who had gone to war. The government, unwilling to antagonize the soldiers who were needed at the front, refrained from taking any action against them or from coming to the aid of the victims (Dubnow, 1920, pp. 100–101).

In the course of these two years, 1903–1904, during which the internal war against the Jews was being exacerbated by the external war against Japan, more than 125,000 Jewish emigrants managed to escape to America (Dubnow, 1920, p. 104).

The year 1905 was a watershed year in the history of the tsarist regime. It was the attempt in November 1904 by the Minister of the Interior, Pyotr Svyatopolk-Mirski, to improve relations with the liberal elements of Russia that brought the movement for political emancipation into the open. For the first time, they could give public utterance to their secret dreams of a constitution. Both a conference of workers and a mass meeting of lawyers and other members of the intelligentsia adopted resolutions calling for the end of the autocratic order and the need to have all segments of the population participate in the work of legislation (Dubnow, 1920, p. 105).

While the government, in response to these demands, reluctantly and slowly granted minor concessions to the population at large, such as small improvements in the legal status of the peasantry, relaxation of the oppressive behaviour of the police and the severity of censorship, the Jews were excluded from any benefits resulting from these changes (Dubnow, 1920, p. 106).

A Tale of Two Histories – 1905–1917

The process of emancipation in Russia, which started when Svyatopolk-Mirski tentatively lifted the lid on authoritarian oppression in 1905, ran a parallel but different course for the two Russian nations which provide the context for this study. While the non-Jewish majority suffered the social and economic consequences of a self-serving oppressive regime, it was never subject to the ethnic cleansing horrors the Jewish community had to endure from both the government and their co-citizens. In spite of all the efforts of the Russian government to combat the revolutionary developments by granting some minor concessions to the general population, it continued to take out all its venom on the Jews by systematically blaming them for all the growing problems besetting the regime while, at the same time, inciting the Russian population by diverting their wrath towards the despised Jewish nation in their midst.

January 9, 1905, which marked the beginning of the open revolution, became known as "Bloody Sunday" following the tragic outcome of the mass demonstration of the striking working men of St. Petersburg, who, when they marched to the Winter Palace to present a petition to the Tsar for economic and political reforms, were greeted with a shower of bullets, resulting in a large number of victims. By replying with bullets to a peaceful appeal for reforms, the Tsar had set off a series of demonstrations, labour strikes and terrorist acts in the provinces. On the same day, Svyatopolk-Mirski was dismissed for his excessive leaning towards liberalism, ending any tendency by the government to give in to the growing demands for democratic reforms (Dubnow, 1920, pp. 106–107).

The general revolutionary movement in Russia was spreading to all sectors of the population. Professional organizations such as the leagues of railroad workers, engineers and lawyers were springing into existence. Railroad strikes and student strikes were occurring with increasing frequency. The government reacted to the demonstrations with rifle shots and Cossack whips. The extreme wing of the Socialist Party escalated their response to terrorist acts such as the assassination on February 17, 1905 of Grand Duke Sergei, the widely detested governor-general of Moscow, by a bomb thrown by a non-Jew, the Social Revolutionist Ivan Kalyayev (Dubnow, 1920, pp. 109–110).

By February 1905, Russian Jewry had decided to place its own demands before the government. Several mass petitions, demanding equal rights for Jews, were addressed to Witte. The thrust of these petitions was the demand for complete rights of national-cultural self-determination instead of the gradual half measures reserved for the Jewish community. The following two passages, from the petitions from the Jewish communities across the country, are typical of the demands voiced nationwide by the Jewish population:

> The Jews are waiting at last for their entire enfranchisement; they are waiting for a radical repeal of all restrictive laws, so that, enjoying freedom and equality with all others, they may shoulder to shoulder with the other citizens of this great country, work for its welfare and prosperity. [...] We expect equal rights, as human beings in whom the feeling of human dignity is alive, as conscience citizens in a modern body politic. (Dubnow, 1920, pp. 108–109)

At this point, the Jews of Russia felt that they needed a non-partisan political organization to expand their struggle for emancipation to all classes of Jewry. At the end of March 1905, at a conference held in Vilna, the League for the Attainment of Equal Rights for the Jewish People in Russia was formed. Its proclaimed object was "the realization to their full extent of the *civil, political, and national rights* of the Jewish people in Russia." According to Dubnow, this was the first attempt by a Jewish organization in modern history to ask not only for the civil and political but also the national emancipation of the Jewish people; the first attempt to obtain liberty for Jewry as a nationality, and not as a mere denominational group forming part of the dominant nation, as had been the case in Western Europe in the nineteenth century. The central bureau of the League was located in St. Petersburg and was composed of twenty-two elective members, half of whom lived in the capital and the other half in the provinces (Dubnow, 1920, pp. 111–112).

At this point, the Russian government feared that the growing demands for freedom, unleashed when Svyatopolk-Mirski lifted the lid off the Pandora's box of Russian oppression, were posing a serious threat to the tsarist government's hold on power. This caused the government of Nicholas II to focus all its attention and energies on reversing the tide by unleashing an all-out war against the burgeoning freedom-seeking efforts of the Russian population (Dubnow, 1920, p. 113).

The revolutionary tide met with ferocious resistance from the Tsar and his underlings. This is where the ultra-nationalist Black Hundreds were enlisted by the authorities to help carry out the repression of the freedom-seeking emancipatory movement. By unleashing the reactionary Russian underworld, the government hoped that it could subdue the progressives and revolutionaries and cast the entire revolutionary movement as the work of the Jews. To achieve the latter, the reactionaries set out to convince the Russian masses that "the enemies of Christ are the only enemies of the Tsar." The proclamation of the Black Hundreds' national society organizations across Russia read as follows:

> The shouts "Down with autocracy!" are the shouts of those blood-suckers who call themselves Zhyds, Armenians, and Poles…. Be on your guard against the Zhyds! All the misfortunes in our lives are due to the Zhyds. Soon, very soon, the great time will come where there will be no Zhyds in Russia. Down with the traitors! Down with the constitution! (Dubnow, 1920, pp. 113–114)

This incitement unleashed an openly organized wave of pogroms, which were often deliberately permitted or even engineered by the police and carried out with the participation of Cossacks and peasants. These pogroms, always fueled by excessive alcohol consumption, followed the usual pattern of plunder, murder and mutilation. The pogrom in the city of Kerch on July 31, 1905 contained all the elements the reactionary government forces had engineered to achieve their purposes. It was preceded, on July 27, by a peaceful political demonstration, in which the Jewish youth had participated. Four days later, the city-governor and gendarmerie chief organized a "patriotic" counter-demonstration during which the "patriotic" mobs, carrying a banner with a portrait of the Tsar and singing the Russian national anthem, destroyed Jewish houses and stores (Dubnow, 1920, pp. 114–117, 120).

During the summer of 1905, following the pattern of the military pogroms of 1904 which had been provoked by the Russian army's defeats on the Manchurian front, the soldiers and Cossacks, incited by the Black Hundreds' depiction of the Jews as the inner enemy, began to wreak their vengeance upon this convenient target by unleashing a series of vicious pogroms in Minsk (May 26), Brest-Litovsk (May 29–31), and Syedletz and Lodz (June 9). On June 30, the soldiery engineered a butchery in Bialystok where, for the entire day, they kept firing into peaceful Jewish crowds (Dubnow, 1920, pp. 119–120).

The months of August, September and October of 1905 were marked by a tug of war between the demands for increased civil liberties by all segments of the population and the determination of the government cabal, backed by their ultra-reactionary Black Hundred cohorts, to resist any infringement on their autocratic rule (Dubnow, 1920, pp. 125–126).

The events during those three months followed a course that was characterized by diametrically opposed objectives and tactics. The demands of the population were expressed openly and peacefully through petitions, non-violent demonstrations and strikes. At first, the government, faced with having to choose between violent repression and appeasing concessions, decided to calm the storm by opting for the latter. On October 17, 1905, an imperial manifesto promised to grant the Russian people the full range of civil liberties, including liberty of speech and assemblage and a legislative assembly (duma), in which all segments of the population would have a voice. While it failed to make all citizens equal before the law or to grant equal rights to the various nationalities, the manifesto achieved its purpose by creating the impression that the revolutionaries had succeeded in transforming Russia from a state based on the rule of power into a body politic based on the rule of law (Dubnow, 1920, pp. 126–127).

The secretly planned government reaction, which had been plotted at the same time that the imperial manifesto was being drafted, set up the newly optimistic population for a rude awakening. On October 18, one day after the manifesto was issued, the carefully concealed army of counter-revolutionaries was unleashed across the country, without any warning, to suppress the rapidly growing freedom-seeking movement (Dubnow, 1920, p. 127).

True to custom, the government, reluctant to tackle the entire Russian population, chose to deflect the public anger at their repressive government by making the Jews the main target of their violent retribution. The wave of pogroms, amounting to several hundred, that swept the country over the course of an entire week (October 18–25, 1905) reached an unprecedented level of Judeophobic violence. By comparison, less than ten percent of the pogroms were directed against Christian members of the civil liberties-seeking movement (Dubnow, 1920, pp. 127–128).

Although it is impossible, within the scope of this study, to provide a full description of each pogrom, it is necessary to appreciate the full gravity of these events to provide a detailed account of the terrible pogrom that took place in Odessa, which lasted four entire days. The rioters were openly assisted by the police and troops and were encouraged by the active support of city governor D. M. Neidhart and the criminal inactivity of the military governor, A. V. Kaulbars. The Jews were able to beat off the hooligans in self-defence but were no match for the troops and police. The battle against the Jews of Odessa resulted in over three hundred dead, thousands of wounded or crippled, one hundred and forty widows, five hundred and ninety-three orphans, and more than forty thousand Jews materially ruined (Dubnow, 1920, p. 129).

The violent counter-revolution, which broke out on October 17, 1905, the day the Tsar's manifesto was promulgated, left the country in a state of near chaos. All hopes of the government relaxing its autocratic hold on power were dashed. This resulted in increased labour strikes and the burning of manors and estates by the emerging peasant movement. The government responded by adopting a policy of extreme repression, including the ongoing propaganda war against the Jews (Dubnow, 1920, pp. 130–131).

Russian Jewry, which had borne the brunt of the October outburst of government vengeance, found itself isolated but not defeated. The progressive elements of Russian society were too preoccupied with their own plight to offer any support to the Jewish people, which had become the scapegoat of the counter-revolution. By now, however, Russian Jewry had shed its quietistic acceptance of its miserable social condition and found strength and courage in the bond of unity they had forged among themselves when, as was noted earlier, they had, in March of the same year, founded the League for the Attainment of Equal Rights for the Jewish People in Russia. In response to the horrible events of October, the League held its second convention in St. Petersburg. During its four-day session (November 22–25), the League gave strong public expression to its feeling of profound national indignation (Dubnow, 1920, p. 131).

The tsarist government and its powerful reactionary members and supporters obstinately continued to suppress the growing efforts of the Russian population to throw off the shackles of tsarist tyranny and kept following up their sporadic minor concessions with brutal and often lethal acts of suppression designed to eradicate any democratic advances. The dumas (imperial legislatures), first established after the 1905 Revolution, were being abolished at the Tsar's whim whenever the progressive elements were asking for or achieving more progress than the regime was willing to grant. The Jewish population was always excluded from any significant progress that was achieved by the non-Jewish population and was uninterruptedly kept in the crosshairs of the Jew-baiting imperial forces. Devastating pogroms continued to be the government's weapon of choice to suppress the Jewish drive for freedom and equality.

One of the main issues facing Russian Jewry, at this time, was the question of legalization. From the time that the government of Nicholas I (1825–1855) had banned the Jewish *Kahal* (community), Russian Jewry had been without legal community organization. Both for practical reasons and as a matter of principle, this problem had become an urgent issue. To deal with it, a Jewish congress was held in Kovno in 1909. It was attended by 120 delegates from 46 cities. In spite of representing politically and socially diverse segments of the Jewish community, the congress was unanimously in favour of seeking its legalization as an administrative body, with the right of taxing its members. While it was a step forward, it was short-lived and ineffectual. The Political Bureau, established as an advisory board to the Jewish deputies to the Fourth State Duma and which had cross-party representation, was far more important (Aronson, 1966, pp. 168–169).

Lawyer and author Jacob Frumkin, who was a member of the political advisory committee to the Jewish delegation in the Fourth Duma from 1914 to 1918, noted that the Political Bureau was set up by the four non-socialist Jewish organizations existing in St. Petersburg for the purpose of maintaining regular contact with the Jewish deputies in the Duma. Although this is not the place to elaborate on the different programmes of these organizations, for the sake of historical accuracy, it will suffice to identify them as the Jewish People's Group, the Zionists, the Folkspartei and the Jewish Democratic. The Political Bureau existed until the revolution in 1917 and was particularly active during the years following the outbreak of World War I in 1914 (Frumkin, 1966, p. 56).

World War I introduced a new tragic chapter in the history of Russian Jewry. When Germany initially occupied Poland in the western provinces, it virtually divided the six million Russian Jewish population in half. The Russians' military setbacks generated a brutal increase of antisemitism at the front, spurred by the army's incompetent command which sought to shift the blame for its failures upon the Jews. This resulted in deportations and charges of spying and treason. In 1915 alone, Jewish relief committees had to support more than 250,000 refugees and deportees (Aronson, 1966, p. 169).

Upon the outbreak of the war, Jews participated enthusiastically in the wave of patriotism that swept the country. Many Jewish youths volunteered for service, among them students who had gone abroad to study because of the quota restrictions that barred them from universities at home. The percentage of Jews in the service, as well as of army causalities, exceeded the percentage of Jews in the country's population. Yet, in spite of this wholehearted manifestation of patriotism, the war still brought untold hardships for the Jews (Frumkin, 1966, p. 58).

A few days after the war began, the local military commanders in front-line zones ordered the total evacuation of Jews. Ten days after the outbreak of the war, the commandant of the Myszensk settlement, near Lodz, ordered all Jews, numbering almost 2,000, to leave the area at once. When the governor overruled the order so that the Jews could return, his ruling was ignored by the commandant. Such mass deportations by order of local authorities were particularly frequent in Russian Poland, where antisemitic feelings ran especially high. False accusations of treasonable acts committed by Jews were circulated on an almost daily basis, leading to antisemitic outbreaks, such as the September 1914 anti-Jewish riots in the city of Suwalki in north-eastern Poland (Frumkin, 1966, pp. 58–59).

Both at the front and in the front-line areas, military authorities charged Jews with espionage and collaboration with the Germans in the occupied sectors of Russian territory. In many cases, the accused were shot without trial or under court-martial sentences, where the accused were entirely without defence. Some of them had no knowledge of Russian and could not understand the charges. Since there was no interpreter, they were quite helpless (Frumkin, 1966, p. 63).

In many areas, the military authorities engaged in the practice of detaining Jews as hostages. On December 4, 1914, twelve hostages were taken at Sokhachev. The hostages were replaced by new men nearly every day. It was suspected that ransom was exacted as a price of release. On December 24, three hostages were executed without any reason being given (Frumkin, 1966, p. 64).

The harshness with which the military command treated the Jewish population in the front-line areas knew no bounds. The combat orders of the 18th Army Corps dated May 14, 1915 included instruction that "The Jews are to be driven out in the direction of the enemy troops" (Frumkin, 1966, p. 64).

Repeated fabricated accusations of treason committed by Jews were used as pretexts for severe punishment. These incidents were so numerous that a detailed description would require a volume of its own. The events in Kuzhi, in the Kovno province, provide a telling example of the treacherous nature of the accusations and of the inhuman execution of the punishment. The General Headquarters of the Supreme Commander in Chief had reported a treacherous act allegedly committed by the Jewish residents. The communication was circulated among all army units and contained the following excerpt:

> On April 30th, at 12:00 noon, the Corps Commander issued orders requesting that all men, down to the last private, be advised of an incident which had taken place on the night of April 25th–26th. [...] While carrying out a combat assignment, 151st Pyatigorsk regiment captured the village of Kuzhi and was billeted there. According to the testimony of participants in the action, a number of German soldiers had been hidden in cellars by Jewish residents before the village was taken over by our troops. At the sound of a single shot, several fires broke out simultaneously throughout the village, and the Germans rushed to the house occupied by the Commander of the Pyatigorsk regiment. At the same time the enemy forces (two battalions supported by cavalry) launched an advance and broke into the village, after destroying two of our pickets. When the flaming house began to collapse, the commander, Col. Danilov, gave orders to burn the regimental colors, all but the brace. After this order had been carried out, Col. Danilov jumped out of the window, but was shot down. Some units of the Pyatigorsk regiment, which had at that moment arrived on the scene, were able to force the enemy to retreat. The remnants of the burned banners were retrieved from the records of the stove. (Frumkin, 1966, p. 65)

Reports describing these alleged acts of treason were published in every newspaper and spread by posters distributed throughout the country (Frumkin, 1966, pp. 65–66). Jacob Frumkin, the author of this account, took an active part in the first authoritative refutation of these charges. He reports that he had learned that Bystritsky, marshal of the landed gentry of Shavli County in which the hamlet of Kuzhi was situated, was in St. Petersburg and that he was indignant over the charge of treason. At Frumkin's request, a meeting was arranged at which Bystritsky met with his colleague from the political bureau, Oscar Gruzenberg, and himself. According to Bystritsky, who said that he knew every house in Kuzhi, very few of them had cellars, and those were suitable for little else but the storage of potatoes. Not even a dozen men could be hidden in such cellars. Moreover, only two houses were owned by Jews; the rest belonged to Lithuanians. In Bystritsky's opinion, what had actually happened was that the commanding officer of the unit which had driven out the Germans and occupied the settlement must have neglected to take security measures for the night. The detachment was then surprised by the Germans. To cover this up, the story of a Jewish betrayal was fabricated and later publicized by the General Headquarters. At Frumkin's and Gruzenberg's request, Bystritsky outlined these facts in a letter to the editor published in the newspaper *Rech*. The subsequent investigation by civil authorities established the falsity of the accusations relating to the Kuzhi incident. Unfortunately, the truth came out too late, as the alleged case of treason had already led to wholesale deportations of Jews from large sectors of the Kovno province in Lithuania and the Courland region in western Latvia (Frumkin, 1966, pp. 66–67).

The deportations were carried out with unprecedented brutality. On the evening of May 3, the Jewish residents of Kovno were notified by the police that they were to leave the city by no later than midnight of May 5. No exceptions were granted. The deportees included hospitalized patients in grave conditions, women about to give birth, inmates of insane asylums, wounded soldiers, and the families of men in active service (Frumkin, 1966, p. 67).

Frumkin noted that the records of the secret sessions held by the Council of Ministers from July 16 through September 2, 1915 showed that the deportations were strongly condemned even in government circles. A. P. Yakhontov, the former assistant office chief for the Council of Ministers, who kept the records, noted that "even irreconcilable antisemites complained to members of the Cabinet, protesting the outrageous handling of the Jews at the front" (Frumkin, 1966, pp. 67–68). Under pressure from the government, which insisted that a wholesale deportation would have serious and damaging consequences, the military command, on May 10 and 11, gave orders to "halt" the deportations. The fact that, by that time, the deportations, which had been completed by May 5, could no longer be "halted" demonstrates the deceitfulness of the military's actions. The deportees, shipped out in east-bound trains, were on their way, crowded into freight cars, many of which had the mark "SPIES" chalked on the outside. Even the terms set by the military authorities for allowing the deportees to come back were totally unacceptable.

The military took a number of rabbis and wealthy Jews as hostages "with a warning that in case of any treasonable acts committed by the Jewish population, the hostages would be hanged." At first, the hostages had been taken forcibly. Now, they were asked to deliver hostages of their own accord as the price for being allowed to return to their hometowns. Frumkin notes that despite their desperate situation, the deportees turned down the humiliating conditions under which they would have been allowed to return to their homes (Frumkin, 1966, pp. 70–71).

As noted in the historical records published by the aforementioned Yakhontov in the *Archive of the Russian Revolution*, the government, headed by Ivan Goremykin, tried hard to persuade the Supreme Commander-in-Chief to revoke the brutal anti-Jewish measures and to refrain from taking further steps in this direction. Yet, in spite of consistent pressure by the civil authorities, General Yanushkevitch, the chief proponent of such measures, remained intransigent and did not hesitate to make the Council of Ministers aware of his position. In his words, "all measures taken against the Jews were woefully inadequate." "Far more drastic steps" were needed, and he was prepared to take them. Prince Shcherbatov, Minister of the Interior, in his statement at the August 4, 1915 session of the Council of Ministers, acknowledged the futility of the efforts exerted by the government in the following words:

> Our attempts to make the General Headquarters see reason remained fruitless. We have exhausted all available means of combating a policy inspired by prejudice... All of us, individually and collectively, have consistently spoken, written, appealed and complained about the matter. But apparently the omnipotent Yanushkevitch does not feel bound by considerations of state. It has been his consistent and deliberate policy to foster a general prejudice in the Army against all Jews and to blame them for our military reverses. Such a strategy was bound to have its effect. Current upsurge of violent antisemitism is affecting the men in the service. I am reluctant to believe this, but – since you are here among our own – I will admit my suspicion that Gen Yanushkevitch perhaps needs this sort of an alibi as suggested at the previous meeting by A.V. Krivoshein. (*Archive of the Russian Revolution*, vol. 18, p. 43, quoted in Frumkin, 1966, p. 72)

Frumkin observed that the less successful the military operations directed by Yanushkevitch were, the more drastic the anti-Jewish measures taken by the Army command became. Trumped-up charges against the Jews increased in scope and number. At a meeting of the Council of Ministers on August 12, Alexander Krivoshein, the Minister of Agriculture, said that Yanushkevitch's presence at the General Headquarters was more dangerous than the German divisions, especially if he had already learned of the threat of his position (Frumkin, 1966, pp. 72–73).

It is not that the Cabinet members sympathized with the Jews. They were strongly opposed to the drastic treatment of the Jews by the military authorities because they realized that such measures were detrimental to the war effort and damaging for the country as a whole. However, reports of excesses attributed to General Yanushkevitch had reached the Allies, and Russia's prestige abroad suffered as a result. At the same time, Germany used the anti-Jewish measures of the Russian military command as a basis for anti-Russian propaganda, especially in the neutral countries (Frumkin, 1966, p. 73).

In August 1915, the Supreme Command was taken over by the Tsar and Grand Duke Nikolay Nikolayevich was transferred to the Caucasus, together with General Yanushkevitch. While, consequently, no further anti-Jewish measures by the military on a scale comparable to the excesses inspired by Yanushkevitch were reported from the other major fronts, explosive antisemitic moods continued to spread in the army as stated at the meeting of the Council of Ministers by Prince Shcherbatov (Frumkin, 1966, p. 76).

Paradoxically, in spite of the fact that the government had vigorously protested against the anti-Jewish acts of General Yanushkevitch, the government itself seemed to follow in his footsteps. The Ministry of Internal Affairs and the Ministry of Finance circulated two appalling memoranda stigmatizing the Jews. The first was signed by the Acting Director of the Department of Police, Kafafov, and became known as the "Kafafov circular" (Frumkin, 1966, p. 76).

This memorandum was addressed to "Governors, City Governors, Chief Regional Administrators and Provincial Security Policy Headquarters." It claimed that the Department of Police had received reports that the Jews were hard at work conducting vigorous revolutionary propaganda through numerous underground organizations. It accused the Jews of using various methods to stir up general unrest in Russia. These included subversive agitation in the Armed Forces and in the major industrial and manufacturing centres of the Russian Empire and the instigation of strikes. The memorandum also accused the Jews of creating shortages of food and high prices to whip up general discontent and hatred of the war. Towards this "sinister" end, the memorandum claimed, Jewish merchants hoarded their wares, delayed shipments and obstructed the unloading of goods at railway terminals. The memorandum goes into great detail about the Jewish efforts to undermine the people's confidence in Russian currency by issuing token money and by spreading persistent rumours that the Russian government was bankrupt and that Jewish agents exacerbated the situation by buying up all available silver and copper coins at inflated prices. The memorandum also cited reports that the Jews were trying to bring about the abolition of the Pale of Settlement through their extensive participation in these "dangerous and subversive activities" (Frumkin, 1966, pp. 76–77).

The second circular, issued by the Ministry of Finance, provided additional fuel to the Judeophobic content of the first one. It claimed that according to "unverified reports" reaching the Department of Police, the Germans were planning to burn the standing crops in various parts of the empire for the purpose of undermining the welfare of Russia's peasant population. According to the same reports, the circular claimed that Germans, listed officially as Russian subjects, were helping to carry out this plan, "which is also aided by Jews, recruited for the purpose through bribery." The circular went on to suggest that tax inspectors, as part of their duties, should acquaint the rural district and village administrations with the contents of the memorandum as "such subversive activities, should they actually take place, must be immediately suppressed – if need be, by the most drastic means" (Frumkin, 1966, pp. 77–78).

These two circulars were of such insidious nature that they triggered an urgent inquiry in the State Duma. On March 8, 1916, the Duma acknowledged the urgency of the inquiry by a vote of 91 to 49. What followed was a vituperative debate between the progressive and conservative factions as to how to deal with the issue. The most egregious outburst came from the extreme right member Zamyslovsky who, throughout his speech, fulminated viciously against "the kikes" and the "kike-inspired inquiry" (Frumkin, 1966, p. 78).

At the next session, explanations were offered by high officials on behalf of the two ministries involved. The Deputy Minister of Finance stated that the circular had been issued without the knowledge of the minister and was rescinded as soon as he found out. Although the Minister of Finance, Pyotr Bark, was not known to be an antisemite, he took no action to discipline his subordinates responsible for circulating the memorandum despite the admittedly doubtful nature of its contents. The Minister of Internal Affairs was represented by Kafafov, above whose signature the circular had been drafted. He claimed that the information it contained had been received from "highly authoritative sources." According to Frumkin, Kafafov was referring to the Supreme Command. To whitewash his actions, Kafafov claimed that, both before and after issuing the circular, he had been signing orders requesting that measures be taken to prevent anti-Jewish riots (Frumkin, 1966, p. 79).

After these explanations, the voices clamouring for the rejection of the inquiry started to gain the upper hand, and, in the end, nothing came of the inquiry. Even Bomash, the Jewish deputy who had been the first to call for an inquiry, declared that since one circular had been rescinded by the Ministry of Finance and the author of the second memorandum had signed a number of circulars directing the prevention of anti-Jewish riots, he would withdraw the inquiry (Frumkin, 1966, p. 80).

Frumkin noted that the outcome of the move against the circulars had a highly disconcerting effect upon the Jewish community. In the Jewish press and at meetings of Jewish societies, the Jewish deputies were criticized for lacking courage. In Frumkin's opinion, they were placed in a difficult position. They had to decide on the spot whether to let the matter be voted upon, which meant certain rejection, or to withdraw the inquiry. He acknowledges that they would perhaps have been more correct if they had chosen the first option but that, in view of the enormous responsibility involved, the deputies could not reasonably be blamed for the decision they had taken (Frumkin, 1966, pp. 80–81).

Less than one year after Kafafov's circular had been debated in the Duma, the February Revolution of 1917 swept away all legal barriers against the Jews. The decree on equal rights was signed on March 20, 1917 and made public two days later, on March 22 (Frumkin, 1966, pp. 82–83).

The October 1917 Revolution sealed the end of the tsarist regime and marked the beginning of a new era in the history of Russia. It is clear from the facts related in this chapter that one major constant during this period was the relentless persecution of Russian Jewry by both the tsarist government and the non-Jewish Russian population. The following story tellingly underscores the never-waning intensity of the moral depravity of the Russian tsarist regime at both the government and the public level.

Shortly before the revolution of 1917, Frumkin and his colleagues learned the story told by a Jewish soldier who was then in a St. Petersburg hospital. According to this soldier, whose name was Medvedovsky and who held three St. George Crosses for valour, his regiment had recently been placed under a new commander – a violent antisemite. Soon after his appointment, a ceremony was held in which a number of soldiers received decorations. When the commander learned that some of the decorated men were Jews, he refused to continue the ceremony and abruptly walked out, leaving his subordinate officer to continue the distribution of awards (Frumkin, 1966, p. 81).

The soldier related that, following this incident, attempts were made to kill off the Jews who held decorations. One of them, whose name was Dankovasky, had been sent out on reconnaissance duty. Before he left, the officer had ordered his sergeant to shoot him during this mission, allegedly for attempting to desert. The second man chosen for this fate was Medvedovsky, whose sergeant had received similar orders from his officer. The sergeant confessed to him and said that he was unable to carry out the order; he would therefore merely wound him. It was as a result of this wound that Medvedovsky was sent to the hospital (Frumkin, 1966, pp. 81–82).

Frumkin and his colleagues thought that his story could not be true and that the soldier must have been suffering from delusions. Frumkin's colleague Oscar Gruzenberg decided to see the soldier at the hospital to verify the story. He spoke to the hospital doctors, who assured him that Medvedovsky showed no symptoms of mental derangement. His conversation with Medvedovsky convinced him that the story was absolutely true. This was confirmed by letters that Medvedovsky received from the regimental priest and his company commander (Frumkin, 1966, p. 82).

Gruzenberg went with the story to General Makarenko, chief military judge and head of the Military Justice Department, with whom he was on excellent terms. Makarenko, however, urged Gruzenberg to refrain from any attempts at initiating an investigation. Pursuing the affair, he said, might result in serious consequences, both for Medvedovsky and for Gruzenberg himself. When Gruzenberg persisted, Makarenko, after consulting with the War Minister, instructed General Lykoshin to investigate the matter. A few weeks before the revolution of 1917, Lykoshin confirmed to Gruzenberg that Medvedovsky had told the truth. The outbreak of the revolution put an end to this affair (Frumkin, 1966, p. 82). The nature and timing of this incident graphically illustrate that the insidious dynamic of virulent antisemitism was, until the very end, a permanent element in the social and political fabric of Tsarist Russia.

The year 1917 witnessed two watershed events in the history of the world and of the Jewish people. The Russian Revolution of October 25, 1917 signified the end of the three-century-long reign of the Romanov dynasty and its oppressive dominion over the diaspora's largest Jewish community. Then, on November 2, 1917, the British government issued the Balfour Declaration to the Jewish people.

Against all hopeful expectations, but in line with the omnipresent systemic symptom of antisemitism, the Bolshevik Revolution of 1917 did not end the persecution of the Jewish population of Russia. Brendan

McGeever, author and lecturer in the sociology of racialization and antisemitism at Birkbeck, University of London, noted that despite the vast literature on the 1917 revolutions, there has been little scholarly interest in the question of antisemitism during this period and that 1917 represents the least analyzed chapter of the waves of antisemitic violence that span the late imperial and revolutionary years (1871–1922). Yet, Russian society in 1917 bore witness to a sharp increase in antisemitism. Violent antisemitism in 1917 was closely connected to the ebb and flow of revolution (McGeever, 2017, p. 236).

In his detailed analysis of the antisemitic manifestations among the various political factions still at loggerheads during the period leading up to the October 25 revolution, McGeever explains that when, in mid-late 1917, the doors were opened wide to tens of thousands of new Bolshevik party members, many of them were politicized for the first time. As a result, the Bolsheviks had truly become a mass party. It was inevitable that, under these circumstances, the Bolshevik project would unwittingly attract racist and antisemitic elements and thus was not always going to be in sync with the thoughts and feelings of the party rank and file as a whole. The seriousness of this problem was demonstrated when, in 1918 and 1919, in many regions of the former Pale of Settlement, the Red Army found swathes of pogromists in their midst marching behind the slogan "Smash the Yids, long live Soviet power!" (McGeever, 2017, p. 248).

A number of prominent voices warned of the danger of increasing antisemitic reactions. On October 15, 1917, a lead article in the liberal Jewish newspaper *Evreiskaia Nedelia* claimed that

> Comrade Lenin and his fellow Bolsheviks call in their speeches and articles on the proletariat to turn their words into action, but […] wherever Slavic crowds gather, the turning of "words into action" means, in reality, "striking out at the Yids." (McGeever, 2017, p. 250)

The following week, the same publication warned that, in the minds of the Petrograd masses, "social revolution" had become synonymous with "Jewish pogrom." As late as October 28, 1917, the Mensheviks' Petrograd Committee issued an appeal to workers in the capital, warning that all forms of protest would inevitably lead to pogroms:

> The Bolsheviks have seduced the ignorant workers and soldiers, and the cry of "All power to the Soviets!" will all too easily turn into "Beat the Jews, beat the shopkeepers." (McGeever, 2017, p. 250)

McGeever noted that, contrary to these alarmist predictions, there were no mass pogroms in the Russian interior in the hours and days immediately following the Bolshevik seizure of power. The revolution did not immediately translate into antisemitic violence, as had been predicted. However, just six months later, in the spring of 1918, in the former Pale of Settlement, the warnings from the previous year began to ring true. In towns and cities of northeast Ukraine, Bolshevik power was consolidated through anti-Jewish violence by the local cadres of the party and Red Guards. While these pogroms did not occur in Petrograd but in the different context of Ukraine, they showed that the fears of the anti-Bolshevik socialist left in late 1917 were not entirely without substance (McGeever, 2017, pp. 250–251).

McGeever noted that the Bolsheviks faced not only the challenge of combating antisemitism among the radical right but also that of how to deal with the overlap between Bolshevik radicalism and antisemitism within the movement itself. In 1918 and 1919, when the Civil War extended to the former Pale of Settlement, where the bulk of the Jewish population resided and where the Red Army was fighting for "Soviet power," distinctions between "antisemite" and "internationalist" and between "revolutionary" and "counter-revolutionary" often collapsed along an axis of antisemitic violence (McGeever, 2017, pp. 251–252).

The story of the ferocious pogroms that ensued in 1918 and 1919 was detailed in McGeever's book (McGeever, 2019), and was covered earlier in dramatic detail by Victoria Khiterer, Associate Professor of History at Millersville University and author. Her research, based on primary sources such as archives and memoirs, draws a stark but illuminating picture of the nature and extent of anti-Jewish pogroms during this turbulent period. She noted that the anti-Jewish violence which followed the outbreak of revolution in the Tsarist Empire in February 1917, and which intensified during the Russian Civil War until November 1920, when the last of the anti-Bolshevik forces were expelled from southern Russia, was on a larger scale than any experienced by Jews in Eastern Europe until the Holocaust. She described the Civil War as a three-way struggle between the Bolsheviks, who had established power in Moscow and Petrograd, the anti-Bolshevik White Russians who had taken control of Kuban in south Russia and subsequently in central and eastern Ukraine, where they were trying to re-establish the pre-war Russian political order, and the peoples of the Baltic and the Caucasus regions, who hoped to use the collapse of the Tsarist Empire to establish independent states. An additional toxic factor was that throughout the Civil War, large parts of the countryside were controlled by peasant anarchist bands (Khiterer, 2015, p. iii).

Khiterer noted the similarity of the wave of pogroms during this period to earlier anti-Jewish outbreaks. It was fueled by the customary suspicion and distrust with which the peasantry regarded the Jews and by the hostility of the Orthodox Church, which now also regarded the Jews as principally responsible for the Bolshevik Revolution. What was new was that the scale was far greater than the pogroms of 1881–1884 and 1903–1097. The fact that Ukraine had been the scene of the shifting Eastern Front in the First World War, with the brutality and expropriations this had entailed, meant that the local Jewish communities, whose cohesiveness had already been undermined by the Russian expulsions of 1914 and 1915, were in a highly vulnerable state. Ukrainian nationalism and modern antisemitism added new sources of hostility to the traditional dislike of the Jews. Many Ukrainians resented the fact that on January 22, 1918, the Jewish parties in the Ukrainian Central Council did not vote for Ukrainian independence. Even though most Jewish political organizations were opposed to Bolshevism, they were still perceived as a threat and were rumoured to be seeking to win power. Ukrainians saw violence as a means of keeping the Jews down (Khiterer, 2015, p. vii).

The estimates of the number of people who died during the anti-Jewish violence accompanying the Civil War support Khiterer's observation noted above that the anti-Jewish violence in the wake of the Russian Revolution was on a larger scale than previously experienced by Jews in Eastern Europe. The "most reliable" estimates she refers to include the admittedly conservative number of 50,000 to 60,000 made by Nakhum Gergel, a former Deputy Minister of Jewish Affairs in the Ukrainian Government; a final number of dead probably exceeding 100,000, according to Sergei Gusev-Orenburgskii, a Kiev researcher who worked for the Russian Red Cross providing aid to pogrom victims; the total of 120,000 given by Elias Heifetz; the total of 100,194 estimated by the Committee for the Jewish Community based on inquiries made in early 1921 in relation to its provision of aid to pogrom victims; and the figure of 150,000 (125,000 in Ukraine and 25,000 in Belarus) estimated by the sociologist Yakov Lestchinsky and included in the study carried out by Z. Mindlin, deputy head of the Jewish Department. These estimates do not include the many more who were wounded or raped, while as many as 200,000 children were orphaned, and many also suffered psychological after-effects (Khiterer, 2015, p. v).

It is beyond the scope of this study to detail the numerous incidences of brutal murders, torture, rapes, public threats and insults inflicted on the Jewish population at the mercy of the intermittently advancing and withdrawing warring factions. These are described at great length in

Khiterer's detailed account. The main reason for including this bloody episode in this book, even though it extends beyond November 2, 1917, the date of the Balfour Declaration, is the fact that it completely invalidates the position of the anti-Zionist leaders of the Anglo-Jewish community who claimed in their submissions to the British War Cabinet in October 1917 that the Russian Revolution had put an end to the plight of Russian Jewry and that, therefore, there was no longer a need for a Jewish homeland in Palestine. The details of these submissions and their effect on the wording of the Balfour Declaration are covered in more depth in *Chapter 6: What's in a Word – Political Word-Craftsmanship*.

Conclusion

The history of the pogroms represents the saga of the resilience of the captive nation of Russian Jewry at the mercy of a genocide-minded tsarist regime, which attempted with all the means available to them at the time, including the systemic Judeophobic attitude of its non-Jewish population that was always ready to burst out, to rid its social fabric of its most civilized and potentially most productive element. As we have seen, while the Jews, through their newly established national body, continued to hope that they could achieve their aim of equal participation in the political life of Russia, the unprecedented outbreak of violence against the Jewish communities, combined with the stated goals of the new government policies, were so harsh as to drive them to consider emigration as the only solution to their predicament. For the impoverished Jewish masses in the shtetls who had not been exposed to the concept of emancipation and the ideas of the equal rights of man, the only hope of survival lay in the escape to more hospitable environments, which in their pre-emancipation minds primarily meant America. For the minority, educated in the modern concept of nationhood, it meant a return to their ancient homeland, which they had never abandoned in their hearts and minds but which they now envisaged as a practical possibility.

It was in this epic struggle that the post-emancipation concept of modern political Zionism was born. Like the birth of a human being, which is the result of the life-giving process that occurs in the womb, the rebirth of the Jewish nation, consecrated by the Balfour Declaration on November 2, 1917, has most of its roots in the tragic but also heroic century-long episode of the martyrdom of the Jewish people during the tsarist regime. How Zionist political thinking arose and developed is the subject of the next chapter, *The Development of Zionist Political Thinking.*

CHAPTER FOUR

THE DEVELOPMENT OF ZIONIST POLITICAL THINKING

Introduction

When the antisemitic outbursts continued to proliferate during the era of enlightenment and emancipation, which had given hope of social acceptance to the Jewish populations in Tsarist Russia as well as in Western Europe, the major Jewish thinkers of the time came to the conclusion that only as a self-governing nation with a Jewish majority could the Jewish people put an end to the relentless persecution they had suffered in the diaspora. The leading philosophical minds who expressed the social implications of this thought process were the forerunners of the political leaders through whom this mindset evolved into the Zionist agenda, which culminated in the promulgation of the Balfour Declaration.

A number of brilliant Jewish thinkers throughout Europe, and especially in Russia, had, throughout the middle decades of the nineteenth century, developed impressive theories about the necessity and ways for the Jews to emerge from their captivity-style ghetto existence and embrace the emancipation era style of life. These include Yehudah Alkalai (1798–1878), Zvi Hirsch Kalischer (1795–1874), Nachman Krochmal (1785–1840) and Moses Hess (1812–1875). While an extensive description of their thoughts and influence falls beyond the scope of this book, it is important to note the common thread that links them to the body of neo-political nationalist thinking that had entered the Jewish world at this time in history. The common denominator that marks their efforts is the realization that the only road to Jewish national redemption is the one that is paved with the political steps that are required to lead the Jews back to the Promised Land by their own practical endeavours and not by impotent prayerful supplications.

A direct sampling of their writings and a discussion of their thinking and of the reasons for their lack of impact in their own time can be found in Arthur Hertzberg's *The Zionist Idea*. Although they were an overture to the history of Zionism, in their time – the middle of the nineteenth century – their work had little influence. They were so quickly forgotten that the Zionism which arose again in the 1880s and 1890s had no sense of indebtedness or linkage to these earlier figures (Hertzberg, 1959, p. 32). All that they produced was theory, with little relation to real life. According to Hertzberg, two major shocks, the Russian pogroms of 1881 and after and the Dreyfus affair in 1894, transformed Zionism from closet philosophy into a mass movement and a maker of history (Hertzberg, 1959, p. 42). The coverage in the previous chapter of the history of Russian Jewry during the tsarist regimes confirms the significance of the Russian pogroms. Attribution of the same weight to the Dreyfus affair, however, is not borne out by the facts, as will become clear from the section in this book devoted to Theodor Herzl and to the developments in Central and Western Europe that shaped his thinking.

For the purpose of tracing back the roots of the Balfour Declaration, we shall identify only the main contributors to the body of modern Zionist thinking that ignited the fires of the Zionist political movement and propelled it onto the path that led to that monumental historical event. Those who joined the ranks after that, while essential to the ultimate outcome of the Zionist project, could chronologically not have influenced the political process that led to the promulgation of the Declaration.

Historically, demands for social change by the oppressed have always been initiated by the few among the intellectual elite who had the opportunity to educate themselves socially and the ability to formulate and express their perceptions of the issues and their visions for a solution. Like pebbles tossed in a pond that cause a ripple effect of widening circles, they caused a political awakening among growing numbers of like-minded followers. They constituted the philosophical wellsprings that fed the growing stream of national self-realization that would eventually achieve the critical mass of a national movement.

The first manifestations of Zionist political activity are generally traced back to the second half of the nineteenth century. The conditions of Jewish life, at that time, were far from uniform throughout the world and were reflective of the socio-political level of development of the societies in which they found themselves. This became a period of first-time developments in the Jewish history of the modern era. For the first time, the seismic movements that were about to alter the geopolitical map of the colonial world also spawned the thought of the possibility of the removal of the suffocating grip of the Ottoman Empire on the Middle Eastern world.

The lure of Palestine was the appeal to which the dominant strain in the Zionist movement spoke. The novelty of Zionism was its ability to integrate the lure of Palestine within what might be regarded as quintessential nineteenth-century nationalism (Gelvin, 2005, p. 44).

How to expand its constituency among an often-sceptical Jewish population was another matter. The existential crisis of the 1881–1882 pogroms in Russia transformed the leading protagonists of Jewish emancipation into the torch lighters and bearers of modern political Zionism. Moshe Leib Lilienblum, Leo Pinsker and Peretz Smolenskin typify this transformation from assimilationists to Zionists.

Moshe Leib Lilienblum

The strongest and perhaps the most articulate supporter of immigration to Palestine who appeared in the pro-*Haskala* Jewish periodical *Razsvet* was Moshe Leib Lilienblum (Berk, 1985, p. 107). Lilienblum was typical of the new generation of educated Russian Jews who ran the gamut of the clashing values that characterized Jewish life in Russia in the turbulent years between 1860 and 1900. Born in 1843, Lilienblum first became a scholar of the Talmud and spent five years (1864–1869) teaching in the yeshivah in the central Lithuanian town of Vilkomir. During this period, he also immersed himself in the current *Haskala* literature which was antithetical to the legalistic rigidity of the Talmud. He came to the conclusion that moderate religious reforms were required to harmonize religion with the spirit of the times. In 1869, he fled to Odessa in search of a thorough secular education. His religious faith was superseded by his concern for the destiny of the individual in concrete material terms. By the end of 1870, he devoted himself exclusively to his secular studies in preparation for entrance into the university, propelled by the belief that the class struggle held the only hope for a better future for all mankind. It was the shock of the 1881 pogroms that shattered this utopian dream (Hertzberg, 1959, pp. 167–168).

Lilienblum's reaction to the 1881 pogroms in Russia, which he perceived as the failure of emancipation to break the pernicious stranglehold of antisemitism on any tendencies to improve the quality of social life of the Jewish populations in the European diaspora, exemplifies a leap forward both in the level of the understanding of the fundamental problems inherent in Judeo-Christian relations at the time as well as in the rational approach to potential solutions. Lilienblum expressed his thoughts prolifically and intensely in his diary and articles. His appeals to his coreligionists in 1882 started to take on the modern characteristics and astute prophetic observations which imbued the architects of the First Zionist Congress in 1897. In an entry in his diary *The Way of Return*, Lilienblum describes his heart-wrenching first-hand experience of the April 15, 1881 pogrom in Elizabethgrad. On March 20, 1881, he was alarmed by a local periodical's report of an impending attack on the Jews during the approaching Easter holiday. On April 17, 1881, he was shocked by the reports of riots and pillaging from the city of Elizabethgrad. On April 28, 1881, he noted equally shocking reports coming from Kiev and other cities. In May, he spoke of his own condition of being under siege and on the effect it had on his opinions and beliefs:

> The situation is terrible and frightening! We are virtually under siege; the courtyards are barred up, and we keep peering through the grillwork of the court gates to see if the mob is coming to swoop down on us. All the furniture is stored in cellars, we all sleep in our clothes without any bedding (also stored in the cellars), so that if we are attacked, we will immediately be able to take the small children, who also sleep in their clothes, and flee. But will they let us flee? What does the future have in store for us? Will they have mercy on the youngsters – who don't even know yet that they are Jews, that they are wretches – and not harm them? Terrible, terrible! How long, oh God of Israel? (Quoted in Hertzberg, 1959, p. 169)

The following excerpts from his diary epitomize his *cri de coeur*, born out of his realization of the futility of pursuing the unrealistic hope of acceptance through emancipation and that the salvation of the Jewish people would only be possible through its reestablishment as a sovereign nation:

> I am glad that I have suffered. At least once in my life I have the opportunity of feeling what my ancestors felt every day of their lives. Their lives were one long terror, so why should I experience nothing of that fright which they felt all their lives? I am their son, their sufferings are dear to me, and I am exalted by their glory.
> When I became convinced that it was not a lack of high culture that was the cause of our tragedy – for aliens we are and aliens we shall remain even if we become full to the brim with culture; when my eyes were opened by the new ideal, and my spirit rose to a new task, in which, if all goes well, lies our eternal salvation – all the old ideals left me in a flash. (Lilienblum, 1881, reprinted in Hertzberg, 1959, pp. 169–170)

In his 1883 article "The Future of our People," Lilienblum concluded that there were three paths open to the Jewish people:

(1) To remain in our present state, to be oppressed forever, to be gypsies, to face the prospect of various pogroms and not be safe even against a major holocaust.

(2) To assimilate, not merely externally but completely within the nations among whom we dwell: to forsake Judaism for the religions of the gentiles, but nonetheless to be despised for many, many years, until some far-off day when descendants of ours who no longer retain any trace of their Jewish origin will be entirely assimilated among the Aryans.

(3) To initiate our efforts for the renaissance of Israel in the land of its forefathers, where the next few generations may attain, to the fullest extent, a normal national life. (Lilienblum, 1883, reprinted in Hertzberg, 1959, p. 177).

Lilienblum ended his article with the call: "Make your choice!" (Lilienblum, 1883, reprinted in Hertzberg, 1959, p. 177). He devoted the rest of his life to the Zionist movement. He was a significant figure in the practical labours of the Hibbat Zion organization, the group which came into being under the impact of the events of 1881 to foster Jewish colonization in Palestine. When political Zionism arose with the appearance of Theodor Herzl, Lilienblum became one of his most active supporters in Russia (Hertzberg, 1959, p. 168).

Leo Pinsker

Of all the leading Jewish thinkers who propelled their reactions to the pogroms in the direction of the political Zionist solution, Berk credited Yehuda Leib (Leo) Pinsker with having had the greatest influence on the movement in support of Palestine as a Jewish homeland (Berk, 1985, pp. 114–115).

Pinsker, a middle-aged Jewish physician from Odessa, had spent his entire adult life endorsing Russification and assimilation as the only way to liberate Russian Jewry from the yoke of antisemitic oppression. It was Pinsker who began the process of organizing the Zionist movement to the point where it could be said that Russian Zionism was an active and at least partially successful political movement during the ten years before Theodore Herzl convened the First Zionist Congress in Basel in 1897 (Berk, 1985, p. 115).

Unlike most of the other leading Jewish thinkers of his time, who started their early years with a ghetto education, Pinsker's father, a distinguished Hebrew scholar, was already "enlightened" and provided his son with the kind of education that was then a rarity for a young Jewish boy. Pinsker, after attending a Russian high school and studying law in

Odessa, obtained a medical degree from the University of Moscow. Following his appointment to the staff of the local city hospital, he became one of the leading physicians of the community. During the Crimean War, he volunteered his services to typhus-stricken soldiers, for which he was honoured by Tsar Nicholas I, a rare distinction for a Jewish person at that time (Hertzberg, 1959, p. 179; Avineri, 2017, p. 77).

Pinsker had always taken a considerable interest in Jewish affairs. In the 1860s and 1870s, he maintained his support for the assimilation of Jewry within liberal Russia. It was the unprecedented nature of the outbreaks of anti-Jewish violence in 1881 that caused Pinsker to give up any hope in emancipation as the solution and to look for "new remedies, and new ways." The question arises as to why the 1881 pogroms had such a greater impact than the previous outbreaks of violence that they constituted an emotional crisis so severe that they irreparably destroyed any hope in the success of emancipation, even in someone as totally committed to it as Pinsker. What drove the situation over the edge this time was the size and composition of the mobs. Within a few months of the assassination of Tsar Alexander II in March 1881, at least 160 cities and villages were the scenes of such outrages that the American Ambassador in St. Petersburg, John W. Foster, reported to the State Department that "the acts which have been committed are more worthy of the Dark Ages than of the present century." The other defining aspect was that all segments of Russian society were involved: the illiterate rabble who carried out the raping and killing; the leading newspapers which had whipped up the frenzy; the educated and prominent Russians who participated in the attacks; and the government which, at the time, justified and encouraged the violence against the Jews. It was immediately following these events that Pinsker abandoned his pro-assimilationist stance and declared that "new remedies and new ways" would have to be found (Hertzberg, 1959, p. 180).

In *Auto-Emancipation*, which Hertzberg referred to as the most significant reaction to the events of 1881 (Hertzberg, 1959, p. 43), Pinsker laid out his views about the real causes of the phenomenon of the abysmal treatment of the Jewish communities in the diaspora. The essence of the problem rested in the fact that, wherever they resided, they formed a segment that could not be assimilated, a distinctive element that could not be readily digested by any nation. The problem, therefore, was to find ways to adjust this exclusive Jewish element to the international body of nations. This required equality in rank and mutually admitted rights and could only be achieved by arrangements based on international law and treaties and upon mutual regard. Only when this basis was established and the equality of the Jews with other nations become a fact could the problem presented by the Jewish Question be considered solved. Unfortunately, this equality, which did exist in the long-forgotten past, could not be restored until the Jewish people acquired the attributes which were a hallmark of a nation: a common language, common customs, and a common land. In his words:

> The Jewish people has no fatherland of its own, though many motherlands; it has no rallying point, no center of gravity, no government of its own, no accredited representatives. It is everywhere a guest and nowhere at home. (Pinsker, 1882, reprinted in Hertzberg, 1959, pp. 182–183)

With the arrival of the age of enlightenment, a number of other dependent and oppressed nationalities were allowed to regain their independence. The Jewish people, therefore, now had the opportunity and the duty to devote their remaining moral force to re-establishing themselves as a living nation. The national consciousness, which until then had existed only in the latent state of sterile martyrdom, burst forth among the Russian and Romanian Jews in the form of irresistible movement towards Palestine (Pinsker, 1882, reprinted in Hertzberg, 1959, pp. 190–191).

It would be very unfortunate, Pinsker asserted, if the Jews were not willing to profit from the practical results of their experience. The most important of these results was the constantly growing conviction that they were nowhere at home and that they finally must have a home, if not a country of their own (Pinsker, 1882, reprinted in Hertzberg, 1959, p. 193). At this stage of his thinking, Pinsker did not look at Palestine as the one and only immediate destination as the Jewish homeland. The need for a secure home for the persecuted Jewish minorities required an immediate solution. In his own words:

> If we would have a secure home, so that we may give up our endless life of wandering and rehabilitate our nation in our own eyes and in the eyes of the world, we must above all not dream of restoring ancient Judea. We must not attach ourselves to the place where our political life was once violently interrupted and destroyed. The goal of our present endeavours must not be the "Holy Land," but a land of our own. We need nothing but a large piece of land for our poor brothers; a piece of land which shall remain our property, from which no foreign master can expel us. Thither we shall take with us the most sacred possessions which we have saved from the shipwreck of our former fatherland, the *God-idea* and the *Bible*. It is only these which have made our old fatherland the Holy Land and not the Jerusalem of the Jordan. Perhaps the Holy Land will again become ours. If so, all the better, but *first of all*, we must determine – and this is the

crucial point – what country is accessible to us, and, at the same time,
adapted to offer the Jews of all lands who must leave their homes a secure
and unquestioned refuge which is capable of being made productive.
(Pinsker, 1882, reprinted in Hertzberg, 1959, p. 194)

Pinsker saw in what was happening in the world at large a unique
opportunity for the Jewish people to take their fate into their own hands.
Such moments rarely occur in the history of a people: "The general history
of the present day seems called to be our ally." The decision to seize the
moment or not would have a decisive influence upon the future of the
Jewish people. The voices of national self-consciousness were triumphing
over the vestiges of traditional statesmanship. Inspired by the great ideas
of the eighteenth and nineteenth centuries, a number of nations had been
gaining their independence. Pinsker granted that nations who were
successful in attaining their national independence, unlike the Jews, lived
on their own soil and spoke one language, which gave them a definite
advantage. The fact that the Jewish position was more difficult should not
act as a deterrent but motivate them to strive even harder to put an
honourable end to their national misery. In Pinsker's own words:

[Until now] we sailed the surging ocean of universal history without a
compass, and such a compass must be invented. Far off, very far off, is the
haven for which our soul longs. As yet we do not even know where it is,
whether in the East or in the West. For a people wandering for thousands
of years, however, no way, no matter how distant, can be too long.
(Pinsker, 1882, reprinted in Hertzberg, 1959, p. 195)

Pinsker emphasized the need for a solid structural foundation in the form
of a national institute convoked by the societies already in existence to
establish a unity of purpose and methods, which would be essential to the
success of their endeavours. This institute needed to comprise the leaders
of the Jewish people – men of finance, scientists, statesmen and publicists
– who needed to unite to move towards the common destination (Pinsker,
1882, reprinted in Hertzberg, 1959, pp. 196–197).

Finally, Pinsker addressed the issue of the type of land required and the
choice of its location. It must be productive and large enough to allow the
settlement of several million Jews. Its ownership must be national and
inalienable. To ensure that this land would meet all the requirements, its
selection must be assigned to a commission of experts selected by the
directorate, because only after a thorough and comprehensive investigation
would such a supreme tribunal be able to render an opinion and make a
final choice as to its location. At this point, its ultimate location was

uncertain; it might be a small territory in North America or in Asiatic Turkey. In the latter case, the directorate would have to secure the assent of the Porte (the Ottoman government) and probably of the other European cabinets as well (Pinsker, 1882, reprinted in Hertzberg, 1959, p. 197).

Pinsker's *Auto-Emancipation* met with mixed responses, many of them negative. To the orthodox, he appeared as lacking in religion; to the liberals, especially outside Russia, he was a traitor to the faith that humanity would prevail over prejudice and hatred. It was among the disillusioned pro-emancipation Russian intelligentsia, whose modernized nationalism remained rooted in the Bible and the prayer book, that Pinsker found the greatest support (Hertzberg, 1959, pp. 180–181). Pinsker's personal prestige and the intellectual force of *Auto-Emancipation* propelled him to the leadership of the new Hibbat Zion movement. After he convened its founding conference in 1884, he devoted his energies to keep the organization alive in spite of the dearth of financial support until his death in 1891. A few colonies were established in Palestine, but it was the educational impact of the movement that led to the wider development of Zionist thought and action in Eastern Europe (Hertzberg, 1959, p. 181).

There is a consensus among the major scholars who addressed the development of Zionist political thought that Pinsker's *Auto-Emancipation* constituted a major breakthrough in the search for a new approach to the fight for freedom and equality. Shlomo Avineri called it one of the seminal essays in modern Jewish thought and a milestone in the evolution of modern Jewish nationalism (Avineri, 2017, p. 77). Stephen Berk noted, when referring to Pinsker's pamphlet:

> Its author almost overnight became one of the great heroes of Russian Jewry of the nineteenth century. [...] The fact that he, a Russian Jew, wrote in German before a foreign public seemed to enhance his position in the eyes of Jewish intellectuals. In this as in so much else Pinsker foreshadowed Theodor Herzl. (Berk, 1985, p. 120)

Louis Greenberg regarded Leo Pinsker's *Auto-Emancipation* as

> the canon of the Zionist movement. [...] The booklet not only formulated the program of Zionism but presented a key analysis of the Jewish position. (Greenberg, 1951, p. 69)

According to Arthur Hertzberg, the personal prestige of the man and his intellectual impact immediately propelled Pinsker to the foreground of the ferment towards creating a Jewish nationalist organization. *Auto-Emancipation* became the first great statement of the torment of the Jew driven to assert his own nationalism because the wider world had rejected him, a theme that was to recur in Theodor Herzl (Hertzberg, 1959, p. 81).

Peretz Smolenskin

In every aspect of his life, Peretz Smolenskin reflects the impact that the ruthless reign of Nicholas I had on the Jewish population of Russia. He was born in the Russian Pale of Settlement. As a child, he saw his oldest brother "snatched" for military service in the Russian army. In 1853, at the age of eleven, one year after losing his father, he followed the traditional Jewish custom of going to study at the yeshivah. While at the yeshivah, he cultivated an already existing interest in "enlightenment" by studying Russian and reading secular books. Since this was regarded as a mortal sin in pious circles, he was persecuted for heresy. This left him with no alternative but to run away. He wandered between various places in the Pale of Settlement and supported himself by singing in choirs and by occasionally preaching in synagogues (Hertzberg, 1959, p. 143). At the age of twenty, he moved to Odessa, home of the most modern Jewish community in Russia, where he spent five years studying music and languages while supporting himself by teaching Hebrew. His Odessa days were the beginning of his literary career. In his autobiographical novel, *Ha-Toe Be-Dareche Ha-Hayim* (The Wanderer in Life's Ways), Smolenskin summarized his own life as well as that of an entire generation. It became the most popular book written in modern Hebrew in the 1870s, as it mirrored the painful experience of a generation of Jews attempting to cling to their identity against the most impossible odds. It resonated with so many as it spoke both to them and for them (Hertzberg, 1959, pp. 143–144).

In 1868, after spending five years in Odessa, Smolenskin moved to Vienna with the intention of entering university. Unfortunately, he lacked the necessary admission fees. He eked out a meagre living, first as a proofreader in a printing house and, after his marriage in 1875, as its manager. Until his death from tuberculosis in 1885, he devoted his major energies to writing for the monthly periodical, *Hashahar* (The Dawn), which he had founded with a collaborator in 1868 (Hertzberg, 1959, p. 144).

Prior to 1881, Smolenskin's writings were, like those of most of his contemporary leading members of the Jewish intelligentsia, primarily focused on advocating the desirability of the modernization of Jewish life as the only way to alleviate the Jewish predicament. Through his writings, which marked the transition in modern Hebrew literature from the period of the enlightenment, which came to an end with the Russian pogroms of 1881, to the age of the development of political Zionism, Smolenskin played a pivotal role in the evolving process of political Zionism thinking (Hertzberg, 1959, p. 144).

On the heels of the pogroms, Smolenskin abandoned his theorizing about Jewish national culture and the definition of Jewry as a spiritual notion to call for the complete evacuation of Eastern Europe. He asked its Jews not to repeat the woeful cycle of history by emigrating to America or to any other lands of exile. There was only one answer: Zionism. He expressed those thoughts in the essay titled *Let us Search our Ways*, which he wrote as an immediate reaction to the pogroms of 1881. Smolenskin argued that Jews should emigrate en masse and together to the same new land, which would allow them to understand and help one another. He saw the land of Israel as the only conceivable destination (Hertzberg, 1959, p. 151).

Smolenskin wrote that he was not trying to convince those Jews who had totally assimilated to the point of ignoring their traditions and deriding their Jewish heritage. Nor did he find any point in arguing with those who waited for the day of miraculous redemption and who were afraid that approaching the Holy Land would amount to blasphemy. Smolenskin stated that his thoughts were aimed at the sensible people who were willing to act out of love for their nation; people who would listen, understand, act and succeed, as there was no other land that would lovingly accept them and offer them justice and lasting peace (Hertzberg, 1959, p. 152).

Smolenskin, having designated the destination, made a strong case for its qualitative and quantitative capacity to absorb large numbers of immigrants. He referred to a number of non-Jewish experts, including distinguished English explorers, who had investigated this land and found that, if cultivated with skill and diligence, it could support fourteen million people. Even if there was room for only half that number, *Eretz Israel* could still contain all those who might wish to take refuge there (Hertzberg, 1959, p. 152).

Smolenskin pointed out that those who cherished the memory of their ancestors would prefer *Eretz Israel* over other destinations, such as North or South America, if they could be assured that they would make a living. In addition, it would also allow them to live together in the manner of their accustomed traditions. Smolenskin added that not all would have to become farmers. To succeed, those who settled in *Eretz Israel* would need it to be a country in which it is possible to make a living from working the land, from commerce and from industry (Hertzberg, 1959, pp. 152–153).

What Smolenskin was essentially telling Russia's persecuted Jewish population was that regaining their sovereignty in their reconstituted ancient homeland would finally provide them with a balanced social and economic environment.

Smolenskin concluded his essay by appealing to his fellow Jews to embrace and propagate the idea of Jewish settlement in the land of Israel. As one of the foremost advocates of the modern Zionist concept, Smolenskin helped launch it on its path towards political realization. Nothing can make this clearer than his closing words:

> The idea of Jewish settlement in the land of Israel must now become the chief topic of conversation among all those who love their people. They must arouse their friends and propagandize the entire Jewish community. It is now too early to tell what steps may be necessary to realize this project and what will be its ultimate results. Now is the time to spread this idea, and to raise funds to help settle those who will go to Eretz Israel. And now, for the sake of resettlement in Zion, let us neither be still nor quiet until the light dawns and causes our healing to begin. (Smolenskin, 1881, reprinted in Hertzberg, 1959, p. 153)

For fifteen years prior to the Congress, the "Lovers of Zion" (*Hibbat Zion*), inspired by the thoughts of Lilienblum and Pinsker, had been actively pursuing the course of establishing a pioneering presence in Palestine. The few Jewish agriculture colonies that had sprung up in Palestine during that period had increased the Jewish population of the Holy Land by some twenty thousand souls. Unfortunately, these moderate achievements were far from meeting the immediate needs of the six million Russian Jews clamouring for relief from their intolerable condition. Yet the staunch opposition of the Ottoman government to allow any form of Jewish presence in Palestine, combined with the desolate physical condition of the land, made it impossible to transfer a considerable portion of Russian Jewry to the Holy Land at that point in time (Dubnow, 1920, p. 42).

It was at this juncture that the charismatic figure of Theodor Herzl appeared on the political scene with his appeal to the Jews to establish a "Jewish state." This appeal arose among the Western European Jewish intelligentsia who had, until then, viewed the sufferings of their eastern brethren strictly from the philanthropic point of view (Dubnow, 1920, p. 42).

All that was needed was the appearance on the stage of a charismatic leader who would carry the message from its parochial environments to the world stage, which brings us to Theodor Herzl.

Theodor Herzl – From Passive Submission to Political Action

A vast amount of scholarship has been devoted to the significance and nature of Herzl's role in raising the consciousness of European Jewry in the nineteenth century from the impotent bottom of the social ladder to the full-blown assertion of its determination to once and for all throw off the paralyzing shackles that had kept it in a state of constant bondage. What people know about his background and activities is limited. Different prominent scholars have given divergent views of the source of his political motivations. Hertzberg, for example, wrote that the major influence that set Herzl firmly on his Zionist path was the Dreyfus affair. In his earlier work, *The Making of Modern Zionism*, published in 1981, Avineri thought likewise when he described in vivid terms the shocking impact of the Dreyfus affair on Herzl's thinking (Avineri, 2017, p. 9). It was only in 1999, after he familiarized himself with Herzl's diaries, that Avineri changed his mind and stated that the Dreyfus affair had not been central to "Herzl's reawakening of a Jewish identity or his development towards Zionism" (Avineri, 1999, p. 1).

Herzl's pivotal role in the development of the concepts that led to the creation of an international political Zionist movement and the formulation of the blueprints for the recreation of a sovereign Jewish state can only be properly assessed within the context of the political developments in Europe during the nineteenth century. He became the catalyst that linked and eventually merged the totally different conditions of the Jewish inhabitants in Western Europe with those of the people in the eastern part of the continent. In Western Europe, the Jews had been emancipated but not assimilated; in Eastern Europe, the Jews had been coercively assimilated without being emancipated.

Once Herzl had come to the conclusion that the reconstitution of a sovereign state in the ancestral homeland was the only permanent solution to diaspora Jewry's torturous existence as a despised and persecuted minority, he pursued this objective with relentless determination. The years covered in his diary, from 1885 to 1895, tell the story of a tragic life, marked by heroic efforts, undeterred by disappointments and failures which would have caused lesser men to give up the fight. The account of his all-consuming odyssey needs to be studied by all those who want to understand how the efforts of one man were able to bring the existential danger threatening the survival of the exiled founders of Western civilization to the attention of the world. The phrase "all-consuming efforts" is not an exaggeration. From the outset, Herzl's physical assets were very limited and his political support nonexistent. His prime emotional capital consisted of his unshakable belief in the rightness and urgency of his cause and of the unique characteristics of his personality. His exceptional skill as a multilingual journalist and his ability to discuss and debate persuasively, engagingly and intelligently at any level of the political world stage were enhanced by his charismatic appearance, imposing physique and confidence-inspiring countenance. One more important characteristic must be added to this complex portrait. Herzl was a man of unshakable moral integrity. Contrary to the duplicity and corruption that was so characteristic of the diplomatic corridors to which his quest for support for his mission took him, Herzl never made a promise he did not intend to keep and never looked for any personal gain.

To understand how this larger-than-life figure accomplished his modern-day mosaic mission, it is best to look at his role in history through his own eyes and mind, as revealed in the diaries which he kept from 1895 until the last entry on May 16, 1904, a few weeks before his death on July 3, 1904. The diaries cover almost two thousand printed pages and constitute a complete self-portrait of Herzl's political development. It provides a daily account of the forces that shaped his public persona and inspired the philosophical building blocks of the movement that he developed into a political structure.

To comprehend Herzl's concept of the state as an abstraction to be turned into a physical realty through the powers of will and determination, it must be remembered that the Jewish people were, in Herzl's time, a fragmented sub-state nation, spread over a number of countries without a sovereign territory of its own. Hence, in his June 16, 1895 entry, he wrote, "no one ever thought of looking for the Promised Land where it actually is – yet it lies so near. This is where it is: within ourselves … for everyone will take across, in himself, a piece of *the* Promised Land – one in his head, another one in his hands, a third in his savings. The Promised Land is where we carry it" (Herzl, 1960a, p. 105).

Herzl confirmed his conviction that the first step towards the creation of a de facto Jewish state was to inculcate the concept of statehood in the hearts and minds of diaspora Jewry when, in his September 3, 1897 entry, he summed up his assessment of the First Zionist Congress held in Basel in August 1897:

> Were I to sum up the Basel Congress in a word – which I shall guard against pronouncing publicly – it would be this: At Basel I founded the Jewish State. If I said this out loud today, it would be answered by universal laughter. Perhaps in five years, and certainly in fifty, everyone will know it. The foundation of a state lies in the will of the people for a

state. [...] Territory is only the material basis; the State, even when it possesses territory, is always something abstract [...] at Basel, then, I created this abstraction which, as such is invisible to the vast majority of people [...] I gradually worked the people into a mood for the state and made them feel that they were its National Assembly. (Herzl, 1960b, p. 581)

As Herzl stated in the opening pages of his diaries, his interest in the Jewish problem started early in his life, before he had found a newspaper as an outlet for his writings. It was triggered by his reading of the German philosopher Eugen Dühring's antisemitic book *The Jewish Question as a Question of the Racial Damage for the Existence, Morals and Culture of the Nations*. Published in 1881, it preached a racial fight against the Jews (Herzl, 1960e, p. 1704). "In one of my old notebooks, now packed away somewhere in Vienna, are my first observations on Dühring's book and on the Question" (Herzl, 1960a, p. 4).

Herzl's faithfully kept diaries provide an insight into the main sources of his ideas about the Jewish problem. While, as the *Neue Freie Presse* correspondent, he had closely followed the first stages of the Dreyfus affair in France, a review of his diaries shows that, contrary to the view held by many scholars, the affair was not the formative trigger of Herzl's realization of the failure of emancipation. From 1895 to the opening of the First Zionist Congress in 1897, Dreyfus' name is only mentioned a few times, and even then, rather tangentially.

For example, when, on November 17, 1895, during a gathering at the home of Zadoc Kahn, the Chief Rabbi of France, one of the guests who, typical of French Jewry's disinterest in Herzl's Zionist ideas, emphasized his French nationality, Herzl retorted:

What? Don't you and I belong to the same nation? Why did you wince when Lueger was elected? Why did I suffer when Captain Dreyfus was accused of high treason? (Herzl, 1960a, p. 273)

This incident is indicative of Herzl's concept of the Jews as a nation and not of the Dreyfus affair having had a major impact on the development of his Zionist persona. The only other time the Dreyfus affair is mentioned in Herzl's diaries is in his report of his audience with the Kaiser in Constantinople on October 19, 1898 when they discussed its impact on the morale of the French army. Herzl noted that while he advanced no opinion one way or the other, it soon became clear that the Kaiser and his Foreign Minister, Prince von Bülow, considered Dreyfus innocent and were totally appalled at the perfidy of the French general staff, which had led to a colossal corruption of justice (Herzl, 1960b, pp. 723–724). This episode took place in 1898 and had nothing to do with Herzl's awakening to the plight of diaspora Jewry.

Herzl was more concerned with the dark clouds of growing antisemitism emerging in the Austrian-Hungarian dual monarchy, which was home to over two million Jews, and with the relentless persecution of the six million Jews in the Tsarist Empire than with the relatively peaceful existence of the one hundred thousand-strong Jewish population of France. The diaries contain numerous entries dealing with much deeper phenomena threatening Jewish life in regions with much vaster Jewish populations than France. As Herzl wrote to his friend Max Nordau on February 23, 1898, when he tried to convince him to hold a Zionist conference in Paris:

> What was possible for me in Vienna, you will be able to do in Paris. I wish I had the facilities here that you have there. You are – despite the Dreyfus trials – in a free country. The proximity of Galicia has no significance whatever in this respect. (Herzl, 1960b, p. 615)

The antisemitic ideas that originated mainly in Germany threatened the fragile liberal-conservative coalition in the Austrian Reichsrat (the Austrian Parliament, which consisted of two houses: a House of Representatives and a House of Lords) (Avineri, 1991, p. 7; Herzl, 1960e, p. 1839). For Herzl, this meant that the stability achieved through the Austro-Hungarian historical comprise was about to disintegrate, and as the destiny of the Jews depended on the ability of the empire to survive, the threat to the empire represented an existential threat to the Jewish population (Avineri, 1991, p. 7).

At the time that Herzl began writing his diaries, matters were starting to take an ominous turn for the worse in the lands which constituted the empire of Franz Josef I. Known as the Habsburg Dual Monarchy, it included, in addition to Austria and Hungary proper, Bohemia, Moravia, Slovakia, Galicia, Bukovina and Transylvania. These regions were home to two million Jews, the largest Jewish population outside the Russian Empire. This modern, multi-religious and multiethnic empire was considered at the time by the Jews to be "the bastion of tolerance and prosperity" (Avineri, 1999, p. 6).

The more Herzl followed these developments, the more he became convinced that the ideological, racist antisemitism that originated in Germany was further undermining the ability of the Austrian regime to mediate among various conflicting national claims. The election in 1895 of Karl Lueger, a member of the antisemitic Christian party, as mayor of Vienna was to Herzl the beginning of the end, something that most of his liberal Jewish contemporaries failed to see. Herzl saw in the election of Lueger, a xenophobic populist demagogue in the capital of an empire that stood for tolerance and moderation, the emergence of the dark clouds that threatened to destabilize the lives of this important segment of European Jewry. For Herzl, the new social and political reality that was beginning to undermine the foundations of the Habsburg monarchy was the alarm bell that triggered his frantic search for a solution to the plight of the large mass of Jews who, until then, had thought that they had found a safe haven under of the wings of the benevolent empire.

Herzl saw a close link between the emergence of antisemitism and the demise of the Austro-Hungarian Empire. He ascribed the rise of antisemitic parties in Hungary, in part, to the prominence of the many Jews in the banking sector and industrial life in that part of the empire. Herzl followed the political struggles between Pan-German and Czech nationalists in the Bohemian lands, especially in Prague. Many Jews felt integrated into the leading German culture of Bohemia, and when Pan-German associations started introducing "Aryan clauses" in their statutes, which effectively barred not only Jews but even converts from their ranks, it appeared that, for many of them, their whole world was about to collapse. When some tried to turn to the Czech national movement, they were equally rebuked, eventually finding themselves in the political crossfire of competing nationalist movements. Herzl discovered a similar problem in Galicia, where the Jewish population was torn between conflicting linguistic claims of the German and Polish language and culture, and the poverty in which many Jews lived in that underdeveloped province of the empire only added to their misery (Avineri, 1999, p. 6).

Herzl saw the structural crisis of the empire as the epitome of the major crisis of European politics and culture and the major threat to the stability of Jewish life in Central and Eastern Europe. The structural problem was exacerbated by the antisemitic views originating in Germany. This crisis of the dual monarchy caused the breakup of the liberal-conservative coalition in the Austrian Reichsrat and led to a virtual impasse in parliamentary life. Observing this from his vantage point as one of Vienna's foremost political journalists, Herzl saw that the stability achieved through the historic Austro-Hungarian Compromise of 1867 was about to disintegrate. And since the destiny of the Jews was inextricably interwoven with the ability of the empire to survive, the threat to the empire meant an existential threat to its Jewish population (Avineri, 1999, pp. 6–7).

Herzl, unlike most of his contemporaries, realized that emancipation could not be achieved by mere legislation proclaiming all men equal. He argued that "when we emerged from the ghetto, we were, and for the time being remained Ghetto Jews. We should have been given time to get accustomed to freedom but the people around us have neither the magnanimity nor the patience. They see only the bad and conspicuous characteristics of a liberated people and they have no idea that these released men have been unjustly punished" (Herzl, 1960a, p. 10).

The name and the figure of Theodor Herzl have risen to the very top of the hierarchy of the architects of political Zionism. As the founder of the World Zionist Organization and convener of the First Zionist Congress in Basel in 1897, Herzl has become identified more than any other person with the emergence of political Zionism.

During the early years of his life, there was nothing to indicate that he would become the architect of the Zionist political movement. Whereas the prominent developers of the modern Zionist concept developed their ideas in response to the life of poverty and persecution that was the fate of the Jews in Tsarist Russia, Herzl was born to a wealthy family. His father was a successful businessman and banker. Both parents were typical products of the modernization of Jewry resulting from the *Haskala*. They sent their son to the Jewish primary school. After the death of his sister in February of 1878, the family moved to Vienna, where he enrolled in the law faculty of the university. He gained his doctorate in 1884, but he gave up his practice as a lawyer a year later for a career as a playwright and feuilletonist (Hertzberg, 1959, p. 201).

At this stage in his life, Herzl outwardly held a conventional view of the Westernized Jewish intellectual in the late nineteenth century, that complete assimilation was both desirable and inevitable. Hertzberg notes that, inwardly, Herzl still carried the traces of his earlier exposure to antisemitism, while still at university, in the racist writings of Eugen Dühring. At the same time, he had also withdrawn from his fraternity when he participated in a Wagner memorial meeting which had turned into an antisemitic demonstration. When he arrived in Paris, antisemitism confronted him again as a rising phenomenon of French life. Edouard Drumont, the author of *La France Juive*, the most notorious and successful of French anti-Jewish writings, had just founded a newspaper and was attracting a noisy, though not yet influential, circle of supporters. Herzl's analytical comments contained in his newspaper account suggested that hatred of the Jew was being used universally as a lightning rod to draw the revolutionary ire of the masses away from the real woes of society. This is how the Jewish problem came to the forefront of his attention (Hertzberg, 1959, p. 202).

Herzl opened his first diary entry in May of 1895 by stating that he had been occupied for some time with a work of "infinite grandeur." It seemed like a mighty dream which had possessed him for days and weeks; it was always at the back of his mind, disturbing him and intoxicating him. If he had to translate this conception into a novel, he would title it "The Promised Land!" Herzl notes that it was a fact at this point that he was not sure whether what he had in mind was literally work for its own sake or a call to action. In that same first entry, he notes that he had actually begun to concern himself with the Jewish Question from the time that he had read Dühring's book (Herzl, 1960a, pp. 3–4).

In his biography of Herzl, Israeli journalist and author Amos Elon stated that it is unclear how Herzl passed from the idea of an earth-shaking novel to a practical programme of political action. Herzl's ecstatic awakening as a man of action emerged from the deepest resources of his soul. Politically, his life had gone full circle – from German nationalism to cosmopolitanism to a belief in a Jewish exodus from Europe. Herzl's soul-searching led to the conclusion that his mission was to liberate diaspora Jewry from the crushing hold of antisemitism. He saw antisemitism as a force of nature and of history, which had "tied victims and culprits to each other in a mutually harmful embrace." To break this vicious circle, it was necessary to find a suitable territory where a properly negotiated Jewish sovereignty could be established. Emigration to the new territory would be organized on a vast scale and executed with modern efficiency as a well-planned scientific operation, "with a full consent of the present host countries." The exodus would be financed by a worldwide Jewish national loan. European governments would willingly subscribe as they would see it as a solution to the Jewish problem (Elon, 1975, p. 131).

Herzl's Meeting with Baron Maurice von Hirsch – June 1895

Herzl's first step was to look for powerful allies. The immensely wealthy financier and philanthropist Baron Maurice von Hirsch was the first powerful personality Herzl approached in his quest for support for his Zionist agenda. After a few letters asking for a meeting, wherein he mentioned that he wanted to submit a plan for a new Jewish policy in which Hirsch could play a significant part, way beyond his role as a philanthropist, he signed as a correspondent for the prestigious *Neue Freie Presse*. These letters had piqued the Baron's curiosity and, in his reply, granted Herzl an interview scheduled for June 2, 1895 at 10:30 a.m. Herzl told the Baron that he needed at least an hour to explain the purpose of his visit, to which Hirsch acquiesced. Herzl started by pointing out that just as Hirsch was originally a banker involved in big business deals who had ended up devoting his time and fortune to the cause of the Jews, he himself had started out as a writer and a journalist, with no thought of the Jews, but that his experiences and observations of the growing pressure of antisemitism had compelled him to interest himself in the problem. After this introduction, Herzl proceeded to explain the plight of the Jews as he saw it. He pointed out that he saw two possible aims: "either we stay where we are or we emigrate somewhere else." As emigration to the Promised Land would not happen overnight but could require twenty or thirty years, either course required that the new generations of Jews would need to be educated with methods different than those used by his interlocutor. Herzl notes that he saw that he was not going to win Hirsch over during this first meeting. Hirsch had argued against uplifting the Jewish character and showed no interest in hearing Herzl out to the full. Nevertheless, Herzl felt that, given enough time and opportunity, he would eventually be able to win him over (Herzl, 1960a, pp. 13–36).

Elon considered this meeting as a great missed opportunity. He presents an interesting counter-factual scenario that could have been realized if Herzl's initial presentation of his revolutionary programme had been better staged and formulated on this occasion. Elon argues that Hirsch might have saved Herzl a host of subsequent troubles and perhaps accelerated the success of Zionism by decades, long before the advent of Arab nationalism. Hirsch's vast fortune might have bought the Zionists a Turkish charter for the colonization of Palestine at a time when such transactions were still possible and not uncommon. Later historians, Elon continues, chastised Hirsch for his short-sightedness and that he "had immortality within his grasp." But Herzl had not really whetted his appetite. He only got through six of his twenty-two prepared notes and did not reach the point where he was going to ask Hirsch to establish an international Jewish congress to plan the establishment of a Jewish state initially under Hirsch's leadership (Elon, 1975, pp. 138–139).

Elon's speculation appears rather inconsequential in view of the fact that Hirsch died on Thursday, April 21, 1896, before Herzl had the opportunity to resume their dialogue and before Herzl's negotiations with the Turkish government in Constantinople in June 1896 and his audience with Sultan Abdul Hamid II on May 18, 1901.

On July 3, 1895, in a brief follow-up letter to the meeting, Hirsch notified Herzl that he would be delighted to meet him again when he was back in Paris, though this would not be for several months and, in any event, he would not change the ideas he had already expressed. In his lengthy reply dated July 5, 1895, Herzl told him that he had given up on him. "You stick to your views and I with equal stubbornness, to mine." Herzl added: "You believe that you can export your Jews, the way you are doing it. I say that you are only creating new markets for antisemitism. *Nous ne nous comprendrons jamais* [we shall never understand each other – P. G. trans.]" (Herzl, 1960a, p. 195).

Nevertheless, on July 26, 1895, when Herzl happened to ride past Hirsch in the street, he decided to write him another letter in which he once more offered him the opportunity to become acquainted with, and possibly involved in, his "perfect plan." When Hirsch did not reply, Herzl finally wrote what he refers to as "a farewell letter." The contents of this letter reflect Herzl's disappointment and frustration in not having been able to rally this powerful magnate to what he had thought was their common cause, as well as his annoyance at having misjudged him:

Dear Sir,
It is part of the Jewish misfortune that you have refused to be enlightened.
I saw in you a useful tool for the important cause, *voilà pourquoi j'ai insisté outre mes habitudes* [this is why I insisted beyond my wont – P. G. trans.].
The legend in circulation about you is obviously false. You engage in the Jewish cause as a sport. Just as you make horses race, you make Jews migrate. And this is what I a protest against most sharply. A Jew is not a plaything.
No, no, you are not interested in the cause. *Elle est bien bonne et j'y ai cru un instant* [It is very nice and I believed it for a minute – P. G. trans.].
For that reason it was an excellent thing that I wrote you once more from Paris and that you did not honour me with a reply. Now any error is out of the question. Some jackass must have told you that I am only a pleasant dreamer, and you believed it. (Herzl, 1960a, pp. 217).

In the end, Herzl changed his mind and did not mail the letter to Hirsch. He thought that he might still be included in his plans at some later date. He also felt that he had to subordinate his indignation and ego to the cause (Herzl, 1960a, p. 219).

Nine months later, when Herzl had expanded his strategy by reaching out to Europe's key governmental leaders, he still felt that Hirsch had the potential, through his wealth, to make a positive difference. He wrote a letter to his most important collaborator and supporter, Max Nordau, in which he gave him the assignment of putting out feelers towards Hirsch, for "with a few million from Hirsch, we can give the project a tremendous resonance and spread some of the money around for baksheesh in Turkey." On the afternoon of April 21, 1896, however, one hour after

Herzl had mailed the letter to Nordau, he learned that Baron Hirsch had died on an estate in Hungary earlier that same day. Herzl recalled his letter to Nordau and noted in his diary that Hirsch's participation could have helped their cause to success "tremendously fast." Herzl called Hirsch's death a loss to the Jewish cause. He noted that, among the rich Jews, Hirsch was the only one who wanted to do something big for the poor. Herzl reflected that perhaps he had not known how to handle Hirsch properly and that he should have asked Nordau to approach Hirsch two weeks earlier (Herzl, 1960a, p. 323).

Herzl's Meeting with Grand Duke Friedrich II of Baden – April 1896

Herzl's audience on April 23, 1896 with Grand Duke Friedrich II of Baden, which had been arranged by the Anglican clergyman William Hechler in preparation for a meeting with Kaiser William II, was his first encounter with a European head of state. Herzl recounted how, during the two and half hours of exhausting conversation, they discussed his ideas about solving the impossible situation in which Jewish people found themselves in their hostile European environments. Inevitably, albeit circuitously, the discussion turned to the possibility of recreating a Jewish state in Palestine and to the benefits this project would bring to the Orient, including Turkey itself. When asked whether his Royal Highness would permit Herzl to tell a few trustworthy men in England that the Grand Duke of Baden had taken an interest in the matter, the latter gave his consent with the stipulation that the matter be discussed only outside the borders of his country. The Duke then asked Herzl if any steps had been taken with the Sultan, to which Herzl replied in the affirmative (Herzl, 1960a, p. 338).

Herzl's Negotiations with the Turkish Government in Constantinople – June 1896

At this point in Herzl's brief but intense political career, he still firmly believed that he could successfully negotiate the creation of a home in Palestine with the Turkish government. The exchange he planned to offer the Sultan was that the Jews of Europe would relieve the Sultan of his financial burdens and his humiliating subservience to French and British creditors by taking over the huge national Turkish debt. In return, Turkey would lease Palestine to the Jews as an independent state or as a vassal territory. With this object in mind, Herzl journeyed to Constantinople, where he arrived on June 17, 1896 (Elon, 1975, pp. 196–198).

His advance man, to whom he was introduced by a Viennese friend, was a Polish nobleman known as Count Philip Michael de Nevlinsky, who operated as a freelancing diplomatic agent and was amazingly well-connected in the Balkan countries and especially in Constantinople. He was a close friend of the Turkish Sultan and enjoyed the unique privilege of being able to see him at almost any time. Herzl and Nevlinsky were very much taken by each other's romantic allure. Herzl, who hoped to purchase Palestine from the Turkish Sultan like Disraeli had bought Cyprus from the Turks in 1878, felt that Nevlinsky could be the proper intermediary. In 1863, at the age of 22, Nevlinsky had joined the Polish mutiny against Russia, and, as a result, his family's estates had been confiscated by the tsarist government. That Herzl was able to hire him for a pittance compared to his going rate may be due to the fact that Nevlinsky was excited by the audacity of Herzl's undertaking, which he may have hoped the Poles might emulate one day.

Herzl's first meeting was with the Grand Vizier, Khalil Rifat Pasha, to whom Herzl laid out his proposed trade. Khair Eddin Bey, Secretary-General to the Grand Vizier, acted as interpreter. When Herzl had the interpreter ask his Highness whether he knew the purpose of his trip and the reply was "no," Herzl presented his proposal to Khair Eddin to have it conveyed to the Grand Vizier, who listened imperturbably. When he asked, "Palestine is large. What part of it do you have in mind?" Herzl, through the interpreter, replied, "That would have to be weighed against the benefits we offer. For more land we shall lay greater sacrifices." When the Grand Vizier inquired about the terms, Herzl told him that he could state the scope of his proposals only to His Majesty. Should they be accepted in principle, Sir Samuel Montagu would submit the financial programme (Herzl, 1960a, p. 376).

Elon marvelled at the audacity of Herzl's undertaking. At this stage, Herzl was, after all, a solitary self-appointed spokesman of the people, without an organization or any binding mandate from anyone, without any financial resources, promising to free Turkey from the burden of international debts amounting to almost 100,000,000 pounds sterling. While Herzl hinted at Jewish money power, his belief that he had its backing was not realistic. While there were, indeed, a few Jewish multimillionaires, they were not interested in politics and certainly not in Jewish politics. At this point, Hirsch had died, and the Rothschilds refused even to speak to Herzl. Sir Samuel Montagu had made no firm commitment, and Herzl was not sure if he could count on him. What drove Herzl to challenge what would seem to be impossible odds was that his courage derived from an unbounded simple faith in the rightness and urgency of his case. Elon suggested that Herzl may have told himself that if he could reach a successful arrangement with the Turks, rich Jews would drop their opposition to his plan (Elon, 1975, pp. 199–200).

In the meantime, the Grand Vizier remained undecided, and another meeting was scheduled for later in the week. By contrast, the next Turkish statesman Herzl met, Mehmet Nuri Bey, Secretary-General of the Foreign Ministry, welcomed Herzl's plan enthusiastically. Son of a Circassian mother and a French father who had converted to Islam, he was ready to relinquish Palestine, which meant little to him, in exchange for Turkish economic independence (Elon, 1975, pp. 199–200).

In the evening, Herzl was told by Nevlinsky that, in a private discussion with the Sultan, the latter had been adamant that any deal for Palestine was out of the question. Herzl notes that he took the blow stout-heartedly. The Sultan had told Nevlinsky to advise Herzl not to take another step in the matter. He could not sell even a foot of land, for it did not belong to him but to his people, who had won the empire with their blood and fertilized it with their blood. As he put it:

> Let the Jews should save their billions. When my Empire is partitioned, they may get Palestine for nothing. But only our corpse will be divided. I will not agree to vivisection. (Herzl, 1960a, p. 378)

Elon noted that while Herzl's expectations had been dashed by the Sultan's position, he did not lose heart. He still insisted on an audience with the Sultan. Even if nothing should come of it, he needed it very badly to keep his movement going and to keep faith in himself as leader. If the Sultan had agreed to his Palestine plan, Herzl would have returned home triumphant, even had he not had a personal audience. Coming back, however, with neither a commitment from the Sultan nor even an audience would cause people to think of Herzl's objective as a crazy dream (Elon, 1975, pp. 199, 201).

During the next few days, Herzl had another round of meetings with the Grand Vizier, Foreign Ministry officials and an assortment of pashas and imperial chamberlains, who took turns encouraging and discouraging him. It was Izzet Bey, the Sultan's secretary and future Vizier and one of the most powerful officials in the Empire, who recommended a new approach. He suggested that the Jews acquire another territory somewhere in the Near East and then trade it for Palestine (with additional payment). Herzl assumed that Izzet spoke for the Sultan and immediately thought of Cyprus. He concluded that the Sultan's refusal to relinquish Palestine was not a matter of sacred principle but a question of face-saving (Elon, 1975, p. 202).

The final outcome, however, was up to the Sultan. He did not receive Herzl but had three more private talks with Nevlinsky, during which Nevlinsky tried to ingratiate Herzl with the Sultan. Herzl was ready to try and help the Sultan with other matters the latter had brought up, but he told Nevlinsky he would be in a much better position to be useful to the Sultan if the latter agreed to give him an audience. He needed it as proof that he had established a foothold and that all was not yet lost (Elon, 1975, pp. 202–203).

The Sultan continued to hedge. Two days later, on June 26, the Sultan spoke again to Nevlinsky about Herzl. He felt that the idea of an exchange, which his trusted secretary Izzet Bey had planted in his mind, was much more plausible. Nevlinsky advised the Sultan to discuss the idea directly with Herzl, who ardently wished to be received by the Sultan. The Sultan did not agree to an immediate meeting, but promised that he would receive Herzl sooner or later. He asked Nevlinsky why the Jews wanted to have Palestine at all costs and why they could not settle in another part of his empire. Nevlinsky answered that Palestine was their cradle and that if they could not have it, they would have to go to Argentina. In that case, Turkey would lose the proposed financial support and would never free itself from its foreign debt. This sagacious hint got the Sultan and Izzet into a lengthy discussion in Turkish. Nevlinsky could only grasp the repeated mentions of Herzl's name (Herzl, 1960a, p. 395)

In spite of Nevlinsky's optimistic reassurance to Herzl that the Turks were willing to trade Palestine and that the Sultan was only playing hardball, Herzl did not obtain the much-coveted rendezvous with the Sultan. Nevertheless, the events during his week-long stay in Constantinople had convinced Herzl that a deal with the Turks was possible, even if at a high cost, and that it was only a question of time. He also felt that he could not go back empty-handed, that the entire movement would lose momentum if he did not obtain some measure of proof of the Sultan's sympathy. Reluctantly, Herzl swallowed his pride and asked Nevlinsky to at least get him a high decoration. Nevlinsky immediately wrote to Izzet Bey, who promptly sent Herzl a box containing the Commander's Cross of the Ottoman Medjidiye Order (Elon, 1975, p. 204).

On the train back from Constantinople, Nevlinsky confirmed Herzl's positive outlook by telling Herzl that his farewell conversation with the Sultan had been quite encouraging. The Sultan could not receive Herzl's visit this time because his plan was no longer a secret and several persons had even made reports about it, including the Grand Vizier and Nuri Bey. Furthermore, since the Sultan could not accept the proposal in its present form, he did not care to talk about it at all. It was when the Sultan ended by saying "the Jews are intelligent. They will soon find a form that will be acceptable" that Nevlinsky believed that the Sultan merely really wanted to save face and that he would accept in the end. Nevlinsky added that the Sultan seemed to have some sort of trade in mind and that, in diplomatic dealings, one must not discuss the heart of the matter too plainly. Nevlinsky also had the impression that Izzet Bey seemed to be working in Herzl's interests (Herzl, 1960a, p. 400).

On balance, Herzl regarded the trip as a "brilliant success." He had established important political connections and grown to feel less intimidated by the "high and mighty." He was a driven man and believed that with tenacity and perseverance, he might reach his goal before the end of the year. After a few hours in Vienna, he went on to London and Paris to seek financial backing for the next round of negotiations with the Turks (Elon, 1975, pp. 205–206).

Herzl's Meetings with Edmond de Rothschild and Sir Samuel Montagu – July 1896

Herzl arrived in London on July 4, 1896. His plan was to assemble a syndicate of Jewish bankers who would offer the Sultan an annual tribute of one million pounds sterling for a Jewish principality in Palestine under the Sultan's suzerainty. He was also scheduled to address a meeting in East London (Elon, 1975, p. 206).

Herzl's first encounter was with Sir Samuel Montagu, the banker and key figure in his scheme who had been so forthcoming on his previous visit. Indeed, when, at the end of November of the previous year, Herzl had had lunch with Montagu, an Orthodox Jew, prominent banker and Liberal Member of Parliament, he had responded enthusiastically to Herzl's case. He had confessed to Herzl that he felt himself more an Israelite than an Englishman and that he would settle in Palestine with all his family. When Herzl mentioned Argentina as a possible alternative, Montagu would not hear of it. He promised his support, both political and financial, for the acquisition of Palestine. He thought that it was possible to buy the country for two million pounds (Elon, 1975, pp. 171–172).

This time, Montagu was at first too busy to see Herzl. When they finally met later in the week, Montagu was reserved and refused to assume any responsibility. He seemed hesitant and anxious to back off. He set down three conditions for his public adherence to Herzl's cause: (1) He would need the prior consent of the Great Powers; (2) The late Baron Hirsch's foundation would have to lend its support to the tune of ten million pounds; and (3) He would require the participation of Edmond de

Rothschild of Paris (whose philanthropy currently supported a few hundred Jewish colonies in Palestine).

Herzl fared no better with other members of the Anglo-Jewish aristocracy. Claude Montefiore, president of the powerful Anglo-Jewish Association, and Frederick Mocatta, an important financier, called on him at his hotel. Herzl presented them with a very moderate programme: the establishment of a "society of Jews" for the purpose of acquiring, under international law, a territory for those Jews unable to assimilate in their present host countries. Their reply was an emphatic "no." They even advised Herzl to stay away from the contemplated meeting in his honour in East London. This was Montagu's parliamentary constituency, and they felt that Herzl's appearance would excite the masses (Elon, 1975, p. 206).

Elon noted that among upper-class Jews in England, the idea of a Jewish restoration in Palestine was not too popular. In 1896, they hoped for the ultimate triumph of reason and tolerance in England and were unwilling to jeopardize a satisfactory status quo for an adventure in statecraft nurtured in the feverish mind of a Viennese man of letters (Elon, 1975, p. 207).

The response to his appearance was totally different among the poor Jews of East London, most of whom had escaped persecution and Russia and Romania in the last decade. On July 12, 1896, Herzl addressed an excited crowd in the Jewish Working Men's Club of Whitechapel at a meeting called in defiance of the existing communal leadership. The huge audience applauded every word and suggestion. Other speakers also hailed him effusively (Elon, 1975, pp. 207–208).

Thus, even though the rich were disappointing him, Herzl was satisfied with the results of his trip. He had been urged by young enthusiasts in London to pressure the reluctant aristocrats by organizing a mass movement among the poor. At the same time, Herzl still preferred an "aristocratic" solution and decided to make one last effort with Edmond de Rothschild in Paris. Even though Rothschild had already intimated that he regarded Herzl as a dangerous adventurer, Herzl did not shy away from applying for an interview. He was surprised that Rothschild received him immediately. According to Elon, their meeting was the turning point in Herzl's career (Elon, 1975, pp. 208–209).

Of all the Rothschilds, Edmond was foremost in his charitable support of Jewish and other causes. The new Jewish colonies in Palestine were among the main beneficiaries of his generosity. He was said to be the richest man in France. For a Jew, his social prominence was unique. When Herzl came to see him, Rothschild was not a Zionist. In his colonies, he was not seeking a national revival; rather, he was conducting a non-

political experiment to see if it was possible to rehabilitate poor East
European city Jews as farmers in Palestine. Although Palestine was a
historic Jewish homeland, the idea of a Jewish state was anathema to him.
He was strongly opposed to Herzl's political activity, fearing that Herzl's
Zionism might expose French Jews like himself to accusations of
disloyalty to France. By arousing Turkish suspicions, Herzl might even
harm the colonies in Palestine (Elon, 1975, pp. 209–210).

Herzl considered Rothschild the kingpin of the plan he had agreed
upon with Samuel Montagu. However, in light of the current attitudes of
both Jewish aristocrats, Herzl's chances of saving the plan were very dim.
Herzl, nevertheless, was so convinced of the rightness of his cause and so
determined to pursue it that he convinced himself that he could win
Rothschild over by rewarding him for his support by handing over the
leadership of the Zionist movement (Elon, 1975, p. 210).

When they met in Rothschild's office, Herzl began by asking how
familiar Rothschild was with his plan. When Rothschild seemed to lose
himself in a disjointed refutation of Herzl's programme, which he knew
only through hearsay, Herzl bluntly told him that he did not know what it
was about and asked Rothschild to let him explain it to him: "A colony is a
small state; a state is a big colony. You want a small state; I want to build
a big colony" (Elon, 1975, p. 210).

Herzl used every argument in his repertoire to present a sensible and
convincing case. His plan was to consolidate the Turkish national debt for
a Jewish vassal state in Palestine. Rothschild did not have to make up his
mind immediately. Only if the plan was successful would Rothschild be
offered the leadership of the movement, from which Herzl would
voluntarily withdraw. If it was impossible to conclude a transaction with
the Turks, the movement would dissolve and there would be no need for
Rothschild's leadership and support (Elon, 1975, pp. 210–211).

Herzl thought that he saw some positive signs in Rothschild's
demeanour; he listened attentively and, at times, with surprise, and Herzl
thought that he occasionally detected admiration in Rothschild's eyes.
Herzl realized how wrong his impression was when Rothschild quickly
made clear that he wanted nothing to do with the project. First, he did not
trust promises from the Turks. Second, he argued that it would be
impossible to control the influx of the masses into Palestine. "The first to
arrive would be a hundred fifty thousand beggars. They would have to be
fed, presumably by me. I don't feel up to that – but perhaps you do!" he
added sarcastically. Rothschild could not assume such responsibility, and
there could also be unforeseen mishaps (Elon, 1975, p. 211).

Herzl retorted that antisemitism was a much greater and permanent mishap, with loss of honour, life and property. In spite of all his efforts, Rothschild would not budge. He had not read Herzl's pamphlet, which included the meticulous preparation for the arrival of the immigrants and which was designed to preclude mishaps and accelerate absorption in the new country. Herzl repeated his favourite argument that modern science and technology permitted a more rational and humane system of colonization than the chaotic settlements of Australia and America (Elon, 1975, p. 211).

Rothschild was piqued by Herzl's condescending remarks, while Herzl was frustrated by Rothschild's uninformed obstinacy. The battle of words continued for about two hours. When Rothschild asked what Herzl wanted him to do, Herzl answered brusquely that Rothschild did not understand him, that he wanted nothing from him, and that he was only inviting him to lend his conditional adherence (Elon, 1975, p. 211).

Herzl's arguments were unsuccessful. Rothschild was not interested in political action. From Herzl's perspective, Rothschild's philanthropic efforts were of little use; in twelve years, only a few hundred families had been resettled, while in Eastern Europe, millions were waiting to be helped (Elon, 1975, p. 212).

In his last words before the conversation ended, Herzl tried to impress the significance of Rothschild's negative response on him. "You were the keystone of the entire combination. If you refuse, everything I have fashioned so far will collapse. I shall then be obliged to do it in a different way. I shall start a mass agitation.... I was going to turn the direction of the entire project over to you...." Herzl then warned Rothschild that the mishaps he was worried about would be nothing compared to the problems that could be caused by Rothschild's refusal if it would lead to Herzl setting the masses in motion through uncontrollable agitation. In spite of Herzl's final passionate appeal, Rothschild remained immovable. On taking his leave, Herzl saw the entire intricate web collapse because of the unimaginativeness of one millionaire. "And the fate of millions is to hang on such a man..." (Elon, 1975, p. 212).

Herzl's failed attempts to involve the wealthy Jewish establishment politically in the Zionist project led him to the conclusion that his success could only come from the plight and poverty of the Jewish masses. He realized through his early efforts that it would be the poor and downtrodden Jews who would be his constituency. His challenge was to turn this insight into a political reality (Avineri, 1999, p. 9).

First Zionist Congress in Basel – August 31, 1897

Herzl was a practical man who understood that if Zionism was to succeed, it needed a permanent institutional structure that could speak in the name of the movement and move its diverse adherents towards consensus. He wrote of the need for a "gestor" (manager) to direct the Jewish political cause and that this would be a task for a single individual. What was needed was a union of several persons, a body corporate. To this end, Herzl issued a call in 1897 for a Zionist congress to create a permanent association and agree on a common programme (Gelvin, 2005, p. 52).

The First Zionist Congress was held in Basel, Switzerland, from August 29 to 31, 1897. It was attended by 197 delegates from many nations. It appointed Herzl the first president of the World Zionist Organization and approved what came to be known as the "Basel Program." It was during the Basel Congress that political Zionism gained significant momentum. In his opening declaration, Herzl underlined his central objective in organizing the historic meeting. "We are here to lay the foundation stone of the house which will shelter the Jewish nation" (Gauthier, 2007, pp. 242–244).

At the conclusion of the Congress, the following resolution relating to the "aim" of Zionism was adopted:

> The aim is to create for the Jewish people a legally assured home in Palestine. In order to attain this object, the Congress adopts the following means:
>
> To promote the settlement in Palestine of Jewish agriculturalists, handicraftsmen, industrialists and men following professions.
>
> The centralization of the entire Jewish people by means of general institutions in accordance with the laws of the land.
>
> To strengthen Jewish sentiment and national self-conscience.
>
> To obtain the sanction of governments necessary to carry out the objects of Zionism. (Gauthier, 2007, p. 244)

Thereafter, this summary of the aims of Zionism was referred to as the "Basel Program." As noted by Dubnow, the First Basel Congress represented a crucial milestone on the march towards the restoration of Jewish statehood. For the first time, the united representatives of Eastern and Western Jewry, in reaction to the continued assaults on their existence – both in the centre of Western assimilation as well as in the crushing reactionary environment of Tsarist Russia – proclaimed before the world that the scattered sections of Jewry looked upon themselves as one national organism striving for national regeneration (Dubnow, 1920, p. 44).

Stein concurred when he postulated that while Zionism had existed as a purely religious concept since the beginning of the Jewish dispersion, its history as an organized and articulate movement with concrete objectives began in 1897 when, under the leadership of Theodor Herzl, the First Zionist Congress set up the Zionist Organization and in the Basel Program defined its purpose as the creation of Palestine as a home for the Jewish people, secured by public law (Stein, 1961, p. 3).

Three of the four articles of the Basel Program adopted by the First Congress deal with the fundamental task of the party, the colonization of large Jewish masses in Palestine, and the political and financial efforts required to that end. Only one voice addressed the need for strengthening the Jewish national feeling and self-respect. The Zionists of the West emphasized the need for political activities and diplomatic negotiations, while the Zionists of the East laid greater emphasis upon internal cultural work along national lines, which they considered as indispensable requisites for national rebirth. These two competing principles became the major subject of debate at each succeeding annual congress (at the second and third held in Basel in 1898 and 1899, at the fourth in London in 1900, and at the fifth in Basel in 1901) (Dubnow, 1920, pp. 44–45).

Herzl devoted the remainder of his life to the sort of diplomatic activities endorsed by the First Zionist Congress. The founding of the World Zionist Organization was a defining event in the history of Zionism. It constituted a critical juncture on the path to the reconstitution of the ancestral Jewish homeland. Now, the Zionist movement had an organization to speak in its name and an institutional structure to plan and coordinate its activities (Gelvin, 2005, pp. 55–56).

In light of the geopolitical considerations the Zionist leadership had to take into account, it comes as no surprise that the World Zionist Organization used the words "a home for the Jewish people" and not a "Jewish state." There is no question that Herzl had a Jewish state in mind. No one reading Herzl's most important work *The Jewish State* can fail to conclude that the vision of a Jewish state was the unequivocal embodiment of the Zionist aspiration. As a matter of fact, "state" was the only word he used throughout the ninety-nine-page text when referring to the envisaged homeland (Herzl, 2010, pp. 1–99).

What took twenty years from the time of the First Zionist Congress' issuing of the Basel Program on August 31, 1897 to the submission of the Zionist Organization to the British government on July 18, 1917 was the forging of a unified leadership and the definition of the Zionist objectives in a manner that would maximize the possibility for these to gain the support of the British government as a first step towards a binding reality under international law. The delegates used the word "home" to dispel the concerns of the Ottoman government, which was unlikely to look favourably on any movement with designs on its territory. Gelvin argues that those concerns could have derailed the plans of the World Zionist Organization for two reasons: first, that the Basel Program stipulated Palestine as the location for the Jewish home, and second, that it should be "secured by public law." Unfortunately for the Zionists, Ottoman authorities were already aware of both their aspirations and the conditions in Eastern Europe. As early as 1882, after the worst pogroms to date in Russia, the Ottoman Sultan issued a ruling granting Jews permission to migrate to the Empire, but under two conditions: they would have to renounce their European citizenship and become Ottoman subjects, and they could immigrate to any place in the Empire except Palestine. Any Jewish immigration to Palestine would, therefore, have to occur secretly and land purchases would have to be made through phantom agents (Gelvin, 2005, p. 53).

Biographers and historians make a great deal of listing the illustrious personalities Herzl was able to meet and how this brought the Zionist struggle to the world's attention. What gets lost in the details of the incessant hustle and bustle these encounters entailed is the identification of the basic motivation underlying this arduous and frenetic activity. What drove this lonely crusader into a quest of such intensity that it cost him his family as well as his life that ended at such an early age? The urgency came from Herzl's premonition that European Jewry was doomed unless a new home was found. While Herzl was alarmed by the populist antisemitic developments in "emancipated" Western Europe, the situation in the East, where the vast majority of Europe's Jewish population was located at the time, was more pressing. For full details on the plight of Russian Jewry, see the previous chapter.

Herzl's Audience with Emperor Wilhelm II in Constantinople – October 19, 1898

Herzl devoted a considerable amount of space in his diary to both his preparation for and his meeting with the Emperor. The draft of the address he was going to deliver in Palestine two weeks later and which he was due to submit the evening before his meeting with the Emperor on October 18, while composed in haste, clearly laid out the aim of the Zionist movement and the purpose of submitting it to the Emperor. As this address was supposed to be delivered in Palestine on November 2, it was written from the perspective of that location. Here are the main excerpts, quoted from the actual text as reproduced in Herzl's diary:

> With deepest reverence a delegation of sons of Israel approaches to German Kaiser in the country which was our fathers' and no longer belongs to us. We are bound to this sacred soil through no valid type of ownership. Many generations have come and gone since this earth was Jewish. If we talk about it, it is only as about the dream of very ancient days. But the dream is still alive, lives in many hundreds of thousands of hearts; because it was and is a wonderful comfort in many an hour of pain for our poor people [...].
>
> The Zionist movement of today is a fully modern one. It grows out of the situations and conditions of present-day life, and aims at solving the Jewish question on the basis of the possibilities of our time [...].
>
> Above all, we have aroused the national consciousness of our scattered brethren. At the Congress of Basel, the program of our movement was formulated before all the world. It is the creation, under public law, of a home for the Jewish people. This is the land of our fathers, the land suitable for colonization and cultivation. Your Majesty has seen the country. It cries out for people to work it. And we have among our brethren a frightful proletariat. These people cry out for a land to cultivate. Now we should like to create a new welfare out of these states of distress – of the land and of the people – by the systematic combination of both. We consider our cause so fine, so worthy of the sympathy of the most magnanimous minds, that we are requesting your Imperial Majesty's exalted aid for the project [...].
>
> We are honestly convinced that the implementation of the Zionist plan must mean welfare for Turkey as well. Energies and material resources will be brought to the country: a magnificent rectification of desolate areas may easily be foreseen; and from all this there will arise more happiness and more culture for many human beings. We are planning to establish a Jewish Land-Company for Syria and Palestine, which is to undertake the great project, and request the protection of the German Kaiser for this company. Our idea offends no one's rights or religious feelings; it breathes long desired reconciliation. We understand and respect the devotion of all faiths to the soil on which, after all, the faith of our fathers, too, arose. (Herzl, 1960b, pp. 719–721)

Herzl reported that when, after all the delays and protocol, he found himself face-to-face with the Emperor, they exchanged friendly greetings, after which the Emperor promptly invited Herzl to state his case. The Emperor's Secretary of State for Foreign Affairs, the "unsympathetic" Prince Bernhard von Bülow, was present throughout the meeting. Herzl notes that the Emperor soon took over the conversation and explained why the Zionist movement appealed to him. It was when Wilhelm remarked that there were elements among "your people" who were usurers at work among the rural population and that these elements could be more useful if they took their possessions and went to settle in the colonies that Herzl started to feel irritated. He notes that he was annoyed by the fact that the Emperor should identify the Jews with a few usurers. Herzl responded with a brief speech attacking antisemitism which, he told the Emperor, had stabbed his people right in the heart and had deeply hurt them. When Bülow noticed that Herzl "was making an attack," he retorted that while the Kaiser, his father and grandfather had always been gracious towards the Jews, Jews were to be seen among all the opposition parties, including the anti-monarchical ones. Bülow called Herzl's attention to the fact that rich Jews were not in favour of his ideas. Bülow added that the major newspapers were not for Herzl's ideas either, particularly his own, and that Herzl should certainly try to win some of them over. Herzl notes that he felt sure that Bülow raised his objections to indicate to the Kaiser that Herzl had no power behind him. However, Bülow stopped at outright rejecting Herzl's proposals as he did not dare to go as far as to oppose the Kaiser himself, who, Herzl felt, seemed to be favourably disposed towards him.

When the conversation turned to the situation in France, the Kaiser, Herzl noted, "took over with verve." The Kaiser told Herzl that he had read in the *Neue Freie Presse* about the projected coup d'état and asked Herzl for his opinion. This is where Herzl remarked that the French Army had suffered greatly because of the Dreyfus incident, and a lengthy conversation about the corruption and treachery of the French government and military ensued (Herzl, 1960b, pp. 727–733).

When Herzl was finally able to bring the conversation back to the purpose of his meeting with the Kaiser, the latter referred – with what Herzl felt was "free-and-easy sympathy and certainly not heartlessness" – to the fact that the Jewish people "have had a pretty bad time of it in Russia during the past couple of hundred years." Later in his notes, Herzl recalls that when the distressing situation of the Jews in the East was mentioned, the Kaiser had added that things would probably turn out worst of all in France. "In that country antisemitism is likely to become strongest for there the Church is behind it, and the Jesuits won't let go once they start a thing like that. Herr von Rothschild seems to know this too, for he is having his art collection shipped to London" (Herzl, 1960b, pp. 733–734).

Herzl recorded that it was at this point that he proceeded to unfold his entire plan before the Kaiser. Herzl believes he presented all the arguments he could muster. He notes that the Kaiser listened to him "magnificently" and with visible strain and effort when Herzl mentioned the complicated forms of the loans he could arrange for Turkey. Finally, Herzl told the Kaiser that, while he might be extremely stubborn about it, the whole thing seemed "completely natural" to him, whereupon the Kaiser looked at him grandly and responded: "To me, too!" Bülow tried to interject by referring to the cost of satisfying the Turkish need for monetary persuasion, but the Kaiser waved him off and remarked that "surely it will make an impression if the German Kaiser concern himself with it and shows an interest in it." "After all," the Kaiser continued, "I am the only one who still sticks by the Sultan. He puts stock in me" (Herzl, 1960b, p. 733).

When the Kaiser glanced at his watch and rose, he saw that Herzl had something else to say and asked him if he had another question. Herzl brought up the specific question about the audience in Palestine, his address, etc. The Kaiser told him to write his address and to give it to Bülow and that he would go over it carefully with him. "Just tell me in a word what I am to ask of the Sultan," the Kaiser added. To which Herzl replied, "A Chartered Company – under German protection." "Good! A Chartered Company!" the Kaiser responded, whereupon he gave Herzl a strong handshake and exited the room (Herzl, 1960b, pp. 733–734).

After the audience, Bülow urged Herzl to talk things over with Adolf Marschall, the German ambassador to Constantinople, to get exact information from him. Bülow told Herzl that he thought the Turks were now unfavourably disposed. Herzl arranged with Bülow that after this conversation with Marschall, he would prepare his address and send it to him. Herzl notes that he was exhausted from the great mental strain and had great difficulty finishing the text of his speech. After a few hours of sleep, he got up and wrote for half an hour, went back to bed exhausted, got up again at 6 o'clock, and then finished as much of his address as he could by half-past eight, at which point he sent it off to Bülow with a covering letter (Herzl, 1960b, pp. 734–735).

Reception by Emperor Wilhelm II of Zionist Delegation in Jerusalem – November 2, 1898

Herzl spent the next few days on board a ship on his way to meeting the Emperor in Jerusalem. His mind was full of doubts and uncertainties. He was wondering how the Turks would regard the matter, which had now become something to take seriously. He felt that he had become a troublesome personage to many a party interested in the Holy Land and wondered at the possibility of some plot being hatched against him in

Palestine. He noted that he was not sharing his anxieties with anyone, not even his travelling companions. To his diary he confided:

> I am obviously approaching the climax of my tragic enterprise. If the expedition to Palestine is successful, the very hardest part of which will be done. Every else would then be simply a matter of execution, something which can be accomplished by others, too [...]. The days I'm now living through are critical days of the first order. (Herzl, 1960b, pp. 736–737)

Several pages in Herzl's diary are devoted to the impressions he gathered on his journey from Constantinople to Palestine, via Alexandria. While it is beyond the scope of this study to replicate the huge volume of details contained in his diary, the following samples will enhance the reader's awareness of his mindset during those daunting days. It is obvious that his main observations are measured against the framework of his Zionist dreams:

> Hot days in Alexandria and Port Said. Alexandria shows how a clever European administration can draw a habitable, comfortable city even out of the hottest soil.
>
> At Port Said I greatly admired the Suez Canal [...]. One must admire the colossal will that executed this simple idea of taking away the sands.
>
> Rishon-le-Zion, for a poor village, is a fairly prosperous place. But if one has imagined it as more than a poor settlement, one is disappointed. Thick dust on the roads, a bit of greenery [...]. The administrator received us with a frightened air, obviously dared to be neither amiable nor unamiable. Fear of Monsieur le Baron hovers over everything. The poor colonists have swapped one fear for another. We were shown to the wine cellars with elaborate ceremony. But I've never doubted that with money one can set up industrial establishments no matter where. With the millions which have been poured into the sand here and stolen and squandered, far different results could have been achieved.
>
> When I remember thee in days to come, O Jerusalem, it will not be with pleasure. The musty deposits of two thousand years of inhumanity, intolerance, and uncleanliness lie in the foul-smelling alleys. The one man who has been present all this time, the amiable dreamer of Nazareth, has only contributed to increasing the hatred. If we ever get Jerusalem and I'm still able to do anything actively at the time, I would begin by cleaning it up. I would clear out everything that is not something sacred, set up workers' homes outside the city, empty the nests of filth and tear them down, burn the secular ruins, and transfer the bazaars elsewhere. Then, retaining the old architectural style as much as possible, I would build around the holy places a comfortable airy new city with proper sanitation.
>
> After we drove away from Rishon, a cavalcade came galloping toward us from the settlement Rehovot: about twenty young fellows [...], lustily

singing Hebrew songs and swarming about our carriage [...]. We had tears in our eyes when we saw those fleet, daring horsemen into whom our young trouser-salesman can be transformed. They reminded me of the Far-West Cowboys of the American plains whom I once saw in Paris. (Herzl, 1960b, pp. 738–748).

Herzl had planned to await the Kaiser the following morning on the highway outside Mikveh Israel. At nine o'clock, the imperial procession, led by fierce-looking Turkish cavalry, appeared on the highway. Herzl notes that when the Kaiser recognized him, even at a distance, he guided his horse in Herzl's direction and pulled up in front of him. The Kaiser leaned down over the neck of his horse and they shook hands. They exchanged cordial greetings. Herzl said that he was having a look at the country. To Herzl's question as to how the journey had agreed with his Majesty so far, the Kaiser replied: "Very hot! But the country has a future." "At the moment it is still sick," Herzl said. "Water is what it needs, a lot of water!" the Kaiser replied. "Yes, Your Majesty! Irrigation on a large scale!" Herzl agreed. After a last handshake from the Kaiser, the imperial procession moved on (Herzl, 1960b, p. 743).

Herzl recalled the train ride from Jaffa to Jerusalem and the frightful heat, with the departure from Jaffa station taking an hour. He describes sitting in the cramped, crowded, scorching compartment as torture. During the ride, Herzl grew more and more feverish and weak. It was already well into the Sabbath when they arrived in Jerusalem. Herzl noted that he would have gladly driven the half-hour distance but that when he saw the long faces around him, he resigned himself to walk into the city, weak with fever though he was. He tottered all over the place on his cane, with his other arm braced alternately against his companions' arms (Herzl, 1960b, p. 744).

Herzl described the three days between his encounter with the Kaiser on October 29, 1898 and their meeting on November 2, at which he would read the text of his script directly to the Kaiser, as a desultory mix of positive and negative impressions and emotions. At first, he had become so enfeebled that he spent the entire day after his arrival admiring Jerusalem's magnificent setting through the windows of his room (Herzl, 1960b, p. 745).

Herzl was shunned by the local Jewish community. After the communal leaders were told that Herzl would very much like to await the Kaiser under their triumphal arch, they declared that there were no more available spaces. The Sephardic Rabbi Meir, who did visit Herzl, explained that the local Grand Rabbis did not want to incur the displeasure of the Turkish government. His visit to the Wailing Wall was equally disappointing.

"Because that place is pervaded by hideous, wretched, speculative beggary, a deeper emotion refuses to come" (Herzl, 1960b, p. 746).

Herzl noted that when he visited the Tower of David, he said to his friends, "It would be a good idea on the Sultan's part if he had me arrested here." They had walked rather quickly through the Via Dolorosa because it was said to be an ill-omened place for Jews. It was also forbidden to set foot in the Mosque of Omar and the Temple area, otherwise it would become subject to excommunication by the rabbis. Herzl remarks that this is what happened to Sir Moses Montefiore. "How much superstition and fanaticism on every side! Yet I'm not afraid of any of these fanatics" (Herzl, 1960b, p. 747).

Herzl next described his visit to a Jewish hospital. He summed up his impression in two words: "Misery and uncleanliness." For appearance's sake, he had to testify in the visitor's book to the hospital's cleanliness. "This is how lies originate" (Herzl, 1960b, p. 747). It is a testimony to Herzl's unshakable belief in the feasibility of his vision that in spite of the dismal picture he found at the time of his visit to the soil of the destined homeland, he reaffirmed in his October 31, 1898 entry that "I am quite firmly convinced that a magnificent New Jerusalem could be built outside the old city walls. The old Jerusalem would still remain Lourdes and Mecca and Yerusholayim. A very pretty, elegant town would be quite possible beside it" (Herzl, 1960b, p. 747).

Eventually, after two days of frustrating delays and bureaucratic meddling, Herzl was summoned to the German Consulate, which wanted further information from Herzl about the audience he had requested. When Herzl arrived at the imperial encampment, the "already very self-possessed" Legation Councillor produced Herzl's corrected address. A number of passages in the draft Herzl had submitted had been crossed out with a pencil. He was told, without being given the source of this decision, that he could not say those deleted items to the Kaiser. The councillor asked Herzl to submit the document to him again, along with the revised manuscript, so that he might compare them and see whether Herzl had done things right. Herzl maintained his self-control, managed to overlook the impertinence, and calmly agreed to comply. It would take too much space here to relate the condescending manner in which the consular staff continued to screen Herzl. It will suffice to say that he felt that they "were all furious that the Kaiser should pay so much attention to a Jew" (Herzl, 1960b, p. 752).

Finally, on November 2, the brief reception with the Kaiser, which, Herzl noted, "will be preserved forever in the history of the Jews, and it is not beyond possibility that it will have historic consequences as well," took place in the imperial tent. When Herzl entered the tent, the Kaiser held out his hand very affably. Bülow stood to one side, holding Herzl's corrected draft in his hand. After Herzl introduced his four companions, he took his script and read it aloud (Herzl, 1960b, p. 755).

The Kaiser thanked Herzl for his communication which, the Kaiser said, had interested him greatly. He observed that the matter still required thorough study and further discussion. He noted that "the land needs, above all, water and shade." His observations had told him that the soil was arable. He noted that there was room for everyone in the country and that the work of the colonists would also serve as a stimulating example to the native population. "Your movement, with which I am thoroughly acquainted, contains a sound idea." He assured Herzl of his continued interest. After having concluded his formal response, the Kaiser gave Herzl his hand but did not yet dismiss Herzl and his companions. Instead, he drew Herzl into a conversation with Bülow. The Kaiser mentioned the extreme heat, whereupon Bülow echoed the Kaiser's observation that water was the main thing. Herzl replied that water could be supplied; it would cost billions, but it would also yield billions. "Well, money is what you have plenty of, more money than any of us," the Kaiser replied. Bülow echoed the Kaiser's words: "Yes, the money which is such a problem for us you have in abundance." Herzl mentioned the water power potential of the Jordan and drew Joseph Seidener, the Russian Jewish engineer and active Zionist leader, into the conversation. Seidener discussed "dams, etc." The Kaiser eagerly took up the subject and expanded on the idea. Herzl tried to prolong the discussion, but he was not able to bring in the other members of his delegation as the Kaiser concluded the audience by once more shaking hands with him. The fact that the Kaiser had said neither yes nor no led Herzl to surmise that a lot had been happening behind the scenes (Herzl, 1960b, pp. 755–757).

Herzl's unease increased when he saw, after his return from Jerusalem, how the German press downplayed his audience with the Kaiser. All the German news agency reported on November 2, 1898 was that the Kaiser had received a Jewish deputation which presented him with an album of pictures of the Jewish colonists established in Palestine and that, in replying to an address by the leader of the deputation, he had expressed a benevolent interest in the improvement of agriculture in Palestine, thus furthering the welfare of the Turkish Empire, with complete respect for the sovereignty of the Sultan. Herzl tried to raise the morale of his very disappointed companions by promising that he would arrange for the publication of a version more suitable to their cause (Herzl, 1960b, p. 767).

In his diary, Herzl noted that in Palestine, Germany did not keep its promise to him and that the lower functionaries shamefully twisted and distorted the Kaiser's actual words in Jerusalem, which had already been greatly toned down (Herzl, 1960b, p. 768). In a further diary entry, Herzl rationalizes that the fact that the Kaiser did not assume the protectorate in Jerusalem was actually an advantage for the future development of the Zionist cause. He reasons that, while the protectorate would have been a clear immediate benefit, in the long run, "we would have to pay most usurious interest for this protectorate" (Herzl, 1960b, pp. 768–769).

Elon notes that Herzl never learned all the reasons that had caused the Kaiser's abrupt change of mind. Elon was able to reconstruct the behind the scenes events from the records preserved in the German and Austrian state archives. These sources confirm that the Kaiser had initially been very much in favour of Herzl's project and that he had in fact urged the Sultan to grant Herzl a charter for Palestine. The records reveal that the Kaiser had raised the matter in Constantinople on more than one occasion, but that each time the Sultan had answered evasively and changed the subject. This led the Kaiser to abandon his efforts to enlist the Sultan's agreement to grant Herzl's charter for Palestine and to turn his attention to what had been the chief purpose of his pilgrimage to the Holy Land, which was to secure a concession for the construction of a strategic railroad to Baghdad (Elon, 1975, p. 301).

In other words, while the idea of a German protectorate over a Jewish Palestine had appealed to him briefly, the Kaiser's main purpose remained the consolidation of a continental block against Britain. The Turks seemed better allies than the Jews, and the Turks did not want any more Jews in Palestine. As a result of these considerations, while Herzl believed himself on the threshold of success, the Kaiser's enthusiasm for the Zionist project turned in other directions (Elon, 1975, pp. 301–302).

What confused matters even further was the fact that the Kaiser's closest advisors worked at cross-purposes. While the Grand Duke of Baden remained an enthusiastic supporter of the Zionist project, the Prince of Hohenlohe, the Imperial Chancellor, considered Herzl "a freak." He accused the Grand Duke of Baden of doing Germany and the Jews a disservice by showing interest in Herzl's cause. Marschall, the ambassador to Constantinople, instead of reporting the friendly attitude of the Turks, as the Grand Duke had erroneously assumed he would, warned the Kaiser against rousing the Sultan's ire. Bülow was especially opposed to Herzl's project. The nature and tone of Bülow's objections speak for themselves, and his remarks to the press included such statements as "These people have no money. The rich Jews don't want to participate and with the lousy

Jews of Poland you can't do a thing." On one occasion, he announced that "beggars are unfit for establishing a state, even for colonization" (Elon, 1975, p. 302).

While hindsight might suggest that Herzl had put too much faith in the Kaiser's power to influence events to meet Herzl's expectations, it should never be forgotten that it was Herzl's unwavering faith in the righteousness of his cause that had driven him from the start and that by holding on to it, undaunted, for the rest of his life, he was able to turn the Zionist aspirations into a potent political force.

Audience with Sultan Abdul Hamid II in Constantinople – May 18, 1901

In June of 1900, before the Fourth Zionist Congress, which was scheduled in August, Herzl felt that he needed a successful development of some sort so as not to face the Congress empty-handed once more. By now, his health had deteriorated and his appearance and gait had significantly aged. He still had hopes of converting the Sultan. Max Nordau had introduced him to a cosmopolitan middleman by the name of Arminius Vámbéry on June 17, 1900, who was a personal friend of the Sultan. Herzl told Vámbéry that he hoped to convert the Sultan to Zionism through a personal audience and asked Vámbéry for his help. Vámbéry was sceptical that Herzl could succeed in winning over the Sultan. Herzl replied that, whatever the outcome, an audience would be useful in itself as a first step, especially if it came before the next Congress, and added that there was always time to discuss details later. All he wanted now was an audience with the Sultan before the Congress in order to maintain the momentum of the cause. He pleaded with Vámbéry to ask the Sultan to receive him. "Tell him that I can render him a service in the world press, and that the mere fact of my appearance will raise his credit with others." He also asked Vámbéry to come along as his interpreter. He told Herzl that the Turks could not be rushed and that, at his age, it was too difficult to travel to Turkey in the summer. Vámbéry asked for time to think it over (Elon, 1975, pp. 321–323).

In the end, Vámbéry did convey Herzl's request to the Sultan, but he warned Herzl that he was not sure if and when his letter would reach its destination and asked Herzl to be patient. It was not until October 15, 1900 that Nuri Bey, Secretary-General of the Turkish Foreign Ministry, contacted Herzl to announce that the Turkish government had "a pressing need for seven or eight hundred thousand Turkish pounds." If Herzl could arrange an immediate loan at 6 or 6.5 percent per annum, he would receive his audience with the Sultan as a reward. Herzl immediately obtained a binding letter of intent from Jacobus Kann's Dutch banking firm (Elon, 1975, p. 326). Kann was a young private banker and the only financier who, in September of 1898, had been ready to participate in the launching of the Jewish Colonial Trust (Elon, 1975, p. 272).

What followed was a protracted correspondence during which Nuri Bey attempted to increase the amount of the loan and to lower the interest rate. According to Elon, Herzl's offer was used by the Turks as a lever to obtain better terms from other possible lenders and as a source of personal income for venal diplomats. While Herzl was involved in elaborate negotiations over the terms of the loan and the fees requested by the Turkish negotiators for their efforts, the Turkish government concluded the loan with the Deutsche Bank, bringing all Herzl's efforts to nought. Although the Deutsche Bank had offered terms that were less beneficial than Herzl's, it had apparently been more lavish in its distribution of *baksheesh* (Elon, 1975, pp. 326–327).

Herzl met with Vámbéry to discuss these developments. Vámbéry again wrote to Constantinople. The only response was an announcement that Turkey opposed the recreation of the Kingdom of Judea and that henceforth Jews would no longer be permitted to enter Palestine. Herzl wrote to Vámbéry on December 28, 1900 that "The whore wants to raise her price, so she says she cannot be had. Am I right?" Vámbéry agreed with him. He had been to Constantinople and met his friend, the Sultan. He wrote to Herzl that the Sultan had expressed himself on the question of Jewish immigration to Palestine quite differently from the official announcement. "He does not give a hoot. All he wants is gold and power" (Elon, 1975, p. 327).

However, in spite of Vámbéry's urging, the Sultan was not yet ready to meet Herzl. After waiting in "agony and suspense," early in May, Vámbéry made another trip to Constantinople to press Herzl's case. For two long weeks, Herzl waited impatiently. Finally, the Sultan agreed to receive him. Herzl, accompanied by his closest collaborator, David Wolffsohn, and one of his faithful adjutants, the architect Oscar Marmorek, took the train to Constantinople for his meeting with the Sultan (Elon, 1975, pp. 327–329).

Herzl arrived at the Hotel Royal in Constantinople on May 13, 1901, where he settled down to wait for his summons. He spent the next few days sightseeing, rehearsing exactly what he was going to tell the Sultan, and dealing with a number of self-appointed middlemen who tried to extract substantial bribes for the imaginary services they claimed they had provided on Herzl's behalf (Herzl, 1960c, pp. 1105–1112).

Finally, on May 18, after spending a whole day attending the customary Friday ceremonies and shows at the palace, Herzl was conducted to the audience chamber for his meeting with the Sultan. Ibrahim Bey, the official greeter of ambassadors, was in attendance as interpreter. After a few minutes discussing a few desultory matters, Herzl tried to steer the discussion to the purpose of his visit. To set the right tone, Herzl said that he was devoted to the Sultan because he was good to the Jews and that Jews all over the world were grateful for this. The Sultan replied that he had always been a friend of the Jews and that, in fact, he only relied on the Muslims and the Jews and did not have the same amount of confidence in his other subjects (Herzl, 1960c, p. 1113).

Herzl then lamented the injustices the Jews experienced throughout the world, to which the Sultan replied that he kept his empire open to Jewish refugees. It was at this point that Herzl used his considerable skills as a communicator and negotiator to raise the issue of the Sultan's main preoccupation, the Turkish national debt, in a way that would not offend the Sultan's sensitivities. Herzl had prepared himself for this challenge by planning to use the old story of Androcles and the Lion, where, euphemistically, he would refer to the Sultan as the lion, the Turkish national debt as the thorn in the lion's foot, and Herzl as Androcles, who would pull the thorn from the Sultan's foot (Herzl, 1960c, p. 1110). The ploy worked, as the Sultan acknowledged the compliment with a smile, and when Herzl asked him if he could speak openly and plainly, the Sultan begged him to do so. "The thorn, as I see it," Herzl continued, "is your *dette publique* [public debt]. If it could be removed, Turkey would be able to unfold afresh in vitality, in which I have faith" (Herzl, 1960c, pp. 1113–1114).

The Sultan ruefully replied that, since the beginning of his reign, he had striven in vain to remove this thorn, which he had inherited from his predecessors and which seemed impossible to get rid of. If Herzl could be of help in this, "it would be ever so nice" (Herzl, 1960c, p. 1114).

Herzl replied that he believed that he could, but that the first and fundamental condition was absolute secrecy. The reason he gave for his insistence on secrecy was that the powers who wanted Turkey weak would try hard to prevent its recovery and would make every effort to frustrate "this operation." The Sultan understood and agreed (Herzl, 1960c, p. 1114).

Herzl noted that from that point, he took the lead in the conversation. He would have this operation carried out by his friends on all the stock exchanges of Europe, provided he had the Sultan's support. When the time came, the support would have to take the form of some measure that was particularly friendly to the Jews and would have to be proclaimed in an appropriate manner. The Sultan gingerly replied that he had a court jeweller who was a Jew and that he might say something favourable about the Jews to him and instruct him to publish it. He would do the same thing with the local Chief Rabbi, the Hakham Bashi (Herzl, 1960c, p. 1114).

Herzl rejected this offer because it would not serve the purpose. "It wouldn't get out into the world in a way that might be useful to us." He told the Sultan that he would like to "put the active sympathies of Jewry to work for the Turkish Empire. Therefore, the proclamation would have to have an imposing character. Words spoken to the Hakham Bashi would only remain in Turkey" (Herzl, 1960c, pp. 1114–1115).

When Herzl noted that the Sultan nodded his agreement to everything he said, he continued by telling the Sultan that all his beautiful country needed was the industrial skill of the Jewish people. The Europeans usually went to Turkey to enrich themselves and then rushed off again with their spoils. An entrepreneur was entitled to make a respectable and honest profit, but after that, he should remain in the country where he had acquired his wealth (Herzl, 1960c, p. 1115).

Nodding contentedly, the Sultan said that unexploited treasures still existed in his country; he had just received a telegram from Baghdad saying that "oil fields have been discovered there, richer than those of the Caucasus." The Sultan told Herzl that he would like to show him the areas served by the Anatolian railroad, the land on both sides of which was like a garden. There was ore and gold and silver mines. During the reigns of his predecessors, gold had been mined, made into ingots, coined and used to pay the soldiers (Herzl, 1960c, p. 1116).

After a discussion of a number of other fundraising ideas, the Sultan refocused on his main priority, which was the removal of the public debt. Herzl notes that, by this time, he was exhausted; the conversation had lasted over two hours. Herzl noted that he felt he had "spun the threads the way I had wanted to." Herzl believed the Sultan would now wish to hear further details from him, so he let the conversation flag. The Sultan, too, found nothing more to say. Herzl stayed a little while longer to recapitulate. Herzl and the Sultan committed themselves once more to keep their intentions and understanding secret. Herzl, with the Congress in mind, told the Sultan that he desired a pro-Jewish proclamation at a moment to be decided by him. He also requested a detailed presentation of the financial situation and the consolidation project. The Sultan promised that all these requests would be granted (Herzl, 1960c, p. 1117).

No sooner had Herzl returned home than he was besieged by a series of contradictory suggestions and demands involving the members of the

Sultan's inner cabinet with whom he had been in contact during his stay in Constantinople. They demanded payment for what they considered was their contribution to Herzl's "successful" meeting with the Sultan and indulged in a series of confusing backstabbing power-play manoeuvres that Herzl found exhausting to deal with, and which he dutifully noted in his diary (Herzl, 1960c, pp. 1119–1126).

On May 19, the day after his meeting with the Sultan, Ibrahim Bey invited Herzl to have lunch with him. Izzet Bey walked in unexpectedly and joined them. After the meal, he identified himself as the man charged with explaining to Herzl the plan for the consolidation of the public debt. To Herzl, it was "obviously a thieves' plan." A syndicate was to supply thirty million pounds, with which the debt could be bought up on the stock exchanges. To Herzl, it looked like "sheer nonsense." He said that he would think it over and then give them his opinion (Herzl, 1960c, p. 1123).

On May 20, Herzl and his party packed their trunks and bags, first thing in the morning, to be able to leave Constantinople at noon. Herzl and Wolffsohn then made their way to the palace, where the Sultan and his ministers were waiting to hear what Herzl had to say after his previous day's meeting with the Sultan. When they arrived at the palace at 9 o'clock, Ibrahim Bey gave Herzl a message from the Sultan stating that he was too busy to see them at this time, but that Herzl should communicate to him without delay whatever he had to say. The Sultan was very curious to learn Herzl's proposals, as the finances at this particular time were in an even sadder condition than at any time since the beginning of his reign. Herzl gave Ibrahim an oral outline, which broke down into two parts and a general rationale, which he had Ibrahim write down for his report to the Sultan. They are noted verbatim in Herzl's diary:

I. Negative Part: (a) Izzet's consolidation plan was impracticable and even to attempt it would be harmful. (b) All loans are inadvisable at present, the main reason being that in her present situation Turkey could only obtain money on the most severely usurious terms – *et encore* [and then]!

II. Positive Part: (a) Buying up the *dette* on the stock exchanges should be carried out in complete secrecy by a trustworthy syndicate, something that under the most favorable circumstances could be accomplished within three years. (b) Meanwhile, immediate requirements must be provided for, and, in particular, steps taken to meet the deficit of 1.5 million pounds by October 1. (c) During this time, however, tapping new sources of revenue should be studied and implemented.

III. General Rationale: We Jews need a protector in the world, and we
would like this protector (the aforementioned lion) to regain his full
strength. (Herzl, 1960c, pp. 1129–1130)

At 11 o'clock, Ibrahim had finished, sealed the report and sent it to the
Sultan. After a short time, Ibrahim was summoned by the Sultan. When he
returned, Tahsin Bey, the Sultan's first secretary, was with him. Ibrahim
was positively amiable this time. He squeezed Herzl's hand with a smile,
regretted that he did not have more time for him and assured him that he
counted on seeing him again soon in Constantinople. A short while later,
the door suddenly opened and Izzet entered, holding in his hand a piece of
paper that Herzl immediately recognized. It was the strictly confidential
report which he had dictated to Ibrahim and which was intended only for
the Sultan. Herzl notes that, a long time ago, the American ambassador
Oscar Straus had told him in Vienna that the Sultan was a scoundrel. "Was
this the "secret, secret" that he had promised me with his eyes solemnly
upturned?" He harshly asked Herzl in what way the plan for consolidating
the debt was harmful. Herzl recognized that his own proposal had thwarted
Izzet's "thievish designs." At first, Herzl tried to be polite. "I am not
saying that it isn't good," Herzl said. "Ah, then it *is* good?" said Izzet
sarcastically, upon which he turned to Ibrahim to take notes so that he
could submit a statement to the Sultan, "garnished with lies" (Herzl,
1960c, pp. 1131–1132).

Herzl immediately realized the danger in Izzet's manoeuvre. As they
were speaking French, Herzl calmly told Ibrahim: "*Oui, Excellence,
ecrivez! L'idee est bonne et belle, comme il serait beau aussi de voler*
[Yes, Your Excellency, write! The idea is good and fine, just as it would
be fine to *voler* (in French, *voler* means both to steal and to fly) – P. G.
trans.]." Herzl notes that a furtive look came into Izzet's eyes. "Did I mean
stealing or flying?" Herzl politely added that he had meant to fly in the air
but that this was impossible under the circumstances. Like in attempting
an impossible aerial flight you might fall and break something, the idea
was harmful. It would only result in raising the price of Turkish bonds on
the stock market – but the operation was impracticable. They would never
find the thirty million pounds needed to begin the redemption. And even if
they found them, the price would go up as a result of the purchases, and
the thirty million would no longer suffice by a long shot (Herzl, 1960c, p.
1132).

Izzet protested that this is not what he had meant. Herzl made it easy
for him to come around as he wanted to win him over. The conversation
continued in a more gentle way. They talked about the revenues to be
created. The Sultan was offering Herzl the exploitation of five monopolies:

mines, oil fields, etc. Herzl presumed that this meant that he and his people were to raise the money for this purpose so that they could "clean us out." Izzet followed this up by saying that his government needed about four million pounds because they had ordered warships, etc. Through all this, Herzl acted as if he believed and trusted them so as to keep the process going. When Izzet asked him what Herzl's idea for raising and covering such a loan was, Herzl notes that he did not want to come right out with the Charter but wanted to let them work up to it and said that he would get back with an answer in three or four weeks, after he had consulted with his friends (Herzl, 1960c, p. 1133).

At this point, the conversation reached an unexpected climax. The Sultan wanted to know about the citizenship of those Jews who wanted to do business with or inside Turkey. Izzet explained that the "Israelites" could come to Turkey, but they must agree to become Ottoman subjects. Whether they bought back bonds of the public debt or whether they came in as colonists, they had to renounce their previous allegiance and have this renunciation documented by the government concerned. They also needed to perform military service if called upon by His Imperial Majesty. "Under these conditions we could let in Israelites of every land." Herzl observed that Izzet uttered these words with the "friendliness of a hyena." Herzl realized that all Izzet and his people were interested in was bringing in poor men and rich men for them to plunder, but he felt that this was not the moment to raise objections with a bunch of villains from whom, eventually, the Charter would have to be bought section by section anyway (Herzl, 1960c, pp. 1134–1135).

Izzet went on in the same vein. "For another thing, colonization must not take place in masses. Instead, let us say five families here and five there – scattered, without connection." Herzl thought to himself that this condition would make it easier for the Turks to plunder and slay these hapless few. Herzl continued to feign agreement but commented that while he would not have the slightest objection to such dispersion, "certain technical and economic difficulties nevertheless militate against it." Herzl told Izzet that precedent had shown that scattered settlements lacked the necessary economic foundation and that, therefore, there was no point to such haphazard emigration. What could be done, instead, was to organize a great land company to which uncultivated territory could be assigned and which could then settle people on it (Herzl, 1960c, p. 1135).

It was at this point that Herzl managed, for the first time, to propound the idea of the Charter:

Surely there is land enough in Palestine which could be used for such a purpose. If this land company, which would no doubt have to be an

Ottoman corporation, were given a suitable concession, it could make the
land arable, settle people, and pay taxes. And on the prospective income of
this land company, money could perhaps be borrowed in advance. You
would have a source of revenue right there. (Herzl, 1960c, p. 1135).

Having made his case, Herzl contented himself with listening to Izzet's
suggestions. He noted that there would be enough time to elaborate on the
matter in the subsequent negotiations and that gold would serve to sweep
away all the misgivings of Izzet and his like (Herzl, 1960c, p. 1136).

At this point, Izzet left to inform the Sultan of everything Herzl had
said. He returned with a farewell greeting from His Royal Majesty, who
expected Herzl's definite proposal within a month. To Herzl, this meant
that he had actually entered into negotiations over the Charter. All he
needed to carry out everything that he had designed was "luck, skill, and
money" (Herzl, 1960c, p. 1136).

This meeting with the Sultan set the tone for a series of ongoing
negotiations, which took from May 20, 1901 to July 18, 1902 to reach a
conclusion. During the first six months of this period, the negotiations
proceeded on a more or less even keel. They consisted of an ongoing
exchange of correspondence discussing the needs and offers of both sides.

On December 19, 1901, Herzl noted that he had written his Congress
speech and that it was essential that he obtain some concession from the
Sultan to use at that important event. On December 20, he wrote to the
Sultan that it might be useful from a financial as well as a political point of
view to make Jews of all countries aware of the generous feeling of the
Sultan for the persecuted Jewish people, and the opportunity to do so was
offered at the end of the month at the annual Zionist Congress in Basel,
which would deliberate on the sad fate of the Jews of the world. Herzl
mentioned that while he intended to speak favourably of the Sultan on that
occasion, the general impression would be so much greater if the Sultan
could reply to Herzl's telegram of loyal homage that he would send to the
Sultan at the opening of the Congress with his own telegram of good
wishes to Herzl. This would be the happiest preparation for the day when
the Sultan would call upon the grateful services of the Jews of the whole
world (Herzl 1960c, pp. 1187–1188).

Herzl sent his wire to the Sultan on the morning of December 25,
1901, the first day of the Congress. He was worried whether he was going
to get the coveted reply from the Sultan. He was relieved when, on the
evening of the following day of the Congress, the answer came. He noted
that with this wire, issued by the Basel telegraph office, his situation was
certified and regularized (Herzl, 1960c, pp. 1189–1190).

The following six months were less propitious from Herzl's perspective. They turned into a protracted vicious circle of proposals and counter-proposals between Herzl and the Sultan, during which the Turks kept hinting that they were willing to negotiate a deal that would provide an autonomous haven for the persecuted Jews of Europe in exchange for a financial bailout of the crushing Turkish national debt. At all times during this process, Herzl knew what his objective was but could not state it clearly up front because he also knew that the Turks were fundamentally opposed to the Jews acquiring autonomy over the area of Palestine. The Sultan's only goal was to extract as much money as possible from the situation so as to relieve the outrageous Turkish national debt. The Sultan's rapacious cabinet entourage exacerbated the situation by their personal intentions to exact as much personal gain as possible from any potential deal. It was only a matter of time before the negotiations reached the stage that both sides' true intentions came to the surface.

The first time the negotiations reached an obvious impasse was during Herzl's meeting on February 15, 1902 in Constantinople, to which he had been summoned by an urgent telegram from Ibrahim Bey. When Herzl, Izzet and Ibrahim met in the latter's office, Izzet came "brusquely" to the point:

> His Imperial Majesty is prepared to open his Empire to Jewish refugees from all countries, on condition that they agree to become Ottoman subjects with all the duties that this imposes, under our laws and military service. [...] Before entering our country they must formally resign their previous nationality and become Ottoman subjects. On this condition they may establish themselves in any of our provinces except – at first – Palestine. (Herzl 1960c, pp. 1218–1219)

Herzl noted that he did not show any reaction to these words; he understood this to be only the first offer and that "they would be open to bargaining." Izzet went on to say that, in return, the Sultan would ask Herzl to form a syndicate for the consolidation of the public debt and offered additional inducements. Izzet concluded the conversation by asking Herzl to prepare a memorandum in reply by the next day (Herzl 1960c, pp. 1218–1219).

In his reply, Herzl summarized the conditions laid out by Izzet and stated that he could only accept this proposition in principle. He also stated that the proposal, as worded, seemed difficult in its realization. To carry it out required sufficient publicity, and this publicity would have a bad effect if the restrictions were added to the generously intended welcome. Furthermore, the capital for the great financial operation would not come from poor colonists. Therefore, a link had to be found between Jewish colonization and the execution of the consolidation of the public debt. This link, in Herzl's opinion, could only be found in the general concession for the formation of a great Ottoman-Jewish company for colonization. In his diary, Herzl notes that the Sultan's proposal had ruined everything (Herzl, 1960c, p. 1221).

The following morning, Herzl handed his letter to Ibrahim, to be translated into Turkish for the Sultan with the help of Ghalib Bey, the Deputy Master of Ceremonies. He had instructions to make a literal translation. After this had been done, Herzl and Ibrahim had a friendly chat and went to lunch together. At this point, Izzet Bey showed up. He had read through Herzl's reply and asked Herzl what he meant by the Ottoman-Jewish colonization company. Was it to have a choice of places for settlement, that is, to be able to buy areas anywhere at all and gather the Jews under it? Herzl replied that yes, this was indispensable. The Jewish people were not concerned with individual protection, which they already had in civilized countries, but with national protection. Herzl explained that this meant that his people needed a great public gesture from the Turks, such as an invitation to immigrate *without any restriction.* After these clarifications, Izzet took the letter to the Sultan (Herzl, 1960c, pp. 1221–1222).

When Izzet returned with the Sultan's decision, it turned out to be unfavourable. The Sultan was willing to open up his empire to all Jews who become Turkish subjects, but the regions to be settled were to be decided by the government each time, and Palestine was to be excluded. The Ottoman-Jewish colonization company was to be allowed to colonize Mesopotamia, Syria, Anatolia, anywhere at all, with the sole exception of Palestine (Herzl 1960c, p. 1222)!

Herzl immediately rejected the idea of a Charter without Palestine and said that he was afraid that he would not find a solution. The next day, he wrote to the Sultan that he regretted that he was not able to accept the existing conditions. The Sultan sent Herzl a message that he could not grant Herzl unlimited immigration under the "Land Company" administration even if he wanted to, for he had reason to fear that he could never win the support of his people for it. Herzl felt that inwardly the Sultan and the people around him had no objections to his proposal and that, as businessmen, they just wanted to make some money. They had to be careful, however, otherwise they might be sent packing (Herzl, 1960c, p. 1226).

Izzet suggested that Herzl and his people should take the Turkish finances in hand and that they would be the boss. Just attend to the banking business, he told Herzl, and you will be given all the necessary concessions. Then he would see what could be done for his colonization request. Whatever other idea Herzl came up with, Izzet kept replying that they would see to that later but that, first of all, they wanted Herzl to attend to their finances. This is how things were left (Herzl, 1960c, p. 1228).

Herzl's notes in his diary on March 1902 reflect his suspicion that the Sultan had taken advantage of Herzl's presence and that he was the Jew who was sent for in order to make the other competitors, such as Maurice Rouvier, more pliable. Rouvier was a former French cabinet minister who enjoyed a considerable advantage over Herzl in that he was supported by one of the Great Powers. The progression of the consolidation deal with Rouvier shows that, in this, the Sultan had succeeded (Herzl, 1960c, p. 1256).

Elon noted that Herzl's comings and goings in the palace for four full days, from February 15 to February 20, 1892, had caused considerable nervousness among other financiers in the wings and that there were press reports that the Sultan had approved the so-called Rouvier project for the consolidation of the debt. If this was the case, it would, in Herzl's eyes, be a veritable disaster. In 1898, the German Kaiser had failed him; now, after what looked like another promising beginning, it was the Sultan. At that moment, Herzl felt that there was nowhere he could turn (Elon, 1975, pp. 346–347).

A few weeks later, Herzl was being pressed by the Turks to get back into the bidding game. The Turkish ambassador returned almost daily with cabled requests from Constantinople that Herzl come without delay. The Rouvier group had made a definite offer to consolidate the national debt at a cost to the Turkish taxpayer of 32 million pounds. If Herzl could offer more advantageous terms, the Sultan would "give the Israelites proofs of sympathy and protection." Although Herzl suspected that he might be used as a bargaining chip, he promised a definite reply within a short time. On July 15, the Sultan requested that Herzl submit his proposal within one day. Herzl replied that he could not carry out such a difficult operation in a fraction of the months it had taken Rouvier. Herzl indicated, however, that his offer would save the Turks two million pounds at the outset and considerably more later on. Herzl urged the Sultan to reject the French proposal because it was advantageous only to the financiers and the imperialist powers backing them (Elon, 1975, p. 356).

Finally, on July 23, accompanied by Wolffsohn, Herzl left for Turkey, where he arrived two days later. Tahsin Bey informed Herzl that the Sultan was very impatient to receive Herzl's offer and demanded an immediate written memorandum. Herzl, exhausted by the long journey, pleaded for an extra day. The Sultan agreed to wait until the morning. In his memorandum, which was in the form of a personal letter to the Sultan, Herzl offered to carry out the consolidation of the Turkish debt for 31.4 million, 1.6 million less than the French financiers had demanded. In return, Herzl demanded "a charter or concession for the Jewish colonization of Mesopotamia, which the Sultan had offered him in February, plus the territory of Haifa and its environs in Palestine." The colonists would pay the Turkish government an annual tribute as well as all regular taxes and levies (Elon, 1975, p. 357).

Herzl arrived at the Palace at noon the following day. Herzl was informed that his memorandum, which he had been rushed to complete the night before, had not yet been translated. Finally, the translation was completed at 12:13 a.m. and taken to the Sultan. Herzl was given an appointment for the next morning. When Herzl showed up, punctually, at ten o'clock, all urgency seemed to have disappeared. After waiting for hours, Tahsin Bey brought a message from the Sultan, asking Herzl to consult with Said Pasha, the Grand Vizier, about his memorandum (Elon, 1975, pp. 357–358).

It was not until Sunday afternoon that Herzl was finally taken to the Grand Vizier's office on the other side of town, where he repeated his proposals. The Grand Vizier asked Herzl if the Jewish colonists would accept Ottoman citizenship and serve in the Army. As he had done so many times before, Herzl declared that they definitely would. Herzl told the Grand Vizier that the potential colonists were poor, persecuted Jews from Russia and Romania; they were neither a danger nor troublesome but a sober, industrious, loyal element bound to the Muslims by racial kinship and affinity (Elon, 1975, p. 358).

After congratulating Herzl for his efforts to aid the persecuted Jews, the Grand Vizier asked Herzl to give him the names of the financiers who formed his syndicate. Herzl replied that he could not do so at this moment; since the deal with Rouvier was said to be almost concluded, such a disclosure would not be ethical. The Grand Vizier conceded the probity of Herzl's claim and did not insist. The meeting came to an end and Herzl was driven back to the Sultan's palace, where, to his surprise, he received word from the Sultan that he should write out the report of his conversation with the Grand Vizier and have it translated by a confidant of his own. It seemed that the Sultan wanted to verify the accuracy of his own minister's report. It took Herzl a whole afternoon to find a suitable translator, who took another twenty-four hours to perform his task. Elon notes that the main result was that the Turks gained more time to exploit

Herzl's visit in their continuing negotiations with the Rouvier group (Elon, 1975, pp. 358–359).

The following day, Herzl was taken again to the Grand Vizier, who raised Herzl's hopes by saying that the Sultan had been very satisfied with his propositions and was prepared "in principle" to go ahead with them. Soon, however, the conversation turned into a meaningless exchange of words, which left the issue unresolved. After two more days of procrastination, with Herzl made to wait endlessly between interviews, he finally became convinced that the Sultan had summoned him to come only to squeeze better terms out of Rouvier. Herzl's conviction was confirmed when, by the end of the week, the Turks concluded their deal with Rouvier (Elon, 1975, p. 359).

It must be remembered that until this moment, the prospect of achieving a Jewish settlement in Palestine through Herzl's negotiations with the Turkish government had unified the various factions within the Zionist movement behind Herzl's leadership. In his novel *Altneuland*, which he started writing in 1899 and which was published in October 1902, Herzl developed an elaborate version of the blueprint provided in *Der Judenstaat* in 1896 in preparation for the First Zionist Congress in 1897. According to one of Herzl's biographers, author and historian Steven Beller, *Altneuland*, which describes a state founded on the most modern technological, economic and scientific foundations, buttressed by the principles of tolerance, justice and freedom, represents Herzl's vision of the complete realization of the Jewish concept of emancipation (Beller, 1991, p. 105).

It would take us too far afield, for the purpose of this study, to describe the clash it provoked and the controversies it created between the main factions of the Zionist movement. According to Beller, it was more than a clash between "West" and "East." It was more the clash between the Central European emancipatory tradition from which Herzl came, with its strongly universalistic interpretation of Judaism, and the more particularistic approach of the Jews of the Russian Pale and Galicia to culture. For Eastern European Jewry, the meaning of the German word *Kultur* (culture) was an organic concept stemming from the roots of the nation. The way Herzl used the term *Kultur* in his diaries carries the general, universal concept of "civilization" applicable to all "progress," especially technological, regardless of national identity (Beller, 1991, p. 108).

In the end, *Altneuland*, instead of bringing all Jews together, which had been Herzl's purpose for writing it, became the symbol of division between the mostly Western and Central European political Zionist supporters of Herzl and the largely Eastern European cultural Zionists,

supporters of the prominent Zionist thinker and founder of cultural
Zionism, Ahad Ha'am (Beller, 1991, p. 111).

Essentially, despite his nationalism and devotion to Palestine, Herzl
remained a rationalist liberal whose main concern was rescuing world
Jewry from moral and physical disaster. For Ahad Ha'am and his
followers, their Zionism was driven by the goal of reclaiming the Jewish
land in Palestine, either as a spiritual centre for all Jews in the world or as
a version of the messianic return. Herzl thought that Zionism was possible
and necessary because of Jewish suffering. Most of the Russian Zionists
felt that suffering was secondary to the prospect of regaining *Eretz Israel*
and creating a viable Jewish culture (Beller, 1991, p. 112).

Until 1902, this difference in approach was not critical, as both sides
were united in their pursuit, by political means, of "A Jewish homeland
recognized by public law in Palestine," as laid down in the Basil Program
of 1897. Calm and unity had been preserved as long as Herzl could
maintain the prospect that he would obtain a charter from the Turks for a
Jewish settlement in Palestine proper. When, in 1902, Herzl realized that,
despite all his unsparing efforts, Turkey's unshakable intransigence on this
crucial Zionist condition was not going to allow him to reach his objective,
he felt that he had no choice but to adjust his strategy. While he would
never abandon the idea of Palestine as the prime destination, until this
became possible, another safe haven would have to be found as a
temporary solution (Beller, 1991, pp. 112–113).

By mid-1902, Herzl's sense of urgency had been reinforced by the
events in Romania. Recent directives against the Jews of Romania
excluded the vast majority of native-born Romanian Jews from Romanian
citizenship. In addition, a new law sought to exclude them from pursuing
any useful livelihood. Reduced to beggary, they would have to emigrate.
The new law led to protest meetings in many European countries as well
as in America. The United States lodged an official protest against these
discriminatory measures, but the Romanian government chose to ignore it
(Elon, 1975, p. 360).

What followed was Herzl's consideration of a number of alternative
possibilities which, in successive order, included Cyprus, the Sinai
Peninsula and the Wadi el Arish, Uganda, as well as various areas of
Africa under Portuguese, Belgian and Italian rule. Each of these involved
complex diplomatic and technical considerations and deliberations. Each
reached different levels of hope of realization, with the Sinai Peninsula
prospect coming closest to a successful conclusion. In the end, none of
them materialized, each for different reasons. The Cyprus plan was firmly
rejected by the delegates at the Third Zionist Congress in 1899. The Sinai

prospect, which had initially received positive consideration by the British government, conditional on the agreement of the Earl of Cromer, consul-general and effective ruler of Egypt, fell apart due to the latter's opposition and the failure to find a solution to the problem of irrigation (Beller, 1991, pp. 112–113).

In April 1903, after the failed negotiations over Sinai, Herzl returned to London to continue to plead his case for that destination with the English Colonial Secretary, Joseph Chamberlain. Fully aware of the failure of the Sinai project, Chamberlain, who had recently returned from a visit to Egypt and East Africa, suggested Uganda as an alternative. Herzl insisted that the Zionist project needed a base in or near Palestine. Chamberlain did not press the issue, but he regretted Herzl's commitment to what he considered to be the politics of sentimentalism. Chamberlain also expressed some reservations about the Zionists' chances of success in the Near East. He feared that there might soon be a showdown there between France, Germany and Russia, and he wondered how that would affect the fate of a Jewish Zionist colony in that area. Herzl replied that this would be a welcome development, as the Powers would find Palestine useful as a buffer state and would thus benefit from its existence (Elon, 1975, p. 371).

By 1903, Herzl was running out of options and was feeling his physical strength weakening under the mounting weight of the challenges he was facing. While he had succeeded in obtaining audiences with the leading political leaders of his time, he had failed to gain their firm support for providing a safe home for his persecuted people. He had also expended a considerable amount of emotional and physical capital to reconcile the divisive cultural rifts among his Zionist associates.

What brought the situation to a new sense of urgency was the unprecedented barbarity of the Kishinev pogrom in April 1903. As we have seen, the Kishinev atrocities were a manifest reminder of the mortal danger faced by Jews in Tsarist Russia, which Herzl had feared and against which he had warned. While the need for a solution was more urgent than ever, the failure of the El Arish project in Sinai, which had come closest to succeeding, still left Zionism without a remedy to the immense distress of its main constituents, the persecuted Jewish masses of the East. It was under these desperate conditions that Herzl started to give serious consideration to the Uganda option.

When Lord Rothschild had suggested Uganda as an option in the summer of 1902, Herzl had rejected it out of hand. When Chamberlain repeated the offer in May 1903, Herzl agreed to negotiate. This significant change in response to the same offer, made one year apart, provides a telling measure of the extent of the changed circumstances. What added to

Herzl's sense of urgency was his steadily deteriorating heart condition. He was desperate to do something for the Jews before he died without having succeeded in doing so. His agreement to consider Uganda, at this stage, makes complete sense when seen against this background of personal and political desperation. Furthermore, while Herzl considered a Jewish colony in East Africa only as an emergency measure, a staging post where Jews could gather under the "flag of Zion" and wait to colonize the homeland, his prime aim was more of a tactical diplomatic nature: to provide a bargaining counter with the Turks while at the same time making the British government, the most powerful and highly respected power in the world at the time with great influence over Middle Eastern politics, an ally of Zionism. Herzl's apparent retreat from Palestine cemented the process by which he and the Zionist Organization had gained official British government recognition as the representatives of the Jewish people, and, as such, constituted a phenomenal diplomatic coup which could only have positive consequences in the future (Beller, 1991, pp. 114–116).

In the meantime, Herzl continued to exert every possible effort to induce Turkey to grant him a charter to settle Palestine. It was for this purpose that he went to Russia on August 8, 1903 for a meeting with Vyacheslav von Plehve, the Russian Minister of the Interior, at which he succeeded in obtaining from him a letter supporting the Zionist policy of Jewish emigration from Russia and a promise to assist with the Turks. The emotional reception he received from the Jews of Vilna and the overwhelming evidence of their desperate situation reinforced his conviction that everything possible should be done to come to their rescue (Beller, 1991, pp. 115–116).

On August 23, 1903, in his opening address to the Sixth Congress, Herzl laid out his assessment of the overall state of affairs which, in light of the events in Kishinev, had reached crisis level. Emigration to Britain and the United States had reached such a high level that both these countries felt the need to impose restrictions on immigration. Negotiations with Turkey had been unsuccessful, and the initially promising El Arish project had failed as well. This left Herzl with only two hopeful messages: the British offer of Uganda and Plehve's letter. The offer of land for an autonomous Jewish colony in East Africa would not have the "historical, poetic-religious and Zionist value" of Palestine, which would always be the "final goal." In view of the current emergency situation, the Uganda offer should be considered as a temporary, stop-gap solution. At the same time, working with the British government on this possibility would add the important political benefit of having the Zionist movement recognized by Britain. Herzl also tried to reassure the Congress by reporting the help promised in Plehve's letter in respect of Turkey's adamant attitude to Palestine. Therefore, while efforts directed towards Palestine needed to be continued, the Congress should respond to the "statesmanlike generosity" of the British by agreeing to send a commission to Africa to review the possibility of establishing a Jewish colony there (Beller, 1991, p. 117).

The vote to send the exploratory expedition was carried by a majority of 295 to 178, with 99 abstaining. While the numbers constituted a victory for Herzl, the opposition, which included most of the Russian contingent, walked out of the Congress. For them, any diversion from Palestine was a betrayal of the Zionist movement and rendered it meaningless. The goal of Zionism had to be the Jewish homeland in Palestine as set out in the Basel Program. Beller points out the irony of the situation; the very same people who Herzl was trying to save by securing a temporary haven without changing the fundamental objective of Palestine now opposed his emergency measure. Leon Trotsky, who observed the scene from the press gallery, predicted the imminent collapse of the Zionist movement (Beller, 1991, p. 117; Elon, 1975, p. 388).

It is at this moment that Herzl's extraordinary personality prevailed and prevented the Zionist movement from falling on its own sword. Beller notes that Herzl managed to swallow his pride and, in an extraordinary effort of self-control and leadership, persuaded the rebels to return to the Congress. He cemented the reconciliation with one of his most famous dramatic gestures when, during his closing speech, he raised his right hand and exclaimed: "If I forget thee, O Jerusalem, may my right hand forget itself" (Beller, 1991, pp. 117–118).

The Uganda controversy illustrated the nature of the ideological division within the Zionist movement. Most of the representatives from Western Europe viewed Zionism as a movement to rescue Jews from persecution and insecurity by setting up their own state so that they could become a normal, even model people. The opponents of the Uganda interim solution, mainly from Russia, were motivated by the religious concept of returning to the soil of the Promised Land. Herzl himself, despite the outward reconciliation, was privately distraught by the stand-off at the Sixth Congress, which he viewed as the abandonment of the humanitarian solution in favour of the Russians' religious-cultural goal. Beller notes that Herzl, while he could not help but admire the "sheer idealism, will power and sheer tenacity in the face of oppression" of his Russian opponents, could not see why they could not accept that, in an emergency, there could be an interim solution (Beller, 1991, p. 118).

In his diary, Herzl noted that after the final session, upon his return from the Congress building, in a state of total exhaustion, he shared his personal thoughts with his closest friends by telling them about the speech he was going to make at the Seventh Congress, if he lived to see it. He writes:

> By then I shall either have obtained Palestine or realized the complete futility of any further efforts. In the latter case, my speech will be as follows:
>
> It was not possible. The ultimate goal has not been reached, and will not be reached within a foreseeable time. But a temporary result is at hand: this land in which we can settle our suffering masses on a national basis and with the right of self-government. I do not believe that for the sake of a beautiful dream or of a legitimistic banner we have a right to withhold this relief from the unfortunate.
>
> But I recognize that this has produced a decisive split in our movement, and this rift is centered about my own person. Although I was originally only a Jewish State man (no matter where) – later I did lift up the flag of Zion and became myself a *Lover of Zion.* Palestine is the only land where our people can come to rest. But hundreds of thousands need immediate help.
>
> There is only one way to solve this conflict: I must resign my leadership. I shall, if you wish, conduct the negotiations of this Congress for you, and at its conclusion you will elect two Executive Committees, one for East Africa and one for Palestine. I shall accept election to neither. But I shall never deny my counsel to those who devote themselves to the work if they request it. And my best wishes will be with those who work for the fulfillment of the beautiful dream.
>
> By what I have done I have not made Zionism poorer, but Jewry richer. Farewell! (Herzl, 1960d, pp. 1547–1548)

In the meantime, the pressure on the unity within the Zionist ranks had become somewhat eased by the changing British attitude on this issue. Beller notes that the British were having second and third thoughts about their Uganda offer. The white settlers already there were aghast at the prospect of a Jewish colony on good land, and their protest had led to a noticeable cooling of British interest in granting an East African charter. Herzl's response was one of relief, for now he could press again for Sinai and redouble his efforts with the Turks. In addition, the attempted assassination of his close associate Max Nordau shifted the sympathy back to Herzl's side (Beller, 1991, pp. 121–122).

Audience with Pope Pius X – January 23–24, 1904

In his January 22, 1904 diary entry, Herzl notes that his long-standing wish to meet the Pope was finally about to be realized. Before the audience, he discussed his objective for the meeting with Count Lippay, a personal friend of the Pope, who acted as an intermediary. Herzl told Lippay that all he was looking for was an encyclical statement from the Pope that he had no objection to Zionism, provided the Holy Places were extraterritorialized (Herzl, 1960d, p. 1591).

The next day, Lippay took him first to meet the Vatican's Secretary of State, Cardinal Merry del Val. Herzl told the Cardinal that he was looking for the goodwill of the Holy See for his cause. The Cardinal replied, "I do not quite see how we can take any initiative in this matter. As long as the Jews deny the divinity of Christ, we certainly cannot make a declaration in their favour. Not that we have any ill will toward them. On the contrary, the church has always protected them. To us they are indispensable witnesses to the phenomenon of God's time on earth. But they deny the divine nature of Christ. How then can we, without abandoning our own highest principles, agree to their being given possession of the Holy Land again?" When Herzl replied that the Jews were only asking for the profane earth and that the Holy Places would be extraterritorialized, the Cardinal responded that "it won't do to imagine them in an enclave of that sort" (Herzl, 1960d, pp. 1593–1594).

A series of arguments and counter-arguments followed, with Herzl pointing out that the Catholic Church could achieve a great moral conquest by declaring itself, if not in favour, at least not against the Zionist enterprise. But the Cardinal stuck to his theme:

> Certainly, a Jew who was himself baptized out of conviction is for me the ideal. In such a person I see the physical characteristics of descent from Christ's people united in spiritual elements […]. The history of Israel is our heritage, it is our foundation. But in order for us to come out for the Jewish people in the way you desire, they would first have to be converted. (Herzl, 1960d, pp. 1593–1594)

When Herzl stated that the Jews had withstood the persecutions but were still there today, the Cardinal acknowledged that Herzl's argument could carry some weight, but he saw no possibility of the Vatican assuming the initiative. Herzl responded:

> No one is asking you to, Your Eminence! The initiative will be taken by one of the Great Powers. You are simply to give your approval […]. I have gone from one Power to another and secured their consent [...]. But I also wish to obtain the spiritual approval of the Roman Church. (Herzl, 1960d, p. 1594)

Herzl showed the Cardinal the last letter he had received from Plehve. Herzl notes that the Cardinal read Plehve's letter thoughtfully and promised that consideration would be given to Herzl's request. He gave him permission to come again and promised to ask the Pope to grant Herzl an audience (Herzl, 1960d, pp. 1594–1595).

The meeting between Herzl and the Pope, on January 25, 1904, started on an awkward note. Herzl notes that the Pope received him standing and held out his hand, which Herzl did not kiss, even though Lippay had told him to do so. Herzl believed that he had incurred the Pope's displeasure by this, for everyone who visits him kneels down and at least kisses his hand. When Herzl briefly placed his request before him and the Pope answered sternly and resolutely, Herzl felt that the Pope was possibly annoyed by his refusal to kiss his hand. The Pope told Herzl that the Church could not give its approval to his movement. While it could not prevent the Jews from going to Jerusalem, it could never sanction it. The Pope concluded:

> The soil of Jerusalem, if it was not always sacred, has been sanctified by the life of Jesus Christ. As the head of the Church I cannot tell you anything different. The Jews have not recognized our Lord, therefore we cannot recognize the Jewish people. (Herzl, 1960d, pp. 1602–1603)

Herzl noted that, at the outset, he tried to be conciliatory. As with the Vatican's Secretary of State, Herzl's argument about the extraterritorialization of the Holy Places did not make much of an impression. Jerusalem, the Pope said, must not get into the hands of the Jews. When Herzl asked him about the present status, the Pope replied:

> I know, it is not pleasant to see the Turks in possession of our Holy Places. We simply have to put up with that. But to support the Jews in the acquisition of the Holy Places, that we cannot do. (Herzl, 1960d, p. 1603)

Herzl mentioned that his focus was on the distress of the Jews and that he wanted to avoid religious issues. The Pope replied that, as the head of the Church, he could not do this. The Pope introduced two possibilities:

> Either the Jews will cling to their faith and continue to await the Messiah who, for us, has already appeared. In that case they will be denying the divinity of Jesus and we cannot help them. Or else they will go there without any religion, then we can be even less favorable to them. The Jewish religion was the foundation of our own; but it was superseded by the teachings of Christ, and we cannot concede it any further validity. The Jews, who ought to have been the first to acknowledge Jesus Christ, have not done so to this day. (Herzl, 1960d, p. 1603)

Herzl replied that "Terror and persecution may not have been the right means for enlightening the Jews." Herzl was impressed by the simplicity of the Pope's rejoinder:

> Our Lord came without power. He was poor... He came in peace. He persecuted no one. He was persecuted. He was forsaken even by his apostles. Only later did he grow in stature. It took three centuries for the Church to evolve. The Jews therefore had time to acknowledge his divinity without any pressure. But they haven't done so to this day. (Herzl, 1960d, p. 1604)

When Herzl raised the fact that the Jews were in terrible straits and that a land was needed for these persecuted people, the Pope asked if it had to be Jerusalem. Herzl answered that they were not asking for Jerusalem but for Palestine – only the secular land. The Pope was adamant: "We cannot be in favour of it." When Herzl asked if His Holiness knew the situation of the Jews, the Pope replied that he had always been on good terms with Jews and that there were other bonds than those of religion: courtesy and philanthropy. These the Church did not deny to the Jews:

> Indeed we also pray for them: that their minds be enlightened ... if you come to Palestine and settle your people there, we shall have churches and priests ready to baptize all of you. (Herzl, 1960d, p. 1604)

This completes Herzl's account of his meeting with Pope Pius X. While Herzl did not obtain the support he was aiming for, the fact that it took place is significant in itself. It showed the true nature of the Judeophobic anti-Zionist motivation of the Catholic Church, which, as we have seen, was similar to the attitude of the Eastern Orthodox Church, which inspired the persecution of the Jews in Tsarist Russia. He had now met face to face and engaged in serious discussions with the main political and spiritual leaders of the time. This cemented his prestige as the recognized leader of the emerging political Jewish nation in exile and also attests to the fact that Herzl continued his fight to rally the world around his project, with unwavering determination in spite of all disappointments, until the end of his life.

After his meeting with the Pope, Herzl returned to the task of restoring unity within the Zionist movement, which had been shaken by the emergence of the Uganda option. He called a meeting of the Greater Actions Committee, which met on April 11, 1904. According to Beller, Herzl's handling of this meeting was his last great performance as a Zionist leader. While he justified the Uganda project as an emergency

measure, he emphatically affirmed his adherence to Palestine as the final
goal. He also pleaded that unity required that the majority decisions of the
Congress be accepted by all participants, including those opposed. In his
closing statement on April 12, he again stressed the need for unity and
expressed what his contribution to Zionism had been. He had turned it
from a loose patchwork of ineffectual idealistic groups into a structured
organization, embodied in the Zionist Congress. In the course of time, he
had learned that the solution to the Jewish problem was only in Palestine.
He appealed to their faith and trust in him and to come back into the fold.
The meeting ended with Herzl promising a free discussion of the Uganda
project at the Seventh Congress and with the Russian delegates accepting
his leadership again. Fortuitously, less than ten weeks before Herzl's death
on July 3, 1904, reconciliation within the Zionist movement had been
achieved (Beller, 1991, p. 122).

Herzl's Death and Legacy

May 1904 marked the beginning of the end of Herzl's life. Two days
before his forty-fourth birthday on May 2, a panel of physicians, alarmed
by the sudden deterioration of his heart muscle, ordered him to the Czech
spa town of Franzensbad for a cure, where he spent two weeks in bed. On
June 3, on his doctor's advice, he entered a sanatorium in Edlach in the
Austrian Alps. His wife Julie accompanied him, staying by his bedside
through the nights. On July 1, he developed pneumonia. When the
Reverend Hechler came to visit him on July 2 and promised Herzl that
they would soon go to Palestine and "see Jerusalem again from the Mount
of Olives," Herzl replied, "Greet Palestine for me. I gave my heart's blood
for my people." He then asked for his mother and children. After he saw
them and exchanged a few words, his strength left him and he fell back on
the bed. Herzl died at 5:00 p.m. on July 3, 1904 of cardiac sclerosis (Elon,
1975, pp. 398–401).

At the site of Herzl's grave, David Wolffsohn, Herzl's successor as
President of the World Zionist Organization, repeated the oath taken by
Herzl at the Sixth Zionist Congress in August 1903: "If I forget thee,
Jerusalem, may my right hand wither." And at the Seventh Zionist Congress
– the first Congress without Herzl – Wolffsohn declared:

> I took this oath during our saddest hour of tribulation, beside Herzl's grave.
> I took it for you all, for all Zionists. We will repeat it, and always think of
> Jerusalem and never forget Zion, but never forget Herzl either. (Fraenkel,
> 1946, pp. 144–145)

In his short eulogy, Wolffsohn swore that Herzl's name would "remain sacred and unforgotten as long as a single Jew lives on this earth." Elon adds that at the same time that Herzl was laid to rest, hundreds of young men were departing from the townlets of Poland, Russia and Romania. The departure of these early Zionists was sporadic and disorganized, but Herzl had started them moving. "Everything remained to be done, but Herzl had cast the mould" (Elon, 1975, p. 403).

Writer and historian Oskar K. Rabinowicz, in his study of Herzl's impact on the achievement of the Balfour Declaration, claimed in 1958 that the efforts made by Zionist leaders in Britain and America during World War I were the result of the foundations which Herzl's genius had established fifteen years previously in the consciousness of the Jews and the world, as well as in the minds of the British statesmen "whom Providence preserved for the fulfillment of the great Zionist leader's dream". This continuity of Herzlian idea, effort and activity, Rabinowicz claimed, has been disregarded in Zionist historiography and has lain dormant, unknown to the new generation. The purpose of his study was to bring to light the greatness of the role of Herzlian Zionism in the achievement of the Balfour Declaration. Rabinowicz notes that his study was based on factual observations and conclusions based on a careful investigation of the contemporary literature and documentary evidence (Rabinowicz, 1958, pp. iii–iv).

The course of Rabinowicz's investigation followed Herzl during his first attempts to appeal to the British public and gradually overcome the walls of ignorance and prejudice, to the Fourth Zionist Congress in London, to the Royal Commission on Alien Immigration, and finally to the offices of the Cabinet ministers and other government officials where "he stood as equals among equals." We have observed, Rabinowicz's states, how Herzl and his colleagues, with tenacity and unabated enthusiasm, won over to the cause of Zionism men of great importance in British public life, such as Chamberlain, Percy, Lansdowne, Balfour, Lloyd George, Churchill, Milner, Grey, Cromer, Wickham Steed and others (Rabinowicz, 1958, pp. 104–105).

Rabinowicz asserted that his investigation clearly brought to light that Herzl had not only established official relations with the British government and achieved recognition for the Zionist Organization as spokesman for Jewry, but had also injected into British public opinion and into its leaders the conception of Zionism in its pure meaning – nationhood and statehood in Palestine. They understood him and became and remained supporters of the cause until the opportune moment for action arrived. Rabinowicz called Herzl the architect of the Balfour Declaration who laid the foundation upon which subsequent Zionist leaders were able in later years to build a structure of the home which eventually became the Jewish state (Rabinowicz, 1958, p. 106).

The question is often raised as to how this man was able, in such a short time, to gain access to so many leaders in the political and financial world while at the same time mobilizing the impoverished and persecuted nineteenth-century Jewish diaspora into a united political force. The two main contributing elements which stand out are his unique personality and his unwavering determination and perseverance.

Herzl combined a complex number of attributes that are rarely found within one person: his appearance and demeanour, his intellectual acumen, his intense but controlled passion for his cause, and his written and verbal communication skills that were continuously honed and practised in his prominent journalistic capacity as chief correspondent for the widely read and influential Viennese paper *Die Neue Freie Presse*, and which also gave him access and exposure to the main political developments of his time. All these merged to create an extremely engaging and charismatic personality, without which the contacts he was able to secure would not have been possible. The fact that he in no way looked and acted the part of the maligned Jewish ghetto stereotype while he was championing the Jewish cause usually came as a surprise to those who met him for the first time and enabled him to be received with respect and, quite often, genuine cordiality. They were compelled by his personality, even when they did not agree with his principles. It is also clear from his diary entries as well as from biographical and other historical accounts that Herzl was more than able to hold his own in battles of wits with friends and foes alike, regardless of their rank or status.

A careful review of Herzl's life reveals a determined struggle, against all the odds, to imbue nineteenth-century diaspora Jewry with the concept that the only way to restore the Jewish nation to sovereign statehood is to lift the eighteen-hundred-year-old yoke of sub-human serfdom in a hostile Christian world. It is this struggle that paved the way towards the historic Balfour Declaration of November 2, 1917. His intellectual acumen made him aware and concerned with the threats of the racist populist reaction to the emancipation of the Jews in Western Europe, and his travels and numerous contacts and meetings throughout the continent made him aware of the suffering of the Jewish masses trapped in Imperial Russia's antisemitic tsarist regime.

Herzl's journey was marked by many disappointments. He failed to convince wealthy Jewish bankers, such as Baron de Hirsh and Rothschild, to provide the funds for the acquisition and development of suitable land in Palestine and for the logistics of moving European Jewry to that destination. He failed to enlist the support of the leading world powers of the day, including the governments of Germany, Russia and Great Britain as well as the Vatican. He also failed to gain support among the emancipated Jewish communities in Western Europe.

Herzl's own accounts of these encounters paint an insightful picture of their role in his practical education in realpolitik and help us understand how they shaped the orientation of the strategy he was forced to develop to raise the Zionist agenda to the world stage. It was his determination and perseverance that helped him rebound from these setbacks while learning what was possible and impossible. Unfortunately, the quasi-Sisyphean nature of his attempts to find international support for the creation of a Jewish state in Palestine, to which he devoted all his time and energy without pause or respite, led to his early demise.

While Herzl was not able to deliver the Promised Land to his people before he died, he left a crucial legacy that allowed the political Zionist dream to develop into a reality. Herzl was the architect who conceived and the engineer who built the bridge that led from Jewish nationhood to Jewish statehood. His spirit would enlighten the path of those that carried the concept forward after he was gone.

From Herzl to Balfour – 1904–1917

During the ten years between Herzl's death in 1904 and the outbreak of World War I in 1914, the geopolitical obstacles which had stymied the Zionist efforts to secure a territorial solution to the desperate plight of European Jewry had not undergone any changes that might have been helpful to the Zionist cause. The major positive developments during those ten years, from the Zionist point of view, occurred within the movement. The internal ideological conflicts which were the main sources of debate during the ensuing Zionist Congresses were gradually being resolved.

During the Seventh Congress, which took place in Basel in 1905, the thorny issue of Uganda was put to rest. The Congress heard the report of the Commission that had been sent to East Africa, which had concluded that Uganda was unsuitable for mass Jewish settlement, and proceeded to vote against a national home anywhere except Palestine and its immediate vicinity. The Congress also discussed practical work in Palestine, e.g. giving support to agricultural settlements and industrial activity (Bard, 2019).

By the time that the Eighth Zionist Congress was convened in The Hague in 1907, the point of view that the establishment of facts on the ground in Palestine should take priority over the objective of first obtaining legal approval for the establishment of a Jewish state was gaining predominance in the Zionist movement. The majority of the Zionist leadership felt that the political activities of the movement were leading nowhere and that if it was not to stagnate and, in the end, die of frustration, it must begin to think less of diplomacy and more of practical work in Palestine. These sentiments were shared by Chaim Weizmann, who attended the Congress as a 32-year-old young man of promise.

The major debate concerned the conflicting approaches of the practical and political Zionists. The political Zionists demanded that a charter be secured before practical work began in Palestine, while the practical Zionists argued that without substantial settlement there was little hope of gaining legal sanction from one or more of the Great Powers. It is at this point that a growing number of delegates, led by Chaim Weizmann, began to adopt what is referred to as synthetic Zionism, which was a synthesis of the two positions.

At this point, it is necessary to introduce Weizmann's background and career path to understand the qualities that propelled him to the leadership of the Zionist movement and his role in the process that led to the Balfour Declaration. Weizmann personifies the quintessential prototype of the evolution of the transformation of the ghetto mentality to the worldwise mindset of the emancipated Jew.

Chaim Weizmann was born in 1874 in the White Russian village of Motol outside Pinsk, where two hundred Jewish families lived amid a larger population of Russian peasants. His father sent him away to attend a Russian gymnasium in Pinsk at the age of eleven. There, he became devoted to science, the course of study that brought him to Berlin, where he was trained as a chemist. Israeli philosopher and political theorist Yoram Hazony traces Weizmann's path from a successful and ambitious student, eager to rise above the pitiful surroundings of his childhood, eventually receiving a doctorate in chemistry in the field of synthetic dyes and devoting much energy to patenting and marketing his discoveries. In 1904, he accepted an invitation to become a research assistant at the University of Manchester – at the very heart of the world of synthetic dyes – which put him on the road to social and financial success (Hazony, 2001, p. 165).

Weizmann turned out to be one of those rare historical figures whose personality, mind and background contributed to a holistic approach to complex socio-political issues. Born in the Pale, educated in the enlightened environment of Western Europe, endowed with valuable scientific skills, and deeply identifying with the plight of the diaspora Jewry and with the liberating objectives of the Zionist Movement, he rose to the top of the Zionist hierarchy and to the position of a respected and influential Zionist protagonist in the pourparlers with the British government. As Weizmann told the Congress in 1907: "If the governments gave us a Charter to-day it will be a scrap of paper. Not so if we work in Palestine; then it will be written and indissolubly cemented with our blood." In any event, the movement supported a number of practical efforts and established a Palestine branch of the World Zionist Organization (Stein, 1961, p. 63; Bard, 2019).

Stein commented that the idea of a charter to be underwritten by the Powers disappeared altogether after the Turkish Revolution of 1908. It was plain that, with their fanatical nationalism, the Young Turks would resist any encroachment on Ottoman sovereignty. Even the most politically-minded Zionists realized at this point that if the Young Turks' distrust of Zionism was to be dispelled, there must be no more talk of a charter or an international guarantee; there should be no room for the suspicion that the real purpose of the Zionist Movement was to detach Palestine from Turkey and turn it into a Jewish state (Stein, 1961, p. 64).

No noteworthy external or internal changes marked the proceedings of the Ninth Congress in Hamburg in 1909. At this point, the question of how to implement the Zionist programme had still not been resolved. The practical lobby accused David Wolffsohn, who had succeeded Herzl as the President of the Zionist Organization, of focusing on political activity and his executive of judging projects by their commercial value. This rival leadership included Menahem Ussishkin, Chaim Weizmann and Nahum Sokolow, who gained support from the representatives of the workers' movement in Palestine (Bard, 2019).

The Tenth Congress held in Basel in 1911 has often been described as the Peace Congress, as it finally laid to rest the debate between the practical and political Zionists, with synthetic Zionism becoming the operational mode of the movement. Considerable attention was given to the question of practical work in Palestine as well as Hebrew culture. Shlomo Kaplansky raised the question of Zionist relations with the Arabs, and, for the first time, a session of the Congress was held in Hebrew (Bard, 2019).

When the Eleventh Congress took place in Vienna in 1913, the Zionist movement was still operating at the theoretical level, as no concrete territorial solution was yet in sight. The delegates spent much of their time discussing settlement activities in Palestine and the work of the organization's office in Jaffa. This Congress also adopted the concept of a Hebrew University in Jerusalem (Bard, 2019).

World War I

On the eve of World War I, as a political movement, Zionism appeared to stand before a blank wall. It could not expect any encouragement from the Turkish or any other government. "The greatest of the Great Powers we have to deal with is the Jewish people. From this Power we expect everything; from the other Powers very little," Weizmann declared at the 1913 Congress (Stein, 1961, p. 65).

The outbreak of the war in the summer of 1914 posed serious problems for the coherent function of the Zionist Organization, which had its base in so many different geographic locales. The Central Office of the Organization and the seat of the Zionist Executive were in Berlin. While it had adherence in all parts of the Jewish world, its main strength was in Russia and Austria-Hungary. Some of its most important institutions – the Jewish Colonial Trust, the Anglo-Palestine Company and the Jewish National Fund – were incorporated in Britain. Of the six members of the Executive, two – Otto Warberg and Arthur Hantke – were Germans, and three – Yechiel Tschlenow, Nahum Sokolow and Victor Jacobson – were Russians. The sixth member, Shmarya Levin, was of Russian origin but had recently acquired Austro-Hungarian nationality. The twenty-five-member General Council included twelve from Germany and Austria-Hungary, seven from Russia, two (Weizmann and Leopold Kessler) from Britain, and one each from Belgium, France, Holland and Romania (Stein, 1961, p. 97).

The circumstances in which the last pre-war Zionist Congress had met in 1913 reflected the Zionist Organization's standing in the Jewish world at the time and how it expected to attain its objectives. Weizmann recalled in his address to the Twelfth Zionist Congress, in the summer of 1921, that the Organization stood before a blank wall that could not be surmounted by ordinary political means. The only way forward was through the gradual extension of the Yishuv in Palestine and the spreading of the Zionist idea throughout the length and breadth of Jewry (Stein, 1961, p. 59).

The weak diplomatic position of the Zionist Movement on the eve of the war was the result of the political climate in France, Germany and Turkey at the time. The French remained convinced that the Zionist Movement was working for Germany, while the Germans had begun to accuse it of working for the enemies. The Turks were adamant in their hostility to the Movement and deaf to Zionist protestations of loyalty and goodwill. The Tenth Zionist Congress in 1911 had announced a change of emphasis by electing a new executive pledged to concentrate on practical work in Palestine – a policy which was reaffirmed by the Eleventh Congress in 1913. It was made clear that "practical work" was intended to include, in addition to colonizing activities, an effective contribution to the revival of the Hebrew language and Jewish culture and to "the strengthening of Jewish sentiment and national consciousness" (Stein, 1961, p. 60).

Even though all the dispersed components of the Zionist Movement were united in their objective of achieving a Jewish homeland in Palestine, they were divided by the national allegiances imposed on them by the countries in which they resided. The requirements of national loyalty were difficult to align with the political agendas of their respective national governments. Should the Organization maintain the principle of neutrality enthusiastically approved a year before at the Eleventh Zionist Congress by abstaining from any political activity during the war, making no attempt in advance to stake a claim to a hearing at the future Peace Conference? If, on the other hand, the Organization did attempt to stake such a claim, might it not find itself on a slippery slope leading to it taking sides in the war? (Stein, 1961, p. 97).

The question that immediately arose was whether the headquarters of the Organization should be left in Berlin or moved to some neutral country. On this point, there were sharp differences of opinion giving rise to a fractured allocation of responsibilities (Stein, 1961, pp. 98–101).

The main reason that the drafting of the Balfour Declaration did not start until the latter part of 1917 was the fact that Zionism had not been on the British political radar until that year, when the developments on the war fronts caused the British to look for any assistance they could muster. The view held in the Foreign Office in the early stages of the War of 1914–18 was that the Zionists and their claims were of little practical importance (Stein, 1961, p. 43). As we have seen, in the Sykes-Picot Agreement of May 1916, the Zionists were still ignored. While the British government and its advisors were alive to the strategic importance of Palestine from both a military and naval point of view and had done their best to keep it out of exclusive French control, in respect of Zionism, the government was still uncommitted (Stein, 1961, p. 115).

The tortuous political developments driven by the dynamics of the Great War drove the almighty British Empire and the fledgeling Zionist movement into the opportunistic partnership that culminated in the issuance of the Balfour Declaration.

The Unlikely Partnership Between the British Empire
and the Zionist Movement

The shift in Jewish populations from the barbaric killing grounds of Tsarist Russia to the less virulently antisemitic environment of the British Isles brought the leadership of the new political Zionist liberation movement face-to-face with the government of the one world power that appeared to hold the keys to the gates to the hitherto inaccessible homeland. No words describe the state of affairs between these two protagonists at the end of 1904 better than those of Joseph Chamberlain; when asked how the salvation of the Jews was to be accomplished without the ruining of the British people at home, he stated:

> [Herzl and I] had agreed that the best solution to the problem of Jewish aliens was 'to find some country in this vast world of ours where these poor exiles can dwell in safety without interfering with the subsistence of others.' (Defries, 2001, p. 45)

Schneer provided a representative example of this pre-WWI state of Jewish social consciousness in his telling description of the situation in Britain at that time. Pre-war indifference to Jewish nationalism was widespread among the British public, including the vast majority of British Jews. Of the 300,000 Jews living in Britain in 1913, only 8,000 belonged to a Zionist organization. The great majority of British Jews were recent immigrants or children of immigrants, refugees from the pogroms of Russia and Eastern and Southern Europe. With physical survival their main priority, such people had little time for Zionists, who spoke to them of a promised land several thousand miles away in Palestine. While few wished to deny their Jewish heritage, they were not ready to join a utopian movement, populated, as they thought, by dreamers and visionaries (Schneer, 2010, p. 110).

While the Jews settled primarily in inner-city areas in major cities such as Manchester and Leeds, they were also to be found in increasing numbers in provincial towns like Sheffield and Leicester, where the manufacturing industry provided employment opportunities. The highest concentration of Jewish settlement was in the East End of London. It has been estimated that by 1914 the Anglo-Jewish population had increased from approximately 65,000 in 1882 to almost 300,000, of which approximately 200,000 were located in London. Defries notes the growing opposition to this substantial increase of Jewish immigrants from Eastern Europe: they were seen as competing with the existing population for housing and work in an economy which was in recession. The trade union movement was fearful that its members would be threatened by immigrants who "would work for lower wages and for longer hours" and "whose presence forced up rents in the working-class areas in which they lived" (Defries, 2001, p. 16).

Restricting immigration became a political issue in the early 1880s. It gathered growing momentum through a series of government and opposition parliamentary bills and culminated with the passing of the Aliens Act, which received royal assent on August 11, 1905. Stein saw this as "a warning that there was a limit to the number of Jews whom the country was prepared to absorb, and that even in England the Jewish Question might arise," as it was already beginning, just about this time, to arise in the United States. Stein finds not only the Act itself disturbing but also the line of argument adopted by some of its leading supporters. He quotes Balfour as having spoken, in a speech on the Bill, of "the undoubted evils that had fallen upon the country from an immigration which was largely Jewish" (Stein, 1961, p. 79).

The asymmetry between the sweeping range of this legislation and the impact of its target on the welfare of Britain suggests a more fundamental source for its motivation than the demagogic political pretexts that brought it to fruition. The alien immigrant community as a whole represented only a very small fraction of the overall population of Britain at this time. In 1901, the census figure for the total United Kingdom population was 41,459,000. The alien population was about 350,000. It has been estimated that the total number of immigrants who settled in the United Kingdom between 1871 in 1911 was 400,000, compared with 6 million British emigrants. It was certainly true that a much larger number of migrants landed in Britain, but these were mostly in transit to the United States. Jewish immigration during this period has been estimated to have totalled around 135,000 and the total Jewish community of the United Kingdom in 1905 at around 250,000, of whom some two-thirds lived in London (Defries, 2001, p. 21).

Defries identified the omnipresent Judeophobic scapegoating attitudes in British society as a determinant policymaking factor. He cited Conservative politician and novelist John Buchan as describing "Jews as members of a world Jewish conspiracy which was bent on the destruction of Christian civilization" and Joseph Chamberlain as telling the Italian foreign minister that he only despised one race, which was the Jews, all of whom he considered to be physical cowards. In the Report of the Royal Commission on Alien Immigration, Jews were accused of creating slum living conditions and furthering vice and crime (Defries, 2001, p. 24). Defries referred to Prime Minister Arthur Balfour's speech in the Commons

in July 1905 in which he stated that some "undoubtable evils" had fallen
upon parts of the country from what was primarily Jewish alien immigration
and that he feared that there would be, in the future, a danger that Britain
could follow the "evil example set by some other countries" of political
antisemitism. The Jews were, according to the Prime Minister, responsible
for the creation of political antisemitism and, more particularly, of
undermining British society by virtue of their maintenance of ethnic
identification (Defries, 2001, p. 28).

In commenting on the outcome of the 1906 general election, Defries
observed that the restriction of alien Jewish immigration had popular
support and electoral advantage. The issue of Jewish immigration became
a hot political issue between the Unionists and the Liberals. Herbert
Gladstone, the Liberal Home Secretary, was to operate the Act, which
came into force on January 1, 1906, more leniently than the Unionist anti-
alienists wished. For example, the aftermath of the 1905 Russian
Revolution resulted in the Home Secretary stipulating that immigration
officers, when considering claims by immigrants that had been subject to
religious or political persecution, should give them the benefit of the doubt
(Defries, 2001, p. 31). Anti-immigration Unionist leaders, on the other
hand, demanded stricter implementation of the Aliens Act, and in
November 1906, Sir Howard Vincent, "Unionist member for Sheffield
Central" (Defries, 2001, p. 18), accused the Board of Deputies of British
Jews of trying to get the government to weaken the administration of the
Act still further (Defries, 2001, p. 31).

The previous March, Walter Rothschild, the unofficial leader of the
British Jewish community, had attacked both the Liberal administration
and the Aliens Act by reporting to a public meeting in Chesham that aliens
who had been refused entry had been shot on their return to Russia. The
conditions of Jews in Russia were worsening, culminating in a pogrom in
Bialystok between June 1 and 3, 1906, which claimed 70 Jewish dead and
90 gravely injured. In the debate on the massacres in the House of
Commons, many Unionists, who opposed Jewish immigration into Britain,
instead expressed support for a Jewish homeland in Palestine or elsewhere
(Defries, 2001, p. 31).

When Great Britain declared war on Turkey on November 5, 1914, the
political engines of the parties involved switched to a new set of tracks
fueled by a clearer set of objectives to which the diplomatic and military
strategies would have to be adjusted. While the Zionists and their claims
took a backseat to the British concerns with the Arabs and the French until
the end of 1916, it was Herbert Samuel, one of the leaders of the Liberal
party and the first person of the Jewish faith to sit in a British Cabinet,

who kept the flame of Zionism alive in the arena of British politics, and the moment Turkey entered the war on the side of the Central Powers, he moved into action.

Turkey's involvement in the war sharpened the focus of the Zionist Movement and moved the centre of gravity of the diplomatic negotiations that would shape the outcome of its aspirations to London, the seat of the British Empire. It was at this stage that the Zionist factions coalesced around the leadership that had emerged from the political wilderness to develop the diplomatic strategies and tactics that they hoped would lead to the fulfilment of the Zionist political objectives. As we have seen, the founding objective, going back to 1897, the year Herzl initiated the First Zionist Congress, was, in Herzl's written and spoken words, the establishment of a Jewish state in Palestine. By the time World War I had erupted, this objective had survived all the Jewish and non-Jewish challenges and become the unequivocal goal of the now politically energized Zionist movement.

The convictions of the leadership that had emerged at this time to carry the Zionist banner in the political arena defined the Zionist perspective on the Balfour Declaration. As mentioned before, Herbert Samuel emerged as the Zionist movement's most effective and highly placed champion. On November 9, 1914, only a week after Turkey entered the war, Samuel expressed the Zionist perspective unequivocally in his meeting with Foreign Secretary Sir Edward Grey. "Perhaps," he told Sir Edward, "the opportunity might arise for the fulfillment of the ancient aspiration of the Jewish people and the restoration [in Palestine] of a Jewish state" (Schneer, 2010, p. 125).

Stein noted that when Turkey entered the war, Samuel had seen that the Zionists might now have a chance of achieving their purpose and was convinced that it would be to Great Britain's advantage to encourage them. Stein also observed that while Chaim Weizmann was of the same mind, the two had never met and were unaware of each other's activities and thoughts. When they met for the first time early in December 1914, Weizmann was astonished to discover that Samuel was committed to the Zionist cause and, in a letter dated March 21, 1915, expressed his appreciation for Samuel's continued support and cooperation (Stein, 1961, p. 116).

Chaim Weizmann's impressive performance in solving some difficult and urgent problems relating to the production of explosives enhanced his personal standing and made him well-known to important ministers and their entourage. This important war work brought him into close personal contact with David Lloyd George and, because of the confidence and respect he inspired, placed him in a strong position for talking about Zionism to a minister who before long was to become the head of the government. His war work, by raising his stature and adding to his prestige, made him so much more effective an advocate of the Zionist cause (Stein, 1961, p. 120). It was because of his belief in himself and his mission that, almost immediately after the outbreak of the war, Weizmann took command of such forces as he could muster and started on the road which was to lead in the end to the Balfour Declaration (Stein, 1961, p. 123).

Weizmann's pre-war tactical differences with other leaders of the Zionist Movement were a reflection of the complexity of the Zionist perspective at that particular time. While fear of Turkish retaliation against any expression of the intention to create a Jewish state in Palestine was foremost in the minds of the Zionist leaders before the outbreak of WWI, it ceased to be a major consideration after Turkey's entry into the war and the ensuing expectation that its ultimate defeat would free Palestine from that threat. This critical turn of events resulted in a strategic change in the attitude of the Zionist leadership.

The Handicap of Cultural Fragmentation

The forging of a unified leadership and the definition of the Zionist objectives in a manner that would maximize the possibility that these would gain the support of the British government ran into a number of significant structural challenges.

Before the Zionist leadership could present a common front in their negotiations with the British government, they had to overcome the serious rift between the pro-Zionist and anti-Zionist factions of British Jewry. As John Strawson, author and law professor at the University of East London's School of Law, pointed out:

> There were stirrings of opposition amongst a small but influential group of anti-Zionist Jews. The most prominent amongst them was Secretary of State for India Edwin Montagu who began to make public protests against government support for Zionism through the pages of *The Times*. (Strawson, 2010, p. 29)

Montagu led a pitched battle between the Zionists and the influential group of British Jews represented by the Conjoint Foreign Committee, the recognized spokesmen of the British Jews in matters affecting Jewish communities abroad. It was through the Conjoint Committee that the two principal lay organs of Anglo-Jewry – the Board of Deputies of British

Jews and the Anglo-Jewish Association – had since 1878 worked together in a sustained effort to secure a more tolerable existence for those Jews, numbering seven million, who, in various parts of the world, especially in Eastern Europe, were still subject to crippling disabilities. In 1914, the fourteen members of the Committee were drawn without exception from the assimilated Jewish bourgeoisie. There were men who, while they felt themselves firmly rooted in Britain, were loyal to a well-established tradition which made it incumbent upon British Jews to take up the cause of oppressed Jews in other parts of the world. None of them was a Zionist, and most of them, though not all, were strongly opposed to the Zionist Movement (Stein, 1961, pp. 172, 442).

In the summer of 1916, James de Rothschild, at the request of his father Baron Edmond of the French branch of the family, tried to break the ice between the Zionists and the Conjoint Foreign Committee by arranging a meeting between Weizmann and Lucien Wolf. A journalist and expert commentator on British foreign affairs, Wolf had come to dominate the Conjoint Foreign Committee and the Board of Deputies of British Jews. It was one of their aims to persuade British policymakers to defend and support Jewish interests outside Great Britain. Wolf believed in Jewish assimilation and took a leading role among the Jews in Britain who opposed Zionism. While Stein notes that, on the Palestine question, the two men had nothing in common and that a single interview was enough to show that there was no point in going further, Baron Edmond was convinced that there was enough common ground for a working arrangement (Schneer, 2010, p. 10; Stein, 1961, p. 443).

With both sides afraid of alienating the Jewish public by provoking an open conflict, discussions began between the Zionists, with Sokolow as their spokesman, and the Conjoint Foreign Committee, represented by Wolf, with a view to re-opening the talks which had broken down in 1915. Lengthy and involved correspondence in which each side tried to improve its tactical position by extracting preliminary assurances from the other began in October 1916 and was brought to an end the following April with Wolf's announcement to Sokolow that his Committee was now at full liberty of action (Stein, 1961, p. 443).

It was now early 1917, and Wolf seems to have realized that the change of government from Herbert Asquith to Lloyd George would be to the advantage of the Zionists and that prompt action was required to neutralize that advantage. In an interview with the new Foreign Secretary, Arthur Balfour, Wolf expressed his concerns with the Zionist agenda and stated that the Committee insisted that the Zionists, with their propaganda and activities in Palestine, should not imperil the rights and status of Jews elsewhere.

> A Jewish nation or State in Palestine must not claim the allegiance of the Jews of Western Europe, who are satisfied with their local nationalities, nor must anything be done – as, for example, by demanding a privileged status for the Jews in Palestine – to compromise the position and aims of Jews in other countries. (Stein, 1961, p. 444)

The core of the Conjoint Committee's concern was that the status of the Jews in Britain, and wherever they felt they enjoyed full equality of rights, was at stake. The Committee was fundamentally concerned that there should be no blurring of the distinction between a Jewish community or Jewish state in Palestine and Palestine as the national home of the Jewish people. The Committee held that on this point there could be no compromise:

> [For] once the Jews were proclaimed to be a people, with Palestine as their national home, the antisemites would have won, since their case would have been conceded. (Stein, 1961, p. 445)

During the controversial exchanges preceding the final rupture between them in the spring of 1917, the Zionists and the Conjoint Committee wrangled endlessly about the true construction of expressions like "nation," "nationality," and "national home." Neither side convinced the other, while ordinary Jews were gravitating in growing numbers towards Zionism from an instinctive feeling that Zionists were moving in the right direction and ought not to be obstructed. At a time when a new world order seemed to be in the making, the idea of a restoration of the Jews to Palestine had an emotional appeal which the Zionists found irresistible. The Conjoint Committee's case, however, was driven by their conviction that the British government's endorsement of Zionism would mean that the British Jews had suffered a kind of rejection and disinheritance which, even though it left their legal rights unimpaired, would be painfully felt (Stein, 1961, pp. 446–447).

The struggle between the Zionists and anti-Zionists as to who would represent the voice of Jewry vis-à-vis the British government at this critical time marks a crucial episode in the development of the Zionist perspective towards the thrust and import of the Balfour Declaration. Stein notes that the battlefield in 1917 was substantially different from what it had been before the war. Whereas the Zionists had previously been a struggling minority, they were now coming into the ascendancy. When, within a month of the March Revolution in Russia, the Provisional Government annulled all restrictions imposed on any class of Russian citizens on account of their religion or nationality, the Russian Jews were relieved of their disabilities and the Conjoint Committee lost one of their main political *raisons d'être,* to the relief of the Foreign Office, which had been wearied and irritated by the Committee's incessant prodding on the Russo-Jewish question, in which the British government, having difficulties enough of its own with its touchy and unreliable Tsarist ally, had been in no position to intervene (Stein, 1961, p. 447).

This left the Committee with one immediate main concern: to dissuade the government from committing itself to the Zionists. Here, too, the Committee was now in a weak position. Not only did the Zionists command the personal sympathies of leading members of the government, there were also important practical considerations which gave them an advantage over the Conjoint Committee. While the Committee had nothing attractive to offer that would serve British interests, the Zionists, on the other hand, could be relied upon to work in support of the British claim to Palestine and were also believed to be able to exert influence by counter-acting both Russia's new regime's intention to abandon the war as well as the apathy about the war in certain circles in the United States. "Not only had the Conjoint Committee no Lloyd George or Balfour on its side but by the test of practical utility it was hopelessly outclassed" (Stein, 1961, p. 447).

Another factor that contributed to the deterioration of the Committee's standing was the changing hierarchy of authority within the Anglo-Jewish community. Since its establishment in 1878, it had been governed by a small and closely-knit group of relatively old and established families. It was primarily due to the prestige attached to wealth and social standing that their leadership had come to be accepted as part of the natural order of things. With the advent of the war, the Committee had become the centre of controversy when elements in Anglo-Jewry, not belonging to the privileged inner circle, started to challenge the established leadership (Stein, 1961, p. 448).

This intra-community struggle came to a head when the Committee publicly exposed its views on the Palestine question and was repudiated by the Board of Deputies, with Zionists and friends of Zionism joining forces with others whose main purpose was to censure the Committee for its behaviour in publishing a statement of this character without having consulted its parent bodies. The strongly pro-Zionist *Jewish Chronicle* remarked that "The battle between Zionists and anti-Zionist was, in fact, mixed up with the struggle for power in the internal politics of Anglo-Jewry" (Stein, 1961, p. 449).

The Conjoint Committee's last-ditch efforts to pre-empt the successful outcome of the Zionists' political agenda failed to derail the course of events. Upon hearing of Sokolow's statement in Paris that the British government had already intimated its approval, in principle, of the Zionist programme, Wolf asked the Foreign Office whether Sokolow's statements were correct, as he pointed out:

> In view of the Conjoint Committee, very serious mischief might result if an agreement on the Palestine question were concluded without their participation, more especially as the gentlemen with whom His Majesty's Government have so far been in negotiation are all foreign Jews having no quality to speak for the native Jews of the United Kingdom. (Stein, 1961, p. 449)

In response, Wolf was informed that

> No new agreement on the Palestine question had been concluded and that the government would act in all matters affecting the Jewish community, not only in its own best interests, but also with a due regard to the wishes and opinions of all its sections, and that they will not depart from these guiding principles. (Stein, 1961, p. 449)

In the same vein, Wolf sought further reassurance, on May 8, in an interview with Lord Robert Cecil, "the parliamentary under-secretary of state for foreign affairs" (Schneer, 2010, xiv). A few days later, on May 16, Claude Montefiore, the anti-Zionist president of the Anglo-Jewish Association, reported to his colleagues that he had seen the influential War Cabinet member Alfred Milner and that Milner had confirmed the assurance of the Foreign Office that the Conjoint Committee would be consulted before anything final was done (Stein, 1961, p. 450).

On May 20, Weizmann assured a Zionist conference in London that the Zionist programme, as he conceived it, had the government's approval. His words reflected the Zionist perspective at this crucial stage in the process that led to the promulgation of the Balfour Declaration, a perspective that was modulated by the tactical adjustments required to accommodate the multitude of political considerations discussed in this chapter. In Weizmann's words:

> States must be built up slowly, gradually, systematically and patiently. We, therefore, say that while the creation of a Jewish Commonwealth is our final ideal…. [T]he way to achieve it lies through a series of intermediary stages. And one of those intermediary stages, which I hope will come about as a result of this war, is that […] Palestine will be protected by such

a mighty and just Power as Great Britain. Under the wing of this Power, Jews will be able to develop and to set up the administrative machinery which, while not interfering with the legitimate interests of the non-Jewish population, would enable us to carry out the Zionist scheme. I am entitled to state in this assembly that His Majesty's Government is ready to support our plans. (Sokolow, 1917, quoted in Stein, 1961, p. 450)

Eager to stem the surging tide of the Zionist cause, the Conjoint Committee was anxious to propagate its cause before it was too late. In this, they felt stymied by the Foreign Office's admonition that any public polemics on the Zionist question would be embarrassing to the government and should be avoided. Early in May, Lord Cecil had intimated to Wolf that he would strongly deprecate any action by the Committee which would involve it in an open controversy with the Zionists. In light of the fact that while the British government was encouraging the Zionist leaders to rally Jewish opinion in the United States and Russia in support of the British claim to suzerainty in Palestine, nothing could be more inopportune than that its own Jewish citizens publicly advertising their differences on the Zionist question (Stein, 1961, p. 451).

The Conjoint Committee and its followers were in a dilemma, which they phrased painfully and accurately:

Did the loyalty British Jews owed to their Government require those for whom Zionism meant a threat of "perpetual alienage" to suppress their fears, and, because British interests appeared to require it, to acquiesce in a policy repugnant to their own wishes and feelings? (Stein, 1961, p. 451)

It was after a number of last-ditch efforts by the Conjoint Committee to plead their case in the press and to respond to what they had been reading in the semi-official Zionist publication *Zionism and the Jewish Future*, which was meant primarily for the enlightenment of the general reader and also as a challenge to anti-Zionist Jews (Stein, 1961, p. 299), that the now public ideological war of words between the Zionists and anti-Zionists reached the point in which the latter were to meet their political Waterloo. The Committee gave vent to its sense of indignation at the Zionist tenets by issuing a strong statement to air its objections to the Zionist proposals. In it, the Committee stated that while it had always been ready to co-operate with the Zionists in a policy "aimed primarily at making Palestine a Jewish spiritual centre by securing for the local Jews, and the colonists who might join them, such conditions of life as would best enable them to develop the Jewish genius on lines of its own," leaving "larger political questions ... to be solved as need and opportunity might render possible," it had learned from the published statements of Zionist leaders that they now favoured a much larger scheme of an essentially political character (Stein, 1961, p. 454).

In their statement, the Committee declared that it would have no objections against a local Jewish nationality establishing itself in Palestine. What it emphatically rejected was the wider Zionist theory, which regards all the Jewish communities in the world as constituting one homeless nationality, incapable of complete social and political identification with the nations in which they dwell, and as needing, therefore, a political centre and an always available homeland in Palestine. This, the Committee declared, must have the effect, throughout the world, of stamping the Jews as strangers in their native lands and of undermining their hard-won position as citizens and nationals of those lands (Stein, 1961, p. 454).

Lucien Wolf and Claude Montefiore were irked both by Rabbi Moses Gaster's statement that "The claim to be an Englishman of the Jewish persuasion – that is, English by nationality and Jewish by faith – is an absolute self-delusion" and also by Weizmann's following remark:

> The efforts of the emancipated Jew to assimilate themselves to the surroundings [...] deceive nobody but himself. The position of the emancipated Jew, though it does not realize it himself, is even more tragic than that of his oppressed brother [...]. The facts of the Jewish position in the East and West alike [...] point to the same fatal source of weakness in the Jewish struggle for existence – the lack of a home [...]. It is this central problem – the homelessness of the Jewish people – that Zionism attacks. (Stein, 1961, p. 454)

Under the headline "Palestine and Zionism – Views of Anglo-Jewry," the statement appeared in *The Times* of May 24 over the signatures of the Presidents of the Board of Deputies of British Jews and the Anglo-Jewish Association – D. L. Alexander, K.C., and Claude Montefiore (Stein, 1961, p. 452). In this statement, the Conjoint Committee created irreparable damage to their cause when they stated that the Zionist proposal to invest the Jewish settlers in Palestine with certain special rights in excess of those enjoyed by the rest of the population, these rights to be embodied in a Charter and administered by a Jewish Chartered Company, would, if implemented, prove a veritable calamity for the whole Jewish people. "In all the countries in which they live, the principle of equal rights for religious denominations is vital for them" (Stein, 1961, p. 455).

The public controversy that broke out following the appearance of this statement was exactly what the Foreign Office had hoped to avoid. There were violent attacks on the Conjoint Committee in the Jewish press, letters on both sides in *The Times*, a *Times* leader giving judgment decisively in favour of the Zionists, a debate at the Council of the Anglo-Jewish Association and, finally, a trial of strength at the Jewish Board of Deputies, ending, though by a narrow margin, in the discomfiture of the Conjoint Committee, followed soon afterwards by its dissolution (Stein, 1961, p. 456).

Stein argued that the strong feeling aroused by the Conjoint Committee's manifesto was due to its being "hopelessly prejudiced by its background and origins." At no time, according to Stein, had the Conjoint Committee shown any constructive interest in the Palestine question; it had, all along, concentrated its efforts on weakening the Zionist movement and making it innocuous. It was general knowledge that the brains of the Committee and the real inspiration of the statement were Montefiore and Wolf, who were the most determined and formidable anti-Zionists in the Anglo-Jewish community. Stein argues that the manifesto might have aroused less indignation if the Committee had kept the controversy within the domestic arena by addressing the Jewish public through the Jewish press. By choosing *The Times* as its forum, the committee scandalized many Jews who felt that this public advertisement of its differences with the Zionists, and the manner in which they were presented, could do the Jewish community no good. Stein argues that it is not surprising that the Zionists and their sympathizers interpreted it as an insidious attempt to discredit the Zionist movement, to misrepresent its aims and outlook to the British public, and to deter the government from supporting it, save to the extent of an emasculated programme to be approved by the Conjoint Committee (Stein, 1961, p. 457).

The fatal blow to the anti-Zionist position came on June 17, 1917, when the Board of Deputies, by a vote of 56 to 51, adopted a resolution expressing its "profound disapproval" of "the views of the Conjoint Committee as promulgated in the communication published in *The Times*" and its "dissatisfaction at the publication thereof," while also declaring that the Committee has lost the confidence of the board (Stein, 1961, p. 458).

The struggle to unify the Jewish world under the Zionist banner came to an end with the dissolution of the anti-Zionist Conjoint Foreign Committee of the Anglo-Jewish Association and the Board of Deputies of British Jews by the resolutions adopted on June 15, 1917 by the Board of Deputies and on September 9 by the Anglo-Jewish Association (Stein, 1961, p. 458). The intra-Jewish cultural and political differences had finally been resolved in favour of the Zionist movement, which would henceforth represent the political voice of the Jewish people vis-à-vis the

British government and the world in their pursuit of the restoration of the ancient Jewish homeland in Palestine.

The Power of Unity

For the Zionist leaders, the fall of the Conjoint Committee came at just the right moment. They were doing their utmost to interest Russian and American Jews in the idea of a Jewish Commonwealth in Palestine under British protection. Their efforts would have been seriously prejudiced, and their standing with the British government impaired, if the anti-Zionists had gained the upper hand in Britain. They could now point to what had happened after the publication of the Conjoint Committee statement as evidence that the body did not speak for Anglo-Jewry, and with their position thus strengthened, they were emboldened to ask the government whether the time had not come for it to identify itself formally and openly with the Zionist cause (Stein, 1961, p. 461).

With the Zionists having consolidated their position as the political voice for the majority of world Jewry, they could now concentrate on reaching the best possible understanding with the British government towards the establishment of a Jewish state after the conclusion of the war and the anticipated defeat of the Ottoman Empire.

Schneer noted that in the summer of 1917, the British Zionists felt that their goal finally lay within their grasp. In consultation with sympathetic officials such as Sir Mark Sykes and Sir Ronald Graham, assistant undersecretary of state at the Foreign Office, Weizmann and Sokolow worked out a method of approach. They would compose a Zionist statement, which, pending approval by the War Cabinet, Balfour would convey to Rothschild by letter. With Weizmann absent in Gibraltar, the London Zionist Political Committee held meetings in London to work on their draft declaration. The participants included, among several others, Sokolow, Ahad Ha'am and, occasionally, the prominent British Zionist leader Harry Sacher. Weizmann's absence at these meetings was due to his being unexpectedly called abroad to Gibraltar to meet with Henry Morgenthau, former United States Ambassador to the Ottoman Empire, to try and convince him to drop an attempt to reach a separate peace between Turkey and the Allies (Schneer, 2010, pp. 264–274, 333–334).

This unforeseen development gives rise to two questions. What led Weizmann to this mission, and how could the leader of the still fledgeling Zionist movement sway the representative of the then most powerful nation on earth to make such a momentous about-face? The details of what transpired might provide a clearer picture of the nature and extent of the influence these two sides exerted on the events leading to the Balfour Declaration.

Weizmann in Gibraltar

Following America's declaration of war against Germany on April 6, 1917, Germany tried to persuade its Turkish ally to join them in that war but could not get Turkey to do more than sever diplomatic relations with the United States. This caused President Wilson to consider the possibility that Turkey was having second thoughts about their involvement in the war altogether, in which case the United States might be able to reach a separate peace (Schneer, 2010, p. 263).

According to Schneer, while Morgenthau sympathized with Zionism, he was not strictly speaking a Zionist. Schneer also calls him impulsive and boastful, like when, in May 1916, he claimed in a speech that he had arranged for the Ottomans to sell Palestine to the Jews. In the same speech, he also warned against the danger from the Arabs if millions of people were placed in Palestine and that it would be best to leave things as they were. These mixed signals from Morgenthau caught Sir Mark Sykes' attention. He warned Rabbi Moses Gaster, one of the leading British Zionists he knew best at the time, of the problem Morgenthau posed (Schneer, 2010, p. 264).

Morgenthau put the following scheme to President Wilson. He would persuade Pashas Enver and Talaat, two of the Pasha triumvirate that ruled the Ottoman Empire during World War I, to allow Allied submarines to pass through the Dardanelles strait to torpedo the German ships that had their guns trained on Constantinople to ensure that the Ottoman Empire would stay on side. This would free the CUP government to conclude a separate peace. Wilson authorized Morgenthau only to listen to what the Turks were willing to offer and to report back to Washington (Schneer, 2010, p. 264).

When British Foreign Secretary Arthur Balfour, who was visiting Washington at the time, was apprised of this scheme by U.S. Secretary of State Robert Lansing, Balfour confirmed that the Turks showed interest in the idea of a separate peace and added that this could lead to very advantageous results. As Schneer observes, while this might have applied to the British, it would work against the objectives of the Zionists who were seeking British support for the Jewish homeland in Palestine, which would be separated from the Ottoman Empire (Schneer, 2010, pp. 264–265).

Britain's chronic political double-dealing is again demonstrated by the fact that when Balfour wired news of Morgenthau's plans to the Foreign Office, no mention was made of the possibility of Zionist objections, although the discussions about the drafting of the Balfour Declaration were in full swing.

With the seeming approval of the British and with Wilson's conditional authorization for his mission in his pocket, Morgenthau's charade was ready to move into operational mode. Having concurred with the British Foreign Office's suggestion that, due to the number of spies in Switzerland, it would be better to carry out the mission in Egypt, Morgenthau also saw this as an opportunity to claim that he was on his way to check the condition of Jews in nearby Palestine. To further camouflage the expedition, Morgenthau planned to invite prominent American Jews to accompany him. These included Harvard Law School professor, Zionist and future Supreme Court Justice Felix Frankfurter, who was working as an assistant to the Secretary of War, Newton Baker. Frankfurter invited his own assistant, the lawyer Max Lowenthal. Also joining the team was Eliahu Lewin-Epstein, treasurer of the Zionist Provisional Executor Committee in New York City. This impressive entourage was intended to create the notion, fostered with leaks to the press, that the mission was a Zionist enterprise. Zionists even began a campaign to raise funds for the mission. At no time were Frankfurter, Lowenthal or Lewin-Epstein aware of Morgenthau's main objective (Schneer, 2010, p. 265).

Before the American mission could make its way to Egypt to explore a separate peace deal with the Ottoman Empire, they needed to have their wartime allies on board. The plan was for the American delegation to stop at Gibraltar and to request that both Britain and France send someone in authority to meet Morgenthau there. Morgenthau also felt that if the British were to send Chaim Weizmann to meet him, it would give further credibility to his cover story. The State Department accepted Morgenthau's suggestion and asked the Foreign Office to send Weizmann to meet their envoy (Schneer, 2010, p. 265).

Morgenthau assumed that Weizmann would fall for his ruse, and so did the State Department. Weizmann, however, learned of Morgenthau's mission, not from the Foreign Office but from Louis Brandeis, the American Zionist and Supreme Court Justice with close ties to President Wilson (Schneer, 2010, pp. 265–266). Brandeis had learned of it first from Frankfurter, who was not aware of its true purpose, and then from Wilson himself, who did explain the mission's real purpose. Brandeis did not hesitate to inform Weizmann of the mission and raise the red flag by suggesting that Weizmann intercept it. Due to his close connection with

Wilson, Brandeis could not be more explicit. Another source of information for Weizmann was the prominent British-Armenian businessman and politician James Malcolm, the British representative on the five-member Armenian National Delegation, which represented Armenian wartime and post-war interest in Europe. Not only had he heard rumours in pro-Turkish circles in London about separate peace initiatives with Turkey, initiated by the Americans in quiet cooperation with the British and the French, but, on June 8, 1917, at an Islamic Society meeting on Muslim interests in Palestine, he had heard open talking and bragging about an early peace with Turkey. From what he heard at that meeting, Malcolm concluded not only that Morgenthau was going to approach the Ottomans but that Aubrey Herbert, the Conservative Turcophile MP and member of the Anglo-Ottoman Society, and a Jewish anti-Zionist, Sir Adam Samuel Block, were involved in a similar initiative (Schneer, 2010, p. 266).

Malcolm wasted no time alerting Weizmann to these developments. The two met at Weizmann's house to fill each other in as to what they had learned. What followed was an ardent attempt by Malcolm and Weizmann to convey their anger to the British government. They felt that William Ormsby-Gore, who in 1917 was Milner's pro-Zionist parliamentary private secretary and subsequently assistant secretary of the Cabinet, working with Sir Mark Sykes, would give them a sympathetic hearing. Ormsby-Gore agreed to Malcolm's urgent request for a meeting, at which they conveyed their criticism and warned that approaching the Turks at this time with peace overtures would imperil the interest of the British Empire. Weizmann openly denounced Morgenthau, whom he practically called a German agent and whose aim Weizmann suggested was an inconclusive peace which would give German capital and German Jews a growing importance in the Turkish Empire and especially in Palestine. At this point, Weizmann was not aware that the Americans had asked for him to be present and ended up suggesting that he should be sent to meet Morgenthau (Schneer, 2010, pp. 267–268).

On June 12, Weizmann and Malcolm visited Sir Ronald Graham separately to continue their pressure. They focused particularly on Morgenthau's intentions. According to Schneer, historians without exception have agreed that their efforts had a dampening effect on the British inclination towards a separate peace with the Turks. As a result of Weizmann's and Malcolm's efforts, the British ended up opposing Morgenthau's approach to the Turks. They felt that the condition of secrecy that was so crucial to Morgenthau no longer existed and that, consequently, his mission would no longer serve a useful purpose and should be postponed. The Americans insisted on pursuing it even though the British no longer believed in it. In addition, the Foreign Office had come to the conclusion that the support of "international Jewry" was necessary to win the war, a feeling that Weizmann assiduously encouraged. With Morgenthau having lost the Foreign Office's confidence and having more trust in Weizmann, they decided to allow Weizmann to go to Gibraltar to head off Morgenthau's mission (Schneer, 2010, p. 268).

In spite of the fact that, as a result of Weizmann's and Malcolm's entreaties, Graham had agreed that the Morgenthau mission should be postponed and that the former thought that he was on the same page as the Zionists on this matter, he had still asked Britain's key diplomat in Switzerland, Horace Rumbold, to cooperate with Aubrey Herbert in his efforts to pursue a separate peace with the Turks, which Graham had convinced Weizmann and Malcolm the British had abandoned. Not only did the Foreign Office not enlighten Weizmann and Malcolm as to what they were up to on the other track, they went to the other extreme when Balfour called Weizmann to his office and instructed him to keep on talking to Morgenthau until he had talked him out of his mission. Weizmann did not know that Balfour was simultaneously sending Aubrey Herbert to Switzerland on another peace mission to the Turks. "Thus the British government tricked Chaim Weizmann" (Schneer, 2010, p. 269). This is another instance in which the British demonstrated their propensity to spin elaborate webs of intrigue to serve their own political ends, regardless of the potential for betrayal and strife this generated.

By July 4, 1917, the British, American and French delegations had arrived in Gibraltar, where, the next day, they all met for discussions. In his report to Sir Ronald Graham, Weizmann relates how the Americans, through their spokesmen Henry Morgenthau and Ashag Schmarvonian, the Turkish Armenian State Department functionary who had been Morgenthau's interpreter in Constantinople, described the conditions in Turkey in the most negative terms. According to Schmarvonian, the Ottoman army was near collapse, the Empire was practically bankrupt, most Turks hated and feared the Germans, and their government leaders were in disunity. Weizmann recalls that Morgenthau thought that with Turkey on the point of collapse, Talaat Pasha might be played off against Enver Bey. When Weizmann asked Morgenthau whether the Turks knew they were beaten in the war and, if so, what their terms for a separate peace would be, neither Morgenthau nor anyone else in the American delegation could answer. At this point, Weizmann conveyed his understanding of the British terms to Morgenthau, which included that Armenia, Mesopotamia, Syria and Palestine were to be detached from the Turkish Empire. While no one at the conference contradicted him, neither did anyone think that the Turks would find such conditions acceptable. Consequently, even though the French seemed to favour making an approach to Turkey, "it was no job at all to persuade Mr. Morgenthau to drop the project" (Schneer, 2010, p. 270).

Weizmann strongly objected to Morgenthau's attempt to cloak his mission in the mantle of Zionism. Weizmann lectured Morgenthau that "on no account must a Zionist organization be in any way identified or mixed up even with the faintest attempts to secure a separate peace... we Zionists feel about this point most strongly and we would like assurances from Mr. Morgenthau that he agrees and understands this position." The assurance was offered. Morgenthau ended up capitulating on all fronts and abandoned his mission (Schneer, 2010, pp. 270–271).

Weizmann's efforts to foil Morgenthau's mission appeared to have been a complete success. Yet, according to Schneer, he had not quite carried off the diplomatic coup he was widely praised for. Weizmann had not put an end to the separate peace idea, only to Morgenthau's version of it. After Weizmann returned to London on July 21, 1917 to report to Graham in person, the latter sent him to Paris to brief Balfour and Lloyd George, who were attending a war conference. While they seemed glad to learn that Weizmann had scotched Morgenthau's mission, they gave no hint to suggest that he had not scored a complete triumph (Schneer, 2010, p. 271).

This episode, like many others that paved the way towards the Balfour Declaration end game, illustrates how Weizmann, having emerged as the perceived representative of not only the British Zionists but of all English Jewry, was being used to serve the political agendas of the Western powers. As noted in Hebrew University professor and English historian Norman Rose's biography of Chaim Weizmann, "Weizmann was more than content to play this game as long as it advanced Zionist interests" (Rose, 1986, p. 174).

Rose's take on Weizmann's trip to Gibraltar can be summarized as follows. Henry Morgenthau, former American Ambassador to Constantinople, had influential contacts in Turkey, and he believed that he could negotiate a separate peace between Turkey and the Allies. While sceptical of Morgenthau's chances, the British agreed to play along for the sake of good relations with their American partners (Rose, 1986, p. 174).

Weizmann, alerted by Brandeis of Morgenthau's intentions, was sceptical that the Turks would agree to any meaningful concessions. Allowing Turkey to maintain control over the Middle East would undermine the Zionist and British policies, which were contingent on the breakup of the Ottoman Empire. Weizmann denounced Morgenthau's initiative to his chief contacts in the Foreign Office, Sir Ronald Graham and William Ormsby-Gore, and suggested sending a "Zionist who we can trust" to ward off Morgenthau. With Harry Sacher, Weizmann's original choice, indisposed, Weizmann volunteered to go himself. Weizmann was also concerned about Germany's competition in courting the Zionists' favour to suit their own political objectives. All told, Weizmann went to Gibraltar to intercept Morgenthau's mission, which, if successful, would nullify Britain's interest in the sought-after declaration. Rose confirms that, in the end, Morgenthau's expedition turned out to be a hollow threat (Rose, 1986, pp. 174–175).

It can be concluded, both from Schneer's account and from Rose's biography, that Morgenthau's position was weak and indecisive and no match for Weizmann's diplomatic skills and persuasiveness. In the end, Weizmann's arguments prevailed, and Morgenthau called his mission off.

Another by-product of Weizmann's trip to Gibraltar was that it caused him to be out of sync with the rest of the Zionist committee on the status of the draft declaration that was being developed.

While Weizmann was absent in Gibraltar, the Political Committee, chaired by Sokolow, worked on preparing the draft, carefully staying within the limits of the general attitude on the subject which prevailed among the leading members of the government. Weizmann recorded the final formula on which the committee had agreed, and which Lord Rothschild handed to Balfour on its behalf on July 18, 1917, as follows:

> His Majesty's Government, after considering the aims of the Zionist Organization, accept the principle of recognizing Palestine as the National Home of the Jewish people and the right of the Jewish people to build up its national life in Palestine under a protection to be established at the conclusion of peace, following upon the successful issue of the war.
>
> His Majesty's Government regard as essential for the realization of this principle the grant of internal autonomy to the Jewish nationality in Palestine, freedom of immigration for Jews, and the establishment of a Jewish National Colonizing Corporation for the re-establishment and economic development of the country.
>
> The conditions and forms of the internal autonomy and a Charter for the Jewish National Colonizing Corporation should, in the view of His Majesty's Government, be elaborated in detail with the representatives of the Zionist Organization. (Weizmann, 1966, p. 203)

While Weizmann's autobiography provides a detailed first-hand account of what transpired during his leadership of the Zionist movement, his narrative contains a serious error with respect to the wording of the July 18, 1917 draft. When, on page 203 of his autobiography *Trial and Error*, he provides the text of the draft that he claims was submitted by Rothschild to Balfour on July 18, 1917, he erroneously cites the text of the formula Sokolow and a group of his advisors had agreed upon a week earlier, on July 12, instead of the text that was actually submitted on July 18 by Rothschild to Balfour. If one uses Weizmann's version as a starting point of the twisting semantic road that led to the actual declaration of November 2, one gets trapped into a chain of non-sequiturs that could end up producing a misleading version of this extremely important episode. Careful scrutiny of the sequence of events as narrated by Stein and Schneer leads to the inevitable conclusion that the July 18 formula they referred to was the correct one (Stein, 1961, p. 470; Schneer, 2010, p. 335).

This serious error in Weizmann's autobiography is due to his being away in Gibraltar while the Zionist committee was working on the draft text in London. His absence caused him to miss the back and forth between Sokolow and Sykes that had resulted in the finalization of the more abbreviated wording which was in fact submitted to Balfour on July 18. This is evidenced by the fact that Lord Milner, a member of the War Cabinet, considered the words "reconstituted" and "secure" too strong and submitted his alternative:

> His Majesty's Government accepts the principle that every opportunity should be afforded for the establishment of a home for the Jewish people in Palestine, and will use its best endeavours to facilitate the achievement of this object, and will be ready to consider any suggestions on the subject which the Zionist Organisation may desire to lay before them. (Ingrams, 2009, p. 9)

He could not have had Weizmann's version in front of him as the words "reconstituted" and "secure" did not appear at all in the draft cited by Weizmann but did so in the version actually submitted on July 18. In any event, the other fact that confirms that the shorter version quoted by Schneer and Stein was the one submitted on July 18 is the cable that Weizmann sent to Brandeis after his meeting with Balfour on September 19, 1917, in which Weizmann stated:

> The following text declaration has been approved [by the] Foreign Office and Prime Minister and submitted [to the] War Cabinet: 1. His Majesty's Government accepts the principle that Palestine should be reconstituted as the National Home of the Jewish people. 2. His Majesty's Government will use its best endeavours to secure the achievement of this object and will discuss the necessary methods with the Zionist Organization. (Weizmann, 1966, p. 204)

With the sending of this cable, Weizmann got back on track with the sequence and timing of the various drafts. We have now entered the phase that would determine the final wording of the British undertaking to assist in the realization of the Zionist dream. From the Zionist perspective, the wording of the sought-after declaration was an agonizingly daunting project. On the one hand, the opportunity of having the leading world power endorse the recovery of a homeland that would free the Jewish nation from the shackles of 1,800 years of worldwide oppression and persecution was so existentially vital that every effort was to be exerted to make that dream come true. At the same time, the Zionist leadership also realized that the utmost caution must be exercised to avoid any missteps that might cause it to fail. As Strawson points out:

> There were differences between the Zionist leaders on what was possible and desirable. The draft was mainly the work of the Nahum Sokolow, who thought that if we want too much, we shall get nothing: on the other hand, if you get some sympathetic declaration, I hope we can get more and more. (Strawson, 2010, p. 29)

The final wording of the Balfour Declaration, while simple on the surface, reflects a number of very complex political considerations. From the Zionist perspective, as we have seen, the ultimate aim was the establishment of a sovereign Jewish state in Palestine. It must also be borne in mind that the overlapping and conflicting commitments made previously by the British to the Arabs and the French were not known to the Zionists, who were therefore at a strategic disadvantage, as the British held a larger, and closed, hand of political cards.

It should also be remembered that the Zionist perspective was shaped by the concern for the effect their negotiations with the British might have on the Jewish communities still living in enemy and/or hostile lands. By being dispersed all over the world, and with Judeophobia being such a universal and enduring phenomenon, the political activities of the Jewish community in one country always ran the risk of negative consequences for Jewish populations living in other countries whose governments were at odds with those activities. Therefore, in the autumn of 1917, when the negotiations leading to the Balfour Declaration were taking place, the Zionist leadership had to take into consideration that Palestine was still firmly in Turkish hands and that the use of explicit sovereignty-oriented wording would risk Turkish ire and serious negative implications for the Jewish communities already residing in the Ottoman Empire.

It is also important to bear in mind that the implementation of the Balfour Declaration was dependent on the outcome of the war. It follows that, from the Zionist perspective, the use of the word *homeland* was a politically induced euphemism for the term *state*. As the Zionists saw it, after the Ottoman Empire was defeated, the Zionists would be able to re-establish a Jewish state in Palestine. The Zionist leadership were not aware of the conflicting promises made by the British to the Arabs and the French, which would inevitably be reflected in the final wording of the Balfour Declaration.

In addition, from the Zionist perspective, what they had always been up against was the pervasive ipso facto handicap of antisemitism which, as we have seen throughout this study, permeated all political and social levels throughout the world, as well as the astronomical asymmetry in human, material and geographic resources between the tiny exiled Jewish nation and the major powers conducting the war.

What the Zionists had going for them was the strength of an unshakable determination based on a deep belief in the rightness and existential nature of their cause and the serendipitous alignment of these dynamic elements with the geopolitical interests of the British government at this unique moment in history.

Characteristically, Harry Sacher, whom Schneer placed in the "maximalist" camp, thought Zionists should ask for as much as possible: "We must control the state machinery in Palestine. If we don't, the Arabs will. Give the Arabs all the guarantees they like for cultural autonomy; but the state must be Jewish." In his narration of the deliberations among the Zionist leaders about the wording of their draft declaration, Schneer notes that "Sokolow overbore Sacher and other maximalists" and that, having remained in constant touch with Sykes and indirectly communicated with Balfour himself, he knew better than his colleagues what the British government would accept and what it would not (Schneer, 2010, p. 334).

Sokolow wrote to Joseph Cowen, former president of the English Zionist Federation, who also took part in the deliberations, to say:

> Our purpose is to receive from the Government a general short approval of the same kind that which I have been successful in getting from the French government. (Schneer, 2010, p. 334)

Sokolow was referring to the letter of support he had requested from the French following his successful negotiations with top French government officials, including the French Foreign Minister, Jules Cambon, and François Georges-Picot, on April 9, 1917, where the French, as Sokolow reported to Weizmann, "had accepted in principle the recognition of Jewish nationality in the capacity of National Home local autonomy, etc." (Schneer, 2010, p. 213). Cambon's letter of June 4, 1917 read as follows:

You were good enough to present the project to which you are devoting your efforts, which has for its object the development of Jewish colonization in Palestine. You consider that, circumstances permitting, and the independence of the Holy Places being safeguarded on the other hand, it would be a deed of justice and of reparation to assist, by the protection of the Allied Powers, in the renaissance of the Jewish nationality in that Land from which the people of Israel were exiled so many centuries ago.

The French government, which entered this present war to defend a people wrongly attacked, and which continues the struggle to assure the victory of right over might, can but feel sympathy for your cause, the triumph of which is bound up with that of the Allies.

I'm happy to give you herewith such assurance. (Schneer, 2010, p. 218)

For practical purposes, this letter filled the void created by the absence of any other concrete approval by the French government of the Balfour Declaration. In the War Cabinet meeting of October 4, 1917, for the purpose of satisfying the Cabinet that the French were in accord, Balfour invoked the Cambon letter as evidence. Thus, by raising the Cambon letter at this critical moment, Balfour was able to weigh the scales in favour of the Declaration. In a lecture Picot delivered in Paris 1918, he stated that a qualified representative of the British government had been heard to say that if he had not been able to produce the Cambon letter to the War Cabinet, it would never have been persuaded to agree to the Balfour Declaration (Stein, 1961, p. 419).

Schneer strengthened this conclusion when he noted that, with this letter, the French government had become the first Great Power to recognize the Jews as a distinct nationality. Not only had Sokolow achieved a Zionist benchmark, the very existence of such a declaration by her primary wartime ally would make it easier for Britain to achieve one too (Schneer, 2010, p. 218).

This is another example of the fact that the British War Cabinet's approval of the Balfour Declaration was contingent upon the backing of all its allies. The French case also highlights how tenuous such support could be and how easily the individual and collective outcomes might have been otherwise.

On July 12, 1917, the London Zionist political committee members reduced half a dozen more complex drafts into a single, albeit still somewhat wordy, paragraph for the British government to sanction. It argued for British recognition of Palestine as the national home for the Jewish people and for the establishment of a "Jewish National Colonizing Corporation," under the aegis of which Jews could immigrate to Palestine freely, live autonomously and develop economically. Sokolow submitted this statement to Sykes and Graham, who responded that it was "too long" and that it contained "matters of detail which would be undesirable to raise at the present moment" (Schneer, 2010, p. 334).

Sokolow reconvened the committee on July 17. The Zionists debated what to cut and what to retain from the earlier paragraph. By now, according to Schneer, Sacher had grasped what kind of statement the Foreign Office wanted and had reconciled himself to the art of the possible. After debating what to cut from the earlier paragraph, they finally reached a consensus. Sacher was the principal architect of the formulation at which they eventually arrived. It read as follows:

(1) His Majesty's Government accepts the principle that Palestine should be reconstituted as the National Home of the Jewish people.

(2) His Majesty's Government will use its best endeavours to secure the achievement of this object and will discuss the necessary methods and means with the Zionist Organization. (Schneer, 2010, p. 335)

Schneer drew attention to the statement's implication of an unbroken link between Jews and Palestine despite the nearly two-thousand-year separation and to the positing of the Zionist Organization as the official representative of Jewish interests (Schneer, 2010, p. 335).

After obtaining approval of this condensed statement from Sykes and Graham, Sokolow passed it along to Lord Rothschild, who sent it to Balfour with the following note:

At last I'm able to send you the formula you asked for. If His Majesty's Government will send me a message on the lines of this formula, if they and you approve of it, I will hand it on to the Zionist Federation and also announce it at the meeting called for that purpose. (Schneer, 2010, p. 335)

From their perspective, the Zionists had every reason to believe that their dedicated efforts were finally going to be rewarded and that the government statement of support would be forthcoming momentarily. They had defeated the Conjoint Committee. They had developed extensive and close relations with department officials and had reason to believe the officials supported them. They had produced the brief statement the Foreign Office desired (Schneer, 2010, p. 335).

Balfour was equally optimistic. He drafted a reply to Rothschild: "I am glad to be in a position to inform you that His Majesty's Government accepts the principle that Palestine should be reconstituted as the national home of the Jewish people." Zionism stood on the verge of an epochal step forward. But Balfour did not send the note (Schneer, 2010, p. 335).

On July 18, 1917, the Zionists felt that their path to a historic restoration of the Jewish homeland had finally reached its destination. As it turned out, a number of new challenges had arisen that threatened the Zionist dream from coming to fruition. The nature of the challenges that caused the three-and-a-half-month delay in the final formulation of the Balfour Declaration will be dealt with in *Chapter 6: What's in a Word – Political Word-Craftsmanship.*

Conclusion

As has been shown in this chapter, it was the nexus between the emancipatory thinkers among the Jewish intelligentsia and the Russian Jewish population desperately striving to escape from the lethal stranglehold of the tsarist government that ignited the Zionist political awakening. The persecution of Russian Jewry had become so severe as to pose an existential threat to its survival as an ethnic identity in their native land. It transformed the leading Jewish pro-assimilationists such as Moshe Leib Lilienblum, Leo Pinsker and Peretz Smolenskin into determined advocates of the Zionist political solution. The Western-educated Theodore Herzl raised the movement to the status of an internationally recognized voice that brought the plight and aspirations of the Jewish diaspora to the attention of the world. He was the linchpin that forged the Zionist political movement that emerged in the second half of the nineteenth century. He brought together the disparate and often divisive parts of the dispersed Jewish nation and forged them into a cohesive, structured organization with a common purpose and common vision: the reconstitution of a Jewish nation state in the ancient homeland.

The Zionist movement was unable to make any progress in the international political arena until the outbreak of World War I. Until then, it occupied itself with reconciling its internal ideological differences through the Zionist Congresses that were held annually for five years starting in 1897 and biannually thereafter until 1913. It was during the ensuing three years that the Zionist movement became engaged in a political dialogue with the British government, which ultimately led to the promulgation of the Balfour Declaration.

One of the challenges encountered by the members of the War Cabinet in 1917, during the drafting process of the Balfour Declaration, was securing the support and approval of the American government. The following chapter, *The American Factor*, analyzes the impact of America's entry into World War I on the diplomatic process which drove the development of the Zionist project.

CHAPTER FIVE

THE AMERICAN FACTOR

Introduction

America's entry into World War I in April of 1917 completely changed the dynamics of that war, as will be shown in this chapter. It also had a major impact on the diplomatic process which drove the development of the Zionist project. It decisively tilted the outcome of the war in favour of the Allies and consolidated the British and Jewish efforts to realize the Zionist dream of the recovery of their ancient homeland.

The American Role in World War I

To understand America's role in World War I, one must appreciate the fact that President Woodrow Wilson's sentiment had been to avoid war, based on the belief that open diplomatic dealings within nations were the secret to avoiding conflict. He understood, however, that the use of force might be necessary in international affairs. In 1915, he had threatened the use of American naval power to bring Germany's unrestricted submarine warfare to a close and had promised the Allies that America would intervene militarily if they accepted his conditions for a peace conference and the Germans did not. In any event, until the spring of 1917, the American President had no intention of joining the war, nor was there any enthusiasm to do so among the American general public (Keegan, 2000, pp. 350–351).

What changed America's outlook were two counterproductive attempts by Germany to keep the Americans out. One was the attempt, via the notorious "Zimmerman telegram," to induce Mexico to ally itself with Germany if America entered the war, in return for which Mexico would regain the territories of Arizona, New Mexico and Texas. This instigative action was intercepted by British naval intelligence and transmitted to the American government. The other was Germany's resumption of unrestricted U-boat attacks, without warning, on merchant shipping in international waters. This policy resulted from the argument of the chief of the German naval staff, Admiral Henning von Holtzendorff, that an all-out attack on British maritime supply was essential for Germany to win the war before blockade by sea and attrition on land had exhausted Germany's ability to continue. The U-boat campaign was launched on February 1, 1917 around the British Isles, the west coast of France, and in the Mediterranean. On February 26, the same day that the Cunard liner *Laconia* was sunk by a German submarine, Wilson asked Congress' permission to arm American merchant ships. On March 15, German submarines sank three American merchant ships. Wilson decided that he could not ignore this direct challenge to the United States' dignity as a sovereign power. On April 6, Congress resolved to declare war against Germany. This was followed by declarations against Austria-Hungary, Turkey and Bulgaria and the enactment of selective military conscription on May 18. Preparations by the armed forces of the United States for operations in Europe were set in motion (Keegan, 2000, pp. 351–352).

By June 1917, an American Expeditionary Force under General John J. Pershing arrived in France, and on July 4, American Independence Day, elements of his 1st Division paraded in Paris. During the following months, fresh American units continued to arrive to meet a target of nearly three million men (Keegan, 2000, p. 372).

Keegan underscored the significance of the American entry into the war when he stated that "rare are the times in a great war when the fortunes of one side or the other are transformed by the sudden accretion of a disequilibrating reinforcement" (Keegan, 2000, p. 373).

It is symptomatic of the political currents and counter-currents that shaped the political landscape of WWI that the perilous military situation in Europe caused the British and French to solicit American participation in the war against the Central Powers while the Germans attempted to keep the Americans out through devastating assaults on the American merchant navy and their abortive attempt to induce Mexico to declare war on the United States.

The effect of the Americans' arrival was deeply depressing for the Germans. After four years of war, during which they had destroyed the Tsar's army, defeated the Italians and Romanians, disheartened the French, and denied the British a decisive victory, they now faced an overwhelming new force, which put paid to their battlefield operations calculations. Germany was not left with sufficient resources to oppose the millions of troops America could bring across the Atlantic. The German military aggression was put in reverse (Keegan, 2002, pp. 411–413).

America and the Balfour Declaration

America's reluctant entry into the World War I theatre also brought the burgeoning issue of Zionism and the Balfour Declaration project into its ambit. With the Americans now in the war, the British policymakers felt that a declaration endorsing Zionist goals might influence American Jews to press the U.S. government to advocate it with greater vigour (Bickerton & Klausner, 1991, p. 41).

The U.S., which had stayed out of the war during its first three years, became a crucial factor during 1917. While the Allies, Britain and France, were exhausting their human and material resources on the Western Front and were anxious for the U.S. to join them, the hope that the imagined Jewish influence in Washington would help sway the Americans was another stimulus behind the British momentum towards the Balfour Declaration. The importance of the U.S. factor was emphasized when Chaim Weizmann went to Gibraltar in July 1917 to intercept Henry Morgenthau, the American Ambassador to Turkey from 1913 to 1916, on his way to Palestine to attempt a separate peace between Turkey and the Allies in order to convince him, successfully, to drop the plan.

The efforts to enlist President Wilson's support for a British protectorate in Palestine for the Jews were also influenced by the fact that the United States was not at war with Turkey and feared that such a commitment would bring the status of Palestine into play with possibly undesirable political consequences for the U.S.-Turkey relationship (Lebow, 1968, pp. 508, 522).

As far as the United States was concerned, its declaration of war on Germany in April 1917 ensured that it would play a decisive part in the shaping of the post-war settlement (Stein, 1961, p. 350). It was, therefore, in the interests of both the Zionist leadership and the British government to persuade the American Jews to endorse the idea of a Jewish Commonwealth in Palestine under British protection (Stein, 1961, p. 358).

Thus started the diplomatic process which led to the United States' endorsement of the Balfour Declaration. On October 4, 1917, the British War Cabinet, concerned about German attempts to capture the support of the Zionists, had put a pro-Zionist declaration back on the front burner. As the United States' endorsement of the Balfour Declaration had become a condition *sine qua non* during the British War Cabinet's deliberations over its final wording, the British government made a renewed appeal to President Wilson by submitting the latest version of the text of the Declaration for his approval.

To obtain Wilson's reaction to the Milner-Amery formula, Balfour telegraphed the text of the October 4 Milner draft to Colonel Edward House, Wilson's aide and chief adviser on foreign affairs, on October 6 with a request for its submission to the President. On the same day, the United States Embassy in London telegraphed Wilson directly, bypassing the State Department, explaining that the British Cabinet was reconsidering a pro-Zionist message in view of reports that the German government was making great efforts in the same direction (Stein, 1961, p. 528).

On October 13, Wilson informed House that the formula was approved. House relayed this to Sir William Wiseman, who wired Balfour's Private Secretary on October 16 that Colonel House had put the formula before the President, who had approved it but had asked that no mention of his approval be made when His Majesty's Government made the formula public, as he had arranged that the American Jews would then ask him for his approval, which he would then give publicly (Stein, 1961, p. 530).

In the end, the War Cabinet did obtain Wilson's approval, which they considered essential for the promulgation of the Declaration. According to Stein, Wilson was at best indifferent to the issue of a national home for the Jews in Palestine, and it was only due to House's efforts, eventually aided by Louis Brandeis, the American Zionist and Supreme Court Justice with close ties to the President, that Wilson was finally brought around to endorsing the Milner-Amery draft declaration. Stein's account has been seriously challenged by American political scientist Richard Ned Lebow, who did extensive research on America's involvement in the history of the Balfour Declaration. In his article "Woodrow Wilson and the Balfour Declaration," Lebow specifically addresses the question of what caused Wilson to change his mind between September 3, 1917, when, having been asked by the British government for his opinion about the advisability of issuing a declaration of sympathy with the Zionist movement, he had replied that the time was not ripe, and October 6, 1917, when, on being asked again, he fully agreed that the British should issue such a declaration.

Lebow noted that scholars who have studied America's involvement in the history of the Balfour Declaration are divided on the influence of the American Zionists in securing President Wilson's support as well on Colonel House's role in Wilson's about-face.

The American historian Selig Adler, whom Lebow referred to as "the first scholar to investigate the problem systematically," credited mainly the American Zionist leadership for winning over the President. According to Adler, Brandeis spoke to Wilson between the two British inquiries and was responsible for his change in attitude. In Adler's opinion, Colonel

House was antisemitic and therefore an anti-Zionist (Lebow, 1968, p. 501).

On the other hand, Leonard Stein, whom Lebow, in December 1968, referred to as the author of the most impressive study to date of Zionist diplomacy during World War I, held a totally different view. Lebow confirmed that, as mentioned earlier in these pages, Stein doubted that Brandeis intervened directly with Wilson. According to Stein, as a result of Brandeis speaking to Colonel House, the latter changed his own attitude towards Zionism, which caused him to prompt President Wilson to approve the British Declaration (Lebow, 1968, p. 501).

The third study Lebow referred to is by Rabbi Herbert Parzen – an active member of the Zionist Organization of America and an author and lecturer on the history of Zionism – who, in 1963, advanced the view that Colonel House had always been pro-Zionist and deserved the credit for winning a reluctant Wilson over to the British proposal. Lebow noted that Parzen believed that the role of the Zionists, including Brandeis, had been overestimated, especially in view of their passive attitude in the crucial month when the fate of Zionism was at stake. According to Parzen, even though Brandeis was aware of Wilson's unfavourable response to the September request, he did not try to approach the President about it (Lebow, 1968, p. 501).

Lebow attributed this great disparity in interpretation to the source materials the three scholars he refers to relied upon. He found that each built his case on documents ignored by the others. Professor Adler relied primarily on the Wilson Papers and on the General Records of the Department of State. Dr. Stein did most of his research in Great Britain, and while he used a prolific number of sources, most came from the papers of the British Zionists. Rabbi Parzen based his argument on documentation contained in British-born journalist and American Zionist leader Jacob de Haas' archives and in the Brandeis Papers. Lebow found the variety of interpretations natural, seeing that none of the sources used provides a complete picture of what happened (Lebow, 1968, p. 502).

Lebow stated that in his own study, in addition to drawing on the sources used by Adler, Stein and Parzen, he reviewed materials from the Colonel Edward House Collection and the William Wiseman Papers as well. He came to the conclusion that the material in these last two collections, which had been overlooked by the other scholars, strongly challenges their interpretations (Lebow, 1968, p. 502).

While this is not the place to provide a detailed account of the history of political Zionism in the United States at the beginning of the twentieth century, a few of the key points raised by Lebow ought to be mentioned to provide some context to his efforts to unravel the riddle of Wilson's apparent vacillation in his position on the draft declaration in favour of a Jewish homeland in Palestine.

One of the salient observations made by Lebow is that when, on April 25, 1917, Brandeis received a cable from James de Rothschild urging that American Zionists secure President Wilson's approval of the British and Zionist plan for Palestine, the American Zionists were caught unprepared. The Provisional Emergency Committee of General Zionist Affairs, created in September 1914 by the Federation of American Zionists to give centralized direction to American Zionism during the war, had been devoting little attention to political matters. Brandeis, the Committee's chairman, had written that it was impossible to forecast the dimensions which the present war had assumed and that the American Zionists hoped that Turkey would not be involved in the war. Consequently, their energies were primarily focused on relief activities, on maintaining their Zionist positions in Palestine, and on trying to save Jewish life in the diaspora (Lebow, 1968, pp. 502–503).

Lebow also mentioned Professor Richard Gottheil, a former president of the Federation of American Zionists, as the only important Zionist leader preoccupied with the political future of Palestine. Lebow noted Gottheil's conviction that Palestine must be freed from Turkish rule and made a British protectorate. His insistent pressing of his position on Brandeis led to the creation, in 1915, of a subcommittee to study war aims. Yet, by April 1917, when the Provisional Committee received the British Zionists' request for help to secure Wilson's approval, they were unprepared to deal with it, as they had never paid attention to Gottheil's subcommittee's deliberations, nor had they established any programme of political objectives (Lebow, 1968, p. 503).

Early in May, when the Provisional Committee of the American Zionists finally took up the question of Palestine's political future, the debates centred on whether they should remain neutral or join the British Zionists in their efforts. Until then, the Provisional Committee had always assumed a policy of neutrality so as not to antagonize the Turks, who they feared would put an end to Jewish relief activities in the Near East or even provoke a massacre in Palestine similar to the Turks' barbaric treatment of the Armenians (Lebow, 1968, p. 504).

In the end, Weizmann's supporters convinced the Provisional Committee that America's entrance into the war, while she was still at peace with Turkey, dissolved the Zionists from any obligation of neutrality and that the objective of a Jewish Palestine was important enough to run the risk of reprisals. Consequently, the Provisional Committee fell behind the diplomatic offensive urged by Weizmann. What Lebow called a London-Moscow-New York axis of Zionists would soon come into being (Lebow, 1968, p. 504).

Now that the American Zionists had thrown their support behind the British plans for Palestine, they no longer felt restricted to relief activities and were ready to raise Weizmann's programme with Wilson and House. Following a long interview with Colonel House on April 9, 1917, during which they discussed the objective of a Jewish Palestine, Rabbi Stephen Wise, a member of Brandeis' group of prominent American Zionist leaders, reported his impressions of the talk to Jacob de Haas in the most enthusiastic terms. He felt that House understood the situation, that the Zionist project had his full backing, and that he was keeping himself ready to move at the right moment (Lebow, 1968, p. 506).

Lebow found that, while the Zionists were convinced of Colonel House's friendship, in reality, the latter was playing a "complicated game with Machiavellian duplicity" and that he told a different story to each group that approached him. According to Lebow, House ingratiated himself with the Zionists and expressed high praise for the British while, simultaneously, counselling President Wilson not to consent to their plans. In his frequent communications with Wise, House expressed his full support of Zionism and its objective for a Jewish homeland in Palestine. He was equally encouraging to the British, as on February 14, 1916, when, referring to his discussions of the Near East question with members of the British War Cabinet in London, he noted in his diary that "we all cheerfully divided up Turkey, both in Asia and in Europe." He suggested as a solution that Constantinople be neutralized (Lebow, 1968, p. 506).

By contrast, back in Washington, whenever House offered his opinion to the President, he persistently advised him against acceding to the British and Jewish plans for Palestine (Lebow, 1968, p. 507).

Meanwhile, encouraged by Wise's optimistic report of his April 9, 1917 meeting with Colonel House, Brandeis approached both Arthur Balfour and President Wilson and came away with positive impressions of the interviews he had with both statesmen. In his May 23 cable to his Zionist colleagues in London, Brandeis wrote that both Balfour and Wilson were in favour of a British protectorate in Palestine for the Jews. The only remaining question was the timing of a public declaration. Balfour suggested that, in view of the sensibilities of the other powers, much more would be obtained if patience was exercised and events were allowed to take their natural course. Brandeis added that Wilson was also not ready to make a public declaration, probably because the United States was not at war with the Ottoman Empire (Lebow, 1968, p. 508).

Lebow found that Adler's suggestion that President Wilson changed his mind on American support for the pro-Zionist declaration from negative on September 3, 1917 to positive on October 6, 1917, as a result of Brandeis having personally intervened and persuaded the President to change his mind, holds no water. Adler bases his opinion on his interpretation of the cable Brandeis sent to Weizmann on September 24, 1917, which stated:

> From talks I have had with the President and from expressions of opinion given closest advisors I feel I can answer you that he is in entire sympathy with Declaration quoted in yours of nineteenth as approved by Foreign Office and the Prime Minister. (Lebow, 1968, p. 514)

According to Lebow, Adler assumed that the talks Brandeis refers to in this cable allude to some conversation between Brandeis and Wilson between September 19, when Brandeis received the draft declaration, and September 24, when Brandeis sent the cable to Weizmann. Lebow reasons that since Brandeis had been in Washington during most of September and early October, whereas Wilson had left Washington on September 1 for New York from where he left on holiday to return to Washington on September 16, Brandeis could only have spoken to Wilson after this date. Yet, Lebow finds that the daily appointment book, in which all visitors to the White House registered, including all their appointments with the President and their duration, makes no mention of Brandeis' visit to the President during this period. The diary of the head usher of the White House does have an entry of a luncheon Wilson had with the Supreme Court on October 1, which, according to Lebow, Brandeis probably attended. But since the luncheon took place a week after Brandeis sent the cable to Weizmann informing him that the President was now backing the Declaration, the luncheon with the Supreme Court could not be the meeting Adler believes Brandeis was referring to. With no evidence of Brandeis meeting Wilson outside the White House or of speaking to him over the phone and with no mention in the meticulously kept Brandeis Papers or in any reports by Brandeis' lieutenants Wise and de Haas of this alleged meeting with the President, Lebow concludes that the conversation alluded to by Adler between Brandeis and Wilson never took place (Lebow, 1968, p. 514–515).

Lebow found it far more likely that the September 24 cable referred instead to the interview Brandeis and Wise had had with Colonel House the day before. Lebow noted that Stein believed that this conversation was responsible for Wilson's change of mind and that after Brandeis had convinced House of the efficacy of the Zionist programme, the latter in turn prompted the President to approve the Declaration (Lebow, 1968, p. 515). Stein bases this contention on a letter he received from Wiseman on November 7, 1952, which stated that "Colonel House was influential in bringing the matter to the President's attention and persuading him to approve" the formula (Lebow, 1968, p. 515).

Rabbi Parzen also credited Colonel House with persuading the President to approve the Balfour Declaration. Parzen bases his opinion on the Brandeis and de Haas papers, according to which the Zionists were convinced of House's friendship and of his favourable advocacy of their cause to the President (Lebow, 1968, p. 515).

Lebow made the case that, by all appearances, House had convinced the Zionists of his support and that they considered him the go-to person whenever they felt it necessary to seek the support of the administration. When, in September, Brandeis learned that the President was not ready to approve the Declaration, the first person to whom he turned for assistance was Colonel House (Lebow, 1968, p. 515).

As noted earlier, when Wise came out of his long interview with House on April 9, 1917, he reported that the Zionist project had House's full backing and that he was keeping himself ready to move at the right moment. Yet, when that moment seemed to come on September 3, 1917, with the British inquiry to the President, House warned Wilson of the high potential for dangers and problems and that the British should be wary of getting too deeply involved. This cold-water advice to Wilson was in stark contrast to his declaration to the War Cabinet in London that he was in favour of "putting Turkey on the scrapheap" and that he approved the British plans for the partition of Turkey (Lebow, 1968, p. 516).

Lebow saw further proof of House's real intentions in his meeting with the Zionists on September 23, 1917, at which "House deliberately misleads the Zionists." At this meeting, he seemed to have convinced Brandeis and Wise of his and Wilson's support for a Jewish Palestine and that they would approve a British declaration to that effect. This motivated Brandeis to assure Weizmann by cable, the next day, of Wilson's full support for the Declaration (Lebow, 1968, p. 516). Yet, in his diary, House records that he had cautioned Brandeis and Wise against pressing the President for any public statement, that he had confessed that the President was willing to go further than he himself thought advisable, and that he had warned the President against a more definite statement than the one he had cabled to Lord Robert Cecil. Lebow asserts that House had not "confessed" this to Brandeis and Wise, for if he had told them so, they would have been astonished. Lebow questions whether, if they had discovered that it was Wilson who actually supported their programme and that it was his advisor who urged against it, they would have continued to confide in the Colonel (Lebow, 1968, p. 516). They only did so because they remained under the impression that House strongly supported their position. Consequently, when Weizmann cabled Brandeis on October 10, stating that the Palestine question was going to be reconsidered by the Cabinet, Brandeis chose to see House instead of Wilson in the belief that it was House who was their real friend. It seems inconceivable to Lebow that the Zionists would have sought House's intervention with Wilson if House had already confessed that he had urged the President to withhold his approval (Lebow, 1968, p. 517).

According to Lebow's account, the instances of House's duplicity kept coming. Stein, relying on Wiseman's records, believes that Brandeis had convinced House to approve the draft declaration, but the evidence suggests a different reality. On October 3, following his discussions with Wise and Brandeis in New York, seven days after Brandeis met House in Washington, the latter wrote to Wilson that "Jews from every tribe have descended in force, and they seemed determined to break in with a jimmy if they are not let in," a remark which seems to show his annoyance with the Zionists for bothering him about Wilson's attitude towards the Palestine question. Lebow quotes the October 13 diary entry in which House recorded his final unequivocal advice to Wilson to the effect that "Turkey must not be partitioned among the belligerents" (Lebow, 1968, p. 518).

In spite of what he told the Zionists and the British, House's real attitude can only be inferred from what he advised the President, and the record shows that during the crucial months of September and October 1917, House, on three occasions, advised President Wilson not to consent to British and Zionist plans for Palestine (Lebow, 1968, p. 519).

At this stage, Lebow's record-straightening exercise still leaves the key question unanswered. In Lebow's own words, "If Brandeis did not intercede and personally change Wilson's mind, and if House, rather than prompt Wilson to approve, advised against acceding to a British declaration, the question still remains: what influenced President Wilson to reverse his decision and acquiesce in the British proclamation?" (Lebow, 1968, p. 520).

To Lebow, it was an indisputable fact that, unlike House, Wilson was genuinely attracted to Zionism and that he had always been consistent, in both his public and private statements, in his support of the Zionist movement. Lebow argues that there were two bases for Wilson's attraction to Zionism. One was his strong belief in national self-determination, which he saw embodied in Zionism's aim to replace Turkish tyranny with democratic government and provide a haven to Jews who were suffering from oppression and persecution. The other motivation was his personal sense of mission which derived from his Presbyterian upbringing and which found expression in what he saw as an opportunity to be "instrumental in the return of the Jews to the land of the prophets." It follows, therefore, that Wilson's change of opinion towards a British declaration was unrelated to his attitude towards Zionism, which had been steady and unwavering throughout (Lebow, 1968, pp. 520–521).

The real reason for Wilson's change of opinion is to be found in the "differing circumstances in which the two British requests were presented." The aforementioned cable from Cecil to Colonel House on September 3, 1917 was nondescript and without any sense of urgency. All it said was that "We are being pressed here for the declaration of sympathy with the Zionist Movement and should be very grateful if you feel able to ascertain if the President favors such a declaration." As this cable did not include any text of a proposed declaration, Wilson had no way of knowing what the requested expression of sympathy was to entail, nor did the cable give any indication as to where the British Cabinet itself stood on the matter. Lebow also notes that in the copy of the cable House passed to the President, the word "unofficially" had been added by House after the words "if you feel able to ascertain," which further toned down the import of the message (Lebow, 1968, p. 521). The fact that, in Stein's version of events, the text sent by Cecil on September 3 included the word "unofficially" and that Stein does not mention that it was added by House gives further credence to Lebow's criticism that Stein's limited research produced an inaccurate account of the facts.

According to Lebow, one of the reasons for the President not approving a declaration of sympathy at that time was that the United States was not at war with Turkey at the time and the two countries were still enjoying friendly relations. A commitment would bring the status of Palestine into play with possibly undesirable political consequences (Lebow, 1968, p. 522).

The British cable of October 6 was quite different from the earlier one. This one was not merely a feeler but an official request which included the text of the proposed declaration. In addition, the second cable came with a much greater sense of urgency. In it, Balfour cited reports that the German government was making great efforts to capture the Zionist movement as the reason for reconsidering the declaration. A declaration now would not only have great propaganda value from the Allied perspective but would also steal the thunder from any contemplated German play for Zionist support. Lebow notes that while it turned out that the Germans were not considering such a move at the time, the fact that Allied statesmen believed that the German government was also considering a pro-Zionist declaration greatly influenced their thinking (Lebow, 1968, pp. 522–523).

Another striking difference between the two requests was the question of publicity. At the time of the September 3 cable received by Wilson, he was concerned that the widely publicized use of the endorsement of the declaration for propaganda purposes would jeopardize American-Turkish relations. By the time Wilson received the second request on October 6, he had found a way around this impediment. He would approve the declaration as long as his approval was not made public. The genuineness of his position was confirmed by the fact that at the end of the war and with the defeat of Turkey, Wilson did make his support for the Declaration public (Lebow, 1968, p. 523).

On the basis of the evidence produced by Richard Lebow, it can be concluded that President Wilson was guided by his own pro-Zionist convictions and that he came out in support of the Balfour Declaration in spite of the disguised attempts by his closest advisor to steer the policy of the American government in a different direction.

It is when the American Zionist leaders saw the contents of the Milner-Amery draft, which Weizmann had telegraphed to Brandeis on October 9, 1917, that the issue of the wording came into play again. They took issue with the words "the rights and political status enjoyed in any other country by such Jews who are fully contented with their existing nationality and citizenship" and preferred to change them to "the rights and civil political status enjoyed by Jews in any other country" (Stein, 1961, pp. 530–531). The American Zionist leaders also wanted to see the words "Jewish race" altered to "Jewish people." On October 16, 1917, Rabbi Stephen Wise informed House of these two changes desired by the Zionist leadership (Stein, 1961, p. 531).

As the declaration was ultimately amended in the way desired by the American Zionists, they were logically under the impression that it was a result of their recommendations. It turned out that Washington had not informed the Foreign Office of the changes proposed by the American Zionists and that Wilson had approved the Milner-Amery draft without any changes. In fact, the same points raised by the American Zionists had been brought up independently by Zionist and other Jewish leaders in Britain, who had been asked by the War Cabinet for their views on the Milner-Amery draft (Stein, 1961, pp. 531–532). In the absence of any demands by any other source for these amendments and in view of the fact that they were approved and incorporated in the final declaration, it follows that this was the result of them having been requested by the Zionist leadership in Britain.

Conclusion

The Americans played a decisive part in the realization of the Balfour Declaration. Without the U.S. entering the war and tilting the balance in favour of the Allies and without President Wilson's approval of the Milner-Amery draft, the Balfour Declaration would either never have materialized or, if issued nevertheless, have turned out to be a stillborn promise.

While securing American support for the Declaration was crucial, it was not the only element that led to its final approval by the British War Cabinet. The nature of the challenges that caused the three-and-a-half-month delay between Walter Rothschild's submission to Balfour of the text of the mutually agreed-to draft declaration on July 18, 1917 and Balfour's reply on November 2, 1917, when he sent Rothschild the substantially differently worded text of the declaration approved by the War Cabinet, is the subject of the next chapter, *What's in a Word – Political Word-Craftsmanship.*

CHAPTER SIX

WHAT'S IN A WORD –
POLITICAL WORD-CRAFTSMANSHIP

Introduction

To have an unambiguous understanding as to what was achieved by the Balfour Declaration, it is essential to have a clear perception of the nature and political etymology of the verbal material that went into its semantically confusing fabric, as each nuance had its roots in the political and ideological motivations that inspired the players involved, both individually and collectively. The progressive exchange of versions of the Balfour Declaration between the Zionist leadership and the British government reflected the considerations that influenced both sides. The Zionists wanted more than the British were prepared to offer, and the British felt obliged to offer less than the Zionists desired. This conceptual tug of war was reflected in the efforts by both sides to end up with wording that represented their respective objectives as closely as possible. For the sake of clarity, we have summarized the sequence of successive drafts and the final text in the Appendix.

While Walter Rothschild had submitted the mutually agreed-to draft declaration to Arthur Balfour on July 18, 1917, Balfour did not reply until November 2, when he sent Rothschild the text of the declaration approved by the War Cabinet, a text which was substantially different from the originally agreed-to July 18 version (Stein, 1961, p. 465).

The questions that will be addressed in this chapter are: Why did it take so long for the wording of the Balfour Declaration to be finalized? What happened to the contents of the Declaration that the Zionists thought had been agreed upon, as Chaim Weizmann had informed Harry Sacher on August 1? In other words, what happened between July 18 and November 2, 1917?

In *Chapter 4: The Development of Zionist Political Thinking*, we saw how the basic tenets of the Zionist goal of the re-establishment of the Jewish homeland in Palestine had expressed themselves in the politically inspired euphemistic language of the Basel Program of 1897. Howard Grief, whose legal analysis and conclusions on the Jewish legal rights to the land of Israel culminated in the book *The Legal Foundation and Borders of Israel under International Law* (Grief, 2008, p. 6), traces two of the key terms of the Balfour Declaration back to the Basel Program of the Zionist Organization approved by the First Zionist Congress on August 30, 1897. Grief argues that, while the cabinet discussions leading to the final approval of the Declaration on October 31, 1917 proved conclusively that the intent was to create a Jewish state in Palestine, those who sought to sabotage the true meaning of the Declaration found ammunition in the terms "home" and "in Palestine," which were taken from the Basel Program (Grief, 2008, p. 74).

As words are the articulation of concepts, it is necessary to start with the text of the first Zionist memorandum of January 1917 that constituted the wellspring of the Balfour Declaration formulation process during the penultimate year of World War I.

The Eight-Month-Long Text Crafting Process

In January 1917, Weizmann submitted a memorandum prepared by the Zionist political committee to Sir Mark Sykes, the Cabinet Secretary. This first official Zionist political committee had been formed in January 1916 and contained, at the beginning, Chaim Weizmann, Nahum Sokolow, Joseph Cowen, Rabbi Moses Gaster and Herbert Bentwich as representatives of the British Zionist Federation. The committee worked in close consultation with the Rothschilds, Herbert Samuel and Ahad Ha'am (Weizmann, 1966, p. 184).

The document was called "Outline of Program for the Jewish Resettlement of Palestine in Accordance with the Aspirations of the Zionist Movement." It was the first memorandum submitted by the Zionist movement to the British government. Its wording constitutes the seminal base for the genealogical study of the wording of the Balfour Declaration. It is also indicative of the socio-political spirit that animated its creation. In Weizmann's own words:

> It represents the efforts of a group of amateur state builders, members of a people which has for many centuries been separated from this type of activity. None of us had had any experience in government and colonization. We have no staff of experts to lean on, no tradition of administration, no civil service, no means of taxation, no national body of land workers. We were journalists, scientists, lawyers, merchants,

philosophers. We were one or two generations removed – if that – from the ghetto. (Weizmann, 1966, p. 186)

The memorandum covered the notions that would become a common thread in the series of draft declarations that would lead to the actual Balfour Declaration of November 2, 1917. The first point stated that:

> The Jewish population of Palestine (which in the program shall be taken to mean both present and future Jewish population), shall be officially recognized by the Suzerain Government as the Jewish Nation, and shall enjoy in that country full civic, national and political rights. The Suzerain Government recognizes the desirability and necessity of a Jewish resettlement of Palestine.

The second point laid down the principle that:

> The Suzerain Government shall grant to the Jews of other countries full and free right of immigration into Palestine. The Suzerain Government shall give to the Jewish population of Palestine every facility for immediate naturalization and for land purchase. (Weizmann, 1966, p. 186)

Shortly after the submission of the memorandum, a meeting took place which Weizmann described as "the first full dress conference leading to the Balfour Declaration" (Weizmann, 1966, p. 238). The meeting took place on February 17, 1917, at the home of Rabbi Moses Gaster. It was attended by Gaster, James Rothschild, Herbert Samuel, Sir Mark Sykes, Nahum Sokolow, Herbert Bentwich and Joseph Cowen. Sykes told the meeting that he was there in a private capacity (Weizmann, 1966, p. 188).

The importance of this meeting in the context of the text crafting process of the Balfour Declaration lies in the fact that "the discussions touched on several points which were to constitute the heart of the problem in the ensuing months." The Zionists wanted a British protectorate with full rights according to the terms of the memorandum submitted to Sykes in January 1917. They also wanted the term "nation" in respect of the emergent Jewish homeland in Palestine applied only to the Jewish homeland and not to the relationship of Jews with the lands in which they lived. Weizmann himself added that the Jews who went to Palestine "would go to constitute a Jewish nation, not to become Arabs or Druses or Englishmen" (Weizmann, 1966, pp. 188–189).

In reviewing the lead-up to the July 18, 1917 submission by the Zionists of a draft declaration to Balfour, Stein noted that the drafting that had already been done, at Balfour's request, by Sacher seemed to Sokolow to be on the wrong lines. The nature of Sokolow's criticism can be inferred from Sacher's comments on July 9: "I am persuaded that my original idea of asking for as much as possible is the right one. I think my own draft erred in not going far enough, not in going too far." Sokolow's reply was that, "if we want too much, we shall get nothing, on the other hand, if we get some sympathetic declaration, I hope we will gradually get more" (Stein, 1961, p. 466).

On July 12, Sokolow and a group of his advisors agreed upon a formula which must have seemed to them to satisfy these requirements:

> His Majesty's Government, after considering the aims of the Zionist Organisation, accepts the principle of recognising Palestine as the National Home of the Jewish people and the right of the Jewish people to build up its national life in Palestine under a protection to be established at the conclusion of peace, following upon the successful issue of the War.
>
> His Majesty's Government regards as essential for the realisation of this principle the grant of internal autonomy to the Jewish nationality in Palestine, freedom of immigration for Jews, and the establishment of a Jewish National Colonising Corporation for the resettlement and economic development of the country.
>
> The conditions and forms of the internal autonomy and the Charter for the Jewish National Colonising Corporation should, in the view of His Majesty's Government, be elaborated in detail and determined with the representatives of the Zionist Organisation. (Stein, 1961, p. 468)

Sokolow submitted this statement to Sykes and Graham, who responded that it was "too long" and that it contained "matters of detail which would be undesirable to raise at the present moment" (Schneer, 2010, p. 334).

Sokolow reconvened the committee on July 17. The Zionists debated what to cut and what to retain from the earlier paragraphs. By now, according to Schneer, Sacher had grasped what kind of statement the Foreign Office wanted and had reconciled himself to the art of the possible. After debating what to cut from the earlier paragraphs, they finally reached a consensus. Sacher was the principal architect of the formulation at which they eventually arrived. It read as follows:

> (1) His Majesty's Government accepts the principle that Palestine should be reconstituted as the National Home of the Jewish people.
>
> (2) His Majesty's Government will use its best endeavours to secure the achievement of this object and will discuss the necessary methods and means with the Zionist Organization. (Schneer, 2010, p. 335; Stein, 1961, p. 470)

Schneer drew attention to the statement's implication, through the use of the word "reconstituted," of an unbroken link between Jews and Palestine despite the nearly two-thousand-year separation and to the positing of the Zionist Organization as the official representative of Jewish interests (Schneer, 2010, p. 335).

This simplified formula was agreed to by Rothschild, accepted by Sykes, and embodied in a letter from Rothschild to Balfour. Stein comments that it had not been easy to satisfy Balfour and that a large number of drafts had already been shown to him and rejected, but that finality had been reached when, a month after Balfour had invited the Zionists to submit a draft declaration, Rothschild wrote a covering letter with the final draft to him on July 18. In his covering letter, Rothschild notes that if the government confirmed its approval of the final draft submitted, he would hand it on to the Zionist Federation and announce it at a meeting called for that purpose.

In the same letter, Rothschild also reminded Balfour of the campaign of the anti-Zionist British Jews to thwart the objectives embodied in the proposed draft declaration. In Rothschild's words:

> I am sorry to say that our opponents commenced their campaign by a most reprehensible manoeuvre, namely to excite a disturbance by the cry of British Jews versus foreign Jews. They commenced this last Sunday, when at the Board of Deputies they challenged the newly elected officers as to whether they were all of English birth (myself among them). (Stein, 1961, p. 470)

The wording of the previously quoted Zionist draft of July 18 was circulated to the ministers concerned at the beginning of August. Three weeks later, the Foreign Office was informed by the Prime Minister's Secretariat that a statement on Palestine was being considered, and, on September 3, the question of policy raised by Rothschild's letter came before the War Cabinet (Stein, 1961, pp. 473-484). At this stage, the War Cabinet still included four of its five original members – David Lloyd George, Andrew Bonar Law, George Curzon and Alfred Milner. The fifth, Arthur Henderson, had been replaced as the Labour representative by George Barnes. During the summer, the War Cabinet had been enlarged by the inclusion of Sir Edward Carson and General Smuts, who had agreed to stay in London to participate in shaping the policy of the Imperial Government (Stein, 1961, p. 473).

In the two-month interval that had passed since the Zionists had been invited by Balfour to submit a draft declaration, some changes disadvantageous to the Zionist cause had taken place, the major one of which was the fact that in the middle of July, Edwin Montagu had become a minister of Cabinet rank in the Lloyd George administration – though not a member of the War Cabinet – on being appointed as Secretary of State for India. As a result, the issue of a pro-Zionist declaration reached the War Cabinet at a time when the only Jew with direct access to the inner circle was an implacable anti-Zionist (Stein, 1961, p. 484).

As we saw in the previous chapter, before the Zionist leadership could present a common front in their negotiations with the British government, they had to overcome the serious rift between the pro-Zionist and anti-Zionist factions of British Jewry. We also traced the struggle between the pro-Zionists and anti-Zionists as to who would represent the voice of Jewry vis-à-vis the British government and how it took most of the first six months of 1917 before the Zionists were able to consolidate their position as the political voice for the majority of world Jewry.

By Weizmann's own account, on June 13, in the wake of the fight between the anti-Zionist and pro-Zionist factions of the Jewish community, he wrote to Sir Ronald Graham, the Assistant Undersecretary of State at the Foreign Office, that "It appears desirable from every point of view that the British Government should give expression to its sympathy and support of the Zionist claims on Palestine. In fact, it need only confirm the view which eminent and representative members of the Government have many times expressed to us, and which have formed the basis of our negotiations throughout the long period of almost three years." A few days later, Weizmann, together with Graham and Rothschild, went to see Balfour and put it to him that "the time had come for the British government to give us a definite declaration of support and encouragement. Mr. Balfour promised to do so, and asked me to submit to him a declaration which would be satisfactory to us, and which he would try and put before the War Cabinet" (Weizmann, 1966, p. 203).

On August 1, Weizmann informed Sacher that he was under the impression that a formula acceptable to both the Zionists and the British government had been reached and that the declaration was imminent (Schneer, 2010, p. 335). However, what from the Zionist perspective looked like the successful last stage of an arduous journey instead turned out to be the beginning of an additional stretch of political roadblocks that had to be negotiated before the Balfour Declaration would see the light of day. As Balfour's niece, Blanche Dugdale (née Blanche Elizabeth Campbell), who authored a two-volume biography of Arthur Balfour and whom Weizmann described as "an ardent, lifelong friend of Zionism" (Weizmann, 1966, p. 154), pointed out about the dynamics of political promises and actions:

It is in fact often easier to have an interview with a Minister, than to get the subject of that interview caught up in the machinery of government, although till that happens, no expressions of sympathy and interest in high quarters will advance the cause one jot. (Dugdale, 1940, p. 26)

To illustrate how Dugdale's insightful observation applies to the episode of political manoeuvering that took the wording of the draft declaration from the text that Rothschild had sent to Balfour on July 18 to the final version adopted on November 2, 1917, we shall start with the text of the July 18 draft, quoted above, and follow how it gradually morphed into the final text of the Declaration. When this draft came before the War Cabinet on September 3, more than two months had passed since the Zionists had been invited by Balfour to submit a draft declaration. This delay resulted mainly from the fact that, as mentioned earlier, the issue of a pro-Zionist declaration reached the government just after Montagu, an implacable anti-Zionist, had been appointed to the Cabinet (Stein, 1961, p. 484).

The September 3 War Cabinet meeting represented an important stage in the development of the wording of the Balfour Declaration due to the range of issues brought up for discussion. These included the correspondence which had passed between Balfour, the Secretary of State for Foreign Affairs, and Lord Rothschild on the question of the policy to be adopted towards the Zionist movement. In addition, the Cabinet had before it an alternative draft prepared by Lord Milner, as well as a memorandum by Montagu entitled "The Anti-Semitism of the Present Government." The Cabinet suggested that a question raising such important issues as to the future of Palestine needed to be discussed with Britain's allies and, more particularly, with the United States (National Archives, CAB 23/4/1).

Montagu voiced his objection to the text of Milner's draft, which was being considered for submission to the United States government for its consideration. Montagu objected to the use of the phrase "the home of the Jewish people." He claimed that it would vitally prejudice the position of every Jew elsewhere and expand the argument contained in his memorandum. The minutes record the counter-argument that the existence of a Jewish state or autonomous community in Palestine would strengthen rather than weaken the situation of Jews in countries where they were not yet in possession of equal rights, and that in countries like Britain, where they possessed such rights and were identified with the nation of which they were citizens, their position would be unaffected by the existence of a national Jewish community elsewhere. In the Cabinet's view, while a small yet influential section of British Jews was opposed to the idea, large numbers were sympathetic to it (National Archives, CAB 23/4/1).

As far as postponing the matter was concerned, Lord Robert Cecil, the Acting Secretary of State for Foreign Affairs, pointed out that this was a question on which the Foreign Office had been very strongly pressed for a long time. He also noted that there was a very strong and enthusiastic organization, more particularly in the United States, who were zealous in this matter, and he believed that it would be of "most substantial assistance to the Allies to have the earnestness of these people enlisted on our side." In his view, to do nothing was to risk a direct breach with them, and it was necessary to face this situation (National Archives, CAB 23/4/1). In the end, the War Cabinet decided that the views of President Wilson should be obtained before any declaration was made and requested the Acting Secretary of State for Foreign Affairs to inform the government of the United States that His Majesty's Government was being pressed to make a declaration in sympathy with the Zionist movement and to ascertain their views as to the advisability of such a declaration being made (National Archives, CAB 23/4/1).

The reference to Montagu's anti-Zionist position in the minutes of the September 3 War Cabinet meeting does not provide a sufficient understanding of the views held by Montagu and the class of his privileged aristocratic Jewish peers in British society. The following subsection thus includes the main details of his memorandum referenced in the War Cabinet minutes and provides a more contextualized understanding of his role in and influence on the Balfour Declaration formulation procedure.

The Montagu Challenge

Sir Edwin Samuel Montagu epitomized the ideological divide between the pro-Zionist and anti-Zionist elements of the Jewish people at the beginning of the twentieth century. Due to his elevated social and political status, he was a voice that could not be ignored. This is what provided him with the opportunity to air his views at the War Cabinet meetings. It took the defeat of his position, after an arduous fight, to overcome his objections and to get the Declaration to safe harbour, albeit not without damage and scars to its original wording and intent.

As Weizmann noted in his autobiography in reference to Montagu's attempts to torpedo the Declaration:

> There cannot be the slightest doubt that without outside interference – entirely from Jews! – the draft would have been accepted early in August, substantially as we submitted it. [...] When the Palestine item was laid before the War Cabinet, Edwin Montagu made a passionate speech against the proposed move... the vehemence with which he urged his views, the

implacability of his opposition, astounded the Cabinet [...]. Certain it was
Montagu's opposition, coupled with the sustained attacks which the tiny
anti-Zionist group had been conducting for months – their letters to the
press, the pamphlets, some of them written pseudonymously by Lucien
Wolf, their feverish interviews with government officials – that was
responsible for the compromise formula which the War Cabinet submitted
to us a few days later. (Weizmann, 1966, pp. 204–206)

The accuracy of Weizmann's assessment of Montagu's influence is
evidenced by the role played by Montagu in the Cabinet and public arenas
during this period. His appointment as Secretary of State for India was
announced in *The Times* on July 18, 1917, just after the text of the draft
declaration Rothschild submitted to Balfour had been agreed upon (Stein,
1961, p. 496). Meeting him late in September, C. P. Scott – *The Manchester
Guardian*'s proprietor and editor – found him still "full of anxiety, first as
to the success of his mission, and, secondly, as to his political future."
Montagu was worried that a pro-Zionist pronouncement by the British
government would embarrass him at the very moment of his appointment
as Secretary of State for India. At this time in his life, he felt that nothing
could be more disastrous for him personally, or for his work in India, than
a British declaration which, as he saw it, would imply that he belonged, as
a Jew, to a separate people, with the real focus of his loyalties in Palestine
(Stein, 1961, pp. 498–499).

Montagu's memorandum referred to in the September 3 War Cabinet
meeting minutes was the result of his reaction to the idea that the Zionists
and Balfour were close to reaching a mutually accepted declaration to the
effect that the British government would endorse the principle that
Palestine should be reconstituted as the national home of the Jewish
people. Montagu was so fired up that he wanted Balfour to redraft his
letter and reject the Zionist statement. He composed a scathing five-page
memorandum titled "The Anti-Semitism of the Present Government"
(Schneer, 2010, p. 337).

The following excerpts provide a sense of the extent and nature of
Montagu's outrage at the idea of a Jewish homeland in Palestine:

I wish to place on record my view that the policy of his Majesty's
Government is anti-Semitic in result and will prove a rallying point for
Anti-Semites in every country in the world.
    [...] This nation will presumably be formed of Jewish Russians, Jewish
Englishmen, Jewish Roumanians, Jewish Bulgarians, and Jewish citizens
of all nations – survivors or relations of those who have fought or laid
down their lives for the different countries which I have mentioned, at a
time when the three years that they have lived through had united their

outlook and thought more closely than ever with the countries of which they are citizens.

Zionism has always seemed to me to be a mischievous political creed, untenable by any patriotic citizen of the United Kingdom.

[…] I assert that there is not a Jewish nation. The members of my family, for instance, who have been in this country for generations, have no sort or kind of community of view or desire with any Jewish family in any other country beyond the fact that they profess to a greater or less degree the same religion.

[…] When the Jews are told that Palestine is their national home, every country will immediately desire to get rid of its Jewish citizens, and you will find a population in Palestine driving out its present inhabitants, taking all the best in the country, drawn from all quarters of the globe, speaking every language on the face of the earth, and incapable of communicating with one another except by means of an interpreter.

[…] I deny that Palestine is today associated with the Jews or properly to be regarded as a fit place for them to live in. The Ten Commandments were delivered to the Jews on Sinai. It is quite true that Palestine plays a large part in Jewish history, but so it does in modern Mohammedan history, and, after the time of the Jews, surely it plays a larger part than any other country in Christian history.

[…] If my memory serves me right, there are three times as many Jews in the world as could possibly get into Palestine if you drove out all the population that remains there now. So that only one-third get back at the most, and what will happen to the remainder?

[…] I feel that the Government are asked to be the instrument for carrying out the wishes of a Zionist organisation largely run, as my information goes, at any rate in the past, by men of enemy descent or birth, and by this means have dealt a severe blow to the liberties, position and opportunities of service to their Jewish fellow-countrymen.

I would say to Lord Rothschild that the Government will be prepared to do everything in their power to obtain for Jews in Palestine complete liberty of settlement and life on an equality with the inhabitants of that country who profess other religious beliefs. I would ask that the Government should go no further. (Montagu, 1966, pp. 7–11)

The inconclusive September 3 War Cabinet meeting ended with a decision to seek President Wilson's views as to the advisability of making such a declaration as was before them. Stein observes that it was decided not to tell Wilson that the British government was in favour of such a declaration. Stein also notes that the idea to consult the President seemed to arise as an afterthought from the discussion on September 3, when the War Cabinet was taken aback by Montagu's protest, but not to the point of dropping the matter entirely. On the contrary, the Foreign Office was anxious to have a declaration approved by the War Cabinet as soon as possible. The War Cabinet hoped that an appeal to Wilson would strengthen its hand. To expedite the matter, it bypassed the proposal that Milner's slightly amended version of the Rothschild formula recommended by Balfour be laid before Wilson and simply asked Washington whether a pro-Zionist declaration would be acceptable in principle (Stein, 1961, p. 503).

Initially, the intermediaries were Sir William Wiseman for the British and Colonel Edward House for the Americans. Wiseman was Head of the British Military Intelligence Service in the U.S.A. Stein notes that he was *persona grata* with the American President and with House and that he was relied upon by the Foreign Office to deal with the declaration at the American end (Stein, 1961, p. 529). House was President Wilson's most intimate confidential advisor (Stein, 1961, p. 350). Wiseman had sought out House and cemented an important wartime relationship with him. Wiseman acted as the main conduit of communications between the two governments (Butts, 2010, p. 115).

On September 4, House informed the President that he had received the following message from Cecil: "We are being pressed here for the declaration of sympathy with the Zionist movement and should be very grateful if you felt able to ascertain unofficially if the President favours such a declaration" (Stein, 1961, p. 504).

On September 7, House wrote to Wilson about Cecil's message of September 4, asking the President if he had made up his mind as to how he would answer Cecil concerning the Zionist movement and admonishing him that there were many dangers lurking into getting too deeply involved with the movement (Stein, 1961, p. 504). Here, the antisemitic patina that has coloured political and social discourses throughout Jewish history manifested itself as a causal factor. Stein sees House's approach to the question as one to be expected of a man moving "in circles in which anti-Semitism was a matter of course" (Stein, 1961, p. 508).

When, a week after telegraphing House, Cecil was still without a reply, the Foreign Office initiated a second round of communications with the Americans when it prepared another message for Wiseman, in which it asked if Colonel House had been able to ascertain whether President favoured a declaration of sympathy with Zionist aspirations, as asked in Cecil's telegram of September 3:

> We should be most grateful for early reply as September 17 is the Jewish New Year and announcement of sympathy by or on that date would have excellent effect. (Dugdale papers, quoted in Stein, 1961, pp. 504–505)

This message was never sent because it was pre-empted by a telegram dated September 11 from House to the Foreign Office, to the effect that Wilson had been approached as requested and had expressed the opinion that the time was not opportune for any definite statement beyond one of sympathy, provided it could be made without conveying any real commitment (Dugdale papers, quoted in Stein, 1961, p. 505).

Stein offered a number of speculations as to the reasons for Wilson's lacklustre response. Perhaps Wilson felt that a declaration of sympathy with Zionist aspirations would point the way towards the expulsion of the Turks from Palestine, and at this point the United States was not yet at war with Turkey. Wilson might also have thought it might still have been possible to coax Turkey out of the war, which would pre-empt any annexationist designs that might stand in the way. It might also simply have been that Wilson was not particularly interested in the matter and that he was content to agree with House that Britain should not be encouraged to enter into a potentially embarrassing commitment. Stein suggests that Louis Brandeis had either not been consulted or, alternatively, been overruled, for it is unlikely that Brandeis would have advised the President to answer the British inquiry in such a frigid manner (Stein, 1961, p. 506).

On September 18, Weizmann wrote to Sacher that he was astonished to hear that Wilson was not ready to support the Declaration. On September 19, Weizmann informed Brandeis that the text declaration submitted to Balfour by Rothschild on July 18 had been approved by the Foreign Office and the Prime Minister and submitted to the War Cabinet. Weizmann expected opposition from assimilationist quarters and concluded that it would greatly help if President Wilson and Brandeis himself supported the text, which he enclosed with the message (Stein, 1961, p. 506).

On September 23, Brandeis saw House to discuss the reply to be sent to Weizmann. The next day, Brandeis wrote to House that, pursuant to their conference the day before, he was sending him a copy of a message he had sent to Weizmann and wired to the British War Office the same day. The message read as follows:

From talks I've had with President and from expressions of opinion given to closest advisors I feel that I can answer that he is in entire sympathy with declaration quoted in yours of 19th as approved by Foreign Office and Prime Minister. I of course heartily agree. – Brandeis. (Stein, 1961, p. 507)

Stein attributed Wilson's volte-face from his position on September 11 (that the time was not opportune for a pro-Zionist declaration) to his reply less than two weeks later (that he was in entire sympathy with the Rothschild formula) to Brandeis' influence. Stein also suggests that it was on House's advice that Wilson approved the proposed declaration. According to Stein, while Brandeis' nomination for the Supreme Court showed how high he stood in the President's esteem, it also added substantial significance to Brandeis' assumption of the Zionist leadership in the United States. Stein adds that the Zionist leaders in London made full use of this asset in their dealings with the British government (Stein, 1961, p. 196).

Stein maintained that while House disliked Jews and was irritated by the Zionists, Brandeis was the one Zionist for whom he had genuine respect and that when he saw House on the Zionist question in September 1917, Brandeis was assured of a respectful hearing. Stein argues that it was as a result of his personal intervention with House that Brandeis found himself in a position to cable Weizmann his reassuring message of September 24 (Stein, 1961, pp. 509–510).

Brandeis sent this message through British official channels to ensure that it would reach the British government directly, with the intention of encouraging the advocates of a pro-Zionist declaration to believe that a further approach to Wilson would be more successful. Indeed, the drive towards a declaration seemed to have reached an impasse with Wilson's negative position, as stated in House's message of September 11 to Robert Cecil, and with Balfour's response on September 24 to a suggestion from Balfour's Foreign Affairs Department that an effort should be made to expedite a pro-Zionist pronouncement. To this, Balfour had replied that, as the Cabinet had, in his absence, decided this question against the Zionists, he could not do anything until the decision was reversed (Dugdale papers, quoted in Stein, 1961, p. 510).

On September 28, Weizmann managed to spend a few minutes with the Prime Minister, who, following Weizmann's representation of urgency, ordered that the Palestine issue be placed on the agenda of the next meeting of the War Cabinet (Stein, 1961, p. 513).

To prevent Montagu from again succeeding in getting the Zionist question shelved, Weizmann prepared a memorandum pressing for a prompt decision in favour of the Zionists. Weizmann's memorandum deplores the one-sided manner in which the divergence of views on Zionism existing in Jewry had been allowed to be presented to the War Cabinet and affirms to have submitted the text of the declaration on behalf of an organization which claimed to represent the will of a "great and ancient, though scattered, people." In anticipation of Montagu's urging of the anti-Zionist view, Weizmann expressed the hope that the Foreign Office and the War Cabinet would consider "our national and Zionist destiny" in light of "Imperial interests and the principles for which the

Entente stands." The memorandum notes that the text of the declaration had been submitted after two years of negotiations and conversations with prominent representatives of the British nation and that, therefore, "we humbly pray that this declaration may be granted to us." The memorandum concludes that such a declaration would enable the Zionist leadership to counteract the demoralizing influence of the enemy's efforts to tip the scales in their favour by holding out vague promises to the Jews and to finally make the necessary preparations for the constructive work that would have to begin as soon as Palestine was liberated (Stein, 1961, p. 514–515).

This appeal, signed by Weizmann and Rothschild, was sent to the Foreign Office on October 3. At the War Cabinet meeting held the next day, all the pro-Zionist policy supporters, with the exception of Smuts, were in attendance. With reports from various sources suggesting that further hesitation about a pro-Zionist declaration might find the British government forestalled by the Germans, the case for the proposal was considerably stronger than it had been on September 3 (Stein, 1961, p. 515).

Montagu, however, was not about to concede defeat. This time, he focused his anti-Zionist views on the effect the British government's favouring of a national home for the Jews in Turkish territory would have on his ability to carry out his mission to India. He argued that if the British government were to refer to Palestine as the national home for the Jews, all the antisemitic organizations and media would challenge the right of a Jewish Englishman with, at best, the status of a natural foreigner to participate in the government of the British Empire (Stein, 1961, pp. 500, 515).

In response, Balfour argued that the Zionist movement had behind it the support of a majority of Jews worldwide and that he saw no inconsistency between "the establishment of a Jewish national focus in Palestine and a complete assimilation and absorption of Jews in the nationality of other countries." He went on to read a very sympathetic pro-Zionist declaration by the French government and confirmed that President Wilson was "extremely favourable to the movement." He also informed the War Cabinet that "the German government were making great efforts to capture the sympathy of the Zionist movement" (Stein, 1961, p. 516).

With regard to this last point, Stein contends that in the autumn of 1917, the Foreign Office believed that the Germans were on the verge of publicly supporting the Zionist cause, which would give them, especially in Russia, a useful political weapon (Stein, 1961, p. 516). When, on

October 4, the War Cabinet again resolved to consult President Wilson, they explained that the issue of a pro-Zionist declaration had been put on the front burner again to preclude any German attempts to capture the support of the Zionists (Stein, 1961, p. 517).

The War Cabinet concluded that two more steps were required before they could finalize a declaration. In light of Montagu's stubborn resistance to the proposed declaration, which he saw as a threat to the vital interests of the British Jews, the War Cabinet decided to give both sides a final hearing by inviting the views of the Zionist leaders and of representative British anti-Zionists. They also wanted to ensure that President Wilson was fully on board this time by seeking his approval of the pro-Zionist declaration they were now considering (Stein, 1961, pp. 517–518).

As we saw in *Chapter 5: The American Factor*, which covers the implications of America's entry into the war in detail, the British government was finally informed, on October 16, 1917, that President Wilson had approved the new Milner draft of October 4, which formed the basis of the final wording of the Balfour Declaration.

The combination of Montagu's relentless filibustering and the insidious salami tactics of the political chiefs who participated in the erosive tweaking of the text of the declaration ended up producing a final version on November 2 that was a far cry from the text of the two-sentence draft statement which Rothschild had sent to Balfour on July 18 and to which Balfour had reacted positively.

The background outlined above allows us to follow how the cumulative minor changes in the wording of each draft ended up producing an end product so drastically different from the initial Zionist draft of July 18.

Sacher, who had been the principal architect of this draft, which, on July 17, 1917, the members of the London Zionist Political Committee had studiously worked on to satisfy Sykes' and Graham's criticism of their previous submission, had managed to retain the essence of the Zionist aspirations. As Schneer notes, the opening sentence of this draft confirms the historic link between Jews and Palestine despite almost two thousand years of forced exile, while the second sentence positions the Zionist Organization as the political representative of the Jewish people (Schneer 2010, pp. 334–335).

Balfour had responded positively with his own slightly amended version, when, in August 1917, he recommended that:

> His Majesty's Government accept the principle that Palestine should be reconstituted as the national home of the Jewish people and will use their best endeavours to secure the achievement of this object and will be ready

to consider any suggestions on the subject which the Zionist Organization
may desire to lay before them. (Stein, 1961, p. 664)

It is clear from these two draft declarations that, at this point, Balfour and
the Zionists were on the same page. The slight amendment in Balfour's
response, where, instead of committing his government to "discuss the
necessary methods and means" to achieve the objective outlined in the
first sentence, he declares his government's readiness "to consider any
suggestions" to that effect from the Zionist Organization, does not
fundamentally digress from the objectives outlined in the Zionist draft of
July 18.

The formula which Milner put before the War Cabinet in August 1917
marks the first significant slide from the qualitative level of the July 18
wording substantially agreed to by the Zionists and Balfour. It read as
follows:

> His Majesty's Government accepts the principle that every opportunity
> should be afforded for the establishment of a home for the Jewish people in
> Palestine and will use its best endeavours to facilitate the achievement of
> this object and will be ready to consider any suggestions on the subject
> which the Zionist organisations may desire to lay before them. (Stein,
> 1961, pp. 520, 664)

In this draft, the term "secure" was replaced by the much weaker
"facilitate," and whereas the Zionists and Balfour had agreed in July to the
principle that Palestine should be "reconstituted as the national home of
the Jews," this major Zionist tenet was omitted from Milner's August draft
altogether and replaced by "the establishment of a home for the Jewish
people in Palestine."

By dropping the terms "secure" and "reconstituted" and by changing
the phraseology of "Palestine as the national home of the Jewish people"
to "a home for the Jewish people in Palestine," this draft significantly
weakened the tenor of the version agreed to in July between the Zionists
and Balfour. Schneer suggests that Milner, by removing the word
"reconstituted," was possibly hoping to assuage the fears of anti-Zionists
such as his friend Claude Montefiore (Schneer, 2010, p. 336).

Just before the War Cabinet meeting of October 4, Milner had asked
Leopold Amery, the War Cabinet secretary, to draft "something which
would go a reasonable distance to meeting the objections both Jewish and
pro-Arab without impairing the substance of the proposed declaration"
(Stein, 1961, p. 520).

The manner in which Milner's alternative draft declaration of October 4 devolved from the Zionist draft submitted to Balfour on July 18 provides a telling example of the salami-slicing strategy referred to earlier. The result read as follows:

> His Majesty's Government views with favour the establishment in Palestine of a national home for the Jewish Race, and will use its best endeavours to facilitate the achievement of this object; it being clearly understood that nothing shall be done which may prejudice the civil and religious rights of existing non-Jewish communities in Palestine, or the rights and political status enjoyed in any other country by such Jews who are fully contented with their existing nationality and citizenship. (National Archives, CAB 23/4/19)

In this formulation, "a home" reverts back to "a national home" and "the Jewish people" become the "Jewish race," while any reference to the role of the Zionist Organization is left out entirely. In addition, the caveats "it being clearly understood that nothing shall be done which may prejudice the civil and religious rights of existing non-Jewish communities in Palestine, or the rights and political status enjoyed in any other country by such Jews who are fully contented with their existing nationality" add two new dimensions which did not appear in the previous drafts. This is the first draft in which mention is made of the non-Jewish communities in Palestine and to the Jews in the diaspora. It is clear that these new considerations were in response to Milner's request, before the War Cabinet meeting of October 4, that Amery produce a draft that would also address the Jewish and pro-Arab objections without affecting the main objectives of the proposed declaration (National Archives, CAB 23/4/19).

The minutes of the October 4 War Cabinet meeting reflect the crystallization of the pro- and anti-Zionist sentiments at the highest political level and the impact they had on the pace and nature of the process. In this sense, the October 4 meeting picked up where the September 3 session had left off.

Balfour's statement at the October 4 meeting encapsulated the Secretary of State for Foreign Affairs' response to the objections raised by Montagu and Curzon. Balfour stated that the German government was making great efforts to capture the sympathy of the Zionist Movement. He affirmed that while this Movement was opposed by a number of wealthy local Jews, it had behind it the support of a majority of Jews, at all events in Russia and America, and possibly in other countries. He saw nothing inconsistent between the establishment of a Jewish national focus in Palestine and the complete assimilation and absorption of Jews in the nationality of other countries. Just as British emigrants to the United States became, either in the first or subsequent generations, American nationals, so, in future, should a Jewish citizenry be established in Palestine, Jews would become either British, American, German, or Palestinian. What was at the back of the Zionist Movement was the intensive national consciousness held by certain members of the Jewish race. They regard themselves as one of the great historic races of the world, whose original home was Palestine, and these Jews had a passionate longing to regain this ancient national home once more. Other Jews had become absorbed into the nations in which they and their forefathers had dwelt for many generations. Balfour then read a very sympathetic declaration which the French government had conveyed to the Zionists, and he stated that he knew that President Wilson was extremely favourable to the Movement (National Archives, CAB 23/4/19).

Montagu again urged strong objections to any declaration in which it was stated that Palestine was the "national home" of the Jewish people. He regarded the Jews as a religious community and himself as a Jewish Englishman. He based his argument on the prejudicial effect of the status of Jewish Britons on a statement that His Majesty's Government regarded Palestine as the national home of the Jewish people. He argued that whatever safeguarding words might be used in the formula, the civil rights of Jews as nationals in the country in which they were born might be endangered. How would you negotiate with the Jewish people of India on behalf of His Majesty's Government if the world had just been told that His Majesty's Government regarded their national home as being in Turkish territory? He especially urged that the only trial of strength by Zionists and anti-Zionists in England had resulted in a very narrow majority for the Zionists, namely, 56 to 51 of the representatives of Anglo-Jewry on the Conjoint Committee. He also claimed that most British-born Jews were opposed to Zionism and that it was supported by foreign-born Jews, such as Dr. Gaster and Dr. Hertz, the two Grand Rabbis who had been born in Romania and Austria respectively, and by Weizmann, President of the British Zionist Federation, who had been born in Russia. He submitted that the Cabinet's first duty was to British Jews and that Colonel House had declared that President Wilson was now opposed to a declaration (National Archives, CAB 23/4/19).

The other strongly opposing voice was that of Lord Curzon, whose objections were based on practical grounds (National Archives, CAB 23/4/19). George Nathaniel Curzon, who had served as Viceroy of India from 1898 to 1905, joined Asquith's coalition government as the Lord Privy Seal in 1915. After Lloyd George had brought him into his own coalition government a year and a half later, Curzon became a prominent member of the War Cabinet in which he served as Lord President of the Council (Schneer, 2010, p. xv). Curzon told the War Cabinet that he recollected from his visit to Palestine that the country was mostly barren and desolate, with sparse cultivation on the terraced slopes, few valleys and streams, and scarce large centres of population, and that a less propitious seat for the Jewish race could not be imagined. Curzon wondered how the existing Muslim inhabitants would be dealt with and the Jews introduced in their place. He also questioned how many Jews would be willing to return and in what pursuits they would engage. In his opinion, it would be a better policy to secure equal civil and religious rights for the Jews already in Palestine than to aim at repatriation on a large scale, which he regarded as sentimental idealism that would never be realized and with which His Majesty's Government should have nothing to do (National Archives, CAB 23/4/19).

The minutes also recorded that during recent years before the war, Jewish immigration into Palestine had been considerably on the increase and that several flourishing Zionist colonies were already in existence (National Archives, CAB 23/4/19).

With these opposition voices in mind, on October 4, 1917, Lord Milner submitted an alternative draft declaration which read as follows:

> His Majesty's Government views with favour the establishment in Palestine of a national home for the Jewish race and will use its best endeavours to facilitate the achievement of this object; it being clearly understood that nothing shall be done which may prejudice the civil and religious rights of the existing non-Jewish communities in Palestine or the rights and political status enjoyed in any other country by such Jews who are fully contented with their existing nationality and citizenship. (National Archives, CAB 23/4/19)

The War Cabinet decided that before coming to a decision, this new draft declaration as read by Lord Milner should be submitted confidentially to President Wilson, to leaders of the Zionist Movement, and to representatives in Anglo-Jewry opposed to Zionism. The War Cabinet further decided that the opinions received on this draft declaration should be collated and submitted to them for decision (National Archives, CAB 23/4/19).

Following the October 4 decision of the War Cabinet to obtain the reactions of the pro- and anti-Zionist factions among the Jewish leadership to the Milner draft, the text was submitted on October 6 to ten representative Jewish leaders. While Montagu's memorandum had already been circulated, the replies from the remaining nine were tabled during the October 17 War Cabinet meeting. According to the minutes of that meeting, six of those replies were regarded as favourable to the declaration, or to the declaration with slight amendments, while three were noted as opposed to a formal declaration acceptable to the Zionists and submitted alternatives. The six favourable to a Zionist form of declaration were listed as:

(1) The Rt. Hon. Herbert Samuel, M.P.
(2) The Chief Rabbi, Dr. J. H. Hertz
(3) Lord Rothschild
(4) Sir Stuart Samuel
(5) Dr. Chaim Weizmann
(6) Dr. Nahum Sokolow

The three unfavourable were:

(1) Sir Philip Magnus, M.P.
(2) C. G. Montefiore, Esq., President, Anglo-Jewish Association.
(3) L. L. Cohen, Esq., Jewish Board of Guardians.

The full texts of these nine responses were attached to the minutes under Appendix I, while various alternative drafts submitted by the respondents were collated in Appendix II (National Archives, CAB 24/4/14).

While unanimous in their approval, the six replies in favour introduced different aspects of the issues involved in presenting their cases. Herbert Samuel's opening remark appealed to Britain's geopolitical self-interest. He argued that if the Turks were left in control of Palestine, the country was likely to fall, in the course of time, under German influence. If Germany, or any other continental power, was dominant there, Egypt would be exposed to constant menace. The best safeguard would be the establishment of a large Jewish population, preferably under British protection. Samuel also stated that he felt no doubt that the policy expressed in the declaration was desired by the mass of the Jewish people, both in Britain and throughout the world. He pointed out that the officers of the Jewish Board of Representatives, which was the nearest approach to a democratically elected body in the Jewish community in Britain, having issued a hostile pronouncement, were censored by their constituents and obliged to resign. Samuel then blended both the British and Jewish perspectives when he argued that if the policy were carried into effect through British influence, it would win for the British Empire the gratitude of Jews throughout the world and create among them a bias favourable to the Empire (National Archives, CAB 24/4/14).

Chief Rabbi Hertz's response was one of unbridled enthusiasm at what he saw as "the intention of His Majesty's Government to lend its powerful support to the re-establishment in Palestine of a national home for the Jewish people." His "profoundest gratification" blinded him to the fact that Milner's draft declaration of October 4 used the words "the establishment in Palestine of a national home for the Jewish race" and not "re-establishment." Fortunately for the pro-declaration side, neither Weizmann nor Sokolow committed Rabbi Hertz's error. Weizmann respectfully proposed to use the word "re-establishment" instead of "establishment." He suggested that, through this small alteration, the historical connection with ancient tradition would be indicated and the whole matter put in its true light. Sokolow similarly suggested that in the phrase "the establishment in Palestine of a national home," the term "re-establishment" be substituted for "establishment" (National Archives, CAB 24/4/14).

The opening remarks in Weizmann's response voiced his deep conviction that the declaration framed by His Majesty's Government would be received "with joy and gratitude by the vast majority of the Jewish people all over the world." He stated that the declaration would supply a powerful impetus towards the regeneration and rejuvenation of an ancient country and an ancient people and would thus form a notable step forward on the path of human progress and display anew the magnanimity of the British Empire. His response is especially noteworthy for the forcefulness with which he challenged the anti-Zionist position of certain members of the Anglo-Jewish establishment. His words to that effect, as recorded in the minutes of the War Cabinet meeting of October 17, speak for themselves:

> Although it is unfortunately true that a certain number of Jews, chiefly in Western countries, are opposed to the idea of a Jewish national home in Palestine, it is no less true that these opponents, who are comparatively few in number, are almost exclusively to be found amongst those Jews who by education and social connections have lost touch with the real spirit animating the Jewish people as a whole. Our opponents, therefore, are entitled to speak in their own name only, but have no right to speak for the Jewish masses whose hopes, aspirations, ideals, and sufferings they do not share. The real motive underlying their opposition is of an eminently individual nature. Our opponents are overcome by fear lest the existence of a Jewish national home compromises to a certain extent their own position in the eyes of the peoples in whose midst they are living and with whom they desired to be totally identified. This motive, which they do not conceal, is in itself an indication that they are conscious of being an

isolated minority in Jewry and of having the bulk of the Jewish people not with but against them. Had it been really their sincere conviction that the great majority of the Jewish people does not sympathise with the establishment of a national home, they would have no reason to be afraid of a scheme which can only be realised by the wholehearted and enthusiastic collaboration of all living forces in Jewry. They would, on the contrary, be content to let the experiment pass unhindered, in order to show by its certain failure how correctly they had interpreted the mind of the Jews in general. (National Archives, CAB 24/4/14)

Sokolow's response, while also couched in grateful terms and in full accord with the spirit of the declaration, included a number of suggestions, on behalf of the Zionist Organization, with regard to the wording of the draft. Although the text of the alternate draft submitted to the War Cabinet by Milner has been reproduced a number of times throughout this chapter, it is useful to insert it again here to follow the drift of Sokolow's suggested alterations:

His Majesty's Government views with favour the establishment in Palestine of a national home for the Jewish race and will use its best endeavours to facilitate the achievement of this object; it being clearly understood that nothing shall be done which may prejudice the civil and religious rights of the existing non-Jewish communities in Palestine or the rights and political status enjoyed in any other country by such Jews who are fully contented with their existing nationality and citizenship.

Sokolow presented his suggested alterations to the above draft as follows:

(1) "The establishment in Palestine of a national home." I would suggest the substitution of "re-establishment" for "establishment." By this slight change the real character of the movement and its historic basis would be recognized.
(2) "The Jewish race" I would suggest to be altered to "the Jewish people." The definition of "race" is a much-disputed question. It would also be questionable whether the word refers to all persons of Jewish origin or only to Jews. "Jewish people" is the best definition.
(3) I would also suggest in substitution for the concluding phrase, "or the rights and political status ... nationality and citizenship," the following more comprehensive expression: "or the rights and political status enjoyed by Jews in any other country of which they are loyal citizens."

Sokolow stated that he recommended these alterations, as he thought that, in this form, a more adequate expression would be given to the principle (National Archives, CAB 24/4/14).

The replies received from the three anti-Zionist leaders were unanimous in their fundamental allegation that the Jews were not a nation and in their rejection of the Zionist claim that the Jews needed a national home of their own. The wording of their responses, as recorded in the minutes of the War Cabinet meeting of October 17, provides a telling picture of the way the majority of the Anglo-Jewish establishment viewed the conditions of the lives of their Jewish coreligionists on the European continent and how they defined their own role and identity in the scheme of things (National Archives, CAB 24/4/14).

Sir Philip Magnus opened his elaborate polemic by asserting that the bond that unites the Jews is not one of race but one of common religion and that the Jews have no national aspirations apart from those of the country of their birth. He disagreed that the Jews regard themselves as a nation and proposed that the term "national" as applied to a community of Jews in Palestine or elsewhere should be withdrawn from the proposed formula. To Magnus, the words "a national home for the Jewish race" in the declaration seemed to be undesirable and inaccurate. On the other hand, a statement to the effect that the British government would take steps to secure for the Jews then resident in Palestine and in the future the freedom to develop their religious culture and observe their religious rites would be welcomed by the Jews and would be consistent with the traditional policy of the British government (National Archives, CAB 24/4/14).

Magnus claimed that the Jews in Turkey had latterly enjoyed many advantages. They had been permitted to found agriculture and commercial colonies and establish Hebrew language schools. Any pronouncement on the part of the British government that they would be prepared to take steps to establish a "national home in Palestine" for Jews and Jews only might be interpreted as implying that the government of Palestine would, under certain conditions, be transferred to the Jews. Such a pronouncement would certainly arouse considerable opposition from other Palestinian communities and might result in the Jews then resident in Palestine receiving the same treatment at the hands of the Turks as had been unhappily experienced by the Armenian Christians (National Archives, CAB 24/4/14).

Magnus asserted that Zionist agitation was a comparatively new phenomenon. The Jews in Spain and Portugal, at the height of their prosperity, made no attempt to use their influence to secure for themselves "a national home in Palestine," nor did they subsequently, when they fled from Spain to Holland and other countries (National Archives, CAB 24/4/14).

Magnus went as far as to utter the self-evident truth that if the Jews of Russia had been permitted to observe their religion and had enjoyed equal civil rights with their fellow citizens, the Zionist movement would not have developed, as if this statement constituted a substantive factor to support his anti-Zionist position. He added that it was more than probable that the agitation would not long outlive the avowed objects of the revolution (National Archives, CAB 24/4/14).

Magnus also speculated that if the rumours in Zionist circles that the conquest of Palestine by Great Britain was desired so that Palestine may become an independent buffer state between Turkey and Egypt and that the declared policy of the Allies was to annex no new territories, the country would be restored to the Jews under a British protectorate. He argues that whether this was the case or not, the British government would have to consult the existing inhabitants of Palestine as to the ruling power under which they would desire to live. Magnus thought it probable that they would elect to be governed by Great Britain or by one of its allies who would hold the balance fairly between the Christian, Jewish and Islamic communities (National Archives, CAB 24/4/14).

In his final remark, Magnus felt that the words "who are fully contented with their existing nationality" failed to express the devotion of Jews to the country of their birth, where they enjoyed equal rights with their fellow citizens. Jews were not fighting in the present war for any distinctly Jewish ideals. They did not need the offer of a national home in Palestine to excite their ardour or to stimulate their courage. They were fighting for the same objects which the British government had so unmistakably defined. If the proposed draft declaration was modified in accordance with his suggestions, it would read as follows:

> His Majesty's Government views with favour the establishment in Palestine of a centre of Jewish culture and will use its best endeavours to facilitate the achievement of this object, it being understood that nothing shall be done which may prejudice the civil and religious rights of existing non-Jewish communities in Palestine or the rights and political status now enjoyed by Jews in any other country. (National Archives, CAB 24/4/14)

C. G. Montefiore's argumentation is practically identical to Magnus'. Montefiore started his submission by stating that he deprecated the expression "a national home" because it assumed that the Jewish race constituted a nation or might profitably become one, both of which propositions he denied. The phrase "national home for the Jewish race" appeared to assume and imply that the Jews generally constitute a nationality. Such an implication, according to Montefiore, was intensely obnoxious to an enormous number of Jews. He had no objection to Jews who *wanted* to form themselves into a nationality in Palestine, but it should be effected without any prejudice to the character and position of the Jews as nationals of other countries (National Archives, CAB 24/4/14).

Montefiore recalled that the idea of a "home" for the Jews was started by the late Dr. Herzl, the founder of Zionism, who, Montefiore claimed, had personally told him that he believed that antisemitism was eternal and that it was hopeless to expect its removal, and also that he believed that the Jewish problem in Russia was insoluble in Russia (National Archives, CAB 24/4/14).

Montefiore noted that he had told Herzl that viewing antisemitism as eternal and irremovable was a libel upon the Jews and upon human nature, and that viewing the Jewish problem as unresolvable within Russian boundaries was too pessimistic. Montefiore claimed that he had not been wrong:

> For if the Revolution in Russia holds and reaction does not set in, the Jewish problem *has* been solved in Russia, and already the majority of the Russian Jews desire cultural autonomy *in* Russia, but not exile *from* Russia. (National Archives, CAB 24/4/14)

In what is obviously a self-delusionary denial of the gruesome realities of the fate of European Jewry outside the British Isles, Montefiore then proffered the sweeping pronouncement that a national home for the Jews on the score of the oppressed condition of the Jews was no longer necessary and that a vast majority of Jews were free citizens of the countries in which they dwelled. He stated that the Polish Jewish question would, with the cooperation of the Allies, doubtless be settled as favourably as the larger Russian Jewish problem had already been settled. The Romanian government would also not be able to resist the pressure of events. With five million Jews fully emancipated in Russia, 250,000 Jews in Romania could not remain pariahs and aliens for much longer.

Montefiore carried on with unrestrained enthusiasm on his fictional path. Despite the well-documented failure of emancipation to bring freedom and equal rights to the despised and persecuted Jewish populations of Europe during Montefiore's lifetime, he claimed that for the true well-being of the Jewish race, emancipation and liberty in the countries of the world were a thousand times more important than a "home," to which he added the incongruous afterthought that, in any case, only a small fraction of the Jews could be collected together in Palestine (National Archives, CAB 24/4/14).

The above summary of Montefiore's response to the War Cabinet's survey covers the gist of his argumentation. The other points of his brief were basically reworded repetitions or echoes of the anti-Zionist cases presented by Montagu and Magnus (National Archives, CAB 24/4/14).

L. L. Cohen, Chairman of the Jewish Board of Guardians, submitted the third of the three replies categorized as unfavourable to a Zionist form of declaration. Like Magnus and Montefiore, Cohen denied that the Jews were a nation. He objected to the expression "by such Jews who are fully contented with their existing nationality and citizenship." He suggested that the promulgation of the proposed declaration would prejudicially affect the prospects of the Jews in Russia and Romania and that His Majesty's Government had always exercised its beneficial influence to improve the lot of the Jews in both those countries and had endeavoured to secure for them equality of treatment with other communities in those countries. He asserted that the Russian Revolution had released the Jews from the shackles which had oppressed them for generations. Cohen was so obsessed with this last point that he reiterated this imaginary wishful belief when he stated that, given the realization of the hopes and aspirations of the Russian and Romanian Jews, "the Jewish question" disappeared (National Archives, CAB 24/4/14).

Cohen argued that the draft declaration would stimulate antisemitism everywhere and that all Jews, including British ones, would suffer from this attempt to settle "the Jewish question." He suggested that while the declaration amounted to a proposal of optional emigration to the new state, with a revival of persecution which was always possible, the Jews might be compulsorily emigrated, and that the words in the declaration relating to the preservation of the political status of Jews in other countries would not protect them in such an eventuality (National Archives, CAB 24/4/14).

Cohen invoked his own version of a time-worn anti-Zionist mantra when he postulated that with a pre-war population in Palestine of under four hundred thousand, and with the number of Jews in Europe being estimated to be nine and a quarter million, if there was a "Jewish question," the creation of a Jewish state in Palestine would scarcely solve it. Cohen followed this up with the statement that it must be acknowledged that the new Jewish population to be attracted to Palestine consisted largely of Jews of the Near East. Consequently, according to Cohen, Jews that at that point in time belonged to the enemy belligerent nations would be numerous amongst the population, and this would establish foci of intrigue on the flank of British interests in Egypt (National Archives, CAB 24/4/14).

One common element that runs through the argumentations of these three anti-Zionist submissions is that the Russian Revolution was putting an end to the plight of the Jews in Russia and that there was, therefore, no longer a need for a separate Jewish homeland. As demonstrated in *Chapter 3: Persecution – Tsarist Russia, the Nineteenth-Century "Egypt,"* this assertion cannot be further from the truth. The unprecedented degree of cruelty, bestiality and depravity that characterized the antisemitic violence that erupted in the wake of the Russian Revolution puts to shame this unwarranted assertion.

In summary, it is clear from the careful reading of the submissions provided by Magnus, Montefiore and Cohen, as well as Montagu's memorandum, that their pleas to block a pro-Zionist declaration by the British government were driven solely by their motivation to protect their privileged conditions in British society. This also explains, if not justifies, the paucity of facts and realism underlying their supporting arguments. In the end, as writer and historian Oskar K. Rabinowicz so aptly put it, "They failed completely to prevent the issue of the declaration, while they succeeded in reducing its scope" (Rabinowicz, 1958, p. 94).

During the War Cabinet meeting of October 25, 1917, War Cabinet Secretary, M. P. A. Hankey mentioned that he was being pressed by the Foreign Office to bring forward the question of Zionism, an early settlement of which was regarded as of great importance. At the outset of the meeting, Lord Curzon stated that he was preparing a memorandum on the subject. This announcement caused the question to be adjourned until Monday October 29, "or some other day early next week" (National Archives, CAB 23/4/31).

On October 31, the War Cabinet had Lord Curzon's memorandum on the subject of the Zionist movement before them. This time, Curzon stated that he admitted the force of the diplomatic arguments in favour of expressing sympathy and agreed that the bulk of the Jews held pro-Zionist rather than anti-Zionist opinions. He added that he did not agree with the attitude taken up by Montagu. On the other hand, he could not share the optimistic views held regarding the future of Palestine. He feared that the suggested declaration would raise false expectations which could never be realized. He also attached great importance to retaining Christian and Muslim Holy Places in Jerusalem and Bethlehem and felt that if this was done effectively, he did not see how the Jewish people could have political capital in Palestine. He recognized, however, that expressing sympathy with the Jewish aspirations would be a valuable adjunct for British propaganda purposes. While giving his support for the declaration for diplomatic reasons, he cautioned that the British government should be guarded in the language used (National Archives, CAB 23/4/35).

With Curzon on board, the point had finally been reached where Balfour could state that everyone was agreed that, from a purely diplomatic and political point of view, it was desirable that some declaration favourable to the aspirations of the Jewish nationalists should now be made. Balfour pointed out that the vast majority of Jews in Russia and America, as, indeed, all over the world, now appeared to be favourable to Zionism. "If we could make the declaration favourable to such an ideal, we should be able to carry on extremely useful propaganda both in Russia and America," Balfour said. He acknowledged the two main arguments that were still being put forward against Zionism: (1) that Palestine was inadequate to form a home for either the Jews or any other people; and (2) the difficulty felt with regard to the future position of Jews in Western countries.

With regard to the first, he understood that there were considerable differences of opinion among experts regarding the possibility of the settlement of any large population in Palestine, but he was informed that, if Palestine were scientifically developed, a very much larger population could be sustained than had existed during the period of Turkish misrule. As to the meaning of the words "national home," to which the Zionists attached so much importance, he understood it to mean some form of British, American or other protectorate, under which full facilities would be given to the Jews to work out their own salvation and to build up, by means of education, agriculture and industry, a real centre of national culture and focus of national life. It did not necessarily involve the early establishment of an independent Jewish state, which was a matter for gradual development in accordance with the ordinary laws of political evolution.

With regard to the second point, he felt that, far from Zionism hindering the process of assimilation in Western countries, the truer parallel was to be found in the position of an Englishman who leaves his country to establish a permanent home in the United States. In the latter case, there was no difficulty with the Englishman or his children becoming full nationals of the United States, whereas, in the present position of Jewry, the assimilation was often felt to be incomplete, and any danger of a double allegiance or non-national outlook would be eliminated (National Archives, CAB 23/4/35).

With reference to Balfour's above-noted remark that the making of a declaration favourable to the Zionist ideal would enable Britain to carry on "extremely useful propaganda both in Russia and America," the American component of this avowed policy objective has been fully covered in *Chapter 5: The American Factor*. For the purpose of explaining the British assumption that the Balfour Declaration was also important for its propaganda value towards enlisting Zionist support for influencing the new revolutionary government in Russia not to abandon the war efforts against the German and Turkish enemies, it is necessary to describe the events in Russia in 1917 which triggered this British belief.

As noted by British scholar and author Sharman Kadish, by the summer of 1917, the collapse of the Russian military, which led to the end of the fighting in the Balkans, constituted a setback to the Allied war effort due to it freeing up substantial German forces for the Western Front. It also lifted the Allied economic blockade by allowing the Central Powers access to Russian supplies, especially to the Ukrainian "breadbasket." It was also feared in the West that the withdrawal of Russia from the Caucasus would strengthen German influence in Turkey, which would thus be enabled to control Syria and Palestine. Such a development would threaten Britain's interests in Egypt and the trade route to India and the Far East. Prime Minister Lloyd George held that the answer was for the British to conquer Palestine first, to which end he launched the "Allenby" offensive in August (Kadish, 1992, pp. 141–142).

It is clear that the situation in Russia, with the dangers it held for British interests, renewed the British government's interest in Zionism. The British felt that Zionism could be manipulated to provide the perfect propaganda pretext for the pursuit of their designs on Palestine. The forthcoming offensive would be depicted as a campaign to liberate Arabs, Armenians and Jews from Turkish rule, with the implication that Jewish national self-determination in Palestine would be promoted under British protection (Kadish, 1992, p. 142).

Kadish also noted Sir Ronald Graham's warning to Balfour on October 24, 1917 to the effect that any further delay to the publication of the Declaration may not only lose the important cooperation of the Zionist forces in Russia and in America but also risk throwing the Zionists into the arms of the Germans. Graham pointed out that:

> Information from every quarter shows the very important role which the Jews are now playing in the Russian political situation. […] Almost every Jew in Russia is a Zionist and if they can be made to realize that the success of the Zionist aspirations depends on the expulsion of the Turks from Palestine, we shall enlist a most powerful element in our favour. (Kadish, 1992, p. 145)

Kadish perceived the Balfour Declaration as a desperate bid to avert the almost certain withdrawal of Russia from the war. He found confirmation of this view in Lloyd George's reflection in his memoirs that:

> The actual timing of the declaration was determined by considerations of war policy [...] the launching of it in 1917 was due [...] to propagandist reasons [...]. In 1917 the issue of the war was still very much in doubt [...]. Public opinion in Russia and America played a great part, and we had every reason at that time to believe that in both countries the friendliness or hostility of the Jewish race might make a considerable difference. (Kadish, 1992, p. 145)

The War Cabinet concluded the October 31 meeting by authorizing the Secretary of State for Foreign Affairs, Arthur Balfour, in whose name the Balfour Declaration was issued, to take a suitable opportunity to make the following declaration of sympathy with the Zionist aspirations:

> His Majesty's Government views with favour the establishment in Palestine of a national home for the Jewish people and will use their best endeavours to facilitate the achievement of this object, it being clearly understood that nothing shall be done which may prejudice the civil and religious rights of existing non-Jewish communities in Palestine, or the rights and political status enjoyed by Jews in any other country. (National Archives, CAB 23/4/35)

On November 1, Sir Ronald Graham sent privately to Weizmann the text of a declaration – a slightly amended version of the Milner alternative formula authorized to be made by the Foreign Secretary. It would be embodied, Graham explained, "in a letter which Mr. Balfour is addressing to Lord Rothschild with a request to communicate it to your Organization" (Stein, 1961, pp. 547–548). The slight amendments referred to here are the replacement of the words "Jewish race" by "Jewish people" and the change from "the rights and political status enjoyed in any other country by such Jews who are fully contented with their existing nationality and citizenship" to "the rights and civil political status enjoyed by Jews in any other country." As noted earlier, these two amendments were the result of having been requested by the Zionist leadership.

The historic end result of the eight-month-long text crafting process described in this chapter was the November 2, 1917 Balfour Declaration which, as noted in the Introduction of this book, was worded as follows:

> His Majesty's Government view with favour the establishment in Palestine of a national home for the Jewish people, and will use its best endeavours

to facilitate the achievement of this object, it being clearly understood that nothing shall be done which may prejudice the civil and religious rights of existing non-Jewish communities in Palestine, or the rights and political status enjoyed by Jews in any other country.

Conclusion

This chapter has traced the difficult process that led to the final wording of the Balfour Declaration. As we have seen, its wording represents the fusion, shaped by the geopolitical environment at the time, of the motivations that drove the British and the Zionists to pursue the establishment of a Jewish homeland in Palestine.

The British efforts to reconcile their self-serving endorsement of the Zionist objective with the conflicting promises made to the Arabs and the French were reflected in the intricate process of wording the Declaration in a manner that would minimize the risks and maximize the rewards on both sides.

From the Zionist perspective, the Balfour Declaration was a necessary step towards the realization of the fundamental objective of a Jewish state. While the Zionist leaders involved in the drafting of the Declaration were motivated by the same fundamental drive, they each had their own thoughts and personalities, which resulted in different approaches towards the political strategies and tactics to be used. To the Zionists, the Balfour Declaration established a firm foothold on the path of a sovereign Jewish state. At the time, those who felt that the chances of obtaining the promise embodied in the Declaration were enhanced by using less explicit language than was used by those who were pressing for an undiluted commitment to a sovereign state prevailed.

It is only by being aware of the political and ideological motivations and considerations that shaped the formulation of the Balfour Declaration that one can appreciate the efforts that went into achieving the contrived ambiguity deemed necessary to accommodate the aspirations and apprehensions that influenced the parties that had a stake in the Declaration and an influence on its wording.

One aspect of the Balfour Declaration formulation process that significantly impacted the shape of its final wording, and which seems to be glaringly ignored in the vast amount of published attention to this historic event, is the astounding asymmetry in size and power between the two parties involved. The fact that the final wording fell far short of the original hopes and expectations of the Zionist movement is not surprising when we consider that what we have here is the greatest power in the world at the time, holding all the cards, negotiating the terms of a historic undertaking with the representatives of a small, persecuted and dispersed nation with no territorial base of its own. What complicated the situation and increased the disadvantages faced by the Zionist representatives was that the British, for reasons unbeknown to their protagonists, were at all times mindful of the necessity to placate the nationalistic and ideological drives of the competing world powers, as well as of the vast populations occupying the enormous territories the Allies expected would soon come under their tutelage.

CONCLUSION

As noted in the Introduction, this book aimed to trace the activities of all the parties involved in the process that led to the historic Balfour Declaration on November 2, 1917. The main protagonists were the Jewish people and the British Empire. The other political entities that played a vital role in this process included the Ottoman Empire, Germany, Russia, the United States and France. Like the multiple parts of precision clockwork, each element, regardless of its shape or size, played an essential part in the functioning of the whole, while the absence of one of them could have altered the outcome of the entire process.

The Balfour Declaration would never have happened if it was not for the auspicious alignment of the essential sine qua nons outlined in this paper. The historical record shows that it sprang from the timely and unique confluence of simmering national and social aspirations that perceived a common cause and seized upon the brief window of opportunity offered by the turn of events that arose in 1917, the third year of World War I. The optimum synergy of this mix of motivational ingredients was reached by the time the Declaration was drafted and promulgated. While the geopolitical components necessary for the development of the Balfour Declaration eventually became interconnected, the process and its outcome were completely unpredictable. Ian Lustick, Professor of Political Science at the University of Pennsylvania, notes in referring to the Balfour Declaration that:

> Trivial accidents of policy, casual ideological or personal prejudices by colonial officers and relevant ministers, and other minor factors, often drove massive impactful interventions. (Lustick, 2017, p. 2)

As the exploration of the British motivation behind the Balfour Declaration in *Chapter 1: The British Motivation* showed, it was the product of a blend of religiously inspired sentiments and self-serving political pragmatism. On close examination, one cannot avoid the sense that the expression "British motivation" might be an oversimplification. Such unqualified appellation might leave the impression that political support for a Jewish homeland was a constant feature of British society at both government and grassroots levels. Calling it instead a temporary British motivation, born of an episodic non-replicable series of disparate social and political events, pulled together under the umbrella of an all-encompassing World War, might be more realistic. That, from the British perspective, it was solely a product of and for the moment was borne out by the fact that, after the war, the promises of the Balfour Declaration morphed into a totally different dynamic, where the principles embodied in the Declaration gave way to the ruthless realpolitik the British resorted to in their attempts to manage the conflicts their World War I double-dealing had spawned. As Niccolò Machiavelli noted in *The Prince*, "The promise given was a necessity of the past. The word broken is a necessity of the present" (Wood, 1893, p. 449).

No statement encapsulates the ultimate objective which motivated the British to issue the Balfour Declaration more than the words of the Duke of Devonshire, Secretary of State for the Colonies, who in 1922, in a memorandum for the consideration of the Cabinet on deciding future policy, stated that "The Balfour Declaration was a war measure ... designed to secure tangible benefits which it was hoped could contribute to the ultimate victory of the Allies" (Ingrams, 2009, p. 173).

The background to the Jewish perspective on the Balfour Declaration is considerably more complex than the British angle. The British were a sovereign world power with all the decisions being made by a democratically elected central government. The Jewish world was the exact opposite, a physically weak and universally despised nation, spread around the world without any unifying sovereign territorial base or governmental structure.

As pointed out in *Chapter 2: Emancipation*, emancipation in Western Europe preceded Russia's de jure enactment by at least a century, while de facto, under the tsarist absolute monarchy, which outlasted its French counterpart by about the same length of time, it never fully emerged from its cocoon. It follows that the social, economic and political impact of emancipation on the Jewish populations in these two regions followed an asymmetric path, both chronologically and qualitatively. Eventually, through the development of a modern Jewish intelligentsia in the East and their exposure to their Western counterparts, these two currents coalesced into the same mainstream of Zionist political development. This allowed the seed of Jewish political nationalism which emerged from the liberating impulse of the French Revolution to eventually reach the intellectual leadership of Russia's Jewish population, which was trapped in the suffocating grip of the absolutist tsarist regime for whom the concept of emancipation was anathema for its own population in general and for its non-Jewish citizenry in particular.

How the relentless genocidal persecution by the tsarist regimes of Russia's Jewish citizenry drove it to abandon any hope of emancipation and civic equality and to look for avenues of physical escape was depicted in detail in *Chapter 3: Persecution – Tsarist Russia, the Nineteenth-Century "Egypt."*

Chapter 4: The Development of Zionist Political Thinking described how the Jewish response to the relentless tsarist persecution helped forge the political Zionist movement which eventually burst forth in the petri dish of WWI. There, it caught the slipstream of British imperial ambitions to emerge as a new reality on the world political scene on November 2, 1917, when the British government proclaimed its official recognition of the Zionist movement when it issued the Balfour Declaration.

These two chapters showed that the path that led the Jews to help forge the Balfour Declaration has its origin in the rising antisemitism in Western Europe and in the anti-Jewish pogroms in Tsarist Russia, and that political Zionism, which held that the only way to freedom and equality was through the recreation of a sovereign national homeland, was the catalyst that forged the ideological union between these two asynchronistic Judeophobic developments. If the Jews of Russia provided the critical mass for the development of political Zionism, Theodore Herzl provided the galvanizing energy and political acumen which lifted it to the international political stage.

It was only when the emerging Zionist movement came to the conclusion that the long-term solution to the two-thousand-year persecution of the Jewish diaspora was the reconstitution of the Jewish homeland in Palestine that the site of the ancient Jewish homeland became the focus of the Zionist leadership's attention. If Palestine was to be the destination, this could not be achieved without the consent of the Turkish government. During Herzl's years of political activism, he devoted the bulk of his physical and emotional energy to obtaining Palestine as a sustainable home for his people. Chapter 4 contains a detailed description of Herzl's efforts to obtain the backing and assistance of the major European powers to succeed in this endeavour. His face-to-face negotiations with Sultan Abdul Hamid II with his coterie of untrustworthy and self-dealing ministers in June 1896 and May 1901, as described in detail in the subsection of Chapter 4 titled "Theodor Herzl – From Passive Submission to Political Action," reveal the picture of an Ottoman government whose degree of corruption, greed and religiously inspired reluctance to grant the Jews any level of political or economic autonomy in Palestine constituted an obstacle to the territorial realization of the Zionist dream that even Herzl's talents and determination could not overcome. In this sense,

Turkey's role in the development of the Zionist agenda was a negative force in terms of practical results for the Zionist cause. This state of stagnation finally came to an end in 1914 with the outbreak of World War I.

This book has demonstrated that the Balfour Declaration was the outcome of the interaction of the major powers that had a significant Jewish presence in their midsts. Until the constitution of a Jewish government in exile, which emerged from the First Zionist Congress in 1897, the role of these powers was limited to their interactions with the Jewish citizens living in their countries. Once Theodor Herzl had started, on behalf of the Jewish diaspora, to negotiate ways of ending their relentless persecution with the reconstitution of their national homeland in Palestine as the prime objective, the activities of the various governments involved started to take on international dimensions, as the location of that homeland triggered a number of geopolitical issues. With the advent of World War I, the road that led to the Balfour Declaration had become an arduous tangled web of international diplomatic and internal political manoeuvres, where the parts played by the major powers involved in that conflict had a direct impact on the fate of the Zionist project.

Of all the entities involved in the World War I conflict, it was the Ottoman Empire that was the main subject of concern for both the Zionists and the British driving forces behind the forging of the historic British promise of the reconstitution of the Jewish homeland. By October 1917, the consensus had been reached among the Allies that its location was to be Palestine. This targeted piece of land happened to lie in the heart of the Ottoman Empire, and with the latter adamantly opposed to any non-Muslim sovereign presence in their realm, the challenge of promising it to the Zionists in the event of an Allied victory, without sparking the ire of the Turks, hung like a threatening cloud over the complex dynamics of the Balfour Declaration-oriented diplomatic manoeuvers driving the process. By the time the formulation of the Balfour Declaration was nearing its completion in October 1917, the fortunes of war had started to turn in favour of the Allies, and it appeared that Turkish control over the Middle East was destined to come to an end and, with it, its role as a major impediment to the reconstitution of the Jewish homeland in Palestine.

To assess the French influence on the Balfour Declaration, it was necessary to assemble a montage of the convoluted discussions and communications between all the parties involved on the French, British and Zionist sides, as was done in Chapters 2 and 6. This assessment leads to the conclusion that what convinced the British War Cabinet that it was acting with the understanding that the French were in full support of the

Balfour Declaration was the Cambon letter of June 4, 1917. As noted in *Chapter 6: What's in a Word – Political Word-Craftmanship*, this letter was the result of Nahum Sokolow's successful negotiations, on April 9, 1917, with top French government officials, including the French Foreign Minister Jules Cambon and French Consul-General in Beirut François Georges-Picot, which led to the French acceptance of the concept of an autonomous Jewish national home in Palestine. The importance of this letter cannot be overstated. It constituted an indispensable link in the chain of events that led to the Balfour Declaration. As mentioned in Chapter 4, in a lecture Picot delivered in Paris 1918, he stated that a qualified representative of the British government had been heard to say that if he had not been able to produce the Cambon letter to the War Cabinet, it would never have been persuaded to agree to the Balfour Declaration. Schneer confirms this conclusion when he notes that, with this letter, the French government had become the first Great Power to recognize the Jews as a distinct nationality. Not only had Sokolow achieved a Zionist benchmark, but the very existence of such a declaration by her primary wartime ally would make it easier for Britain to make one too (Schneer, 2010, p. 218).

Germany, while being on the opposing side in World War I and neither a supporter nor a participant in the deliberations leading to the Balfour Declaration, was nevertheless a factor in the considerations that informed the Allied and Jewish agendas. As noted in *Chapter 1: The British Motivation,* it was the competing territorial ambitions of the British and the Germans that triggered the devastating conflict of WWI and the ensuing drives by both sides to enlist support from existing and potential allies. As detailed in this chapter, it led to the duplicitous political deal-making between the British and the Arabs, the British and the French, the British and the Jews, and the British and the Ottomans. The German impact was felt again in the penultimate year of World War I, when the perilous military situation in Europe caused the British and French to pursue the American participation in the war against the Central Powers, while the Germans attempted to keep the Americans out through devastating assaults on the American merchant navy and the abortive attempt to induce Mexico to declare war on the United States. One of the developments that emerged from this convoluted hodgepodge of political interactions was the concept that supporting the Zionist dream might somehow enhance the fortunes of war. The fear that Germany's promises of acting in favour of the realization of the Jewish homeland, for the purpose of currying favour with the Zionist movement, might tilt the balance of the war in Germany's favour acted as an accelerant in the British endeavours to proclaim its own promise.

An additional dimension of Germany's impact on the Balfour Declaration process derived from the fact that it was Turkey's decision to tie its fate to that of Germany that led Turkey to join Germany in being defeated in World War I, thus allowing Britain to inherit the bulk of the Ottoman Empire and to promise Palestine to the Jewish people. It begs the question as to what would have happened if Turkey had been allied with Britain on the winning side. It is fair to surmise that Turkey would have maintained control over Palestine, that there would have been no promise of a Jewish homeland in Palestine by the British, and that the post-WWI history of the Jewish people and of the Middle East, as we know it today, would not have existed. It is clear that Germany's territorial ambitions and its drawing of Turkey to its side unintentionally enabled the Balfour Declaration process to run its course.

The impact of Russia on the Balfour Declaration manifested itself in two stages, both of which are covered in *Chapter 3: Persecution – Tsarist Russia, the Nineteenth-Century "Egypt."* The first stage was the quasi-genocidal persecution of Russian Jewry under the tsars, which gave rise to political Zionism and drove its centre of gravity to the political hub of the British Empire, where it became an active participant in the British policy-making process with regard to both sides' strategic objectives in the Middle East. The growing Jewish immigration to Great Britain as a result of their increasingly vicious persecution in Russia is a vital component of the investigation of the roots of the Zionist perspective in respect of the Balfour Declaration. One of the fundamental messages, within the theme of this study, is that the persecution of the Jews in Tsarist Russia had triggered mass immigration to the West, and the concept of Zionism which was conceived in reaction to that persecution rode the tide of that exodus to find in Britain a fertile ground for its development.

The second stage of Russia's impact on the Balfour Declaration was triggered by the Russian Revolutions of 1917. The collapse of the Russian military in the summer of 1917 led to the promise by the Bolshevik regime to take Russia out of the war, which would end the fighting in the Balkans. This constituted a setback to the Allied war effort by freeing up substantial German forces for the Western Front. It also broke the Allied economic blockade by allowing the Central Powers access to Russian supplies. It was feared in the West that the withdrawal of Russia from the Caucasus would strengthen German influence in Turkey, which would thus be enabled to maintain control over Syria and Palestine. Such a development would threaten Britain's interests in Egypt and the trade route to India and the Far East. These negative, from the Allied perspective, developments in Russia led the British to play the Zionist card in the hope that it would help to keep Russia in the war and provided them with an additional impetus to issue the Balfour Declaration.

As we saw in *Chapter 5: The American Factor*, America's entry into World War I in April of 1917 completely changed the dynamics of the war. It had a major impact on the diplomatic process that drove the development of the Zionist project. It decisively tilted the outcome of the war in favour of the Allies and consolidated the Jewish efforts to realize the Zionist dream of the recovery of their ancient homeland. Without the U.S. entering the war and tilting the balance in favour of the Allies, the Balfour Declaration would either never have materialized or, if issued nevertheless, turned out to be a stillborn promise.

This book is also heedful of the caveat that the political currents that moulded the British motivation behind the Balfour Declaration should be appraised only in the context of the political developments that preceded it and not obfuscated by the wisdom of hindsight inspired by the knowledge of what transpired thereafter. As we saw in *Chapter 6: What's in a Word – Political Word-Craftsmanship*, the wording of the Declaration was forged in such a way as to leave the British room for future political manoeuvering while trying to accommodate the Zionist aspiration for a Jewish homeland.

As demonstrated in this study, the Balfour Declaration was the culmination of a 128-year-long process of social change in the Jewish diaspora. This process began in 1789, when the French Revolution liberated the politically blindfolded Jewish minds from the confines of the ghetto, and came to fruition in 1917, when this historic promise signalled the restoration of sovereign Jewish nationhood.

Appendix

The Balfour Declaration:
Successive Drafts and Final Text

Zionist Draft: July 12, 1917

His Majesty's Government, after considering the aims of the Zionist Organisation, accepts the principle of recognising Palestine as the National Home of the Jewish people and the right of the Jewish people to build up its national life in Palestine under a protection to be established at the conclusion of peace, following upon the successful issue of the War.

His Majesty's Government regards as essential for the realisation of this principle the grant of internal autonomy to the Jewish nationality in Palestine, freedom of immigration for Jews, and the establishment of a Jewish National Colonising Corporation for the resettlement and economic development of the country.

The conditions and forms of the internal autonomy and the Charter for the Jewish National Colonising Corporation should, in the view of His Majesty's Government, be elaborated in detail and determined with the representatives of the Zionist Organization.

Zionist Draft: July 18, 1917

His Majesty's Government accepts the principle that Palestine should be reconstituted as the National Home of the Jewish people.

His Majesty's Government will use its best endeavours to secure the achievement of this object and will discuss the necessary methods and means with the Zionist Organisation.

Balfour Draft: August 1917

His Majesty's government accept the principle that Palestine should be reconstituted as the national home of the Jewish people and will use their best endeavours to secure the achievement of this object and will be ready to consider any suggestions on the subject which the Zionist organization may desire to lay before them.

Milner Draft: August 1917

His Majesty's Government accepts the principle that every opportunity should be afforded for the establishment of a home for the Jewish people in Palestine and will use its best endeavours to facilitate the achievement of this object and will be ready to consider any suggestions on the subject which the Zionist organization may desire to lay before them.

Milner Alternative Draft: October 4, 1917

His Majesty's Government views with favour the establishment in Palestine of a National Home for the Jewish Race and will use its best endeavours to facilitate the achievement of this object; it being clearly understood that nothing shall be done which may prejudice the civil and religious rights of the existing non-Jewish communities in Palestine, or the rights and political status enjoyed in any other country by such Jews who are fully contented with their existing nationality and citizenship.

Final Text: November 2, 1917

His Majesty's Government view with favour the establishment in Palestine of a national home for the Jewish people, and will use their best endeavours to facilitate the achievement of this object, it being clearly understood that nothing shall be done which may prejudice the civil and religious rights of existing non-Jewish communities in Palestine, or the rights and political status enjoyed by Jews in any other country.

REFERENCES

Anderson, S. (2012). *Lawrence in Arabia*. McClelland & Stewart Ltd.

Antonius, G. (1939). *The Arab Awakening: The Story of the Arab National Movement*. Lippincot.

Aronson, G. (1966). Ideological Trends Among Russian Jews. In J. Frumkin, G. Aronson & A. Goldenweiser (Eds.), *Russian Jewry 1860–1917* (pp. 144–171). Thomas Yoseloff.

Aronson, I. M. (1990). *Troubled Waters: The Origins of the 1881 Anti-Jewish Pogroms in Russia*. University of Pittsburgh Press.

Avineri, S. (1991). *Herzl: Theodor Herzl and the Foundation of the Jewish State*. Weidenfeld & Nicolson.

Avineri, S. (1999). Theodor Herzl's Diaries as a Bildungsroman. *Jewish Social Studies, 5*(3), 1–46.

Avineri, S. (2017). *The Making of Modern Zionism: The Intellectual Origins of the Jewish State*. Basic Books.

Bard, M. G. (2019). *Zionist Congress: First to Twelfth Zionist Congress (1897–1921)*. https://www.jewishvirtuallibrary.org/first-to-twelfth-zionist-congress-1897-1921

Beller, S. (1991). *Herzl*. Peter Halban Publishers Ltd.

Berk, S. M. (1985). *Year of Crisis, Year of Hope: Russian Jewry and the Pogroms of 1881–1882*. Greenwood Press.

Bickerton, I. & Klausner, C. (1991). *A Concise History of the Arab Israeli Conflict*. Prentice Hall.

Butts, R. H. (2010). *An Architect of the American Century: Colonel Edward M. House and the Modernization of United States Diplomacy* (Order No. 3443311) [Doctoral dissertation, Texas Christian University]. ProQuest Dissertations & Theses Global. https://search-proquest-com.mgs-ariel.macam.ac.il/docview/854839987

Defries, H. (2001). *Conservative Party Attitudes to Jews 1900–1950*. Frank Cass.

Dowty, A. (2012). *Israel/Palestine* (3rd ed.). Polity Press.

Dubnow, S. M. (1916). *History of the Jews in Russia and Poland: From the Earliest Times until the Present Day, Volume I*. The Jewish Publication Society of America.

Dubnow, S. M. (1918). *History of the Jews in Russia and Poland: From the Earliest Times until the Present Day, Volume II*. The Jewish Publication Society of America.

Dubnow, S. M. (1920). *History of the Jews in Russia and Poland: From the Earliest Times until the Present Day, Volume III*. The Jewish Publication Society of America.

Dugdale, B. E. C. (1940). *The Balfour Declaration: Origins and Background*. The Jewish Agency for Palestine.

Elon, A. (1975). *Herzl*. Holt, Rinehart and Winston.

Fraenkel, J. (1946). *Theodor Herzl, A Biography*. Ararat Publishing Society Limited.

Frederic, H. (1892). *The New Exodus: The Study of Israel in Russia*. G. P. Putnam's Sons.

Friedman, I. (1968). Lord Palmerston and the Protection of Jews in Palestine 1839–1851. *Jewish Social Studies, 30*(1), 23–41.

Fromkin, D. (2009). *A Peace to End all Peace*. Henry Hold and Company.

Frumkin, J. (1966). Pages from the History of Russian Jewry (Recollections and Documentary Material). In J. Frumkin, G. Aronson & A. Goldenweiser (Eds.), *Russian Jewry 1860–1917* (pp. 18–84). Thomas Yoseloff.

Gauthier, J. P. (2007). *Sovereignty over the Old City of Jerusalem*. [Doctoral dissertation, Université de Genève].

Gelvin, J. L. (2005). *The Israel-Palestine Conflict – One Hundred Years of War*. Cambridge University Press.

Goldberg, B. Z. (1961). *The Jewish Problem in the Soviet Union, Analysis and Solution*. Crown Publishers, Inc.

Greenberg, L. (1944). *The Jews in Russia, Volume I – The Struggle for Emancipation*. Yale University Press.

Greenberg, L. (1951). *The Jews in Russia, Volume II – The Struggle for Emancipation, 1881–1917*. Yale University Press.

Grief, H. (2008). *The Legal Foundation and Borders of Israel Under International Law: A Treatise on Jewish Sovereignty Over the Land of Israel*. Mazo Publishers.

Hazony, Y. (2001). *The Jewish State: The Struggle for Israel's Soul*. Basic Books.

Hertzberg, A. (1959). *The Zionist Idea*. Doubleday & Company Inc.

Herzl, T. (1960a). *The Complete Diaries of Theodor Herzl, Volume I*. Thomas Yoseloff.

Herzl, T. (1960b). *The Complete Diaries of Theodor Herzl, Volume II*. Thomas Yoseloff.

Herzl, T. (1960c). *The Complete Diaries of Theodor Herzl, Volume III*. Thomas Yoseloff.

Herzl, T. (1960d). *The Complete Diaries of Theodor Herzl, Volume IV*. Thomas Yoseloff.

Herzl, T. (1960e). *The Complete Diaries of Theodor Herzl, Volume V*. Thomas Yoseloff.

Herzl, T. (2010). *The Jewish State*. Penguin Group.

Hughes, M. (1999). *Allenby and British Strategy in the Middle East, 1917–1919*. Frank Cass.

Ingrams, D. (2009). *Palestine Papers 1917–1922: Seeds of Conflict*. Eland Publishing Limited.

Joseph, S. (1914). *Jewish Immigration to the United States from 1881–1910*. Columbia University.

Kadish, S. (1992). *Bolsheviks and British Jews: The Anglo-Jewish Community, Britain and the Russian Revolution*. Frank Cass.

Karsh, E. (2015). *The Tail Wags the Dog: International Politics and the Middle East*. Bloomsbury.

Keegan, J. (2000). *The First World War*. Vintage Books.

Khiterer, V. (2015). *Jewish Pogroms in Kiev During the Russian Civil War 1918–1920*. The Edwin Mellen Press.

Lebow, R. (1968). "Woodrow Wilson and the Balfour Declaration." *The Journal of Modern History, 40*(4), 501–523.

Lewis, D. M. (2010). *The Origin of Christian Zionism – Lord Shaftesbury and Evangelical Support for a Jewish Homeland*. Cambridge University Press.

Lustick, I. S. (2017). The Balfour Declaration as a Radical and Accidentally Relevant Document. Quoted with author's permission from a paper prepared for presentation at the annual meeting of the Association for Israel Studies, Brandeis University, Waltham, MA, June 12–14, 2017.

Makovsky, M. (2007). *Churchill's Promised Land: Zionism and statecraft*. Yale University Press.

Mathew, W. M. (2011). War-time Contingency and the Balfour Declaration of 1917: An Improbable Regression. *Journal of Palestine Studies, 40*(2), 26–42.

McGeever, B. (2017). Revolution and antisemitism: The Bolsheviks in 1917. *Patterns of Prejudice, 51*(3–4), 235–252.

McGeever, B. (2019). *Antisemitism and the Russian Revolution*. Cambridge, UK: Cambridge University Press.

Montagu, E. S. (1966). *Edwin Montagu and the Balfour Declaration*. Arab League Office.

National Archives at Kew. https:discovery.nationalarchives.gov.uk. Record type: Conclusion. Former reference: WC227. Date: 03 September 1917. Reference: CAB 23/4/1. War Cabinet and Cabinet: Minute 2.

National Archives at Kew. https:discovery.nationalarchives.gov.uk. Record type: Conclusion. Former reference: WC245. Date: 04 October 1917. Reference: CAB 23/4/19. War Cabinet and Cabinet: Minute 18.

National Archives at Kew. https:discovery.nationalarchives.gov.uk. Record type: Memorandum. Former reference: G164. Date: 17 October 1917. Reference: CAB 24/4/14. War Cabinet and Cabinet: Memoranda.

National Archives at Kew. https:discovery.nationalarchives.gov.uk. Record type: Conclusion. Former reference: WC257. Date: 25 October 1917. Reference: CAB 23/4/31. War Cabinet and Cabinet: Minute 12.

National Archives at Kew. https:discovery.nationalarchives.gov.uk. Record type: Conclusion. Former reference: WC261. Date: 31 October 1917. Reference: CAB 23/4/35. War Cabinet and Cabinet: Minute 12.

Noelle-Neumann, E. (1993). *The Spiral of Silence: Public Opinion – Our Social Skin*. University of Chicago Press.

Rabinowicz, O. (1958). *Herzl, Architect of the Balfour Declaration*. Herzl Press.

Reynold, N. (2014). *Britain's Unfulfilled Mandate for Palestine*. Lexington Books.

Rose, N. (1986). *Chaim Weizmann: A Biography*. Viking.

Schneer, J. (2010). *The Balfour Declaration – The Origins of the Arab-Israeli Conflict*. Random House.

Shahar, D. (2013). *Israel – A Jewish and Democratic State*. Kinneret-zmora-Bitan-Dvir.

Stein, L. (1961). *The Balfour Declaration*. Vallentine Mitchell & Co.

Strawson, J. (2010). *Partitioning Palestine: Legal Fundamentalism in the Palestinian-Israeli Conflict*. Pluto Press.

Tuchman, B. W. (1956). *Bible and Sword: England and Palestine from the Bronze Age to Balfour*. Random House.

Tuchman, B. W. (2004). *The Guns of August*. Presidio Press.

Weizmann, C. (1966). *Trial and Error – the Autobiography of Chaim Weizmann*. Schocken Books.

Witte, S. (1921). *The Memoirs of Count Witte*. Doubleday, Page & Company.

Wood, J. (1893). *Dictionary of Quotations from Ancient and Modern English and Foreign Sources*. Frederick Warne and Co.

INDEX